LIVES OF THE GREAT ROMANTICS

GENERAL EDITOR: JOHN MULLAN
VOLUME EDITORS: JOHN MULLAN
CHRIS HART
PETER SWAAB

William Holl (1807–71), portrait of Percy Bysshe Shelley
By courtesy of the National Portrait Gallery, London

William Holl, the son of an engraver of the same name, made a living engraving mainly portraits. All the many portraits of Shelley engraved in the nineteenth century derive in the end from the painting of Shelley by Amelia Curran, begun in May 1819, but completed after his death. Mary Shelley obtained it from the artist in 1825, and Jane Williams had a copy made by George Cling, with reference to a water-colour of the poet by Edward Williams, apparently the only other portrait taken from life. (The Curran and Clint portraits are both now in the National Portrait Gallery.)

LIVES OF THE GREAT ROMANTICS
BY THEIR CONTEMPORARIES

VOLUME
1

SHELLEY

EDITED BY
JOHN MULLAN

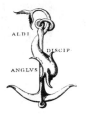

LONDON
WILLIAM PICKERING
1996

Published by Pickering & Chatto (Publishers) Limited

21 Bloomsbury Way, London, WC1A 2TH

Old Post Road, Brookfield, Vermont 05036, USA

BRITISH LIBRARY CATALOGUING IN PUBLICATION DATA
Lives of the great romantics: Shelley, Byron and Wordsworth
by their contemporaries
1. Shelley, Percy Bysshe, 1792–1822 – Criticism and interpretation
2. Byron, George Gordon Byron, Baron, 1788–1824 – Criticism and
interpretation   3. Wordsworth, William, 1770–1850 – Criticism and
interpretation   4. Poets, English – 19th century   5. English poetry –
19th century – History and criticism   6. Romantics – 19th century –
History and criticism
I. Mullan, John   II. Hart, Chris   III. Swaab, Peter
821.7′09′145

Set ISBN 1–85196–270–0
This volume ISBN 1–85196–271–9

LIBRARY OF CONGRESS CATALOGING-IN-PUBLICATION DATA
Lives of the great romantics : Shelley, Byron and Wordsworth / by
contemporaries ; edited with introduction and notes by John Mullan,
Christopher Hart, Peter Swaab.
    p.   cm.
Includes bibliographical references.
Contents: v. 1. Shelley –– v. 2. Byron –– v. 3. Wordsworth.
ISBN 1–85196–270–0 (set)
1. Poets, English––19th century––Biography.   2. Shelley, Percy
Bysshe, 1792–1822––Biography.   3. Byron, George Gordon Byron, Baron.
1788–1824––Biography.   4. Wordsworth, William, 1770–1850––Biography.
5. Romanticism––Great Britain.   I. Mullan, John.   II. Hart,
Christopher.   III. Swaab, Peter.
PR105.L58   1996
821′.709––dc20
[b]   95–21350
                                                             CIP

Printed and bound in Great Britain by
Biddles Ltd
Guildford

To my parents

CONTENTS

ACKNOWLEDGEMENTS

I am grateful for the assistance that I have been given at the British Library, Cambridge University Library, Dartmouth College Library, and the University of London Library. This anthology relies a good deal on the scholarship of others, and I would like to acknowledge, in particular, my debts to the editors of two scrupulously annotated collections of correspondence: *The Letters of Percy Bysshe Shelley*, 2 vols (Oxford: Clarendon Press, 1964), edited by Frederick L. Jones and *The Letters of Mary Wollstonecraft Shelley*, 3 vols (Baltimore: The Johns Hopkins University Press, 1980–88), edited by Betty T. Bennett. I would like to thank Peter Swaab and Chris Hart, the editors of the two accompanying volumes in this edition, on Wordsworth and Byron, for their advice, and Bridget Frost, for her patience and know-how. Special thanks to Harriet Stewart, for her help in everything.

INTRODUCTION

On June 15th, 1893, *The Times* reported a ceremony that could be seen as the culmination of all the efforts made by Shelley's family, friends, and admirers, since his death in 1822, to have him accepted as one of his nation's greatest poets.

THE SHELLEY MEMORIAL AT OXFORD

The memorial to the poet Shelley which has been presented to University College, Oxford, by Lady Shelley, was opened yesterday in the presence of a distinguished company. It is the work of Mr. Onslow Ford, and a cast of the monument was exhibited at the Royal Academy last year... Amongst those present at the ceremony were Lady Shelley, the Bishop of Southwark, the Master of the University (Dr. Bright), the Master of Balliol (Professor Jowett), Sir William Markby, the Warden of All Souls, the Resident of Magdalen, the Warden of Merton, the Rector of Exeter, Mr. Arthur Sedgwick, Mr. Onslow Ford, Canon St. John, Dr. Garnett, Mr. William Esdaile (grandson of the poet). Mr. Hamilton Aïdé, Mr. Champneys (who designed the chamber in which the memorial is placed), and Mr. H. M. Burge.

The university and the college from which Shelley had been expelled over eighty years earlier for his inflammatory pamphlet *The Necessity of Atheism* were welcoming him back. Near the end of a century in which his beliefs and his way of life had as often been a matter of dispute as the merits of his poetry, his status and respectability were being acknowledged. Other poets, as well as many readers, might long since have proclaimed their respect for him. (Browning had recorded his admiration of Shelley, and indeed of 'the whole personality of the poet shining forward from the poems', in his 'Essay on Shelley' of 1852 (Browning, p. 1005). Tennyson too, while thinking Shelley 'too much in the clouds', was happy to call himself an admirer (Tennyson, p. 657; see also p. 475).) Now the very institution of learning against which Shelley had rebelled, the custodian of a nation's literary and intellectual traditions, was commemorating his achievements.

As *The Times* says, the memorial – which resides to this day in its specially designed chamber at University College – had been donated by Lady Shelley. She was the widow of Sir Percy Shelley, the poet's son and only surviving child by Mary Shelley. For her the ceremony was the fulfilment of decades of unwearying promotion of Shelley's reputation. Here was official recognition.

> Having handed a gold key of the chamber to Dr. Bright, Lady Shelley said she begged to thank the Master and Fellows of University College, and the distinguished artist who designed the memorial, for enabling her to fulfil one of the dearest wishes of her heart. For more than 40 years she had been a student of Shelley, and so far as she was able had striven to give the world a just impression of his character. She had lived in the companionship of his noble-minded wife and of his son, and she had been acquainted with most of his friends, none of whom, she believed, were now survivors. They were much mistaken who fancied that Shelley and Mary were regardless of the duties of life. Men of great genius could not always be reduced to rule. They erred sometimes, but they were not therefore to be deprived of the love and admiration of their countrymen.

As the newspaper report indicates, Lady Shelley's advocacy could not wish away, and yet somehow had to minimize, Shelley's unconventional beliefs and conduct. As she herself says, having the poet's 'genius' widely recognized had meant establishing 'a just impression of his character'. Some of her own work to this end is recorded in this anthology. As self-appointed guardian of Shelley's memory on behalf of the family into which she had married, her aims had been more determinedly celebratory (and thus, frequently, more dishonest) than any of Shelley's other memoirists. The project of justifying his 'character', however, was not singular. For one writer after another through the nineteenth century, such justification was a necessary condition for the establishment of his literary reputation. His life was attacked and was defended, but rarely was it suggested that the work might be judged separately from it. For those who had known him, almost all of whom had once shared some of his ideals and habits, the necessity to defend his 'character' was strongest.

The unveiling of the Oxford memorial is a good place to begin and end an account of the making of Shelley's posthumous reputation for other, though connected, reasons. One is that, as Lady Shelley here remarks, it comes at a point when the last of his 'friends' have all died: Claire Clairmont in 1879, in Florence, pursued to the last by hunters after Shelley manuscripts; Edward Trelawny in 1881, celebrated by the obituary writers as the bosom friend of great poets; Jane Hogg in 1884, the last and most reticent of the 'Pisa Circle', also harried in her old age by Shelley biographers. From now on there would be no more actual witnesses – no one to make a name by remembering what Shelley said or did (in Trelawny's case, apparently remembering in ever greater detail as the years went by). From now on, biographers and critics would work from what was written. And here is another reason why an event that crowns Lady Shelley's efforts is a natural punctuation mark in the story not only of Shelley's reputation but also of the making of the canon of his poems. For the previous year, 1892, Lady Shelley had marked the centenary of the poet's birth by offering the Bodelian Library a large number of the relics and manuscripts of Shelley in the family's possession. Her hold over all this material (which included many of the letters of both Shelley and Mary) was not entirely relinquished, for one box of letters was to be kept sealed until 1922, the centenary of Shelley's death (when eventually opened, it proved to contain little that was not already in print). The gift, however, might be seen as the making available to scholarship of the private Shelley, jealously guarded by Lady Shelley for almost half a century. (She left some papers to the descendants of Shelley's brother, John, and to those of her own adopted daughter: eventually these too came to the Bodleian.) When she died, aged seventy-nine, in 1899, Shelley really had been returned to the University from which he had once been driven. With the pioneering editorial work of H. Buxton Forman in the 1870s and 1880s, he had already begun to pass into the hands of scholars. The story of this scholarship goes on, and it is worth noting that over a century after Forman's first attempts to bring rigorous textual scholarship to Shelley's work, there is still no reliable and complete edition of his poetry (for a succinct account and explanation of this, see Matthews and Everest, Introduction). However, the story of the struggles of memorialists to leave to posterity that 'just impression of his character' had ended.

The nature of the memorial that Lady Shelley and the assembled dignitaries were opening remains, in all its grotesque sentimentality, a demonstration of how, in the eyes of some beholders, death could romanticise the poet's life. In bronze and marble, the monument depicts the drowned Shelley – not, of course, in the state in which his body was actually found, but as one of the beautiful dead beloved of nineteenth-century art. In fact, it had originally been commissioned by Lady Shelley for the poet's tomb, and was to have been installed in the Protestant Cemetary in Rome where his ashes were interred. However, Trelawny had bought the plot, and had had his own ashes buried next to Shelley's. His daughter, Laetitia Call, refused to allow Lady Shelley to pursue her scheme, saying that her father had given strict instructions to 'resist every innovation' (Norman, p. 258). So University College was offered it instead. The cemetary piece was just as suitable for its new setting, for the tragedy of a cruelly curtailed life (Shelley was twenty-nine when he was drowned) had become familiar to Victorian poetry lovers, in part through some of the texts represented in this volume. The poet had been cut off when his visionary enthusiasm was still in full spate. 'Men of great genius... erred sometimes', but this genius's premature death allowed his supposed errors to be seen as the excesses of youthful idealism – an idealism forever preserved.

For the representative of Oxford University on this satisfying yet potentially awkward occasion, the task was to dissolve any sense that there was
something incongrous in this gathering of academics and clergymen to
celebrate the work of English Literature's most notorious rebel and atheist.
Dr Bright made the best of his obligation.

The MASTER of the UNIVERSITY returned thanks on behalf of the corporation
of which he was the head for the generous gift which Lady Shelley had
bestowed on them, adding that the gift received fresh charms from the tender
way in which she had delivered it over to them. It was not often that a college
in Oxford had a modern work of art given to it. The reason of that was, he
thought, that there was a sort of erroneous fancy that Oxford belonged
completely to the old. If Oxford was to be what it claimed to be – the very
centre and heart of the growth of young England – it seemed to him clear that
Oxford must advance with the world, must expand and be open to all new
influences, and he could not conceive any more true emblem of the present
century than the great poet whose effigy they had now received. For if they
came to think of what really happened to him, he thought it was this – that he
was prophetic in all directions of what was to come to the world. Their thanks
were very largely to do with this fact – that the gift of the memorial was a sort
of emblem and symbol to them of a rubbing out of old ill-wills and old ill-
feelings, and of a perfectly peaceful feeling towards that great man. He did not
think they ought to judge of their predecessors very harshly, or to say that the
action of the college was very extraordinarily wrong, for he believed there was
hardly any place in Oxford which would not have acted in the same way as
University College acted. But what they had to observe was this – that the very
greatness of the man had rendered open to that kind of treatment. It was
because there was in him such a well-spring of hatred of all that was false and
oppressive, and because he had such a strong feeling of all that was gloomy
and sad in the history of the world and mankind, that he could not but
become a rebel. But the rebel of 80 years ago was the hero of the present
century. In other words, the great aspirations which he had, the intense love
of the human race which he had, the intense admiration of all objects that met
his eyes in the natural world, the intense hatred of all that was evil and all that
was sad, what was it but the very thing they had been learning for these last 80
years? And when at this time they had constant repetitions of very sad and
pessimistic views as to what the world was going to become, it was very
cheerful to come across a prophet who prophesied good things and not bad.
Although it probably was true that the great giant lay still chained upon the
hilltops, and although Jupiter, the emblem of what was false and conventional,
still in some degree reigned, it must be confessed that the prophecies he
uttered had been hastening towards their fulfilment, and that, in some way or
other – though it might not be as he fancied it – the human race was coming,
as they all hoped, to something like a condition of happiness in universal and
divine equality and love.

Rebel to hero: Dr Bright confirmed the transformation that Victorian Shel-leyans had worked hard to bring about.

We might also notice that, with his reference to 'Jupiter, the emblem of what was false and conventional', he shows some knowledge of Shelley's most ambitious and demanding work: *Prometheus Unbound*. The 'condition of happiness in universal and divine equality and love' of which he speaks, however, has been changed from the radical dream of that poem to the strangely confident kind of pronouncement that we can only call 'Victorian'. The Romantic poet turns out to have prophesied Victorian progress (readers of the relevant extracts will find that this is the thought of Lady Shelley's *Shelley Memorials*). By the end of the nineteenth century, with a map of Romantic literature – and, indeed, the term 'Romanticism' – established, the poet can be looked back on as a 'prophet'. For Romanticism itself had surely singled out 'the Poet' as a culture's best kind of prophet. (Although the Master of the University's expression of relief at coming across 'a prophet who prophesied good things and not bad' turns his reclaiming of a great rebel into something close to bathos.) When Samuel Johnson had written his *Lives of the English Poets* near the end of the eighteenth century, he had composed salutary narratives of the petty vanities and material pressures of authors' lives – especially the authors whose poetry he most admired. One of the successes of Romanticism with Victorians was to make poets better than this. Individual genius was emphasised, and therefore the life of the writer dignified. The memorialists whose accounts are represented in this volume and others in this edition were contributing to an idea of authorship at the heart of Romanticism.

In Shelley's case, the poetry seemed to force biography on the curious reader, and often to tempt the hostile critic to reflection on the poet's life. This was not only because the lyrical verse beloved of Victorian readers seemed to speak directly of particular occasions of rapture or dejection. It was also because some of his most self-consciously idealistic writing seemed – and, indeed, still seems – to insist that ideals should be practised, that manners of living and writing should not be dissociated. For Shelley, we could say, the personal was the political. He was not the first English poet to write with passion of the poverty and powerlessness of the labouring classes. However, he was the first to stake the creative claims of atheism, and, with the possible (and still obscure) exception of Blake, was the first to turn a politics of sexual liberation into poetry. How could the poet's life not matter, when his earliest long poem, *Queen Mab* (1813), privately distri-buted by Shelley but popular in pirated editions from the early 1820s, spoke so strongly against marriage and in favour of free love? Working to make his verse carry his ideas (*Queen Mab* is subtitled 'A Philosophical Poem') Shelley appended lengthy 'Notes' to the poem, keyed to particular lines.

One of these declares, 'Love withers under constraint: its very essence is liberty: it is compatible neither with obedience, jealousy, nor fear' (Matthews and Everest, p. 368). Any law, therefore, binding a husband and wife 'for one moment after the decay of their affection' can only be 'intolerable tyranny'.

> Constancy has nothing virtuous in itself, independently of the pleasure it confers... Love is free: to promise for ever to love the same woman, is not less absurd than to promise to believe the same creed: such a vow, in both cases, excludes us from all enquiry (Matthews and Everest, p. 370).

It is true that Shelley was not quite twenty-one when he wrote this (and, it might be added, still apparently happy with his wife Harriet, whom he had married almost two years earlier). But the idea that political freedom should be accompanied by a liberation from the 'system of constraint' governing sexual relations – that the pursuit of sexual satisfaction outside marriage might even be, as is implied in the passage above, a kind of intellectual exploration – was pursued in his mature poetry. 'Love is celebrated everywhere as the sole law which should govern the moral world', proclaims the last sentence of the Preface to Shelley's longest poem, *The Revolt of Islam*, published in January 1818 (see Hutchinson, p. 37). 'Love' here, as elsewhere in Shelley's writing, includes both what the Preface calls 'love of mankind' – that feeling stirred in the 'most generous and amiable natures' by the first phases of the French Revolution, of which this poem is in part an allegory – and sexual passion. In its first incarnation, as *Laon and Cythna; or, The Revolution of the Golden City: A Vision of the Nineteenth Century*, the poem was more 'revolutionary' than the version eventually published. In this earlier version the two lovers of the title were brother and sister, and several highly wrought passages of *The Revolt of Islam* (see particularly Canto VI, stanzas xxix–xxxviii) were once apparent celebrations of an incestuous passion, consumated. When the poem, although already printed, was suppressed before publication by the publisher, Charles Ollier, it was because of his worries about this aspect of the narrative, rather than because of its political radicalism or its hostility to established religion. Shelley wrote to Thomas Moore a few weeks before *The Revolt of Islam* appeared saying that the alterations 'consist in little else than the substitution of the words *friend* or *lover* for that of *brother & sister*' (Jones, *Letters*, I, p. 582). (Although Richard Holmes points out that 'Shelley was being less than frank', as he also cancelled rather more lines with 'controversial references to God, Hell, Christ, republicanism and atheism': Holmes, p. 391). The 'seclusion of my habits', he explained, had made him oblivious to what 'revolts & shocks many who might be inclined to sympathise with me in my general views'.

Even with this fundamental rebellion against sexual taboo excised, the implicit and explicit advocacy of free love remained. When Cythna, in the guise of Laone ('most eloquently fair'), makes a rousing speech to her fellow revolutionaries in Canto V, the rhetoric of *Queen Mab* returns in her celebration of intellectual progress, vegetarianism, and free love:

> 'My brethren, we are free! the plains and mountains,
> The gray sea-shore, the forests and the fountains,
> Are haunts of happiest dwellers; – man and woman,
> Their common bondage burst, may freely borrow
> From lawless love a solace for their sorrow

(Canto V, stanza li, verse 4: unless otherwise stated, all references to Shelley's poems are to the one-volume Oxford text, ed. Hutchinson).

Shelley's Preface calls his poem 'an experiment on the temper of the public mind, as to how far a thirst for a happier condition of moral and political society survives, among the enlightened and refined, the tempests which have shaken the age in which we live' (Hutchinson, p. 32). The 'happier condition' would be one of equality between the sexes (thus the point of having a brother and sister as leading characters). Laon fixes his bond with Cythna when he realizes that

> Never will peace and human nature meet
> Till free and equal man and woman greet
> Domestic peace
>   (II, xxxvii).

Incest was necessary to the original design because the poem was dreaming of an equality between the sexes that could involve both intellectual affinity and sexual passion. This idea returns in some of the memoirs that follow when the braver biographers try to justify Shelley's abandonment of his first wife for Mary Godwin: Harriet was youthful infatuation; Mary was intellectual soul-mate.

The Revolt of Islam was dedicated 'To MARY — —' (and was clearly much influenced by Shelley's reading of the writings of her mother, Mary Wollstonecraft). His dedicatory verses make only slightly abstracted reference to his own quest for the sympathies and satisfactions envisioned in the poem, and, it is implied, privately experienced in his relationship with Mary.

> Alas, that love should be a blight and snare
> To those who seek all sympathies in one! –
> Such once I sought in vain
>   (Dedication, vi).

In his search for this 'one', 'never found I one not false to me,/Hard hearts, and cold'. Until Mary.

Thou Friend, whose presence on my wintry heart
Fell, like bright Spring upon some herbless plain
(Dedication, vii).

One does not have to be one of Shelley's nineteenth-century antagonists to feel that a reading of such a poem might need to be set against the life of its author. In this century, even the most sympathetic critics have flinched from Shelley's assertion that all before Mary were 'false', when tested against what we now know of his relationship with and separation from Harriet. Whatever our verdicts, and those of the memoirists included in this anthology, it is impossible to deny that Shelley makes his life, and what Victorians would have called his 'conduct', a matter of enquiry.

His conduct had, in one particular respect, become public a year earlier when, after the discovery of Harriet Shelley's suicide in December 1816 and the marriage of Shelley and Mary Godwin at the end of the same month, Harriet's father, John Westbrook, had filed a Bill of Complaint in Chancery for the appointment of guardians for Harriet's children by Shelley, Charles and Ianthe. Shelley lost his struggle for custody, and was quick to see the court's judgement as having been made, as he wrote in a letter to Byron, 'on the ground of my being a REVOLUTIONIST, and an *Atheist*' (Jones, *Letters*, I, p. 530). Eliza Westbrook, Harriet's sister and often the target of Shelley's hostility, had 'whilst she lived in my house... possessed herself of such papers as go to establish these allegations'. That this interpretation was self-serving would be evident even without the later confirmation of Shelley's friend Thomas Love Peacock, included in this volume. John Westbrook had in fact put together more ordinary evidence of Shelley's supposed unfitness as a guardian, including his failure to visit the children after his separation from his wife (see Holmes, pp. 356–7). It is a sign of Shelley's (at this time understandable) inability to examine his own part in 'unexpected and overwhelming sorrows' that, in the same letter to Byron, he wrote that Eliza Westbrook 'may be truly said (though not in law, yet in fact) to have murdered her [Harriet] for the sake of her father's money'. The basis for this conviction – that Harriet had been driven from the family home and into despair by her sister's machinations – seems to have been solely Shelley's desire to believe it true. Yet even if his own role was, in the immediate aftermath of Harriet's suicide, invisible to him, it was certainly not, after the Chancery case, a private affair.

Characteristically, four years later Shelley turned the effects of this tragedy into part of a poem in which an autobiography of love is treated as an allegory of the yearnings of the human soul. The poem in which readers have frequently found this autobiography is another which seems to speak in favour of free love: *Epipsychidion*. It is addressed to 'EMILIA V – ': in fact,

Emilia Viviani, the nineteen year-old daughter of Count Viviani, the Governor of Pisa, who was confined in a convent while her parents attempted to arrange her marriage. 'Discovered' by Claire Clairmont, she was introduced to Shelley in December 1820. The Shelleys visited and corresponded with her and, writing to Claire, Shelley confessed himself her admirer: 'She continues to to enchant me infinitely' (Jones, *Letters*, II, p. 254). This enchantment spoke itself in *Epipsychidion*, composed in January and February 1821 and published by Ollier (anonymously) in the Summer of the same year. The most autobiographical passage of the poem speaks of that same pursuit of love described in the Dedication to *The Revolt of Islam*.

> In many mortal forms I rashly sought
> The shadow of that idol of my thought
> (ll. 267–8).

Now the pursuit has taken a new dirction. Mary Godwin, once consumation of all hopes, seems to appear as the Moon, who 'makes all beautiful on which she smiles' (l. 282), but is also 'cold' and 'chaste' (as if acknowledging the association, in her Journal entries for 5 and 10 October 1822 Mary Shelley refers to herself as 'moonshine', and in October 1822 ends a letter to Byron by saying, 'now I am truly *cold moonshine*: Bennett, *Letters*, I, p. 284). The death of Harriet is surely the substance of the part of the poem where 'storms' obscure the Moon, and Shelley's first wife the 'She' of these lines:

> when She,
> The Planet of that hour, was quenched, what frost
> Crept o'er those waters, till from coast to coast
> The moving billows of my being fell
> Into a death of ice, immovable
> (ll. 312–16).

Epipsychidion goes on to speak of the 'Comet beautiful and fierce,/ Who drew the heart of this frail Universe/ Towards thine own' (ll. 368–70) – apparently an idealization of Claire Clairmont – and then directly to address 'Emily' as 'my heart's sister', invited to share some imagined 'Elysian isle' with the poet (ll. 415 and 539). It ends with an ecstatic expression of the 'passion in twin-hearts' that he and she will enjoy: 'Our breath shall intermix, our bosoms bound,/ And our veins beat together' (ll. 565–6). Perhaps it is unsurprising that it is the only lengthy poem that Mary Shelley was to print entirely without comment when she produced her edition of Shelley's *Poetical Works* in 1839. (Shelley's feelings for 'Emily' had already ebbed by the Spring of 1821, and in July she wrote to Shelley, perhaps at her family's bidding, to ask the Shelleys not to visit her again – although she was to write asking him for money that Autumn. She was married to a presentable husband in September 1821.) It is in *Epipsychidion* that Shelley seems to speak most clearly of his personal adherence to a belief in free love.

> I never was attached to that great sect,
> Whose doctrine is, that each one should select
> Out of the crowd a mistress or a friend,
> And all the rest, though fair and wise, commend
> To cold oblivion, though it is in the code
> Of modern morals
>
> (ll. 149–54).

'True Love in this differs from gold and clay,/ That to divide is not to take away' (ll. 161–2): neat rhyme for a doubtable proposition. In a first draft of the passage he had written not 'True Love' but 'Free love' (see Hutchinson, p. 426).

It has always, then, been particularly difficult to apply in Shelley's case the argument that the titillating details of the writer's private life are not relevant to his poetry. Yet, surprisingly, only occasionally in Shelley's lifetime did hostile reviewers refer to the poet's own conduct. John Taylor Coleridge, Coleridge's nephew, did describe Shelley as a man 'who thinks even adultery vapid unless he can render it more exquisitely poignant by adding incest to it' in a review of Leigh Hunt's *Foliage* (*The Quarterly Review*, 18 May 1818) – the 'incest' presumably being a reference to Shelley's rumoured liason with his wife's 'sister' (in fact her step-sister) Claire Clairmont. The same critic was to end an antagonistic review of *The Revolt of Islam* a year later by implying a scandal which he would not specify: 'if we might withdraw the veil of private life, and tell what we *now* know about him, it would be indeed a disgusting picture that we should exhibit, but it would be an unanswerable comment on our text' (*The Quarterly Review*, April 1819, in Barcus, p. 135). Yet this review drew down on Coleridge the anger of the anonymous reviewer of *Alastor* in the conservative *Blackwood's Magazine*. The reviewer, who might have been John Gibson Lockhart, disdained him as 'a dunce rating a man of genius'. 'If that critic does not know that Mr. Shelley is a poet, almost in the very highest sense of that mysterious word, then, we appeal to all those whom we have enabled to judge for themselves, if he be not unfit to speak of poetry before the people of England' (ibid, p. 103). 'He *exults* to calumniate Mr. Shelley's moral character, but he *fears* to acknowledge his genius'.

In *The Examiner*, Leigh Hunt vigilantly surveyed responses to Shelley's poetry and defended his achievements; his efforts at biography represented in this volume were but a posthumous continuation of the campaign on behalf of Shelley that he began with his 'Young Poets' article of 1 December 1816, and pursued vigorously in his periodical between 1818 and 1822. John

Taylor Coleridge's review of *The Revolt of Islam* brought angry replies from Hunt in *The Examiner* of 26 September 1819; 3 October 1819; and 10 October 1819 (see Barcus, pp. 135–43). Hunt declared that Shelley was much more remarkable for 'Christian benevolence' than his supposedly Christian critics (ibid, p. 140), and denounced the assault on 'the private life of an author'. 'Failing in the attempt to refute Mr. Shelley's philosophy, the Reviewers attack his private life'. Rejecting all notion that Shelley might be 'dissolute in his conduct', Hunt described him living a life of asceticism and high-minded intellectual enquiry – 'nor have we ever known him, in spite of the malignant and ludicrous exaggerations on this point, deviate, notwithstanding his theories, even into a single action which those who differ with him might think blameable' (ibid, p. 143).

In his collection of contemporary criticism of Shelley, *The Unextinguished Hearth*, Newman Ivey White points out that Hunt's partisanship might not have always helped Shelley. 'Gallant as Leigh Hunt's long championship of Shelley seems today, it was certainly more disastrous than beneficial during Shelley's lifetime' (p. 20). It was the association with Hunt that often drew the fire of critics. Thus another *Blackwood's* article berates Shelley for having 'the same pernicious purposes' as the 'COCKNEY SCHOOL', but finds in him the poetic genius that Hunt and Keats lack (Barcus, pp. 115–6). Yet even here, despite 'the author's execrable system', the critic finds the poetry 'impressed every where with the more noble and majestic footsteps of footsteps of his genius' (ibid, p. 116). After all, Shelley is not really a 'COCKNEY'.

> Mr. Shelley, whatever his errors may have been, is a scholar, a gentleman, and a poet; and he must therefore despise from his soul the only eulogies to which he has hitherto been accustomed – paragraphs from the *Examiner*, and sonnets fron Johny Keats. He has it in his power to select better companions; and if he does so, he may very securely promise himself abundance of better praise (ibid, p. 122).

What will often seem surprising to modern readers about contemporary reviews is their willingness to find merit (even if it is only 'poetic') in what Shelley was writing. Hunt might have needed to believe this unlikely ('the bigot will be shocked, terrified, and enraged; and fall to providing all that is said against himself': *The Examiner*, 1 February 1818, p. 75) but even John Taylor Coleridge concedes 'beautiful passages' (see Barcus, p. 125). The efforts of Shelley's friends and admirers to celebrate his poetry and justify his life were never simple and necessary responses to contemporary hostility or stupidity. As will be seen from the following pages, certain biographical issues were difficult for them because, at the very least, they seemed to indicate contradictions between ideals and actions, and these in the life of the most idealistic of writers. Some of the difficulties are different for different memoirists, although all need either to explain or (more often) carefully to avoid being clear about Shelley's separation from Harriet, and his adultery with Mary Godwin. Because of the embarrassment of Shelley's first biographers, the facts of the matter were only debated with any precision when Peacock entered the memoirists' fray almost forty years after the poet's death (see the headnotes in this volume to extracts from his 'Memoirs of Percy Bysshe Shelley').

When narrating this part of Shelley's life, twentieth-century biographers have also had to take account of testimonies that might have been influential upon those who wrote memoirs, but which remained private in the nineteenth century. Contradicting the 'official' story that Shelley and his first wife had separated before he commenced his relationship with Mary Godwin, for instance, Claire Clairmont told Trelawny, when he was preparing his *Records* in 1878 and had written to her asking about Harriet's suicide, that 'It was no fault of her's that S— quitted her – he fell desperately in love with Mary' (in K. N. Cameron, *Shelley and His Circle 1773–1822*, vol. 4, p. 787; readers will find the information about Harriet Shelley's death, and reactions to it, expertly marshalled in this volume, pp. 769–802). Claire went on to say that Harriet's 'lover' after the separation was 'a Captain in the Indian or Wellington army' (ibid, p. 788). (She had this story from her mother, who was apparently given the details by Eliza Westbrook.) In this letter to Trelawny she added that he should not believe rumours that Harriet had 'a connexion with some low man': this might be implied in William Michael Rossetti's 'Memoir' of 1870, but he wrote 'to suit Lady Shelley's predilections – and she is a warm partisan of Shelley and Mary, and like all warm partisans does not care much about Truth'.

To Claire we also owe the report, transmitted via Mrs Godwin, that Shelley persuaded Mary to stay with him 'by declaring that Harriet did not really care for him; that she was in love with a Major Ryan; and the child she would have was certainly not his' (ibid, p. 772). Since White's 1940 biography, scholars have worried over whether, if this was so, Shelley was deceiving Mary, or deceiving himself. As White says, 'In no normal sense of the word does it seem possible for Shelley himself to have believed her unfaithful at this time... In all subsequent references to Harriet's two children he plainly assumed paternity. Charles Clairmont [Mrs Godwin's son], who drew his information from Shelley, later expressly exonerated Harriet from this charge while condemning her on other grounds' (I, p. 346). Mary's father, who ostracized Shelley after the elopement with his daughter and step-daughter, needed to believe some such chain of events once the two men were reconciled at the end of 1816. In a letter of 12 May 1817 to William Baxter, he wrote that Harriet 'had proved herself unfaithful to her husband before their separation. Afterwards, she was guilty of repeated acts of levity, & had latterly lived in open connection with a colonel Maxwel' (Cameron, p. 787). Baxter's daughter Isabel had been a friend of Mary's, but her family had forbidden all contact after Mary's elopement with Shelley. Godwin's attempt to persuade Baxter to reconsider this ban – which is, of necessity, also an attempt to justify his own acceptance of his new son-in-law – manages to sound, as William St Clair notes, almost pleased by Harriet Shelley's death:

> My first information you will be very glad to hear. Mrs. Shelley died in November last and on the 30th December Shelley led my daughter to the altar. I shall always look with poignant regret upon the preceding events but you can scarcely imagine how great a relief this has brought to mine and Mrs. God-win's mind. Mary has now (most unexpectedly) acquired a status and character in society
>
> (in St Clair, *The Godwins*, p. 417).

Godwin's testimony as to Harriet's character and conduct can surely be worth very little.

In a letter to Mary the day after being informed of his first wife's suicide, Shelley wrote that 'this poor woman – the most innocent of her abhorred & unnatural family – was driven from her father's house, & descended the steps of prostitution' (Jones, *Letters*, I, p. 521). Both parts of this seem unlikely, although Shelley sometimes wrote of 'prostitution' rather loosely, using the word to refer to any case of cohabitation without 'love'. At this stage he actually knew very little of his wife's fate, and did not have the most vivid and sad testimony to her last days, a letter that she wrote shortly before her death, adressed, in turn, first to her sister, and then to her husband. 'Too wretched to exert myself lowered in the opinion of everyone why should I drag on a miserable existence embittered by past recollections & not one ray of hope to rest on for the future' (Cameron, p. 805: the letter is also given in Jones, *Letters*, I, p. 520). Harriet Shelley's last request of her husband went against the grain of his rooted hostility to her sister: 'let me conjure you by the remembrance of our days of happiness to grant my last wish – do not take your innocent child [Ianthe] from Eliza who has been more than I have, who has watched over her with such unceasing care' – Shelley's contesting of the Chancery case, of course, went against this wish. More painfully, her letter, in its address to Shelley, made that connection between her fate and his actions that his memoirists would find difficult: '. . .if you had never left me I might have lived but as it is, I freely forgive you & may you enjoy that happiness which you have deprived me of'.

Clearly, none of Shelley's memoirists could ignore the history of his two marriages. Lack of documentary evidence that has since become available meant, however, that they could more easily deal with – or avoid dealing with – other questions about the poet's life. In particular, Shelley's relationship with Claire Clairmont, still a matter of controversy, is either ignored or treated as unproblematic. Since the 1930s, we have known that, in early 1815, Hogg, with Shelley's encouragement, courted Mary, who was, when the would-be love affair commenced, heavily pregant (for Mary's letters to Hogg at this time, see Bennett, *Letters*, I, pp. 6–14). She wrote that her 'affection' for him was not 'exactly as you would wish', but thought that it would 'dayly become more so – then what can you have to add to your happiness' (ibid, p. 8). It would seem that, with Shelley's full knowledge, she was contemplating a sexual relationship (although it is unlikely that it was consumated). Inevitably, the extraordinary correspondence between Mary and Hogg, and Shelley's evident willingness to share his lover with his friend, has provoked speculation about Shelley's relationship with Claire, with whom, often to Mary's disgruntlement, he was spending much of his time. At least some contemporary witnesses, perhaps including Godwin, seem to have assumed that the two were, or had been, lovers (see St Clair, *The Godwins*, pp. 420–1) – although such assumptions cannot quite be evidence. Speculation was given another twist, in this century, by the discovery that, in Naples in December 1818, Shelley registered a baby girl, falsely, as his child by Mary. The true parentage of Elena Adelaide Shelley, who died eighteen months later, remains a matter of dispute (see White, II, pp. 71–83 for the earliest and most painstaking account), but a possibility frequently entertained is that this child was, in fact, Shelley's daughter by Claire, who was in Naples with the Shelleys at the time. This possibility was the subject of the 'malicious reports' to which Lady Jane Shelley refers in an extract in this volume (see p. 339). There is still sometimes sharp disagreement about this.

The likelihood, or otherwise, of a sexual relationship at some time beween Shelley and Claire Clairmont is frequently discussed in modern biographies not only of these two, but also of Mary Shelley, who in recent decades has become an important literary character in her own right and the subject of many biographical studies. To browse through a few of these is to encounter some of the necessary illusions that bolster biographers, in the twentieth as much as in the nineteenth century, for they usually express equal but incompatible certainties about the relationship between Shelley and Claire. This is true of even the more scholarly accounts. The first important biography of Mary Shelley to be produced after her dalliance with Hogg became clear, R. Glynn Grylls' *Mary Shelley. A Biography* (1938), did not imagine what later biographers have often thought obvious, but then it found Claire such 'a feather-brain' that any real intimacy between her and Shelley seemed beyond consideration. More recently, Claire has had her advocates, with their different sympathies. In her invaluable edition of Claire Clairmont's *Journals*, Marion Kingston Stocking decides that 'a sexual union between Claire and Shelley' would have not have been 'inconsistent with their principles, provided that they had been genuinely and deeply in love. I can find, however, no evidence that they were' (p. 97). Nineteenth-century biographers struggled to make Shelley true to his principles; in the second half of the twentieth century, writers have tried to do the same for Mary and Claire.

Some of the principles that most trouble Shelley's admirers in the the following pages now give rather less pause to readers. In every tone from apology to endorsement, those who produced memoirs of the poet dealt with the poet's atheism – proclaimed not only in his poetry and polemical prose, but in his life. His adventures had, after all, begun with the publication of *The Necessity of Atheism* (appropriately, a rare copy of the original edition of this pamphlet was part of Lady Shelley's bequest to the Bodleian). Frequently it was found necessary to convert Shelley into an essentially Christian, or essentially religious, person: his acts of charity and his devout wonderment at the beauties of Creation are therefore constant themes. The man once reviled for blasphemy was to become the 'divine' poet, drawn upwards from the sublunary world into a heaven of ideals that, however impractical, were always admirable. Not that the sense of a man with his mind on higher things was merely wishful. Hogg's version, for instance, of Shelley at Oxford – one biographical 'explanation' of his atheism in its early shape – has always, with its recollections of electrical experiments and audacious, sceptical talk, simply rung true. Like plenty of other anecdotes in the memoirs in this anthology, its details have been preserved in more recent and disinterested accounts.

And here we come to an odd fact about the little industry of commemoration whose climax was the opening of the Shelley Memorial at University College, Oxford. However untrustworthy and mutually hostile the memoirs excerpted in this volume, they have nevertheless contributed a great deal to our knowledge of the poet. This is not only because they are sometimes our clearest evidence, even in their evasions, about certain aspects of Shelley's life. (After all, most of the testimonies to which any biographer returns will be *parti pris*.) It is also because they often do seem, despite their deceptions or self-delusions, to bear the impressions of real memory – to catch, if not the character of the writer, at least a recall of the effects of knowing him. In this way, their efforts to make the best of his life could be thought to do a kind of justice to him. In part, this is because of a kind of unanimity in their verdicts, if not in their 'facts': Shelley undoubtedly inspired loyalty and affection that even the reader attentive to the memoirists' likely distortions must recognize. It is also because only a remarkable writer – and a writer who made his life remarkable in his writings – could command such efforts at explanation. In 'Julian and Maddalo', a poem in which we can find a vivid depiction of his friendship with Byron, Shelley provides one of the many self-characterizations to be found in his writing, apparently inviting biographical criticism. He is Julian, 'passionately attached to those philosophical notions which assert the power of man over his own mind, and the immense improvements of which, by the extinction of certain moral superstitions, human society may yet be susceptible' ('Julian and Maddalo', Preface). He is also, it is to be confessed, 'rather serious'. As if foreseeing all those posthumous memoirs, the poem's preface wryly invites us to test the ideals against the character: 'Julian, in spite of his heterodox opinions, is conjectured by his friends to possess some good qualities. How far this is possible the pious reader will determine'. It is an invitation that has proved difficult to refuse.

BIBLIOGRAPHY

References to works are by author's or editor's names, and volume and page number. If a person is author or editor of more than one work, an abbreviated form of the work's title is used (e.g. St Clair, *Trelawny*, p. 150).

Primary texts

[Dix, J.,] *Pen and Ink Sketches of Poets, Preachers, and Politicians* (London, 1746)

Hazlitt, William, 'On Paradox and Common-place', in *Table-Talk; or, Original Essays*, (London, 1821)

[Hogg, Thomas Jefferson,] 'Shelley at Oxford', in *The New Monthly Magazine* (January, February, April, July, October, December 1832; May 1833)

Hogg, Thomas Jefferson, *The Life of Percy Bysshe Shelley*, 2 vols (London: Edward Moxon, 1858)

Hunt, Leigh, *Lord Byron and Some of His Contemporaries; with Recollections of the Author's Life, and of His Visit to Italy* (London: Henry Colburn, 1828)

Hunt, Leigh, *The Autobiography of Leigh Hunt; with Reminiscences of Friends and Contemporaries*, 3 vols (London, 1850)

Hunt, Thornton, 'Shelley. By One Who Knew Him', in *The Atlantic Monthly* (Boston) February, 1863: pp.183–203

Medwin, Thomas, *Journal of the Conversations of Lord Byron: Noted During a Residence with his Lordship at Pisa, in the Years 1821 and 1822* (London, 1824)

Medwin, Thomas, *The Life of Percy Bysshe Shelley*, 2 vols (London: T.C. Newby, 1847)

Medwin, Thomas, *The Shelley Papers. Memoir of Percy Bysshe Shelley by T. Medwin, Esq. and Original Poems and Papers by Percy Bysshe Shelley Now First Collected* (London, 1833)

Peacock, Thomas Love, 'Memoirs of Shelley', in *Fraser's Magazine*, June 1858, January 1860, and March 1862

Polidori, John, *The Diary of Dr. John William Polidori 1816*, ed. William Michael Rossetti (London: Elkin Mathews, 1911)

Shelley, Lady Jane (ed.), *Shelley Memorials: from Authentic Sources* (London, 1859)

[Shelley, Mary (ed.)] *Posthumous Poems of Percy Bysshe Shelley* (London, 1824)

Shelley, Mary (ed.), *Essays, Letters from Abroard, Translations and Fragments, by Percy Bysshe Shelley*, 2 vols (London, 1840)

Trelawny, E. J., *Recollections of the Last Days of Shelley and Byron* (London: Edward Moxon, 1858)

Trelawny, E. J., *Records of Shelley, Byron, and the Author*, 2 vols (London: Basil Montagu Pickering, 1878)

Secondary texts

Barcus, James E. (ed.), *Shelley. The Critical Heritage* (London: Routledge & Kegan Paul, 1975)

Bennett, Betty T. (ed.), *The Letters of Mary Wollstonecraft Shelley*, 3 vols (Baltimore: The Johns Hopkins University Press, 1980–88)

—— (ed.), *Selected Letters of Mary Wollstonecraft Shelley* (Baltimore: The Johns Hopkins University Press, 1995)

Browning, Robert, 'Essay on Shelley' in *The Poems, Volume I*, ed., John Pettigrew (Penguin: Harmondsworth, 1981)

Butler, Marilyn, *Peacock Displayed. A Satirist in His Context* (London: Routledge & Kegan Paul, 1979)

Cameron, K. N. (ed.), *Shelley and His Circle 1773–1822*, Vol. II (Cambridge, Mass.: Harvard University Press, 1961)

—— (ed.), *Shelley and His Circle 1773–1822*, Vol. III (Cambridge, Mass.: Harvard University Press, 1970)

—— (ed.), *Shelley and His Circle 1773–1822*, Vol. IV (Cambridge, Mass.: Harvard University Press, 1970)

Engelberg, Karsten Klejs, *The Making of the Shelley Myth. An annotated bibliography of criticism of Percy Bysshe Shelley, 1822–1860* (London: Mansell Publishing, 1988)

Feldman, Paula R. and Diana Scott-Kilvert (eds), *The Journals of Mary Shelley 1814–1844*, 2 vols (Oxford: Clarendon Press, 1987)

Forman, H. Buxton (ed.), *The Life of Percy Bysshe Shelley*, by Thomas Medwin (London: Oxford University Press, 1913)

Garnett, Richard, 'Shelley in Pall Mall', in *Macmillan's Magazine*, No. 8 (June, 1860) pp. 100–110

—— (ed.), *Relics of Shelley* (London: Edward Moxon & Co., 1862)

Grylls, R. Glynn, *Mary Shelley. A Biography* (London: Oxford University Press, 1938)

Holmes, Richard, *Shelley. The Pursuit* (London: Weidenfeld & Nicolson, 1974)

Hutchinson, Thomas (ed.), *Shelley. Poetical Works*, rev. G.M. Matthews (London: Oxford University Press, 1970)

Ingpen, Roger, *Shelley in England: New Facts and Letters from the Shelley-Whitton Papers*, 2 vols (London: Kegan Paul, Trench, Trubner & Co., 1917)

Jones, Frederick L. (ed.), *The Letters of Percy Bysshe Shelley*, 2 vols (Oxford: Clarendon Press, 1964)

—— (ed.), *Maria Gisborne & Edward E. Williams, Shelley's Friends. Their Journals and Letters* (Norman, Ok.: University of Oklahoma Press, 1951)

Jones, Stanley, *Hazlitt: A Life* (Oxford: Clarendon Press, 1989)

Lovell, Ernest J., *Captain Medwin: Friend of Byron and Shelley* (Austin, Tx: University of Texas Press, 1962)

—— (ed.), *Medwin's Conversations of Lord Byron* (Princeton, N.J.: Princeton University Press, 1966)

Marchand, *Byron. A Biography*, 3 vols (New York: Alfred A. Knopf, 1957)

Matthews, Geoffrey, and Kelvin Everest (eds), *The Poems of Shelley. Volume I 1804–1817* (London: Longman, 1989)

Medwin, Thomas, *The Angler in Wales*, 2 vols (London: Richard Bentley, 1834)

Miller, Barnette, *Leigh Hunt's Relations with Byron, Shelley and Keats* (New York: Columbia University Press, 1910)

Norman, Sylva, *Flight of the Skylark. The Development of Shelley's Reputation* (Norman, Ok.: University of Oklahoma Press, 1954)

Redpath, Theodore, *The Young Romantics and Critical Opinion 1807–1824* (London: Harrap, 1973)

Reiman, Donald H. (ed.), *Shelley and His Circle 1773–1822*, Vol. V (Cambridge, Mass.: Harvard University Press, 1973)

Rolleston, Maud, *Talks with Lady Shelley* (London: George G. Harrap & Co., 1925)

St Clair, William, *Trelawny. The Incurable Romancer* (New York: The Vanguard Press, 1977)

——, *The Godwins and the Shelleys. The Biography of a Family* (London: Faber & Faber, 1989)

Smith, Robert M., *The Shelley Legend* (New York: Charles Scribner's Sons, 1945)

Stocking, Marion Kingston (ed.), *The Journals of Claire Clairmont* (Cambridge, Mass.: Harvard University Press, 1968)

Sullivan, Alvin (ed.), *British Literary Magazines. The Romantic Age, 1789–1836* (Westport, Conn.: Greenwood Press, 1983)

Taylor, Charles H., Jr., *The Early Collected Editions of Shelley's Poems* (New Haven, Conn.: Yale University Press, 1958)

Tennyson, Hallam, *Alfred Lord Tennyson. A Memoir*, 1st ed. 1897 (London, 1899)

Thompson, James R., *Leigh Hunt* (Boston, Mass.: Twayne, 1977)

White, Newman Ivey, *Shelley*, 2 vols, first published 1940, 2nd ed. (London: Secker & Warburg, 1947)

—— (ed.), *The Unextinguished Hearth. Shelley and His Contemporary Critics* (1938; rpt. London: Frank Cass & Co., 1966)

CHRONOLOGY

1792 (4 August) Percy Bysshe Shelley born.

1798 Enters the school of the Rev. Edwards, the local vicar.

1802 Begins boarding at Syon House Academy, Isleworth, Middlesex.

1804 (September) Is sent to Eton College, where he remains for the next six years.

1809 Meets and begins a correspondence with his cousin, Harriet Grove.

1810 (March) *Zastrozzi*, a Gothic novel, published. (October) Shelley begins at University College, Oxford, and meets Thomas Jefferson Hogg.

1811 (February) 'The Necessity of Atheism' published. (March) Shelley writes to Leigh Hunt for the first time; Shelley and Hogg expelled from University College. (April) Shelley becomes friendly with Harriet Westbrook and her sister, Eliza. (May) Shelley meets Leigh Hunt. (August) Shelley and Harriet Westbrook elope to Edinburgh where, though both under legal age, they are married on 29 August. (November) The Shelleys leave York for the Lake District with Eliza Westbrook after Hogg attempts to seduce Harriet.

1812 (January) Shelley writes to Godwin for the first time. (February) The Shelleys travel to Ireland with Eliza Westbrook, returning to Wales in April. (June) They travel to Lynmouth, Devon, where they live for two months. (October) The Shelleys are in London, and Shelley first meets Godwin. (November) Shelley meets Thomas Love Peacock and Mary Godwin; his friendship with Hogg is restored. (December) Shelley returns to Wales with Harriet and Eliza, living for three months at Tremadoc, a model community created by philanthropist and MP William Madocks.

1813 (April) After another trip to Ireland, the Shelleys are back in London. (May) *Queen Mab* is printed. (June) The Shelleys' first child, Eliza Ianthe, is born. (July) The couple are staying in Bracknell, Berkshire, near their friend Mrs Boinville. (December) They move to Windsor, though Shelley continues to spend much of his time with the Boinvilles.

1814   (22 March) Shelley re-marries Harriet in London, possibly because
        of doubts about the legality of their Scottish wedding. (May) Shelley
        meets Mary Godwin again. (July) Harriet comes to London, and
        Shelley tells her that he is in love with Mary Godwin. On 28 July, he,
        Mary, and Claire Clairmont leave for France. They spend August
        and early September travelling through France, Switzerland, Ger-
        many and Holland, before returning to London. Godwin refuses to
        meet Shelley, who lives with Mary and Claire Clairmont at various
        London addresses. (30 November) Harriet Shelley gives birth to a
        son, Charles.

1815   (January) Hogg commences an amorous correspondence with Mary.
        (22 February) Mary gives birth, prematurely, to a girl, who dies two
        weeks later. (August) Shelley and Mary rent a house at Bishopsgate,
        near Windsor. *Alastor* is written by the end of 1815.

1816   (24 January) Mary gives birth to a son, William. (February) *Alastor*
        published. (March) Claire Clairmont begins an affair with Byron; she
        is now living in London with Shelley and Mary. (May) The three of
        them leave England for the Continent and travel to Geneva. (June)
        They move to a small house at Cologny; Byron stays nearby at Villa
        Diodati. They travel in the locality, visiting Mont Blanc at the end of
        July. (September) The Shelley party returns to England. (October)
        Fanny Imlay, Mary Godwin's half-sister, commits suicide. (10 De-
        cember) Harriet Shelley's body found in the Serpentine; Shelley is
        informed by Thomas Hookham on 15 December. On 30 December
        he and Mary are married, and he is soon on friendly terms once more
        with Godwin.

1817   (January) The commencement of the Chancery hearing to settle
        custody of Ianthe and Charles Shelley; on 12 January, Claire Clair-
        mont's daughter by Byron is born, and called Alba – later, at Byron's
        request, Allegra. 'Hymn to Intellectual Beauty' published in *The
        Examiner*. The Shelleys stay with the Hunts. (March) They move to
        Marlow, where Peacock lives. (September) Mary gives birth to a
        daughter, Clara. (November) *Laon and Cythna* printed, but with-
        drawn from publication. Shelley agrees to make alterations to it.

1818   (January) *The Revolt of Islam*, the altered and retitled *Laon and
        Cythna*, is published. 'Ozymandias' appears in *The Examiner*. The
        Shelleys return to London. (March) *Frankenstein* published anony-
        mously. The Shelleys, with their two children, Claire Clairmont, and
        her daughter, Allegra, depart for Italy. After travel around Northern
        Italy, they settle in Bagni di Lucca in June. (July) Shelley translates
        the *Symposium*. (September) Shelley begins *Prometheus Unbound*.

Clara Shelley dies. (October) The Shelleys in Venice, where Shelley spends time with Byron and begins 'Julian and Maddalo'. (November) The Shelley party, including Claire Clairmont, travels to Rome and Naples. (December) 'Elena Adelaide Shelley' registered in Naples as the Shelleys' child.

1819   (28 February) The Shelleys and Claire Clairmont leave Naples They stay in Rome until mid-June. (7 June) William Shelley dies. (August) Shelley completes *The Cenci*; later this month he hears of the Peterloo Massacre, which inspires 'The Mask of Anarchy'. The Shelleys spend the next four months in Florence, where 'Ode to the West Wind' is composed. (November) The Shelleys' son, Percy Florence, is born on 12 November.

1820   (January) The Shelleys move to Pisa. (March) *The Cenci* is published. (June) Elena Adelaide Shelley dies in Naples. (August) *Prometheus Unbound: A Lyrical Drama in Four Acts, with Other Poems* is published. (October) Thomas Medwin arrives. (December) The Shelleys meet Emilia Viviani.

1821   (January) Edward and Jane Williams arrive in Pisa. Shelley completes 'The Witch of Atlas' and commences *A Defence of Poetry*. (February) Shelley writes *Epipsychidion*; Keats dies on 23 February. (May) The Shelley household moves to Bagni di Pisa, where they live for six months. (June) Shelley writes *Adonais*, an elegy to Keats. (August) Shelley in Ravenna with Byron. Mary Shelley writes to her friend Mrs Hoppner denying rumours about the true parentage of Elena Adelaide Shelley. (September) Emilia Viviani marries. (November) Byron arrives in Pisa. Shelley completes *Hellas*.

1822   (January) Trelawny arrives in Pisa. (February) *Hellas* published. The building of Byron's boat, the *Bolivar*, and Shelley's, the *Don Juan*, begins. (April) Allegra dies. The Shelleys move, with the Williamses, to Casa Magni, Lerici, near La Spezia. (May) The Hunts sail from England. Shelley begins work on his *Triumph of Life*. (June) Mary Shelley suffers a miscarriage. (1 July) Shelley sails to Leghorn to meet the Hunts. (8 July) They set off on the return journey with deckhand Charles Vivian. (17 July) Williams's body is washed ashore, and the next day so are Shelley's and Charles Vivian's. Williams and Shelley are buried in quicklime. (19 July) Trelawny tells Mary Shelley and Jane Williams of the discovery of the bodies. They travel to Pisa with Claire Clairmont. On 16 August, Shelley's body is exhumed and cremated, under Trelawny's supervision, on the beach near Viareggio, where it was washed ashore. Byron and Hunt are present, but Medwin arrives just too late to witness the ritual. In January 1823,

Shelley's ashes are buried in the Protestant Cemetery in Rome. In April 1823, Trelawny arrives in Rome to organize the reburial of the ashes and the erection of a gravestone with Leigh Hunt's suggested epitaph (COR CORDIUM) and his own addition of lines from *The Tempest* ('Nothing of him that doth fade...').

COPY TEXTS

The following extracts are reproduced in facsimile except in one case
(indicated in the headnote) where the text has been reset due to the poor
quality of the original. Breaks between excerpts (which may cover paragraphs or whole volumes) are indicated by three asterisks:

☆ ★ ☆

In order to fit texts comfortably to the pages of this edition certain liberties
have been taken with the format of the original: occasionally right-hand
pages have become left-hand pages (and vice versa) and text from consecu-
tive pages has been fitted onto a single page. Endnotes in this edition refer
to Pickering & Chatto page and line numbers. Readers wishing to consult
the passages in the original are referred to the table below.

TEXT NO.	PROVENANCE	ORIGINAL PAGE NUMBERS	P&C page no. ff
1.	BL	354–9	3
2.	BL	iii–viii	11
3.	CUL	248–59	20
4.	CUL	174–8, 182–8, 202–5, 227–9	36
5.	CUL	January 1832: 91–6	55
		February 1832: 137–8, 139–40	61
		April 1832: 346–51	64
		July 1832: 67–73	70
		December 1832: 509–13	77
		May 1833: 23–9	82
6.	CUL	9–10, 25–9, 41–51, 104–6	93
7.	CUL	I: xiii–xvi, xxiv–xxviii; II: 344–52	118
8.	CUL	140–44	137
9.	CUL LL	I: 27–34, 147–52, 185–99, 324–31; II: 24–6	145
10.	CUL	II: 188–200; III: 16–22	185

TEXT NO.	PROVENANCE	ORIGINAL PAGE NUMBERS	P&C page no. ff
11.	*CUL*	I: v–xii, 136–41, 444–52, 457–60; II: 1–8, 300–10, 414–20, 536–8	209
12.	*BL*	20–3, 57–6, 70–75, 115–35, 139–43	267
13.	*LL*	June 1858: 643–4, 652–9	311
14.	*BL*	iii–vi, 21–3, 61–6, 67–8, 160–64	324
15.	*LL*	January 1860: 92–104, 109 March 1862: 343–6	345 358
16.	*BL*	186–9, 196–8	365
17.	*CUL*	I: v–xvii, 107–17, 156–62; II: 14–20, 240–45	374
18.	reset	101, 106–8, 112–13, 127–8	419

Texts are reproduced by kind permission of: *BL* – the British Library Board; *CUL* – the Syndics of Cambridge University Library; *LL* – the London Library.

William Hazlitt, 'On Paradox and Common-place', in *Table-Talk; or, Original Essays*, 2 vols (London, 1821)

Hazlitt's description of Shelley is unusual in having been published during the poet's lifetime. Other accounts based on personal knowledge of Shelley were posthumous: attempts either to form or to exploit his reputation. Written by friends and followers, these memoirs presented themselves as sympathetic, even if sympathy was characterized by the effort to exculpate Shelley from the misconduct or intellectual folly of which his opponents accused him. Hazlitt's portrait is written by a member of the liberal, literary circles in which Shelley moved for a time, but is satirical rather than admiring. He was often enough mocked by those who did not know him and were his natural ideological foes; this text is interesting (and unique) because its satire comes from a writer who did know him, and who might have been expected to have shared his political discontent.

Hazlitt became acquainted with Shelley shortly after Harriet Shelley's suicide and his marriage to Mary. In February 1817, he and Mary were staying with Leigh Hunt and his family in Hampstead. During their stay, they met many of Hunt's literary acquaintances, including Keats, Charles Lamb, and Charles Ollier, who was to become Shelley's publisher (Holmes, p. 359). Mary Shelley's *Journal* records meeting Hazlitt twice. On the first occasion, there was clearly animated discussion: 'Sunday 9th. . . Several of Hunt's acquaintances come in the evening – Music – after Supper a discussion untill 3 in the morning with Hazlitt concerning monarchy & republicanism' (Feldman and Scott-Kilvert, I, p. 163). At this time the Shelleys also frequently visited Godwin, in whose company they almost certainly met Hazlitt again. Indeed, in a letter to them in July 1821, Leigh Hunt implies as much when he tries to explain Hazlitt's motivation for penning the portrait given here: 'Did Shelley ever cut him up at Godwin's table? Somebody says so, and that this is the reason of Hazlitt's attack' (Jones, *Letters*, II, p. 383). Hunt clearly saw the essay as an act of betrayal, and says in the same letter, 'I wrote him an angry letter about Shelley – the first one I ever did; and I believe he is very sorry: but this is his way. Next week, perhaps, he will write a panegyric upon him. He says that Shelley provokes him by his going to a *pernicious* extreme on the liberal side, and so hurting it'.

At the time that he met Shelley, Hazlitt was almost forty, and was at a peak of productivity as a writer of essays and reviews for periodicals. It is difficult not to hear in his description of the 'shrill-voiced' intellectual enthusiast that he encountered at the Hunts' the resentment of the jobbing writer for the aristocratic dilettante. Yet we should not forget that, for all the immediacy of Hazlitt's characteristic present tense, the essay dates from four years after the meetings on which it was based. Hazlitt's resentment is likely to have become greater in the interim. By the time that he wrote 'On Paradox and Common-place', the living that he was attempting to earn from periodical journalism and from giving lectures on literary topics had become more precarious than ever (see Jones, *Hazlitt*, pp. 304–6). The Shelleys were now in Italy, and Hazlitt was absorbed by the unrequited passion for his landlady's daughter (and the arrangement of his separation from his wife) that he turned into his strangely confessional *Liber Amoris* (1823). In fact, he wrote most of *Table-Talk* at an inn outside Edinburgh, having travelled North seeking a Scottish divorce. It was, we might say, a difficult time.

The essay from which the passage below is taken sets out to distinguish between 'originality' (which is admirable) and its pale mimic, 'singularity' (which is merely the capacity to manufacture paradoxes). The unthinking prejudices of those who rely entirely on 'custom and authority' are but mirrored by the 'paradoxes' of those who, 'under the influence of novelty and restless vanity', try to think or say what is 'singular' (I, p. 350). This comparison structures the whole essay: 'With one party, whatever is, is right: with their antagonists, whatever is, is wrong. These swallow every antiquated absurdity: those catch at every new, unfledged project – and are alike enchanted with the velocipedes or the French Revolution' (p. 352). Shelley is taken as a prime specimen of the latter sort.

The author of the Prometheus Unbound (to take an individual instance of the last character) has a fire in his eye, a fever in his blood, a maggot in his brain, a hectic flutter in his speech, which mark out the philosophic fanatic. He is sanguine-complexioned, and shrill-voiced. As is often observable in the case of religious enthusiasts, there is a slenderness of constitutional *stamina*, which renders the flesh no match for the spirit. His bending, flexible form appears to take no strong hold of things, does not grapple with the world about him, but slides from it like a river—

> " And in its liquid texture mortal wound
> Receives no more than can the fluid air."

The shock of accident, the weight of authority make no impression on his opinions, which retire like a feather, or rise from the encounter unhurt, through their own buoyancy. He is clogged by no dull system of realities, no earth-bound feelings, no rooted prejudices, by nothing that belongs to the mighty trunk and hard husk of nature and habit, but is drawn up by irresistible levity to the regions of mere speculation and fancy, to the sphere of air and fire, where his delighted spirit floats in " seas of pearl and clouds of amber." There is no *caput mortuum* of worn-out, thread-bare experience to serve as ballast to his mind; it is all volatile intellectual salt of tartar, that refuses to combine its evanescent, inflammable essence with any thing solid or any thing lasting. Bubbles are to him the only realities:—touch them, and they vanish. Curiosity is the only proper category of his mind, and though a man in knowledge, he is a child in feeling. Hence he puts every thing into a metaphysical crucible to judge of it himself and exhibit it to others as a subject of interesting experiment, without first making it over to the ordeal of his common sense or trying it on his heart. This faculty of speculating at random on all questions may in its overgrown and uninformed state do much mischief without intending it, like an overgrown child with the power of a man. Mr. Shelley has been accused of vanity—I think he is chargeable with extreme levity; but this levity is so great, that I do not believe he is sensible of its consequences. He strives to overturn all established creeds and systems: but this is in him an effect of constitution. He runs before the most extravagant opinions, but this is because he is held back by none of the merely mechanical checks of sympathy and habit. He tampers with all sorts of obnoxious subjects, but it is less because he is gratified with the rankness of the taint, than captivated with the intellectual phosphoric light they emit. It would seem that he wished not so much to convince or inform as to shock the public by the tenor of his productions, but I suspect he is more intent upon startling himself with his electrical experiments in morals and philosophy; and though they may scorch other people, they are to him harmless amusements, the coruscations of an Aurora Borealis, that " play round the head, but do not reach the heart." Still I could wish that he would put a stop to the incessant, alarming whirl of his Voltaic battery. With his zeal, his talent, and his fancy, he would do more good and less harm, if he were to give up his wilder theories, and if he took less pleasure in feeling his heart flutter in unison with the panic-struck apprehensions of his readers. Persons of this class, instead of consolidating useful and acknowledged truths, and thus advancing the cause of science and virtue, are never easy but in raising doubtful and disagreeable questions, which bring the former into disgrace and discredit. They are not contented to lead the minds of men to an eminence overlooking the prospect of social amelioration, unless, by forcing them up slippery paths and to the utmost verge of possibility, they can dash them down the precipice the instant they reach the promised Pisgah. They think it nothing to hang up a beacon to guide or warn, if they do not at the same time frighten the community like a comet. They do not mind making their principles odious, provided they can make themselves notorious. To win over the public opinion by fair means is to them an insipid, common-place mode of popularity: they would either force it by harsh methods, or seduce it by intoxicating potions. Egotism, petulance, licentiousness, levity of principle (whatever be the source) is a bad thing in any one, and most of all, in a philosophical reformer. Their humanity, their wisdom is always " at the horizon." Any thing new, any thing remote, any thing questionable, comes to them in a shape that is sure of a cordial welcome—a welcome cordial in proportion as the object is new, as it is apparently impracticable, as it is a doubt whether it is at all desirable. Just after the final failure, the completion of the last act of the French Revolution, when the legitimate wits were crying out, " The farce is over, now let us go to supper," these provoking reasoners got up a lively hypothesis about introducing the domestic government of the Nayrs into this country as a feasible set-off against the success of the Boroughmongers.

The practical is with them always the antipodes of the ideal; and like other visionaries of a different stamp, they date the Millennium or New Order of Things from the Restoration of the Bourbons. Fine words butter no parsnips, says the proverb. "While you are talking of marrying, I am thinking of hanging," says Captain Macheath. Of all people the most tormenting are those who bid you hope in the midst of despair, who, by never caring about any thing but their own sanguine, hair-brained Utopian schemes, have at no time any particular cause for embarrassment and despondency because they have never the least chance of success, and who by including whatever does not hit their idle fancy, kings, priests, religion, government, public abuses or private morals, in the same sweeping clause of ban and anathema, do all they can to combine all parties in a common cause against them, and to prevent every one else from advancing one step farther in the career of practical improvement than they do in that of imaginary and unattainable perfection.

NOTE

p. 3, ll. 14–15: 'And in its liquid texture . . .', *Paradise Lost*, VI, ll. 348–9, slightly adapted.

Mary Shelley, Preface to *Posthumous Poems of Percy Bysshe Shelley* (London, 1824)

On 22 August 1824, two years after Shelley's death, Mary Shelley wrote from London to Leigh Hunt who was still in Italy with his family (thinking of the distance between the two countries, she commented, '... it seems to me as if I wrote to Paradise from Purgatory'). As in many of her letters from the years immediately after Shelley's death, financial concerns are uppermost. With Peacock's help, she has, she says, begun a 'Negociation' with her father-in-law, Sir Timothy Shelley. In return for 'sacrificing a small part of my future expectations on the will' (by which she means the money that will come to her on his death) 'I shall ensure myself a sufficiency, for the present' (Bennett, *Letters*, I, 444). There is, however, a condition – a condition with which she has no choice but to comply. 'I have been obliged however as an indispensable preliminary, to suppress the Post. Poems – More than 300 copies had been sold so this is the less provoking, and I have been obliged to promise not to bring dear S's name before the public again during Sir. T—'s life. There is no great harm in this, since he is above 70, & from choice I should not think of writing memoirs *now*'. She adds that, by the account that she has had from Sir Timothy's lawyer, 'Sir T. writhes under the fame of his incomparable son as if it were a most grievous injury done to him'.

In some ways, Mary's position was to become unexpectedly more secure two years later when Charles, Shelley's son by Harriet, died of consumption, aged eleven. Now her son Percy was the Shelley heir, and she could not easily be disowned by the family. Yet her efforts as a writer of novels, tales, and essays brought little financial reward. She and her son remained financially dependent upon her father-in-law for the next twenty years: he lived into his nineties, dying in 1844. Until she was permitted to produce an edition of Shelley's *Poetical Works* in 1839, the *Posthumous Poems* volume was her most significant attempt to shape her husband's reputation and the signed preface to the collection was her only published statement about him. Yet even in her enforced silence she was not inactive. She privately confessed that her novel *The Last Man*, published in 1826 as 'by the Author of Frankenstein', contained, in the character of Adrian, a portrait of 'my lost Shelley': 'I have endeavoured, but how inadequately to give some idea of him... the sketch has pleased some of those who best loved him' (letter to John Bowring, in Bennett, *Letters*, I, 512). She secretly encouraged the Paris publishers of the Galignani edition of the works of Coleridge, Keats, and Shelley, which appeared in 1829 (see her correspondence with Cyrus Redding and William Galignani in Bennett, *Letters*, II). This collection contained a biographical sketch of Shelley that borrowed largely from her own preface to *Posthumous Poems*, and Leigh Hunt's *Lord Byron and Some of His Contemporaries* (see the extracts in this volume). Perhaps most influentially, she promoted the romantic tale of the circumstances in which *Frankenstein* was produced in a Preface to a new edition of that novel, published in 1831. In doing so, she managed to imply that she and Shelley had been married when they went to Switzerland in 1816 (see St Clair, 485).

Even if *Posthumous Poems* was quickly suppressed in the face of Sir Timothy's displeasure, Mary Shelley still remembered it, fifteen years later, as a labour of love. In December 1838, when she wrote to Edward Moxon to accept his terms for the publication of the *Poetical Works*, she described how she had composed the earlier collection from 'fragments of paper which in the hands of an indifferent person would never have been de-cyphered – the labour of putting it together was immense' (Bennett, *Letters*, II, 300). By the time that she recalled this, she had obtained permission from Sir Timothy to produce an edition of Shelley's writing, provided that no memoir were attached. Famously, in the *Poetical Works* of 1839 she kept to his stipulation by turning her knowledge and opinions to the 'Notes' that framed Shelley's poems. These have been preserved in many subsequent editions, even where the texts of the poems themselves have been amended. Most importantly, they have been reprinted in the Oxford Standard Authors collection, which has been the standard edition of Shelley's poetry for much of this century. (For a short history of editions, see the Introduction to *The Poems of Shelley. Volume I 1804–1817*, eds Geoffrey Matthews and Kelvin Everest.) For this reason, they have not been reprinted in this volume.

When she produced *Posthumous Poems*, Mary Shelley still imagined that there would eventually be an authorised biography of Shelley – either written by herself, or by someone, probably Leigh Hunt, whom she could trust and prompt. The Notes and Preface to her 1839 edition of Shelley's *Poetical Works* indicate, however, that, fifteen years later, she was not unhappy to leave this biography unwritten, and that Sir Timothy's edict was therefore not so unwelcome.

I abstain from any remark on the occurences of his private life, except inasmuch as the passions which they engendered inspired his poetry. This is not the time to relate the truth; and I should reject any colouring of the truth. No account of these events has ever been given at all approaching reality in their details, either as regards himself or others; nor shall I further allude to them than to remark that the errors of action committed by a man as noble and generous as Shelley, may, as far as he only is concerned, be fearlessly avowed by those who loved him, in the firm conviction that, were they judged impartially, his character would stand in fairer and brighter light than that of any contemporary (Hutchinson, p. xxi).

So she wrote in her 1839 Preface. The defensiveness here (so quick to mention those 'errors') concedes that the poet's life has been a matter of controversy, but in order to imply that only small minds will fail to see beyond this. None of the accounts of the life that have been given are to be trusted, but, turning a necessity into a source of pride, Shelley's widow declares that she is not going to enter the biographical fray. She will speak only of his 'qualities': his philanthropy, his idealism, his 'extreme sensibility' (ibid, p. xxii).

Sir Timothy's ban on a memoir might even have made it easier for the 1839 edition to imagine Shelley as, in its editor's words, 'a pure-minded and exalted being' (ibid, p. xxiii). She can only hint at the misfortunes with which he had to struggle, so his poetry can be seen all the more clearly as a transcendance of difficulties that would have broken an ordinary spirit. Her note on *The Revolt of Islam*, for instance, describes it as a poem of reborn hopes after the 'saddest events' of late 1816 and early 1817 – by which she must mean the suicide of Harriet Shelley and the case to decide the custody of Shelley's two children (ibid, p. 156). Yet her own reticence about Shelley's life, and 'the persecutions he underwent', matches her celebration of a poem in which the poet's 'deep unexpressed passion' and 'sense of injury' engender a creation freed from 'the weakness and evil which cling to real life'. Indeed, what embarrassment Mary Shelley seems to feel when she is finally allowed to produce an edition of Shelley's poems is caused by their political content. The respectable widow does have to explain that the noble poet was 'the victim of the state of feeling inspired by the reaction of the French Revolution' (ibid, p. xxi), though she can take refuge in her certainty that, as her Note to *The Mask of Anarchy* puts it, 'Days of outrage have passed away'.

So Mary Shelley was spared the difficulties – and presumably the evasions – to be found in most memoirs of Shelley. This is striking when one looks at her letters and her journals, now available to us. Without the pressure (sensed by the other contributors to this volume) of public explanation, Mary Shelley was able to sustain it these private documents a consistent rhetoric of reverence and devotion. The high tone of the following preface to *Posthumous Poems* is therefore quite consistent with her references to her husband in her private writings. It would have been put under much more strain if she had undertaken to be Shelley's biographer rather than his editor.

PREFACE.

It had been my wish, on presenting the public with the Posthumous Poems of Mr. SHELLEY, to have accompanied them by a biographical notice; as it appeared to me, that at this moment, a narration of the events of my husband's life would come more gracefully from other hands than mine, I applied to Mr. LEIGH HUNT. The distinguished friendship that Mr. SHELLEY felt for him, and the enthusiastic affection with which Mr. LEIGH HUNT clings to his friend's memory, seemed to point him out as the person best calculated for such an undertaking. His absence from this country, which prevented our mutual explanation, has unfortunately rendered my scheme abortive. I do not doubt but that on some other occasion he will pay this tribute to his lost friend, and sincerely regret that the volume which I edit has not been honoured by its insertion.

The comparative solitude in which Mr. SHELLEY lived, was the occasion that he was personally known to few; and his fearless enthusiasm in the cause, which he considered the most sacred upon earth, the improvement of the moral and physical state of mankind, was the chief reason why he, like other illustrious reformers, was pursued by hatred and calumny. No man was ever more devoted than he, to the endeavour of making those around him happy; no man ever possessed friends more unfeignedly attached to him. The ungrateful world did not feel his loss, and the gap it made seemed to close as quickly over his memory as the murderous sea above his living frame. Hereafter men will lament that his transcendant powers of intellect were extinguished before they had bestowed on them their choicest treasures. To his friends his loss is irremediable : the wise, the brave, the gentle, is gone for ever! He is to them as a bright vision, whose radiant track, left behind in the memory, is worth all the realities that society can afford. Before the critics contradict me, let them appeal to any one who had ever known him : to see him was to love him; and his presence, like Ithuriel's spear, was alone sufficient to disclose the falsehood of the tale, which his enemies whispered in the ear of the ignorant world.

His life was spent in the contemplation of nature, in arduous study, or in acts of kindness and affection. He was an elegant scholar and a profound metaphysician : without possessing much scientific knowledge, he was unrivalled in the justness and extent of his observations on natural objects ; he knew every plant by its name, and was familiar with the history and habits of every production of the earth; he could interpret without a fault each appearance in the sky, and the varied phœnomena of heaven and earth filled him with deep emotion. He made his study and reading-room of the shadowed copse, the stream, the lake and the waterfall. Ill health and continual pain preyed upon his powers, and the solitude in which we lived, particularly on our first arrival in Italy, although congenial to his feelings, must frequently have weighed upon his spirits; those beautiful and affecting " Lines, written in dejection at Naples," were composed at such an interval; but when in health, his spirits were buoyant and youthful to an extraordinary degree.

Such was his love for nature, that every page of his poetry is associated in the minds of his friends with the loveliest scenes of the countries which he inhabited. In early life he visited the most beautiful parts of this country and Ireland. Afterwards the Alps of Switzerland became his inspirers. "Prometheus Unbound" was written among the deserted and flower-grown ruins of Rome, and when he made his home under the Pisan hills, their roofless recesses harboured him as he composed "The Witch of Atlas," " Adonais" and " Hellas." In the wild but beautiful Bay of Spezia, the winds and waves which he loved became his playmates. His days were chiefly spent on the water; the management of his boat, its alterations and improvements, were his principal occupation. At night, when the unclouded moon shone on the calm sea, he often went alone in his little shallop to the rocky caves that bordered it, and sitting beneath their shelter wrote " The Triumph of Life," the last of his productions. The beauty but strangeness of this lonely place, the refined pleasure which he felt in the companionship of a few selected friends, our entire sequestration from the rest of the world, all contributed to render this period of his life one of continued enjoyment. I am convinced that the two months we passed there were the happiest he had ever known : his health even rapidly improved, and he was never better than when I last saw him, full of spirits and joy, embark for Leghorn, that he might there welcome LEIGH HUNT to Italy. I was to have accompanied him, but illness confined me to my room, and thus put the seal on my misfortune. His vessel bore out of sight with a favourable wind, and I remained awaiting his return by the breakers of that sea which was about to engulph him.

He spent a week at Pisa, employed in kind offices towards his friend, and enjoying with keen delight the renewal of their intercourse. He then embarked with Mr. WILLIAMS, the chosen and beloved sharer of his pleasures and of his fate, to return to us. We waited for them in vain; the sea by its restless moaning seemed to desire to inform us of what we would not learn :——but a veil may well be drawn over such misery. The real anguish of these moments

transcended all the fictions that the most glowing imagination ever pourtrayed : our seclusion, the savage
nature of the inhabitants of the surrounding villages,
and our immediate vicinity to the troubled sea, combined to embue with strange horror our days of uncer-
tainty.   The truth was at last known,—a truth that
made our loved and lovely Italy appear a tomb, its sky
a pall. Every heart echoed the deep lament, and my
only consolation was in the praise and earnest love that
each voice bestowed and each countenance demonstrated for him we had lost,—not, I fondly hope, for
ever : his unearthly and elevated nature is a pledge
of the continuation of his being, although in an altered form.   Rome received his ashes ; they are
deposited beneath its weed-grown wall, and " the
world's sole monument" is enriched by his remains.

   I must add a few words concerning the contents
of this volume.   " Julian and Maddalo," " The
Witch of Atlas," and most of the Translations, were
written some years ago, and, with the exception of
" The Cyclops," and the Scenes from the " Magico
Prodigioso," may be considered as having received
the author's ultimate corrections.   " The Triumph
of Life " was his last work, and was left in so unfinished a state, that I arranged it in its present form
with great difficulty.   All his poems which were
scattered in periodical works are collected in this
volume, and I have added a reprint of " Alastor, or
the Spirit of Solitude :"—the difficulty with which a
copy can be obtained, is the cause of its republica-

tion. Many of the Miscellaneous Poems, written on the spur of the occasion, and never retouched, I found among his manuscript books, and have carefully copied : I have subjoined, whenever I have been able, the date of their composition.

I do not know whether the critics will reprehend the insertion of some of the most imperfect among these ; but I frankly own, that I have been more actuated by the fear lest any monument of his genius should escape me, than the wish of presenting nothing but what was complete to the fastidious reader.   I feel secure that the Lovers of SHELLEY's Poetry (who know how more than any other poet of the present day every line and word he wrote is instinct with peculiar beauty) will pardon and thank me : I consecrate this volume to them.

The size of this collection has prevented the insertion of any prose pieces.   They will hereafter appear in a separate publication.

MARY W. SHELLEY.

London, June 1st, 1824.

Journal of the Conversations of Lord Byron: Noted During a Residence with his Lordship at Pisa, in the Years 1821 and 1822, by Thomas Medwin, Esq. of the 24th Light Dragoons, Author of 'Ahasuerus the Wanderer' (London, 1824)

There is a telling entry in the Index of Newman Ivey White's *Shelley* (1940), the single most important and influential twentieth-century biography of the poet. Under the heading for Thomas Medwin's *The Life of Percy Bysshe Shelley* it simply says '*citations too numerous to specify*' (II, lxi). White's expression of his debt to Medwin is all the more significant as he is using H. Buxton Forman's 1913 edition of Medwin's text, which provides a detailed commentary on Medwin's almost innumerable errors and confusions. White, the most dedicated and scholarly of researchers, announces his reliance on the most careless of biographers – a writer mocked for his inaccuracies from the first appearance of his *Conversations of Lord Byron* in 1824. This paradox is characteristic of Medwin's role as a memoirist of Shelley: though constantly wrong on matters of detail, he has often been felt to be fundamentally truthful, his very mistakes a sign of his lack of guile. 'Muddled and confused' is White's (in context) rather kind judgement on Medwin, whose 'general good faith' he still trusts (I, 437). It is a kindness that is particularly striking when we consider that Medwin's first memoir of Shelley, given below, appears as a lengthy footnote to a passage of the *Conversations* that tells a peculiarly audacious lie.

Medwin's surprising authority derived in part from his knowledge of Shelley as a child and adolescent, a knowledge unique amongst the poet's memoirists. He was Shelley's second cousin, and his family home was in Horsham, only a couple of miles from Shelley's at Field Place. The two were boyhood friends, and for a while attended school together at Syon House (although Medwin, born in 1788, was four years older). Medwin matriculated at Oxford in 1805, and left without a degree before Shelley's arrival in 1810, but the two seem to have remained intimate during this period, and certainly met again in London in 1811, after Shelley's expulsion from Oxford. In his two later memoirs, *The Shelley Papers* (1833) and *The Life of Percy Bysshe Shelley* (1847), Medwin was to make claims upon this early intimacy.

In 1812, Medwin joined the 24th Light Dragoons. He sailed for India in August of that year, and served there with his regiment until 1819. As he tells the story, his interest in his poetic cousin was re-awakened when, just before he sailed from Bombay, he discovered a copy of *The Revolt of Islam* on a Parsee book-stall. He was 'astonished at the greatness of his genius' (Lovell, *Captain Medwin*, 55). After his return, he retired on half-pay, and arrived in Geneva in September 1819. Here he rented a house with another half-pay lieutenant whom he had known in India, Edward Williams, and his 'wife', Jane. (They named their first child, born in 1820, Edward Medwin Williams.) He began a correspondence with Shelley, and in October 1820 travelled to meet him in Pisa (the Williams following a couple of months later). He was back in Geneva in August 1821, but returned to Pisa in November and was introduced by Shelley to Byron. He soon became Byron's fervent admirer, and began taking notes of the conversations that the two men had over the next few months. Is March 1822, he left the 'Pisa circle', and was in Geneva once again when news reached him of Shelley's death. Though setting out immediately for Italy, he arrived shortly after the famous cremation of Shelley's body. As will be seen below, by altering the date of this event, he falsified his account so that he could make himself a witness to the dramatic ritual.

After stays in Paris and London, he was once again in Geneva, where he composed the *Conversations* in 1824. Mary Shelley was to write to John Cam Hobhouse in November 1824, shortly after its publication, saying that she had refused Medwin's request that she correct his manuscript. (Hobhouse had himself asked for her comments on his pamphlet 'Exposure of the Misstatements Contained in Captain Medwin's Pretended Conversations of Lord Byron', which was eventually published anonymously in the *Westminster Review* a year later.)

> He afterwards sent me his Memoir of Shelley – I found it one mass of mistakes – I returned it uncorrected – earnestly entreating him not to publish it – as it would be highly injurious to my interests to recall in this garbled manner past facts at a time that I was endeavoring to bring Sir T.S. to reason. When I have the book I will point out a few of these mistatements – The book has been a source of great pain to me & will be of more. (Bennett, *Letters*, I, 455)

Some of the mistakes that Medwin makes in the footnote memoir of Shelley, given here in its entirety, concern matters of fact that will continue to embarrass the poet's admirers. He says that Shelley returned to England in 1816 because of his wife Harriet's death, when, in fact, he had already returned, but was living, with Mary, separately from her. He says that Shelley married Mary the year after Harriet's death, but in fact the wedding took place only a fortnight after Shelley first received news of Harriet's suicide on December 15th, 1816. They seem convenient errors. His omissions, such as not mentioning that Mary Godwin (and Claire Clairmont) accompanied Shelley to Switzerland in 1816, are characteristic of Shelley's memoirists, as are his apologies for the poet's 'visionary' speculations.

Perhaps because of the antagonism that they aroused, Medwin's *Conversations* seems to have been rather successful (see Lovell, 176–92, for its reception). It went through six English editions within eight years, and was almost immediately published in America and translated into both French and German. As the first book-length memoir of Byron, it was both particularly influential and particularly open to attack. (For the picture that it gives of Byron, see *Byron*, in this edition.) Inevitably, it was Byron's reputation, rather than Shelley's, over which his antagonists took issue. It was Shelley's after-life, however, that continued to preoccupy Medwin. The headnotes in this volume to extracts from *The Shelley Papers* and *The Life of Percy Bysshe Shelley* describe this preoccupation, and Medwin's life after 1824.

18th August, 1822.—On the occasion of Shelley's melancholy fate I revisited Pisa, and on the day of my arrival learnt that Lord Byron was gone to the sea-shore, to assist in performing the last offices to his friend.* We came to a spot marked by an old and withered trunk of a fir-tree; and near it, on the beach, stood a solitary hut covered with reeds. The situation was well calculated for a poet's

---

* It is hoped that the following memoir, as it relates to Lord Byron, may not be deemed misplaced here.

Percy Bysshe Shelley was removed from a private school at thirteen, and sent to Eton. He there shewed a character of great eccentricity, mixed in none of the amusements natural to his age, was of a melancholy and reserved disposition, fond of solitude, and made few friends. Neither did he distinguish himself much at Eton, for he had a great contempt for modern Latin verses, and his studies were directed to any thing rather than the exercises of his class. It was from an early acquaintance with German writers that he probably imbibed a romantic turn of mind ; at least, we find him before fifteen publishing two Rosa-Matilda-like novels, called 'Justrozzi' and 'The Rosicrucian,' that bore no marks of being the productions of a boy, and were much talked of, and reprobated as immoral by the journalists of the day. He also made great progress in chemistry. He used to say, that nothing ever delighted him so much as the discovery that there

grave.   A few weeks before I had ridden with him and
Lord Byron to this very spot, which I afterwards visited

---

were no *elements* of earth, fire, or water : but before he left school
he nearly lost his life by being blown up in one of his experiments,
and gave up the pursuit.   He now turned his mind to metaphysics,
and became infected with the materialism of the French school.
Even before he was sent to University College, Oxford, he had entered into an epistolary theological controversy with a dignitary of
the Church, under the feigned name of a woman ; and, after the
second term, he printed a pamphlet with a most extravagant title,
'The Necessity of Atheism.'   This silly work, which was only a reca-
pitulation of some of the arguments of Voltaire and the philosophers of
the day, he had the madness to circulate among the bench of Bishops,
not even disguising his name.   The consequence was an obvious
one :—he was summoned before the heads of the College, and, refusing to retract his opinions, on the contrary preparing to argue
them with the examining Masters, was expelled the University.   This
disgrace in itself affected Shelley but little at the time, but was fatal
to all his hopes of happiness and prospects in life ; for it deprived
him of his first love, and was the eventual means of alienating him
for ever from his family.   For some weeks after this expulsion his
father refused to receive him under his roof; and when he did,
treated him with such marked coldness, that he soon quitted what
he no longer considered his home, went to London privately, and

more than once.   In front was a magnificent extent of the
blue and windless Mediterranean, with the Isles of Elba

---

thence eloped to Gretna Green with a Miss Westbrook,—their united
ages amounting to thirty-three.   This last act exasperated his
father to such a degree, that he now broke off all communication
with Shelley.   After some stay in Edinburgh, we trace him into
Ireland ; and, that country being in a disturbed state, find him publishing a pamphlet, which had a great sale, and the object of which
was to soothe the minds of the people, telling them that moderate
firmness, and not open rebellion, would most tend to conciliate, and
to give them their liberties.

He also spoke at some of their public meetings with great fluency
and eloquence.   Returning to England the latter end of 1812, and
being at that time an admirer of Mr. Southey's poems, he paid a visit
to the Lakes, where himself and his wife passed several days, at
Keswick.   He now became devoted to poetry, and after imbuing himself with ' The Age of Reason,' ' Spinosa,' and ' The Political Justice,'
composed his ' Queen Mab,' and presented it to most of the literary
characters of the day—among the rest to Lord Byron, who speaks of
it in his note to ' The Two Foscari' thus:—" I shewed it to Mr.
" Sotheby as a poem of great power and imagination.   I never wrote
" a line of the Notes, nor ever saw them except in their published
" form.   No one knows better than the real author, that his opinions

and Gorgona,—Lord Byron's yacht at anchor in the offing:
on the other side an almost boundless extent of sandy

" and mine differ materially upon the metaphysical portion of that
" work; though, in common with all who are not blinded by baseness
" and bigotry, I highly admire the poetry of that and his other produc-
" tions." It is to be remarked here, that ' Queen Mab ' eight or ten
years afterwards fell into the hands of a knavish bookseller, who published it on his own account; and on its publication and subsequent
prosecution Shelley disclaimed the opinions contained in that work, as
being the crude notions of his youth.

His marriage, by which he had two children, soon turned
out (as might have been expected) an unhappy one, and a separation ensuing in 1816, he went abroad, and passed the summer of that year in Switzerland, where the scenery of that romantic country tended to make Nature a passion and an enjoyment;
and at Geneva he formed a friendship for Lord Byron, which
was destined to last for life. It has been said that the perfection of
every thing Lord Byron wrote at Diodati, (his Third Canto of ' Childe
Harold,' his ' Manfred,' and ' Prisoner of Chillon,') owed something
to the critical judgment that Shelley exercised over those works, and
to his dosing him (as he used to say) with Wordsworth. In the
autumn of this year we find the subject of this Memoir at Como,
where he wrote ' Rosalind and Helen,' an eclogue, and an ode to the

wilderness, uncultivated and uninhabited, here and there interspersed in tufts with underwood curved by the sea-

---

Euganean Hills, marked with great pathos and beauty. His first visit to Italy was short, for he was soon called to England by his wife's melancholy fate, which ever after threw a cloud over his own. The year subsequent to this event he married Mary Wolstonecraft Godwin, daughter of the celebrated Mary Wolstonecraft and Godwin; and shortly before this period, heir to an income of many thousands a-year and a baronetage, he was in such pecuniary distress that he was nearly dying of hunger in the streets! Finding, soon after his coming of age, that he was entitled to some reversionary property in fee, he sold it to his father for an annuity of 1000*l.* a-year, and took a house at Marlow, where he persevered more than ever in his poetical and classical studies. It was during his residence in Buckinghamshire that he wrote his 'Alastor, or the Spirit of Solitude;' perhaps one of the most perfect specimens of harmony in blank verse that our language possesses, and full of the wild scenes which his imagination had treasured up in his Alpine excursions. In this poem he deifies Nature much in the same way that Wordsworth did in his earlier productions.

Inattentive to pecuniary matters, and generous to excess, he soon found that he could not live on his income; and, still unforgiven by his family, he came to a resolution of quitting his native country, and never returning to it. There was another circumstance also that tended to disgust him with England: his children were taken from him

breeze, and stunted by the barren and dry nature of the
soil in which it grew.   At equal distances along the coast

---

by the Lord Chancellor, on the ground of his Atheism.   He again
crossed the Alps, and took up his residence at Venice.   There he strengthened his intimacy with Lord Byron, and wrote his ' Revolt of Islam,'
an allegorical poem in the Spenser stanza.   Noticed very favourably in
Blackwood's Magazine, it fell under the lash of ' The Quarterly,'
which indulged itself in much personal abuse of the author, both
openly in the review of that work, and insidiously under the critique
of Hunt's ' Foliage.'   Perhaps little can be said for the philosophy of
' The Loves of Laon and Cythra.'   Like Mr. Owen of Lanark, he
believed in the perfectibility of human nature, and looked forward to
a period when a new golden age would return to earth,—when all the
different creeds and systems of the world would be amalgamated into
one,—crime disappear,—and man, freed from shackles civil and religious, bow before the throne " of his own aweless soul," or " of the
Power unknown."

Wild and visionary as such a speculation must be confessed to be in
the present state of society, it sprang from a mind enthusiastic in its
wishes for the good of the species, and the amelioration of mankind
and of society : and however mistaken the means of bringing about
this reform or " revolt" may be considered, the object of his whole life
and writings seems to have been to develope them.   This is particularly observable in his next work ' The Prometheus Unbound,' a bold

stood high square towers, for the double purpose of guarding the coast from smuggling, and enforcing the quaran-

---

attempt to revive a lost play of Æschylus. This drama shews an acquaintance with the Greek tragedy-writers which perhaps no other person possessed in an equal degree, and was written at Rome amid the flower-covered ruins of the Baths of Caracalla. At Rome also he formed the story of ' The Cenci ' into a tragedy, which, but for the harrowing nature of the subject, and the prejudice against any thing bearing his name, could not have failed to have had the greatest success,—if not on the stage, at least in the closet. Lord Byron was of opinion that it was the best play the age had produced, and not unworthy of the immediate followers of Shakspeare.

After passing several months at Naples, he finally settled with his lovely and amiable wife in Tuscany, where he passed the last four years in domestic retirement and intense application to study.

His acquirements were great. He was, perhaps, the first classic in Europe. The books he considered the models of style for prose and poetry were Plato and the Greek dramatists. He had made himself equally master of the modern languages. Calderon in Spanish, Petrarch and Dante in Italian, and Goëthe and Schiller in German, were his favourite authors. French he never read, and said he never could understand the beauty of Racine.

tine laws. This view was bounded by an immense extent of
the Italian Alps, which are here particularly picturesque

Discouraged by the ill success of his writings—persecuted by the
malice of his enemies—hated by the world, an outcast from his family,
and a martyr to a painful complaint,—he was subject to occasional fits
of melancholy and dejection. For the last four years, though he
continued to write, he had given up publishing. There were two
occasions, however, that induced him to break through his resolution.
His ardent love of liberty inspired him to write ' Hellas, or the
Triumph of Greece,' a drama, since translated into Greek, and
which he inscribed to his friend Prince Maurocordato; and his
attachment to Keats led him to publish an elegy, which he entitled
' Adonais.'

This last is perhaps the most perfect of all his compositions, and
the one he himself considered so. Among the mourners at the
funeral of his poet-friend he draws this portrait of himself; (the
stanzas were afterwards expunged from the Elegy :)

> " 'Mid others of less note came one frail form,—
> A phantom among men,—companionless
> As the last cloud of an expiring storm,
> Whose thunder is its knell. He, as I guess,
> Had gazed on Nature's naked loveliness

from their volcanic and manifold appearances, and which
being composed of white marble, give their summits the
resemblance of snow.

> Actæon-like ; and now he fled astray
> With feeble steps on the world's wilderness,
> And his own thoughts along that rugged way
> Pursued, like raging hounds, their father and their prey.
>
> His head was bound with pansies overblown,
> And faded violets, white and pied and blue ;
> And a light spear, topp'd with a cypress cone,
> (Round whose rough stem dark ivy tresses shone,
> Yet dripping with the forest's noonday dew,)
> Vibrated, as the ever-beating heart
> Shook the weak hand that grasp'd it.   Of that crew
> He came the last, neglected and apart,—
> A herd-abandon'd deer, struck by the hunter's dart !"

The last eighteen months of Shelley's life were passed in daily intercourse with Lord Byron, to whom the amiability, gentleness, and elegance of his manners, and his great talents and acquirements, had en-
deared him. Like his friend, he wished to die young : he perished in the
twenty-ninth year of his age, in the Mediterranean, between Leghorn
and Lerici, from the upsetting of an open boat. The sea had been to him,

As a foreground to this picture appeared as extraordinary a group. Lord Byron and Trelawney were seen standing

---

as well as Lord Byron, ever the greatest delight; and as early as 1813, in the following lines written at sixteen, he seems to have anticipated that it would prove his grave.

> " To-morrow comes :
> Cloud upon cloud with dark and deep'ning mass
> Roll o'er the blacken'd waters ; the deep roar
> Of distant thunder mutters awfully :
> Tempest unfolds its pinions o'er the gloom
> That shrouds the boiling surge ; the pitiless fiend
> With all his winds and lightnings tracks his prey ;
> The torn deep yawns,—the vessel finds a grave
> Beneath its jagged jaws."

For fifteen days after the loss of the vessel his body was undiscovered; and when found, was not in a state to be removed. In order to comply with his wish of being buried at Rome, his corpse was directed to be burnt; and Lord Byron, faithful to his trust as an executor, and duty as a friend, superintended the ceremony which I have described.

The remains of one who was destined to have little repose or happiness here, now sleep, with those of his friend Keats, in the burial-

over the burning pile, with some of the soldiers of the guard ; and Leigh Hunt, whose feelings and nerves could not carry him through the scene of horror, lying back in the carriage, —the four post-horses ready to drop with the intensity of the noonday sun.   The stillness of all around was yet more felt by the shrill scream of a solitary curlew, which, perhaps attracted by the body, wheeled in such narrow circles round the pile that it might have been struck with the hand, and was so fearless that it could not be driven away.   Looking at the corpse, Lord Byron said,

" Why, that old black silk handkerchief retains its form
" better than that human body ! "

Scarcely was the ceremony concluded, when Lord Byron, agitated by the spectacle he had witnessed, tried to dissipate, in some degree, the impression of it by his favourite re-creation.   He took off his clothes therefore, and swam off to his yacht, which was riding a few miles distant.   The heat of the sun and checked perspiration threw him into a fever, which he felt coming on before he left the water,

---

ground near Caius Cestus's Pyramid ;—" a spot so beautiful," said he, " that it might almost make one in love with death."

and which became more violent before he reached Pisa. On his return he immediately ordered a warm bath.

" I have been very subject to fevers," said he, " and am " not in the least alarmed at this. It will yield to my usual " remedy, the bath."

The next morning he was perfectly recovered. When I called, I found him sitting in the garden under the shade of some orange-trees, with the Countess. They are now always together, and he is become quite domestic. He calls her *Piccinina*, and bestows on her all the pretty diminutive epithets that are so sweet in Italian. His kindness and attention to the Guiccioli have been invariable. A three years' constancy proves that he is not altogether so unmanageable by a sensible woman as might be supposed. In fact no man is so easily led : but he is not to be driven. His spirits are good, except when he speaks of Shelley and Williams. He tells me he has not made one voyage in his yacht since their loss, and has taken a disgust to sailing.

NOTES

p. 22, l. 17: 'The Age of Reason' – Thomas Paine's *The Age of Reason*, Part I of which was published in 1794, Part II in 1795, and Part III in 1807. A collection of Paine's *Political Works* had been published in 1817.

p. 22, l. 17: 'The Political Justice' – William Godwin's *An Enquiry concerning Political Justice*, first published in 1793, and revised by Godwin for new editions in 1796 and 1798.

p. 27, l. 11: 'Prince Maurocordato' – Prince Mavrocordato was an exiled Greek nationalist leader whom Shelley met in Pisa in 1821. Later in the year, shortly before Shelley began writing *Hellas*, he returned to Greece to take part in the armed struggle against the occupying Turks.

Leigh Hunt, *Lord Byron and Some of His Contemporaries* (London, 1828)

Leigh Hunt's admiring portrait of Shelley is also testimony to Shelley's admiration of Hunt, whom he always looked up to as a campaigner for 'Liberty'. Indeed, it was politics that first drew the two together. On March 2nd, 1811, some three weeks before he was sent down from Oxford, Shelley wrote from University College to 'Leigh Hunt, Editor of *The Examiner*, London'. He wished to congratulate 'one of the most fearless enlighteners of the public mind at the present time' on the 'triumph' of his acquittal on charges of libel brought by the goverment (he had published an article on the brutality of corporal punishment in the army) (Jones, *Letters*, I, p. 54). Shelley, at his most forward when he thought that he had detected a fellow-thinker, enclosed an 'address' on the subject of organizing 'a methodical society' that would resist 'the enemies of liberty' and promote '*rational liberty*'. A couple of months later, he was proudly telling Hogg that he had been invited to breakfast with Hunt, who was clearly more flattered than alarmed by his introduction of himself. He earnestly reported his attempts to persuade Hunt out of Deism and into Atheism: 'Hunt is a man of cultivated mind, & certainly exalted notions; – I do not entirely despair of rescuing him out of this damnable heresy from Reason' (Jones, *Letters*, I, p. 77). Hunt's wife, Marianne, he added, was 'a most sensible woman, she is by no means a Xtian, & rather atheistically given'.

From his reading of *The Examiner*, Shelley clearly expected a meeting of minds with its editor. Hunt's journal, published with his elder brother, John, was trenchantly opposed to Tory politics at a time of Tory ascendancy. It promoted causes such as Catholic emancipation, Parliamentary reform, abolition of the slave trade and child labour, liberty of the press, and universal education. Its editor, born in 1784, the son of a clergyman, had been educated at Christ's Hospital, and had worked as a clerk in the War Office between 1803 and 1808, before committing himself to a life of letters. He began various politically motivated periodicals, but none achieved the notoriety of *The Examiner*. In part this was because, the year after his meeting with Shelley, it included a bitter attack on the Prince Regent ('a violator of his word, a libertine over his head and ears in debt and disgrace, a despiser of domestic ties, the companion of gamblers and demireps') that led to Hunt and his brother being convicted of libel (*The Examiner*, 22 March, 1812, No. 221). The Hunts were heavily fined and sentenced to two years' imprisonment. Shelley, who appears not to have built a friendship with Hunt on that first meeting, followed the trial closely (Jones, *Letters*, I, p. 346). In a letter to Thomas Hookham, he said that he was 'boiling with indignation at the horrible injustice & tyranny of the sentence' and that he intended to begin a subscription for the Hunts (ibid., I, p. 353).

The real intimacy between the two men began in 1816, clearly founded on Shelley's early admiration. In October 1816, he submitted his '*Hymn to Intellectual Beauty*' to the *Examiner*, and, on December 1st, Hunt published an article on 'Young Poets' in which Shelley was praised as 'a very striking and original thinker' (the poem appeared in the journal on January 19th, 1817). As a correspondence began between the two men, Hunt took the opportunity to ask Shelley for financial help, which he appears to have given willingly (Holmes, p. 350). Hunt usually had money troubles. In early December, Shelley was staying with the Hunts in Hampstead. The relationship between Shelley and Hunt was intensified by Harriet Shelley's suicide, and its consequences, in particular the Chancery case for custody of Shelley's two children by Harriet, Charles and Ianthe. While this was under way, Shelley and Mary, now married, spent a good deal of time with the Hunts, and would later often recall their kindness. The friendship continued until the Shelleys left for Italy in March 1818. Hunt kept up a correspondence with Shelley, became his main advocate and defender in England (see, for example, the extract from the *Examiner* in Jones, *Letters*, II, p. 134), and was the dedicatee of *The Cenci*, completed in 1819. Eventually, he was persuaded to bring his family (he had six children) to join the Shelleys in Italy.

The Hunts arrived in Genoa in June, 1822, and then travelled on to Livorno, to where Shelley sailed on July 1st. After meeting his friends again, Shelley went with them and Byron to Pisa, where they discussed their projected periodical the *Liberal* (four issues of the journal were to appear after Shelley's death). It was on his return journey from this reunion that Shelley, along with Edward Williams and Charles Vivian, capsized and drowned. Hunt was one of those who witnessed the cremation of Shelley's body when it was finally recovered. (In *Lord Byron and Some of His Contemporaries* he was to object to Medwin's misrepresentation of his involvement, denying that his 'feelings and nerves could not carry him through the scene of horror' (p. 97).) In the aftermath of this disaster, he and his family found themselves dependent on Byron for financial support; the relationship between Hunt and Byron suffered as a consequence. The Hunts remained in Italy for two more years. When they returned to England, they were again badly in need of funds, and Hunt's best asset appeared to be his recollections of Byron, who had recently died. The publisher Colburn, who was feeding a market hungry for Byroniana, advanced him money on the prospect of these.

In his Preface to *Lord Byron and Some of His Contemporaries*, which was published in 1828, Hunt himself indicated that only pressure from his publisher had induced him to make Byron the main subject of his memoirs. While protesting the absolute truthfulness of his account, he also found it necessary to signify a certain distaste for the work to which financial exigencies had forced him. 'I must even confess, that such is my dislike of these personal histories, in which it has been my lot to become a party, that had I been rich enough, and could have repaid the handsome conduct of Mr. Colburn with its proper interest, my first impulse on finishing the work would have been to put it in the fire' (ibid., p. iv). His hostile account of Byron did indicate provoke much anger – but also excellent sales, and further editions. Amongst the controversy over his picture of what he called 'the infirmities of Lord Byron' (Hunt, *Lord Byron*, p. vi), his enthusiastic portraits of Shelley and Keats were unlikely to attract much attention. His allegiance to Shelley is evident in the following extracts, and was to remain throughout his life (for his later career, see the headnote in this volume to extracts from his *Autobiography*). Although his protests about Shelley's supposed religiosity might seem rather too loud, he tackles the poet's opinions and ideals more directly than most later memoirists.

MR. SHELLEY.

WITH A CRITICISM ON HIS GENIUS, AND

MR. TRELAWNEY'S NARRATIVE OF HIS LOSS AT SEA.

MR. SHELLEY, when he died, was in his thirtieth year. His figure was tall and slight, and his constitution consumptive. He was subject to violent spasmodic pains, which would sometimes force him to lie on the ground till they were over; but he had always a kind word to give to those about him, when his pangs allowed him to speak. In this organization, as well as in some other respects, he resembled the German poet, Schiller. Though well-turned, his shoulders were bent a little, owing to premature thought and trouble. The same causes had touched his hair with grey: and though his habits of temperance and exercise gave him a remarkable degree of strength, it is not supposed that he could have lived many years. He used to say, that he had lived three times as long as the calendar gave out; which he would prove, between jest and earnest, by some remarks on Time,

> " That would have puzzled that stout Stagyrite."

Like the Stagyrite's, his voice was high and weak. His eyes were large and animated, with a dash of wildness in them; his face small, but well-shaped, particularly the mouth and chin, the turn of which was very sensitive and graceful. His complexion was naturally fair and delicate, with a colour in the cheeks. He had brown hair, which, though tinged with grey, surmounted his face well, being in considerable quantity, and tending to a curl. His side-face upon the whole was deficient in strength, and his features would not have told well in a bust; but when fronting and looking at you attentively, his aspect had a certain seraphical character that would have suited a portrait of John the Baptist, or the angel whom Milton describes as holding a reed "tipt with fire." Nor would the most religious mind, had it known him, have objected to the comparison; for, with all his scepticism, Mr. Shelley's disposition may be truly said to have been any thing but irreligious. A person of much eminence for piety in our times has well observed, that the greatest want of religious feeling is not to be found among the greatest infidels, but among those who never think of religion but as a matter of course. The leading feature of Mr. Shelley's character, may be said to have been a natural piety. He was pious towards nature, towards his friends, towards the whole human race, towards the meanest insect of the forest. He did himself an injustice with the public, in using the popular name of the Supreme Being inconsiderately. He identified it solely with the most vulgar and tyrannical notions of a God made after the worst human fashion; and did not sufficiently reflect, that it was often used by a juster devotion to express a sense of the great Mover of the universe. An impatience in contradicting worldly and pernicious notions of a supernatural power, led his own aspirations to be misconstrued; for though, in the severity of his dialectics, and particularly in moments of despondency, he sometimes appeared to be hopeless of what he most desired,—and though he justly thought, that a Divine Being would prefer the increase of benevolence and good before any praise, or even recognition of himself, (a reflection worth thinking of by the intolerant,) yet there was in reality no belief to which he clung with more fondness than that of some great pervading " Spirit of Intellectual Beauty ;" as may be seen in his aspirations on that subject. He said to me in the cathedral at Pisa, while the organ was playing, " What a divine religion might be found out, if charity were really made the principle of it, instead of faith !"

Music affected him deeply. He had also a delicate perception of the beauties of sculpture. It is not one of the least evidences of his conscientious turn of mind, that with the inclination, and the power, to surround himself in Italy with all the graces of life, he made no sort of attempt that way ; finding other use for his money, and not always satisfied with himself for indulging even in the luxury of a boat. When he bought elegancies of any kind, it was to give away. Boating was his great amusement. He loved the mixture of action and repose which he found in it; and delighted to fancy himself gliding away to Utopian isles, and bowers of enchantment. But he would give up any pleasure to do a deed of kindness. " His life," says Mrs. Shelley, " was spent in the contemplation of nature, in arduous study, or in acts of kindness and affection. He was an elegant scholar, and a profound metaphysician. Without possessing much scientific knowledge, he was unrivalled in the justness and extent of his observations on natural objects : he knew every plant by its name, and was familiar with the history and habits of every production of the earth : he could interpret, without a fault, each appearance in the sky ; and the varied phenomena of heaven and earth filled him with deep emotion. He made his study and reading-room of the shadowed copse, the stream, the lake, and the waterfall." — *Preface* to his Posthumous Poems, p. 14. " The comparative solitude," observes the same lady, "in which Mr. Shelley lived, was the occasion that he was personally known to few ; and his fearless enthusiasm in the cause which he considered the most sacred upon earth, the improvement of the moral and physical state of mankind, was the chief reason why he, like other illustrious reformers, was pursued by hatred and calumny. No man was ever more devoted than he to the endeavour of making those around him happy; no man ever possessed friends more unfeignedly attached to him. Before the critics contradict me, let them appeal to any one who had ever known him. To see him was to love him."—*Ibid.* This is a high cha- racter, and I, for one, know it was deserved. I should be glad to know, how many wives of Mr. Shelley's calumniators could say as much of their husbands ; or how many of the critics would believe them, if they did.

Mr. Shelley's comfort was a sacrifice to the perpetual contradiction between the professions of society and their practice ; between " the shows of things and the desires of the mind." Temperament and early circumstances conspired to make him a reformer, at a time of life when few begin to think for themselves ; and it was his misfortune, as far as immediate reputation was concerned, that he was thrown upon society with a precipitancy and vehemence, which rather startled them with fear for themselves, than allowed them to become sensible of the love and zeal that impelled him. He was like a spirit that had darted out of its orb, and found itself in another planet. I used to tell him that he had come from the planet Mercury. When I heard of the catas- trophe that overtook him, it seemed as if this spirit, not sufficiently constituted like the rest of the world, to obtain their sympathy, yet gifted with a double portion of love for all living things, had been found dead in a solitary corner of the earth, its wings stiffened, its warm heart cold; the relics of a misunderstood nature, slain by the ungenial elements.

That the utility, however, of so much benevolence was not lost to the world, whatever difference of opinion may exist as to its occasional mode of showing itself, will be evinced, I hope, by the following pages.

☆ ★ ☆

Conceive a young man of Mr. Shelley's character, with no better experience of the kindness and sincerity of those whom he had perplexed, thrown forth into society, to form his own judgments, and pursue his own career. It was " *Emilius out in the World,*" but formed by his own tutorship. There is a Novel, under that title, written by the German, La Fontaine, which has often reminded me of him. The hero of another, by the same author, called the " *Reprobate,*" still more resembles him. His way of proceeding was entirely after the fashion of those guileless, but vehement hearts, which not being well replied to by their teachers, and finding them hostile to inquiry, add to a natural love of truth all the passionate ardour of a generous and devoted protection of it. Mr. Shelley had met with Mr. Godwin's " Political Justice ;" and he seemed to breathe, for the first time, in an open and bright atmosphere. He resolved to square all his actions by what he conceived to be the strictest justice, without any consideration for the opinions of those, whose little exercise of that virtue towards himself, ill-fitted them, he thought, for better teachers, and as ill warranted him in deferring to the opinions of the world whom they guided. That he did some extraordinary things in consequence, is admitted : that he did many noble ones, and all with sincerity, is well known to his friends, and will be admitted by all sincere persons. Let those who are so fond of exposing their own natures, by attributing every departure from ordinary conduct to bad motives, ask themselves what conduct could be more extraordinary in their eyes, and at the same time less attributable to a bad motive, than the rejection of an estate for the love of a principle. Yet Mr. Shelley rejected one. He had only to become a yea and nay man in the House of Commons, to be one of the richest men in Sussex. He declined it, and lived upon a comparative pittance. Even the fortune that he would ultimately have inherited, as secured to his person, was petty in the comparison.

We will relate another anecdote, which the conventional will not find it so difficult to quarrel with. It trenches upon that extraordinary privilege to indulge one sex at the expense of the other, which they guard with so jealous a care, and so many hypocritical faces. The question, we allow, is weighty. We are far from saying it is here settled: but very far are they themselves from having settled it; as their own writings and writhings, their own statistics, morals, romances, tears, and even jokes will testify. The case, I understood, was this; for I am bound to declare that I forget who told it me; but it is admirably in character, and not likely to be invented. Mr. Shelley was present at a ball, where he was a person of some importance. Numerous village ladies were there, old and young; and none of the passions were absent, that are accustomed to glance in the eyes, and gossip in the tongues, of similar gatherings together of talk and dress. In the front were seated the rank and fashion of the place. The virtues diminished, as the seats went backward; and at the back of all, unspoken to, but not unheeded, sat blushing a damsel who had been seduced. We do not inquire by whom; probably by some well-dressed gentleman in the room, who thought himself entitled nevertheless to the conversation of the most flourishing ladies present, and who naturally thought so, because he had it. That sort of thing happens every day. It was expected, that the young squire would take out one of these ladies to dance. What is the consternation, when they see him making his way to the back benches, and handing forth, with an air of consolation and tenderness, the object of all the virtuous scorn of the room! the person whom that other gentleman, wrong as he had been towards her, and " wicked" as the ladies might have allowed him to be towards the fair sex in general, would have shrunk from touching!—Mr. Shelley, it was found, was equally unfit for school-tyrannies, for universities, and for the chaste orthodoxy of squires' tables.   So he went up to town.

The philosophic observer will confess, that our young author's experiences in education, politics, and gentlemanly morality, were not of a nature to divert him from his notions of justice, however calculated to bring him into trouble. Had he now behaved himself pardonably in the eyes of the orthodox, he would have gone to London with the resolution of sowing his wild oats, and becoming a decent member of society; that is to say, he would have seduced a few maid-servants, or at least haunted the lobbies; and then bestowed the remnant of his constitution upon some young lady of his own rank in life, and settled into a proper church-and-king man, perhaps a member of the Suppression of Vice.   This is the proper routine, and gives one a right to be didactic.   Alas! Mr. Shelley did not do so; and bitterly had he to repent, not that he did not do it, but that he married while yet a stripling, and that the wife whom he took was not of a nature to appreciate his understanding, or perhaps to come from contact with it, uninjured in what she had of her own.   They separated by mutual consent, after the birth of two children.   To this measure his enemies would hardly have demurred ; especially as the marriage was, disapproved by Mr. Shelley's family, and the lady of inferior rank. It might have been regarded even as something like making amends. But to one thing they would strongly have objected. He proceeded, in the spirit of Milton's doctrines, to pay his court to another lady. We wish we could pursue the story in the same tone : but now came the greatest pang of Mr. Shelley's life. He was residing at Bath, when news came to him that his wife had destroyed herself. It was a heavy blow to him ; and he never forgot it. Persons who riot in a debauchery of scandal, delighting in endeavouring to pull down every one to their own standard, and in repeating the grossest charges in the grossest words, have taken advantage of this passage in Mr. Shelley's life, to show their total ignorance of his nature, and to harrow up, one would think, the feelings of every person connected with him, by the most wanton promulgation of names, and the most odious falsehoods. Luckily, the habitual contempt of truth which ever accompanies the love of calumny, serves to refute it with all those whose good opinion is worth having. So leaving the scandal in those natural sinks, to which all the calumnies and falsehoods of the time hasten, we resume our remarks with the honourable and the decent. As little shall we dwell upon the conduct of one or two persons of better repute, who instead of being warned against believing every malignant rumour by the nature of their own studies, and as if they had been jealous of a zeal in behalf of mankind, which they had long been accused of merging in speculations less noble, did not disdain to circulate the gossip of the scandalous as far as other countries, betraying a man to repulses, who was yearning with the love of his species ; and confounding times, places, and circumstances, in the eagerness of their paltry credulity. Among other falsehoods it was stated, that Mr. Shelley, at that time living with his wife, had abruptly communicated to her his intention of separating; upon which the other had run to a pond at the end of the garden, and drowned herself. The fact, as we have seen, is, that they had been living apart for some time, during which the lady was accountable to no one but herself. We could relate another story of the catastrophe that took place, did we not feel sincerely for all parties concerned, and wish to avoid every species of heart-burning. Nobody could lament it more bitterly than Mr. Shelley. For a time, it tore his being to pieces; nor is there a doubt, that however deeply he was accustomed to reason on the nature and causes of evil, and on the steps necessary to be taken for opposing it, he was not without remorse for having no better exercised his judgment with regard to the degree of intellect he had allied himself with, and for having given rise to a premature independence of conduct in one unequal to the task. The lady was greatly to be pitied; so was the survivor. Let the school-tyrants, the University refusers of argument, and the orthodox sowers of their wild oats, with myriads of unhappy women behind them, rise up in judgment against him. Honester men will not be hindered from doing justice to sincerity, wherever they find it; nor be induced to blast the memory of a man of genius and benevolence, for one painful passage in his life, which he might have avoided, had he been no better than his calumniators.

On the death of this unfortunate lady, Mr. Shelley married the daughter of Mr. Godwin; and resided at Great Marlow, in Buckinghamshire, where he was a blessing to the poor. His charity, though liberal, was not weak. He inquired personally into the circumstances of the petitioners; visited the sick in their beds, (for he had gone the round

of the Hospitals on purpose to be able to practise on occasion) ; and
kept a regular list of industrious poor, whom he assisted with small sums
to make up their accounts.* At Marlow he wrote the *Revolt of Islam.*

* " Another anecdote remains, not the least in interest." (I was speaking, in the Literary Examiner, of an adventure of Mr. Shelley's, at the time he was on a visit to me at
Hampstead.) Some years ago, when a house (on the top of the Heath) " was occupied
by a person whose name I forget, (and I should suppress it in common humanity, if I did
not,) I was returning home to my own, which was at no great distance from it, after the
Opera. As I approached my door, I heard strange and alarming shrieks, mixed with the
voice of a man. The next day, it was reported by the gossips, that Mr. Shelley, no Christian,
(for it was he, who was there,) had brought some ' very strange female ' into the house, no
better of course than she ought to be. The real Christian had puzzled them. Mr. Shelley,
in coming to our house that night, had found a woman lying near the top of the hill, in fits.
It was a fierce winter night, with snow upon the ground ; and winter loses nothing of its
fierceness at Hampstead. My friend, always the promptest as well as most pitying on these
occasions, knocked at the first houses he could reach, in order to have the woman taken in.
The invariable answer was, that they could not do it. He asked for an outhouse to put her
in, while he went for a doctor. Impossible ! In vain he assured them she was no impostor. They would not dispute the point with him ; but doors were closed, and windows were shut down. Had he lit upon worthy Mr. Park, the philologist, he would assuredly have come, in spite of his Calvinism. But he lived too far off. Had he lit upon you,
dear B——n, or your neighbour D——e, you would either of you have jumped up from amidst
your books or your bed-clothes, and have gone out with him. But the paucity of Christians is astonishing, considering the number of them. Time flies ; the poor woman is in convulsions ; her son, a young man, lamenting over her. At last my friend sees a carriage driving up to a house at a little distance. The knock is given ; the warm door opens ; servants
and lights pour forth. Now, thought he, is the time. He puts on his best address, which
any body might recognize for that of the highest gentleman as well as an interesting individual, and plants himself in the way of an elderly person, who is stepping out of the carriage
with his family. He tells his story. They only press on the faster. ' Will you go and see
her ?' ' No, Sir ; there 's no necessity for that sort of thing, depend on it : impostors swarm
every where : the thing cannot be done : Sir, your conduct is extraordinary.' ' Sir,' cried
Mr. Shelley at last, assuming a very different appearance, and forcing the flourishing householder to stop out of astonishment, ' I am sorry to say that *your* conduct is *not* extraordinary :
and if my own seems to amaze you, I will tell you something that may amaze you a little

Queen Mab was an earlier production, written at the age of seventeen or eighteen, when he married; and it was never published with his consent. He regretted the publication when it did take place some years afterwards, and stated as much in the newspapers, considering it a crude performance, and as not sufficiently entering into the important questions it handled. Yet upon the strength of this young and unpublished work, he was deprived of his two children.

more, and I hope will frighten you. It is such men as you who madden the spirits and the patience of the poor and wretched : and if ever a convulsion comes in this country, (which is very probable,) recollect what I tell you;—you will have your house, that you refuse to put the miserable woman into, burnt over your head.' ' God bless me, Sir ! Dear me, Sir !' exclaimed the frightened wretch, and fluttered into his mansion. The woman was then brought to our house, which was at some distance, and down a bleak path; and Mr. S. and her son were obliged to hold her, till the doctor could arrive. It appeared that she had been attending this son in London, on a criminal charge made against him, the agitation of which had thrown her into the fits on her return. The doctor said that she would inevitably have perished, had she lain there a short time longer, The next day my friend sent mother and son comfortably home to Hendon, where they were well known, and whence they returned him thanks full of gratitude. Now go, ye Pharisees of all sorts, and try if ye can still open your hearts and your doors like the good Samaritan. This man was himself too brought up in a splendid mansion, and might have revelled and rioted in all worldly goods. Yet this was one of the most ordinary of his actions."

☆ ★ ☆

The writer who criticised the " Posthumous Poems," in the " Edinburgh Review," does justice to the excellence of Mr. Shelley's intentions, and acknowledges him to be one of those rare persons called men of genius; but accuses him of a number of faults, which he attributes to the predominance of his will, and a scorn of every thing received and conventional. To this cause he traces the faults of his poetry, and what he conceives to be the errors of his philosophy. Furthermore, he charges Mr. Shelley with a want of reverence for antiquity, and quotes a celebrated but not unequivocal passage from Bacon, where the Philosopher, according to the advice of the Prophet, recommends us to take our stand upon the ancient ways, and see what road we are to take for progression. He says Mr. Shelley had " too little sympathy with the feelings of others, which he thought he had a right to sacrifice, as well as his own, to a grand ethical experiment; and asserts that if a thing were old and established, this was with him a certain proof of its having no solid foundation to rest upon : if it was new, it was good and right : every paradox was to him a self-evident truth : every prejudice an undoubted absurdity. The weight of authority, the sanction of ages, the common consent of mankind, were vouchers only for ignorance, error, and imposture. Whatever shocked the feelings of others, conciliated his regard; whatever was light, extravagant, and vain, was to him a proportionable relief from the dulness and stupidity of established opinions." This is caricature; and caricature of an imaginary original.

Alas! Mr. Shelley was so little relieved by what was light and vain, (if I understand what the Reviewer means by those epithets,) and so little disposed to quarrel with the common consent of mankind, where it seemed reasonably founded, that at first he could not endure even the comic parts of Lord Byron's writings, because he thought they tended to produce mere volatility instead of good; and he afterwards came to relish them, because he found an accord with them in the bosoms of society. Whatever shocked the feeling of others so little conciliated his regard, that with the sole exception of matters of religion (which is a point on which the most benevolent Reformers, authors of " grand ethical experiments," in all ages, have thought themselves warranted in hazarding alarm and astonishment,) his own feelings were never more violated than by disturbances given to delicacy, to sentiment, to the affections. If ever it seemed otherwise, as in the subject of his tragedy of the Cenci, it was only out of a more intense apprehensiveness, and the right it gave him to speak. He saw, in every species of tyranny and selfish will, an image of all the rest of the generation. That a love of paradox is occasionally of use to remind commonplaces of their weakness, and to prepare the way for liberal opinions, nobody knows better or has more unequivocally shown than Mr. Shelley's critic; and yet I am not aware that Mr. Shelley was at all addicted to paradox; or that he loved any contradiction, that did not directly contradict some great and tyrannical abuse. Prejudices that he thought innocent, no man was more inclined to respect, or even to fall in with. He was prejudiced in favour of the dead languages; he had a theoretical antipathy to innovations in style; he had almost an English dislike of the French and their literature, a philosopher or two excepted: it cost him much to reconcile himself to manners that were not refined; and even with regard to the prejudices of superstition, or the more poetical sides of popular faith, where they did not interfere with the daily and waking comforts of mankind, he was for admitting them with more than a spirit of toleration. It would be hazardous to affirm that he did not believe in spirits and genii. This is not setting his face against " every received mystery, and all traditional faith." He set his face, not against a mystery nor a self-evident proposition, but against whatever he conceived to be injurious to human good, and whatever his teachers would have forced down his throat, in defiance of the inquiries they had suggested. His opposition to what was established, as I have said before, is always to be considered with reference to that feature in his disposition, and that fact in his history. Of antiquity and authority he was so little a scorner, that his opinions, novel as some of them may be thought, are all to be found in writers, both ancient and modern, and those not obscure ones or empirical, but men of the greatest and wisest, and best names,—Plato and Epicurus, Montaigne, Bacon, Sir Thomas More. Nothing in him was his own, but the genius that impelled him to put philosophical speculations in the shape of poetry, and a subtle and magnificent style, abounding in Hellenisms, and by no means exempt (as he acknowledged) from a tendency to imitate whatever else he thought beautiful, in ancient or modern writers.

But Mr. Shelley was certainly definite in his object: he thought it was high time for society to come to particulars: to know what they would have. With regard to marriage, for instance, he was tired with the spectacle continually presented to his eyes, of a community always feeling sore upon that point, and cowed, like a man by his wife, from attempting some real improvement in it. There was no end, he thought, of setting up this new power, and pulling down that, if the one, to all real home purposes, proceeded just as the other did, and nothing was gained to society but a hope and a disappointment. This, in his opinion, was not the kind of will to be desired, in opposition to one with more definite objects. We must not, he thought, be eternally generalizing, shilly-shallying, and coquetting between public submission and private independence; but let a generous understanding and acknowledgment of what we are in want of, go hand in hand with our exertions in behalf of change; otherwise, when we arrive at success, we shall find success itself in hands that are but physically triumphant—hands that hold up a victory on a globe, a splendid commonplace, as a new-old thing for us to worship. This, to be sure, is standing *super vias antiquas;* but not in order to " make progression." The thing is all to be done over again. If there is " something rotten in the state of Denmark," let us mend it, and not set up Sweden or Norway, to knock down this rottenness with rottenness of their own; continually waiting for others to do our work, and finding them do it in such a manner, as to deliver us bound again into the hands of the old corruptions. We must be our own deliverers. An Essay on the Disinterestedness of Human Action is much; but twenty articles to show that the most disinterested person in the world is only a malcontent and a fanatic, can be of no service but to baffle conduct and resolution, in favour of eternal theory and the talking about it.

☆ ★ ☆

So do not end the pleasures given us by men of genius with great and beneficent views. So does not end the pleasure of endeavouring to do justice to their memories, however painful the necessity. Some good must be done them, however small. Some pleasure cannot but be realized, for a great principle is advocated, and a deep gratitude felt. I differed with Mr. Shelley on one or two important points ; but I agreed with him heartily on the most important point of all,—the necessity of doing good, *and of discussing the means of it freely.* I do not think the world so unhappy as he did, or what a very different and much more contented personage has not hesitated to pronounce it,— a " vale of blood and tears." But I think it quite unhappy enough to require that we should all set our shoulders to the task of reformation ; and this for two reasons: first, that if mankind can effect any thing, they can only effect it by trying, instead of lamenting and being selfish; and second, that if no other good come of our endeavours, we must always be the better for what keeps human nature in hope and activity. That there are monstrous evils to be got rid of, nobody doubts : that we never scruple to get rid of any minor evil that annoys us, any obstacle in our way, or petty want of comfort in our dwellings, we know as certainly. Why the larger ones should be left standing, is yet to be understood. Sir Walter Scott may have no objection to his " vale of blood and tears," provided he can look down upon it from a decent aristocratical height, and a well-stocked mansion ; but others have an inconvenient habit of levelling themselves with humanity, and feeling for their neighbours : and it is lucky for Sir Walter himself, that they have so ; or Great Britain would not enjoy the comfort she does in her northern atmosphere. The conventional are but the weakest and most thankless children of the unconventional. They live upon the security the others have obtained for them. If it were not for the reformers and innovators of old, the Hampdens, the Miltons, and the Sydneys, life in this country, with all its cares, would not be the convenient thing it is, even for the lowest retainers of the lowest establishment. A feeling of indignation will arise, when we think of great spirits like those, contrasted with the mean ones that venture to scorn their wisdom and self-sacrifice; but it is swallowed up in what absorbed the like emotions in their own minds, —a sense of the many. The mean spirit, if we knew all, need not be denied even his laugh. He may be too much in want of it. But the greatest unhappiness of the noble-minded has moments of exquisite relief. Every thing of beautiful and good that exists, has a kind face for him when he turns to it; or reflects the happy faces of others that enjoy it, if he cannot. He can extract consolation out of discomfiture itself,—if the good he sought otherwise, can come by it. Mr. Shelley felt the contumelies he underwent, with great sensibility ; and he expressed himself accordingly; but I know enough of his nature to be certain, that he would gladly have laid down his life to ensure a good to society, even out of the most lasting misrepresentations of his benevolence. Great is the pleasure to me to anticipate the day of justice, by putting an end to this evil. The friends whom he loved may now bid his brave and gentle spirit repose ; for the human beings whom he laboured for, *begin to know him.*

NOTE

'That would have puzzled that stout Stagyrite': see note on p. 204.

Thomas Jefferson Hogg, 'Shelley at Oxford', in *The New Monthly Magazine* (January, February, April, December, 1832, and May, 1833)

Hogg's memoir, later to be absorbed into his controversial *Life of Percy Bysshe Shelley* (1858), is the first in which the meeting and subsequent friendship of poet and memoirist is the focus of interest. As Hogg describes in the first of these articles, published a decade after Shelley's death, the two young men met as fellow undergraduates at University College, Oxford. Hogg was a lawyer's son from Durham (and would eventually become a lawyer himself). He was, he says, fascinated by 'a character so extraordinary, and indeed almost preternatural' (*New Monthly Magazine*, February, 1832, p. 136). He declares, indeed, that he immediately felt 'reverence' for Shelley. The impressions that he recalls in these articles are, of course, shaped by his sense, by 1832, of the poet's greatness. Yet he was clearly gripped by Shelley, and rapidly became a kind of follower as well as a close friend. While the account that he gives here is scarcely disinterested, it has been treated by later biographers as essentially reliable. Pictures such as that of Shelley's college rooms in the second of these extracts seem too vivid and too unusual to be invented. Our idea of Shelley the student – the galvanic experimenter and dabbler in sceptical thought – still derives almost entirely from these articles.

The period that they cover is one of less than five months, from a first meeting in November to their joint expulsion from Oxford in March 1811 for their co-authored tract, *The Necessity of Atheism*. Hogg saw a great deal of Shelley over the next three years, and indeed lived with him for certain periods. (Their friendship at this time, and Hogg's relationships with, first, Harriet Shelley, and then Mary Godwin, are described in the headnote in this volume to passages from Hogg's *Life of Percy Bysshe Shelley* in this volume.) However, intimacy between him and Mary became a muted antagonism, and from 1815 onwards, he and Shelley were to meet only occasionally. After Hogg was called to the bar in 1817, his attention was diverted to his career. Shelley, however, tried to persuade Hogg to join him in Italy, and continued to describe him in letters as, along with Hunt and Peacock, one of his very few true friends in England. By this time Hogg was the sedulous lawyer that his family had always wished him to be.

Shelley's death had one odd and important consequence for Hogg. Jane Williams, common-law wife of Edward Williams, who had drowned with Shelley, left Italy for England in September 1822, with a letter of introduction to Hogg from Mary Shelley. 'I would say do all in your power to be of use to her, but to know her is sufficient to make the desire of serving her arise in an unselfish mind. Do what little you can to amuse her' (Bennett, *Letters*, I, p. 258). For all Mary Shelley's initial disbelief, an attachment grew between the two, and they began living together as husband and wife in the Spring of 1827. Shelley's widow stayed a close friend of Jane Williams Hogg, and friendly relations between her and Hogg were re-established. In 1841, writing to the publisher Edward Moxon about an amended edition of Shelley's poetry, Mary was to suggest that it might include a piece by Hogg: 'an Essay on Shelley's life & writings – original – though it might embody the substance of his Articles in the New Monthly' (Bennett, *Letters*, III, p. 17). Evidently she believed that the articles in the *New Monthly* gave a proper impression of the poet's youthful idealism (and perhaps as palatable an explanation of his expulsion from Oxford as was ever likely).

Hogg published six articles about Shelley in *The New Monthly Magazine*. Extracts below are taken from all but one: the article that appeared in October 1832. The issues in which the following passages appeared were those for January, February, April, July, and December, 1832, and May 1833. A note at the head of the December, 1832, article indicated that it would be the last. Evidently the description of the expulsion of Hogg and Shelley from Oxford published in May 1833 was either Hogg's or his editor's after-thought. It is also the most self-important and least entirely credible of all the articles.

At the commencement of Michaelmas term, that is, at the end of October, in the year 1810, I happened one day to sit next to a fresh man at dinner: it was his first appearance in hall. His figure was slight, and his aspect remarkably youthful, even at our table, where all were very young. He seemed thoughtful and absent. He ate little, and seemed to have no acquaintance with any one. I know not how it was that we fell into conversation, for such familiarity was unusual, and, strange to say, much reserve prevailed in a society where there could not possibly be occasion for any. We have often endeavoured in vain to recollect in what manner our discourse began, and especially by what transition it passed to a subject sufficiently remote from all the associations we were able to trace. The stranger had expressed an enthusiastic admiration for poetical and imaginative works of the German school. I dissented from his criticisms. He upheld the originality of the German writings. I asserted their want of nature. " What modern literature," said he, " will you compare to theirs?" I named the Italian. This roused all his impetuosity ; and few, as I soon discovered, were more impetuous in argumentative conversation. So eager was our dispute, that when the servants came to clear the tables, we were not aware that we had been left alone. I remarked, that it was time to quit the hall, and I invited the stranger to finish the discussion at my rooms. He eagerly assented. He lost the thread of his discourse in the transit, and the whole of his enthusiasm in the cause of Germany ; for as soon as he arrived at my rooms, and whilst I was lighting the candles, he said calmly, and to my great surprise, that he was not qualified to maintain such a discussion, for he was alike ignorant of Italian and German, and had only read the works of the Germans in translations, and but little of Italian poetry, even at second hand. For my part, I confessed, with an equal ingenuousness, that I knew nothing of German, and but little of Italian ; that I had spoken only through others, and like him, had hitherto seen by the glimmering light of translations. It is upon such scanty data that young men reason ; upon such slender materials do they build up their opinions. It may be urged, however, that if they did not discourse freely with each other upon insufficient information—for such alone can be acquired in the pleasant morning of life, and until they educate themselves—they would be constrained to observe a perpetual silence, and to forego the numerous advantages that flow from frequent and liberal discussion. I inquired of the vivacious stranger, as we sat over our wine and dessert, how long he had been at Oxford, how he liked it, &c.? He answered my questions with a certain impatience, and resuming the subject of our discussion, he remarked, that " Whether the literature of Germany, or of Italy, be the most original, or in the purest and most accurate taste, is of little importance ! for polite letters are but vain trifling ; the study of languages, not only of the modern tongues, but of Latin and Greek also, is merely the study of words and phrases ; of the names of things ; it matters not how they are called ; it is surely far better to investigate things themselves." I inquired, a little bewildered, how this was to be effected ? He answered, " through the physical sciences, and especially through chemistry ;" and raising his voice, his face flushing as he spoke, he discoursed with a degree of animation, that far outshone his zeal in defence of the Germans, of chemistry and chemical analysis. Concerning that science, then so popular, I had merely a scanty and vulgar knowledge, gathered from elementary books, and the ordinary experiments of popular lecturers. I listened, therefore, in silence to his eloquent disquisition, interposing a few brief questions only, and at long intervals, as to the extent of his own studies and manipulations. As I felt, in truth, but a slight interest in the subject of his conversation, I had leisure to examine, and I may add, to admire, the appearance of my very extraordinary guest. It was a sum of many contradictions. His figure was slight and fragile, and yet his bones and joints were large and strong. He was tall, but he stooped so much, that he seemed of a low stature. His clothes were expensive, and made according to the most approved mode of the day ; but they were tumbled, rumpled, unbrushed. His gestures were abrupt, and sometimes violent, occasionally even awkward, yet more frequently gentle and graceful. His complexion was delicate, and almost feminine, of the purest red and white ; yet he was tanned and freckled by exposure to the sun, having passed the autumn, as he said, in shooting. His features, his whole face, and particularly his head, were, in fact, unusually small ; yet the last *appeared* of a remarkable bulk, for his hair was long and bushy, and in fits of absence, and in the agonies (if I may use the word) of anxious thought, he often rubbed it fiercely with his hands, or passed his fingers quickly through his locks unconsciously, so that it was singularly wild and rough. In times when it was the mode to imitate stage-coachmen as closely as possible in costume, and when the hair was invariably cropped, like that of our soldiers, this eccentricity was very striking. His features were not symmetrical, (the mouth, perhaps, excepted,) yet was the effect of the whole extremely powerful.

They breathed an animation, a fire, an enthusiasm, a vivid and pre-ternatural intelligence, that I never met with in any other coun-tenance. Nor was the moral expression less beautiful than the intellectual; for there was a softness, a delicacy, a gentleness, and especially (though this will surprise many) that air of profound religious veneration, that characterizes the best works, and chiefly the frescoes, (and into these they infused their whole souls,) of the great masters of Florence and of Rome. I recognized the very peculiar expression in these wonderful productions long afterwards, and with a satisfaction mingled with much sorrow, for it was after the decease of him in whose countenance I had first observed it. I admired the enthusiasm of my new acquaintance, his ardour in the cause of science, and his thirst for knowledge. I seemed to have found in him all those intellectual qualities which I had vainly expected to meet with in an University. But there was one physical blemish that threatened to neutralize all his excellence. "This is a fine, clever fellow!" I said to myself, "but I can never bear his society; I shall never be able to endure his voice; it would kill me. What a pity it is!" I am very sensible of imperfections, and especially of painful sounds—and the voice of the stranger was excruciating: it was intolerably shrill, harsh, and discordant; of the most cruel intension—it was perpetual, and without any remission—it excoriated the ears. He continued to discourse of chemistry, sometimes sitting, sometimes standing before the fire, and sometimes pacing about the room; and when one of the innumerable clocks that speak in various notes during the day and the night at Oxford, proclaimed a quarter to seven, he said suddenly that he must go to a lecture on mine-ralogy, and declared enthusiastically that he expected to derive much pleasure and instruction from it. I am ashamed to own that the cruel voice made me hesitate for a moment; but it was impossible to omit so indispensable a civility—I invited him to return to tea; he gladly assented, promised that he would not be absent long, snatched his cap, hurried out of the room, and I heard his footsteps, as he ran through the silent quadrangle, and afterwards along the High-street. An hour soon elapsed, whilst the table was cleared, and the tea was made, and I again heard the footsteps of one running quickly. My guest suddenly burst into the room, threw down his cap, and as he stood shivering and chafing his hands over the fire, he declared how much he had been disappointed in the lecture. Few persons attended; it was dull and languid, and he was resolved never to go to another. "I went away, indeed," he added, with an arch look, and in a shrill whisper, coming close to me as he spoke—"I went away, indeed, before the lecture was finished. I stole away; for it was so stupid, and I was so cold, that my teeth chattered. The Professor saw me, and appeared to be displeased. I thought I could have got out without being observed; but I struck my knee against a bench, and made a noise, and he looked at me. I am determined that he shall never see me again."

"What did the man talk about?"

"About stones! about stones!" he answered, with a downcast look and in a melancholy tone, as if about to say something excessively profound. "About stones!—stones, stones, stones!—nothing but stones!—and so drily. It was wonderfully tiresome—and stones are not interesting things in themselves!"

We took tea; and soon afterwards had supper, as was usual. He discoursed after supper with as much warmth as before of the wonders of chemistry; of the encouragement that Napoleon afforded to that most important science; of the French chemists and their glorious discoveries; and of the happiness of visiting Paris, and sharing in their fame and their experiments. The voice, however, seemed to me more cruel than ever. He spoke likewise of his own labours and of his apparatus, and starting up suddenly after supper, he proposed that I should go instantly with him to see the galvanic trough. I looked at my watch, and observed that it was too late; that the fire would be out, and the night was cold. He resumed his seat, saying that I might come on the morrow, early, to breakfast, immediately after chapel. He continued to declaim in his rapturous strain, asserting that chemistry was, in truth, the only science that deserved to be studied. I suggested doubts. I ventured to question the pre-eminence of the science, and even to hesitate in admitting its utility. He described in glowing language some discoveries that had lately been made; but the enthusiastic chemist candidly allowed that they were rather brilliant than useful, asserting, however, that they would soon be applied to purposes of solid advantage. "Is not the time of by far the larger proportion of the human species," he inquired, with his fervid manner and in his piercing tones, "wholly consumed in severe labour? and is not this devotion of our race—of the whole of our race, I may say (for those who, like ourselves, are indulged with an exemption from the hard lot are so few, in comparison with the rest, that they scarcely deserve to be taken into the account,) absolutely necessary to procure subsistence; so that men have no leisure for recreation or the high improvement of the mind? Yet this incessant toil is still inadequate to procure an abundant supply of the common necessaries of life: some are doomed actually to want them, and many are compelled to be content with an insufficient provision. We know little of the peculiar nature of those substances which are proper for the nourishment of animals; we are ignorant of the qualities that make them fit for this end. Analysis has advanced so rapidly of late that we may confidently anticipate that we shall soon discover wherein their aptitude really consists; having ascertained the cause, we shall next be able to command it, and to produce at our pleasure the desired effects. It is easy, even in our present state of ignorance, to reduce our ordinary food to carbon, or to lime; a moderate advancement in chemical science will speedily enable us, we may hope, to create, with equal facility, food from substances that appear at present to be as ill adapted to sustain us. What is the cause of the remarkable fertility of some lands, and of the hopeless sterility of others? a spadeful of the most productive soil, does not to the eye differ much from the same quantity taken from the most barren. The real difference is probably very slight, by chemical agency the philosopher may work a total change, and may transmute an unfruitful region into a land of exuberant plenty. Water, like the atmospheric air, is compounded of certain gases : in the progress of scientific discovery a simple and sure method of manufacturing the useful fluid,

in every situation and in any quantity, may be detected; the arid
deserts of Africa may then be refreshed by a copious supply, and may
be transformed at once into rich meadows, and vast fields of maize and
rice. The generation of heat is a mystery, but enough of the theory
of caloric has already been developed to induce us to acquiesce in the
notion that it will hereafter, and perhaps at no very distant period, be
possible to produce heat at will, and to warm the most ungenial climates
as readily as we now raise the temperature of our apartments to whatever degree we may deem agreeable or salutary. If, however, it be
too much to anticipate that we shall ever become sufficiently skilful
to command such a prodigious supply of heat, we may expect, without the fear of disappointment, soon to understand its nature and the
causes of combustion, so far at least as to provide ourselves cheaply
with a fund of heat that will supersede our costly and inconvenient
fuel, and will suffice to warm our habitations for culinary purposes
and for the various demands of the mechanical arts. We could not
determine, without actual experiment, whether an unknown substance
were combustible; when we shall have thoroughly investigated the
properties of fire, it may be that we shall be qualified to communicate to clay, to stones, and to water itself, a chemical recomposition
that will render them as inflammable as wood, coals, and oil; for the
difference of structure is minute and invisible, and the power of feeding flame may perhaps be easily added to any substance, or taken
away from it. What a comfort would it be to the poor at all times,
and especially at this season, if we were capable of solving this problem alone, if we could furnish them with a competent supply of
heat! These speculations may appear wild, and it may seem improbable that they will ever be realized, to persons who have not extended their views of what is practicable by closely watching science
in its course onward; but there are many mysterious powers, many
irresistible agents, with the existence and with some of the phenomena of which all are acquainted. What a mighty instrument
would electricity be in the hands of him who knew how to wield it,
in what manner to direct its omnipotent energies; and we may command an indefinite quantity of the fluid: by means of electrical kites
we may draw down the lightning from heaven! What a terrible organ would the supernal shock prove, if we were able to guide it; how
many of the secrets of nature would such a stupendous force unlock!
The galvanic battery is a new engine; it has been used hitherto to
an insignificant extent, yet has it wrought wonders already; what will
not an extraordinary combination of troughs, of colossal magnitude,
a well-arranged system of hundreds of metallic plates, effect? The
balloon has not yet received the perfection of which it is surely capable; the art of navigating the air is in its first and most helpless in-
fancy; the aerial mariner still swims on bladders, and has not mounted even the rude raft: if we weigh this invention, curious as it is,
with some of the subjects I have mentioned, it will seem trifling, no
doubt—a mere toy, a feather, in comparison with the splendid anticipations of the philosophical chemist; yet it ought not altogether to be
contemned. It promises prodigious facilities for locomotion, and will
enable us to traverse vast tracts with ease and rapidity, and to ex-
plore unknown countries without difficulty. Why are we still so

ignorant of the interior of Africa ?—why do we not despatch intrepid aeronauts to cross it in every direction, and to survey the whole peninsula in a few weeks ? The shadow of the first balloon, which a vertical sun would project precisely underneath it, as it glided silently over that hitherto unhappy country, would virtually emancipate every slave, and would annihilate slavery for ever"

With such fervor did the slender, beardless stranger speculate concerning the march of physical science : his speculations were as wild as the experience of twenty-one years has shown them to be ; but the zealous earnestness for the augmentation of knowledge, and the glowing philanthropy and boundless benevolence that marked them, and beamed forth in the whole deportment of that extraordinary boy, are not less astonishing than they would have been if the whole of his glorious anticipations had been prophetic ; for these high qualities, at least, I have never found a parallel. When he had ceased to predict the coming honours of chemistry, and to promise the rich harvest of benefits it was soon to yield, I suggested that, although its results were splendid, yet for those who could not hope to make discoveries themselves, it did not afford so valuable a course of mental discipline as the moral sciences ; moreover, that if chemists asserted that their science alone deserved to be cultivated, the mathematicians made the same assertion, and with equal confidence, respecting their studies ; but that I was not sufficiently advanced myself in mathematics to be able to judge how far it was well founded. He declared that he knew nothing of mathematics, but treated the notion of their paramount importance with contempt. "What do you say of metaphysics ?" I continued ; " is that science, too, the study of words only ?"

" Ay, metaphysics," he said, in a solemn tone, and with a mysterious air, " that is a noble study indeed ! If it were possible to make any discoveries there, they would be more valuable than any thing the chemists have done, or could do ; they would disclose the analysis of mind, and not of mere matter !" Then rising from his chair, he paced slowly about the room, with prodigious strides, and discoursed of souls with still greater animation and vehemence than he had displayed in treating of gases—of a future state—and especially of a former state—of pre-existence, obscured for a time through the suspension of consciousness—of personal identity, and also of ethical philosophy, in a deep and earnest tone of elevated morality, until he suddenly remarked that the fire was nearly out, and the candles were glimmering in their sockets, when he hastily apologised for remaining so long. I promised to visit the chemist in his laboratory, the alchemist in his study, the wizard in his cave, not at breakfast on that day, for it was already one, but in twelve hours—one hour after noon—and to hear some of the secrets of nature ; and for that purpose, he told me his name and described the situation of his rooms. I lighted him down-stairs as well as I could with the stump of a candle which had dissolved itself into a lamp, and I soon heard him running through the quiet quadrangle in the still night. That sound became afterwards so familiar to my ear, that I still seem to hear Shelley's hasty steps.

☆ ★ ☆

Books, boots, papers, shoes, philosophical instruments, clothes, pistols, linen, crockery, ammunition, and phials innumerable, with money, stockings, prints, crucibles, bags, and boxes, were scattered on the floor and in every place; as if the young chemist, in order to analyze the mystery of creation, had endeavoured first to re-construct the primeval chaos. The tables, and especially the carpet, were already stained with large spots of various hues, which frequently proclaimed the agency of fire. An electrical machine, an air-pump, the galvanic trough, a solar microscope, and large glass jars and receivers, were conspicuous amidst the mass of matter. Upon the table by his side were some books lying open, several letters, a bundle of new pens, and a bottle of japan ink, that served as an inkstand; a piece of deal, lately part of the lid of a box, with many chips, and a handsome razor, that had been used as a knife. There were bottles of soda water, sugar, pieces of lemon, and the traces of an effervescent beverage. Two piles of books supported the tongs, and these upheld a small glass retort above an argand lamp. I had not been seated many minutes before the liquor in the vessel boiled over, adding fresh stains to the table, and rising in fumes with a most disagreeable odour. Shelley snatched the glass quickly, and dashing it in pieces among the ashes under the grate, increased the unpleasant and penetrating effluvium. He then proceeded, with much eagerness and enthusiasm, to show me the various instruments, especially the electrical apparatus; turning round the handle very rapidly, so that the fierce, crackling sparks flew forth; and presently standing upon the stool with glass feet, he begged of me to work the machine until he was filled with the fluid, so that his long, wild locks bristled and stood on end. Afterwards he charged a powerful battery of several large jars; labouring with vast energy, and discoursing with increasing vehemence of the marvellous powers of electricity, of thunder, and lightning; describing an electrical kite that he had made at home, and projecting another and an enormous one, or rather a combination of many kites, that would draw down from the sky an immense volume of electricity, the whole ammunition of a mighty thunderstorm; and this being directed to some point would there produce the most stupendous results.

In these exhibitions and in such conversation the time passed away rapidly and the hour of dinner approached. Having pricked *æger* that day, or in other words, having caused his name to be entered as an invalid, he was not required, or permitted, to dine in hall, or to appear in public within the college, or without the walls, until a night's rest should have restored the sick man to health.

☆ ★ ☆

It seemed but too probable that in the rash ardour of experiment he would some day set the college on fire, or that he would blind, maim, or kill himself by the explosion of combustibles. It was still more likely indeed that he would poison himself, for plates and glasses, and every part of his tea equipage were used indiscriminately with crucibles, retorts, and recipients, to contain the most deleterious ingredients. To his infinite diversion I used always to examine every drinking-vessel narrowly, and often to rinse it carefully, after that evening when we were taking tea by firelight, and my attention being attracted by the sound of something in the cup into which I was about to pour tea, I was induced to look into it. I found a seven-shillings piece partly dissolved by the *aqua regia* in which it was immersed. Although he laughed at my caution, he used to speak with horror of the consequences of having inadvertently swallowed, through a similar accident, some mineral poison, I think arsenic, at Eton, which he declared had not only seriously injured his health, but that he feared he should never entirely recover from the shock it had inflicted on his constitution. It seemed probable, notwithstanding his positive assertions, that his lively fancy exaggerated the recollection of the unpleasant and permanent taste, of the sickness and disorder of the stomach, which might arise from taking a minute portion of some poisonous substance by the like chance, for there was no vestige of a more serious and lasting injury in his youthful and healthy, although somewhat delicate aspect.

I knew little of the physical sciences, and I felt therefore but a slight degree of interest in them; I looked upon his philosophical apparatus merely as toys and playthings, like a chess-board or a billiard-table. Through lack of sympathy, his zeal, which was at first so ardent, gradually cooled; and he applied himself to these pursuits, after a short time, less frequently and with less earnestness. The true value of them was often the subject of animated discussion; and I remember one evening at my own rooms, when we had sought refuge against the intense cold in the little inner apartment, or study, I referred, in the course of our debate, to a passage in Xenophon's "Memorabilia," where Socrates speaks in disparagement of Physics. He read it several times very attentively, and more than once aloud, slowly and with emphasis, and it appeared to make a strong impression on him.

Notwithstanding our difference of opinion as to the importance of chemistry, and on some other questions, our intimacy rapidly increased, and we soon formed the habit of passing the greater part of our time together; nor did this constant intercourse interfere with my usual studies. I never visited his rooms until one o'clock, by which hour, as I rose very early, I had not only attended the college lectures, but had read in private for several hours. I was enabled, moreover, to continue my studies afterwards in the evening, in consequence of a very remarkable peculiarity. My young and energetic friend was then overcome by extreme drowsiness, which speedily and completely vanquished him; he would sleep from two to four hours, often so soundly that his slumbers resembled a deep lethargy; he lay occasionally upon the sofa, but more commonly stretched upon the rug before a large fire, like a cat; and his little round head was exposed to such a fierce heat, that I used to wonder how he was able to bear it. Sometimes I have interposed some shelter, but rarely with any permanent effect; for the sleeper usually contrived to turn himself, and to roll again into the spot where the fire glowed the brightest. His torpor was generally profound, but he would sometimes discourse incoherently for a long while in his sleep. At six he would suddenly compose himself, even in the midst of a most animated narrative or of earnest discussion; and he would lie buried in entire forgetfulness, in a sweet and mighty oblivion, until ten, when he would suddenly start up, and rubbing his eyes with great violence, and passing his fingers swiftly through his long hair, would enter at once into a vehement argument, or begin to recite verses, either of his own composition or from the works of others, with a rapidity and an energy that were often quite painful. During the period of his occultation I took tea, and read or wrote without interruption. He would sometimes sleep for a shorter time, for about two hours; postponing for the like period the commencement of his retreat to the rug, and rising with tolerable punctuality at ten; and sometimes, although rarely, he was able entirely to forego the accustomed refreshment.

☆ ★ ☆

The sympathies of Shelley were instantaneous and powerful with those who evinced in any degree the qualities for which he was himself so remarkable—simplicity of character, unaffected manners, genuine modesty, and an honest willingness to acquire knowledge, and he sprung to meet their advances with an ingenuous eagerness which was peculiar to him ; but he was suddenly and violently repelled, like the needle from the negative pole of the magnet, by any indication of pedantry, presumption, or affectation.   So much was he disposed to take offence at such defects, and so acutely was he sensible of them, that he was sometimes unjust, through an excessive sensitiveness, in his estimate of those who had shocked him by sins of which he was himself utterly incapable.   Whatever might be the attainments, and however solid the merits of the persons filling at that time the important office of instructors in the University, they were entirely destitute of the attractions of manner ; their address was sometimes repulsive, and the formal, priggish tutor was too often intent upon the ordinary academical course alone to the entire exclusion of every other department of knowledge : his thoughts were wholly engrossed by it, and so narrow were his views, that he overlooked the claims of all merit, however exalted, except success in the public examinations.   " They are very dull people here," Shelley said to me one evening soon after his arrival, with a long-drawn sigh after musing awhile; " a little man sent for me this morning and told me in an almost inaudible whisper that I must read : ' you must read,' he said many times in his small voice.   I answered that I had no objection.   He persisted ; so to satisfy him, for he did not appear to believe me, I told him I had some books in my pocket, and I began to take them out.   He stared at me, and said that was not exactly what he meant : ' you must read *Prometheus Vinctus*, and Demosthenes *de Coronâ*, and Euclid.'   Must I read Euclid?   I asked sorrowfully. ' Yes, certainly ; and when you have read the Greek works I have mentioned, you must begin Aristotle's Ethics, and then you may go on to his other treatises.   It is of the utmost importance to be well acquainted with Aristotle.'   This he repeated so often that I was quite tired, and at last I said, must I care about Aristotle ? what if I do not mind Aristotle?   I then left him, for he seemed to be in great perplexity."

Notwithstanding the slight he had thus cast upon the great master of the science, that has so long been the staple of Oxford, he was not blind to the value of the science itself. He took the scholastic logic very kindly, seized its distinctions with his accustomed quickness, felt a keen interest in the study, and patiently endured the exposition of those minute discriminations, which the tyro is apt to contemn as vain and trifling. It should seem that the ancient method of communicating the art of syllogizing has been preserved, in part at least, by tradition in this university. I have sometimes met with learned foreigners, who understood the end and object of the scholastic logic, having received the traditional instruction in some of the old universities on the Continent; but I never found even one of my countrymen, except Oxonians, who rightly comprehended the nature of the science : I may, perhaps, add, that in proportion as the self-taught logicians had laboured in the pursuit, they had gone far astray. It is possible, nevertheless, that those who have drunk at the fountainhead, and have read the " Organon" of Aristotle in the original, may have attained to a just comprehension by their unassisted energies; but in this age, and in this country, I apprehend the number of such adventurous readers is very inconsiderable. Shelley frequently exercised his ingenuity in long discussions respecting various questions in logic, and more frequently indulged in metaphysical inquiries. We read several metaphysical works together, in whole, or in part, for the first time, or after a previous perusal, by one, or by both of us. The examination of a chapter of Locke's " Essay on the Human Understanding" would induce him, at any moment, to quit every other pursuit. We read together Hume's " Essays," and some productions of Scotch metaphysicians, of inferior ability—all with assiduous and friendly altercations, and the latter writers, at least, with small profit, unless some sparks of knowledge were struck out in the collision of debate. We read also certain popular French works, that treat of man, for the most part in a mixed method, metaphysically, morally, and politically. Hume's " Essays" were a favourite book with Shelley, and he was always ready to put forward, in argument, the doctrines they uphold. It may seem strange that he should ever have accepted the sceptical philosophy, a system so uncongenial with a fervid and imaginative genius, which can allure the cool, cautious, abstinent reasoner alone, and would deter the enthusiastic, the fanciful, and the speculative. We must bear in mind, however, that he was an eager, bold, and unwearied disputant ; and although the position in which the sceptic and the materialist love to entrench themselves offers no picturesque attractions to the eye of the poet, it is well adapted for defensive warfare ; and it is not easy for an ordinary enemy to dislodge him, who occupies a post that derives strength from the weakness of the assailant. It has been insinuated, that whenever a man of real talent and generous feelings condescends to fight under these colours, he is guilty of a dissimulation, which he deems harmless, perhaps even praiseworthy, for the sake of victory in argument. It was not a little curious to observe one, whose sanguine temper led him to believe implicitly every assertion, so that it was improbable and incredible, exulting in the success of his philosophical doubts, when, like the calmest and most suspicious of analysts, he refused to admit, without strict proof, propositions, that many, who are not deficient in metaphysical prudence, account obvious and self-evident. The sceptical philosophy had another charm ; it partook of the new and the wonderful, inasmuch as it called into doubt, and seemed to place in jeopardy, during the joyous hours of disputation, many important practical conclusions. To a soul loving excitement and change, destruction, so that it be on a grand scale, may sometimes prove hardly less inspiring than creation. The feat of the magician, who, by the touch of his wand, could cause the great pyramid to dissolve into the air, and to vanish from the sight, would be as surprising as the achievement of him who, by the same rod, could instantly raise a similar mass in any chosen spot. If the destruction of the eternal monument was only apparent, the ocular sophism would be at once harmless and ingenious : so was it with the logomachy of the young and strenuous logician, and his intellectual activity merited praise and reward. There was another reason, moreover, why the sceptical philosophy should be welcome to Shelley at that time : he was young, and it is generally acceptable to youth. It is adopted as the abiding rule of reason throughout life by those only who are distinguished by a sterility of soul, a barrenness of invention, a total dearth of fancy, and a scanty stock of learning. Such, in truth, although the warmth of juvenile blood, the light burthen of few years, and the precipitation of inexperience, may sometimes seem to contradict the assertion, is the state of the mind at the commencement of manhood, when the vessel has as yet received only a small portion of the cargo of the accumulated wisdom of past ages, when the amount of mental operations that have actually been performed is small, and the materials, upon which the imagination can work, are insignificant ; consequently the inventions of the young are crude and frigid. Hence the most fertile mind exactly resembles in early youth the hopeless barrenness of those, who have grown old in vain, as to its actual condition, and it differs only in the unseen capacity for future production. The philosopher who declares that he knows nothing, and that nothing can be known, will readily find followers among the young, for they are sensible that they possess the requisite qualification for entering his school, and are as far advanced in the science of ignorance as their master. A stranger, who should have chanced to have been present at some of Shelley's disputes, or who knew him only from having read some of the short argumentative essays, which he composed as voluntary exercises, would have said, " Surely the soul of Hume passed by transmigration into the body of that eloquent young man ; or rather, he represents one of the enthusiastic and animated materialists of the French school, whom revolutionary violence lately intercepted at an early age in his philosophical career." There were times, however, when a visitor, who had listened to glowing discourses delivered with a more intense ardour, would have hailed a young Platonist breathing forth the ideal philosophy, and in his pursuit of the intellectual world entirely overlooking the material, or noticing it only to contemn it. The tall boy, who is permitted for the first season to scare the partridges with his new fowling-piece, scorns to handle the top, or the hoop of his younger brother ; thus the man, whose years and studies are mature, slights the first feeble aspirations after the higher departments of knowledge, that were deemed so important during his residence at College. It seems laughable, but it is true, that our knowledge of Plato was derived solely from Dacier's translation of a few of the dialogues, and from an English version of that French translation ; we had never attempted a single sentence in the Greek. Since that time however, I believe, few of our countrymen have read the golden works of that majestic philosopher in the original language more frequently and more carefully than ourselves ; and few, if any, with more profit than Shelley. Although the source, whence flowed our earliest taste of the divine philosophy, was scanty and turbid, the draught was not the less grateful to our lips : our zeal in some measure atoned for our poverty. Shelley was never weary of reading, or of listening to me whilst I read, passages from the dialogues contained in this collection, and especially from the Phædo, and he was vehemently excited by the striking doctrines which Socrates unfolds, especially by that which teaches that all our knowledge consists of reminiscences of what we had learned in a former existence. He often rose, paced slowly about the room, shook his long wild locks, and discoursed in a solemn tone and with a mysterious air, speculating concerning our previous condition, and the nature of our life and occupations in that world where, according to Plato, we had attained to erudition, and had advanced ourselves in knowledge so far that the most studious and the most inventive, or in other words, those who have the best memory, are able to call back a part only, and with much pain and extreme difficulty, of what was formerly familiar to us.

It is hazardous, however, to speak of his earliest efforts as a Platonist, lest they should be confounded with his subsequent advancement ; it is not easy to describe his first introduction to the exalted wisdom of antiquity without borrowing inadvertently from the knowledge which he afterwards acquired. The cold, ungenial, foggy atmosphere of northern metaphysics was less suited to the ardent temperament of his soul, than the warm, bright, vivifying climate of the southern and eastern philosophy ; his genius expanded under the benign influence of the latter, and he derived copious instruction from a luminous system, that is only dark through excess of brightness, and seems obscure to vulgar vision through its extreme radiance. Nevertheless in argument, and to argue on all questions was his dominant passion, he usually adopted the scheme of the sceptics, partly, perhaps, because it was more popular and is more generally understood : the disputant, who would use Plato as his text-book in this age, would reduce his opponents to a small number indeed.

The study of that highest department of ethics, which includes all the inferior branches, and is directed towards the noblest and most important ends, of Jurisprudence, was always next my heart ; at an early age it attracted my attention. When I first endeavoured to turn the regards of Shelley towards this engaging pursuit, he strongly expressed a very decided aversion to such inquiries, deeming them worthless and illiberal. The beautiful theory of the art of right and the honourable office of administering distributive justice have been brought into general discredit, unhappily for the best interests of humanity, and, to the vast detriment of the state, into unmerited disgrace in the modern world by the errors of practitioners. An ingenuous mind instinctively shrinks from the contemplation of legal topics, because the word law is associated with and inevitably calls up the idea of the low chicanery of a pettifogging attorney, of the vulgar oppression and gross insolence of a bailiff, or, at best, of the wearisome and unmeaning tautology that distends an act of Parliament, and the dull dropsical compositions of the special pleader, the conveyancer, or other draughtsman. In no country is this unhappy debasement of a most illustrious science more remarkable than in our own; no other nation is so prone to, or so patient of abuses; in no other land are posts in themselves honourable so accessible to the meanest. The spirit of trade favours the degradation, and every commercial town is a well-spring of vulgarity, which sends forth hosts of practitioners devoid of the solid and elegant attainments which could sustain the credit of the science, but so strong in the artifices that insure success, as not only to monopolize the rewards due to merit, but sometimes even to climb the judgment-seat. It is not wonderful, therefore, that generous minds, until they have been taught to discriminate, and to distinguish a noble science from ignoble practices, should usually confound them together, hastily condemning the former with the latter. Shelley listened with much attention to questions of natural law, and with the warm interest that he felt in all metaphysical disquisitions, after he had conquered his first prejudice against practical jurisprudence. The science of right, like other profound and extensive sciences, can only be acquired completely when the foundations have been laid at an early age: had the energies of Shelley's vigorous mind taken this direction at that time, it is impossible to doubt that he would have become a distinguished jurist. Besides that fondness for such inquiries, which is necessary to success in any liberal pursuit, he displayed the most acute sensitiveness of injustice, however slight, and a vivid perception of inconvenience. As soon as a wrong, arising from a proposed enactment, or a supposed decision, was suggested, he instantly rushed into the opposite extreme; and when a greater evil was shown to result from the contrary course which he had so hastily adopted, his intellect was roused, and he endeavoured most earnestly to ascertain the true mean that would secure the just by avoiding the unjust extremes. I have observed in young men that the propensity to plunge headlong into a net of difficulty, on being startled at an apparent want of equity in any rule that was propounded, although at first it might seem to imply a lack of caution and foresight, which are eminently the virtues of legislators and of judges, was an unerring prognostic of a natural aptitude for pursuits, wherein eminence is inconsistent with an inertness of the moral sense and a recklessness of the violation of rights, however remote and trifling. Various instances of such aptitude in Shelley might be furnished, but these studies are interesting to a limited number of persons only.

As the mind of Shelley was apt to acquire many of the most valuable branches of liberal knowledge, so there were other portions comprised within the circle of science, for the reception of which, however active and acute, it was entirely unfit. He rejected with marvellous impatience every mathematical discipline that was offered; no problem could awaken the slightest curiosity, nor could he be made sensible of the beauty of any theorem. The method of demonstration had no charms for him ; he complained of the insufferable prolixity and the vast tautology of Euclid and the other ancient geometricians; and when the discoveries of modern analysts were presented, he was immediately distracted, and fell into endless musings.

With respect to the Oriental tongues, he coldly observed that the appearance of the characters was curious. Although he perused with more than ordinary eagerness the relations of travellers in the East, and the translations of the marvellous tales of oriental fancy, he was not attracted by the desire to penetrate the languages which veil these treasures. He would never deign to lend an ear, or an eye, for a moment to my Hebrew studies, in which I had made at that time some small progress; nor could he be tempted to inquire into the value of the singular lore of the Rabbins. He was able, like the many, to distinguish a violet from a sunflower, and a cauliflower from a peony; but his botanical knowledge was more limited· than that of the least skilful of common observers, for he was neglectful of flowers. He was incapable of apprehending the delicate distinctions of structure which form the basis of the beautiful classification of modern botanists. I was never able to impart even a glimpse of the merits of Ray, or Linnæus, or to encourage a hope that he would ever be competent to see the visible analogies that constitute the marked, yet mutually approaching *genera*, into which the productions of nature, and especially vegetables, are divided. It may seem invidious to notice imperfections in a mind of the highest order, but the exercise of a due candour, however unwelcome, is required to satisfy those who were not acquainted with Shelley, that the admiration excited by his marvellous talents and manifold virtues in all who were so fortunate as to enjoy the opportunity of examining his merits by frequent intercourse, was not the result of the blind partiality that amiable and innocent dispositions, attractive manners, and a noble and generous bearing sometimes create.

☆ ★ ☆

The prince of Roman eloquence affirms, that the good man alone can be a perfect orator, — and truly, for without the weight of a spotless reputation, it is certain that the most artful and elaborate discourses must want authority, the main ingredient in persuasion. The position is, at least, equally true of the poet, whose grand strength always lies in the ethical force of his compositions; and these are great in proportion to the efficient greatness of their moral purpose. If, therefore, we would criticise poetry correctly, and from the foundation, it behoves us to examine the morality of the bard. In no individual, perhaps, was the moral sense ever more completely developed than in Shelley; in no being was the perception of right and of wrong more acute. The biographer who takes upon himself the pleasing and instructive, but difficult and delicate task of composing a faithful history of his whole life, will frequently be compelled to discuss the important questions, whether his conduct, at certain periods, was altogether such as ought to be proposed for imitation; whether he was ever misled by an ardent imagination, a glowing temperament, something of hastiness in choice, and a certain constitutional impatience; whether, like less gifted mortals, he ever shared in the common portion of mortality,—repentance; and to what extent? Such inquiries, however, do not fall within the compass of a brief narrative of his career at the University. The unmatured mind of a boy is capable of good intentions only, and of generous and kindly feelings, and these were pre-eminent in him. It will be proper to unfold the excellence of his dispositions, not for the sake of vain and empty praise, but simply to show his aptitude to receive the sweet fury of the Muses. His inextinguishable thirst for knowledge, his boundless philanthropy, his fearless, it may be, his almost imprudent, pursuit of truth, have been already exhibited. If mercy to beasts be a criterion of a good man, numerous instances of extreme tenderness would demonstrate his worth. I will mention one only.

We were walking one afternoon in Bagley Wood; on turning

a corner, we suddenly came upon a boy, who was driving an ass. It was very young, and very weak, and was staggering beneath a most disproportionate load of faggots, and he was belabouring its lean ribs angrily and violently with a short, thick, heavy cudgel. At the sight of cruelty Shelley was instantly transported far beyond the usual measure of excitement : he sprang forward, and was about to interpose with energetic and indignant vehemence. I caught him by the arm, and to his present annoyance held him back, and with much difficulty persuaded him to allow me to be the advocate of the dumb animal. His cheeks glowed with displeasure, and his lips murmured his impatience during my brief dialogue with the young tyrant. "That is a sorry little ass, boy," I said ; "it seems to have scarcely any strength."—"None at all; it is good for nothing."—"It cannot get on ; it can hardly stand ; if any body could make it go, you would ; you have taken great pains with it."—"Yes, I have ; but it is to no purpose !"—"It is of little use striking it, I think."—"It is not worth beating ; the stupid beast has got more wood now than it can carry ; it can hardly stand, you see !"—"I suppose it put it upon its back itself?" The boy was silent : I repeated the question. "No ; it has not sense enough for that," he replied, with an incredulous leer. By dint of repeated blows he had split one end of his cudgel, and the sound caused by the divided portion had alarmed Shelley's humanity : I pointed to it, and said, "You have split your stick ; it is not good for much now." He turned it, and held the divided end in his hand. "The other end is whole, I see ; but I suppose you could split that too on the ass's back, if you chose ; it is not so thick." —"It is not so thick, but it is full of knots; it would take a great deal of trouble to split it, and the beast is not worth that ; it would do no good !"—"It would do no good, certainly ; and if any body saw you, he might say that you were a savage young ruffian, and that you ought to be served in the same manner yourself." The fellow looked at me with some surprise, and sank into solemn silence. He presently threw his cudgel into the wood as far as he was able, and began to amuse himself by pelting the birds with pebbles, leaving my long-eared client to proceed at its own pace, having made up his mind, perhaps, to be beaten himself, when he reached home, by a tyrant still more unreasonable than himself on account of the inevitable default of his ass. Shelley was satisfied with the result of our conversation, and I repeated to him the history of the injudicious and unfortunate interference of Don Quixote between the peasant, John Haldudo, and his servant, Andrew. Although he reluctantly admitted, that the acrimony of humanity might often aggravate the sufferings of the oppressed by provoking the oppressor, I always observed, that the impulse of generous indignation, on witnessing the infliction of pain, was too vivid to allow him to pause and consider the probable consequences of the abrupt interposition of the knight errantry, which would at once redress all grievances. Such exquisite sensibility and a sympathy with suffering so acute and so uncontrolled may possibly be inconsistent with the calmness and forethought of the philosopher, but they accord well with the high temperature of a poet's blood.

As his port had the meekness of a maiden, so the heart of the young virgin who has never crossed her father's threshold to encounter the rude world, could not be more susceptible of all the sweet domestic charities than his: in this respect Shelley's disposition would happily illustrate the innocence and virginity of the Muses. In most men, and especially in very young men, an excessive addiction to study tends to chill the heart, and to blunt the feelings, by engrossing the attention. Notwithstanding his extreme devotion to literature, and amidst his various and ardent speculations, he retained a most affectionate regard for his relations, and particularly for the females of his family: it was not without manifest joy that he received a letter from his mother, or his sisters. A child of genius is seldom duly appreciated by the world during his life, least of all by his own kindred. The parents of a man of talent may claim the honour of having given him birth, yet they commonly enjoy but little of his society. Whilst we hang with delight over the immortal pages, we are apt to suppose that the gifted author was fondly cherished; that a possession so uncommon and so precious was highly prized; that his contemporaries anxiously watched his going out and eagerly looked for his coming in; for we should ourselves have borne him tenderly in our hands, that he might not dash his foot against a stone. Surely such an one was given in charge to angels, we cry: on the contrary, Nature appears most unaccountably to slight a gift that she gave grudgingly; as if it were of small value, and easily replaced. An unusual number of books, Greek or Latin classics, each inscribed with the name of the donor, which had been presented to him, according to the custom on quitting Eton, attested that Shelley had been popular among his schoolfellows. Many of them were then at Oxford, and they frequently called at his rooms: although he spoke of them with regard, he generally avoided their society, for it interfered with his beloved study, and interrupted the pursuits to which he ardently and entirely devoted himself.

In the nine centuries that elapsed from the time of our great founder, Alfred, to our days, there never was a student who more richly merited the favour and assistance of a learned body, or whose fruitful mind would have repaid with a larger harvest the labour of careful and judicious cultivation. And such cultivation he was well entitled to receive. Nor did his scholar-like virtues merit neglect; still less to be betrayed, like the young nobles of Falisci, by a traitorous schoolmaster, to an enemy less generous than Camillus. No student ever read more assiduously. He was to be found book in hand at all hours; reading in season and out of season; at table, in bed, and especially during a walk: not only in the quiet country, and in retired paths; not only at Oxford, in the public walks, and High-street, but in the most crowded thoroughfares of London. Nor was he less absorbed by the volume that was open before him, in Cheapside, in Cranbourn-alley, or in Bond-street, than in a lonely lane, or a secluded library. Sometimes a vulgar fellow would attempt to insult or annoy the eccentric student in passing. Shelley always avoided the malignant interruption by stepping aside with his vast and quiet agility. Sometimes I have observed, as an agreeable contrast to these wretched men, that persons of the humblest station have paused and gazed with respectful wonder as he advanced, almost unconscious of the throng, stooping low, with bent knees and outstretched neck, poring earnestly over the volume; which he extended before him : for they knew this, although the simple people knew but little, that an ardent scholar is worthy of deference, and that the man of learning is necessarily the friend of humanity, and especially of the many.   I never beheld eyes that devoured the pages more voraciously than his : I am convinced that two-thirds of the period of day and night were often employed in reading.   It is no exaggeration to affirm, that out of the twenty-four hours, he frequently read sixteen.   At Oxford, his diligence in this respect was exemplary, but it greatly increased afterwards, and I sometimes thought that he carried it to a pernicious excess : I am sure, at least, that I was unable to keep pace with him. On the evening of a wet day, when we had read with scarcely any intermission from an early hour in the morning, I have urged him to lay aside his book.   It required some extravagance to rouse him to join heartily in conversation ; to tempt him to avoid the chimney-piece, on which commonly he had laid the open volume.   "If I were to read as long as you do, Shelley, my hair and my teeth would be strewed about on the floor, and my eyes would slip down my cheeks into my waistcoat pockets ; or at least I should become so weary and nervous, that I should not know whether it were so or not."   He began to scrape the carpet with his feet, as if teeth were actually lying upon it, and he looked fixedly at my face, and his lively fancy represented the empty sockets ; his imagination was excited, and the spell that bound him to his books was broken, and creeping close to the fire, and, as it were, under the fire-place, he commenced a most animated discourse.   Few were aware of the extent, and still fewer, I apprehend, of the profundity of his reading ; in his short life, and without ostentation, he had, in truth, read more Greek than many an aged pedant, who, with pompous parade, prides himself upon this study alone.   Although he had not entered critically into the minute niceties of the noblest of languages, he was thoroughly conversant with the valuable matter it contains.   A pocket edition of Plato, of Plutarch, of Euripides, without interpretation or notes, or of the Septuagint, was his ordinary companion ; and he read the text straightforward for hours, if not as readily as an English author, at least with as much facility as French, Italian, or Spanish.   " Upon my soul, Shelley, your style of going through a Greek book is something quite beautiful !" was the wondering exclamation of one who was himself no mean student.

As his love of intellectual pursuits was vehement, and the vigour of his genius almost celestial, so were the purity and sanctity of his life most conspicuous.   His food was plain and simple as that of a hermit, with a certain anticipation, even at this time, of a vegetable diet, respecting which he afterwards became an enthusiast in theory, and in practice an irregular votary.   With his usual fondness for moving the abstruse and difficult questions of the highest theology, he loved to inquire, whether man can justify, on the ground of reason alone, the practice of taking the life of the inferior animals, except in the necessary defence of his life and of his means of life, the fruits of that field, which he has tilled, from violence and spoliation. " Not only have considerable sects," he would say, " denied the right altogether, but those among the ten-der-hearted and imaginative people of antiquity, who accounted it lawful to kill and eat, appear to have doubted, whether they might take away life merely for the use of man alone. They slew their cattle not simply for human guests, like the less scrupulous butchers of modern times, but only as a sacrifice, for the honour and in the name of the deity; or rather of those subordinate divinities, to whom, as they believed, the supreme being had assigned the creation and conservation of the visible material world; as an incident to these pious offerings, they partook of the residue of the victims, of which, without such sanction and sanctification they would not have pre-sumed to taste. So reverent was the caution of a humane and pru-dent antiquity !" Bread became his chief sustenance, when his regi-men attained to that austerity, which afterwards distinguished it. He could have lived on bread alone without repining. When he was walking in London with an acquaintance he would suddenly run into a baker's shop, purchase a supply, and breaking a loaf, he would offer half of it to his companion. " Do you know," he said to me one day with much surprise, " that such an one does not like bread; did you ever know a person who disliked bread?" and he told me that a friend had refused such an offer. I explained to him, that the indi-vidual in question probably had no objection to bread in a moderate quantity, at a proper time and with the usual adjuncts, and was only unwilling to devour two, or three, pounds of dry bread in the streets and at an early hour. Shelley had no such scruple; his pockets were generally well-stored with bread. A circle upon the carpet, clearly defined by an ample verge of crumbs, often marked the place where he had long sat at his studies, his face nearly in contact with his book, greedily devouring bread at intervals amidst his profound abstractions. For the most part he took no condiment; sometimes, however, he ate with his bread the common raisins, which are used in making pud-dings, and these he would buy at little mean shops. He was walk-ing one day in London with a respectable solicitor, who occasion-ally transacted business for him; with his accustomed precipitation he suddenly vanished, and as suddenly reappeared : he had entered the shop of a little grocer in an obscure quarter, and had returned with some plums, which he held close under the attorney's nose, and the man of fact was as much astonished at the offer, as his client, the man of fancy, was at the refusal. The common fruit of the stalls, and oranges and apples, were always welcome to Shelley; he would crunch the latter as heartily as a schoolboy. Vegetables and especially sallads, and pies and puddings, were acceptable : his beverage con-sisted of copious and frequent draughts of cold water, but tea was ever grateful, cup after cup, and coffee. Wine was taken with sin-gular moderation, commonly diluted largely with water, and for a long period he would abstain from it altogether; he avoided the use of spirits almost invariably and even in the most minute portions. Like all persons of simple tastes, he retained his sweet tooth; he would greedily eat cakes, gingerbread, and sugar; honey, preserved or stewed fruit, with bread, were his favourite delicacies, these he thankfully and joyfully received from others, but he rarely sought for them or provided them for himself. The restraint and protracted duration of a convivial meal were intolerable; he was seldom able to keep his seat during the brief period assigned to an ordinary family dinner.

These particulars may seem trifling, if indeed any thing can be little, that has reference to a character truly great; but they prove how much he was ashamed that his soul was in body, and illustrate the virgin abstinence of a mind equally favoured by the Muses, the Graces and Philosophy. It is true, however, that his application at Oxford, although exemplary, was not so unremitting, as it afterwards became, nor was his diet, although singularly temperate, so meagre, however his mode of living already offered a foretaste of the studious seclusion and absolute renunciation of every luxurious indulgence, which ennobled him a few years later. Had a parent desired that his children should be exactly trained to an ascetic life and should be taught by an eminent example to scorn delights and to love laborious days; that they should behold a pattern of native innocence and genuine simplicity of manners; he would have consigned them to his house as to a temple, or to some primitive and still unsophisticated monastery. It is an invidious thing to compose a perpetual panegyric, yet it is difficult to speak of Shelley, and impossible to speak justly, without often praising him; it is difficult also to divest myself of later recollections; to forget for a while what he became in days subsequent, and to remember only what he then was, when we were fellow-collegians. It is difficult, moreover, to view him with the mind which I then bore,—with a young mind; to lay aside the seriousness of old age; for twenty years of assiduous study have induced, if not in the body, at least within, something of premature old age. It now seems an incredible thing and altogether inconceivable, when I consider the gravity of Shelley and his invincible repugnance to the comic, that the monkey tricks of the schoolboy could have still lingered, but it is certain that some slight vestiges still remained. The metaphysician of eighteen actually attempted once, or twice, to electrify the son of his scout, a boy like a sheep, by name James, who roared aloud with ludicrous and stupid terror, whenever Shelley affected to bring by stealth any part of his philosophical apparatus near to him.

As Shelley's health and strength were visibly augmented if by accident he was obliged to accept a more generous diet than ordinary, and as his mind sometimes appeared to be exhausted by never ending toil, I often blamed his abstinence and his perpetual application. It is the office of an University, of a public institution for education, not only to apply the spur to the sluggish, but also to rein in the young steed, that being too mettlesome, hastens with undue speed towards the goal. " It is a very odd thing, but every woman can live with my lord and do just what she pleases with him, except my lady!" Such was the shrewd remark, which a long familiarity taught an old and attached servant to utter respecting his master, a noble poet. We may wonder in like manner, and deeply lament, that the most docile, the most facile, the most pliant, the most confiding creature, that

ever was led through any of the various paths on earth, that a tracta-
ble youth, who was conducted at pleasure by anybody, that approached him, it might be, occasionally, by persons delegated by no legitimate authority, was never guided for a moment by those, upon whom
fully and without reservation that most solemn and sacred obligation
had been imposed, strengthened moreover by every public and private, official and personal, moral, political and religious tie, which the
civil polity of a long succession of ages could accumulate. Had the
University been in fact, as in name, a kind nursing mother to the
most gifted of her sons ; to one, who seemed to those that knew
him best—

" Heaven's exile straying from the orb of light ;"

had that most aweful responsibility, the right institution of those, to
whom are to be consigned the government of the country and the
conservation of whatever good human society has elaborated and ex-
cogitated, duly weighed upon the consciences of his instructors, they
would have gained his entire confidence by frank kindness, they
would have repressed his too eager impatience to master the sum of
knowledge, they would have mitigated the rigorous austerity of his
course of living, and they would have remitted the extreme tension of
his soul by reconciling him to a liberal mirth, convincing him, that if
life be not wholly a jest, there are at least many comic scenes occsion-
ally interspersed in the great drama. Nor is the last benefit of trifling
importance, for as an unseemly and excessive gravity is usually the
sign of a dull fellow, so is the prevalence of this defect the characteristic of an unlearned and illiberal age. Shelley was actually offended,
and indeed more indignant than would appear to be consistent with
the singular mildness of his nature, at a coarse and awkward jest, especially if it were immodest, or, uncleanly ; in the latter case his anger
was unbounded, and his uneasiness pre-eminent ; he was, however,
sometimes vehemently delighted by exquisite and delicate sallies,
particularly with a fanciful, and perhaps somewhat fantastical faceti-
ousness, possibly the more because he was himself utterly incapable
of pleasantry.

In every free state, in all countries that enjoy republican institutions, the view, which each citizen takes of politics, is an essential ingredient in the estimate of his ethical character. The wisdom of a
very young man is but foolishness, nevertheless if we would rightly
comprehend the moral and intellectual constitution of the youthful
poet, it will be expedient to take into account the manner in which
he was affected towards the grand political questions at a period
when the whole of the civilized world was agitated by a fierce storm
of excitement, that, happily for the peace and well-being of society, is
of rare occurrence.

☆ ★ ☆

The passionate fondness of the Platonic philosophy seemed to sharpen his natural affection for children, and his sympathy with their innocence. Every true Platonist, he used to say, must be a lover of children, for they are our masters and instructors in philosophy : the mind of a new-born infant, so far from being, as Locke affirms, a sheet of blank paper, is a pocket edition, containing every dialogue, a complete Elzevir Plato, if we can fancy such a pleasant volume; and, moreover, a perfect ency-clopedia, comprehending not only the newest discoveries, but all those still more valuable and wonderful inventions that will hereafter be made !

One Sunday we had been reading Plato together so diligently, that the usual hour of exercise passed away unperceived : we sallied forth hastily to take the air for half an hour before dinner. In the middle of Magdalen Bridge we met a woman with a child in her arms. Shelley was more attentive at that instant to our conduct in a life that was past, or to come, than to a decorous regulation of the present, according to the established usages of society, in that fleeting moment of eternal duration, styled the nineteenth century. With abrupt dexterity he caught hold of the child. The mother, who might well fear that it was about to be thrown over the parapet of the bridge into the sedgy waters below, held it fast by its long train. "Will your baby tell us anything about pre-existence, Madam ?" he asked, in a piercing voice, and with a wistful look. The mother made no answer, but perceiving that Shel-ley's object was not murderous, but altogether harmless, she dismissed her apprehension, and relaxed her hold. "Will your baby tell us any thing about pre-existence, Madam ?" he repeated, with unabated earnest-ness. "He cannot speak, Sir," said the mother, seriously. "Worse and worse," cried Shelley, with an air of deep disappointment, shaking his long hair most pathetically about his young face ; "but surely the babe can speak if he will, for he is only a few weeks old. He may fancy perhaps that he cannot, but it is only a silly whim ; he cannot have forgotten entirely the use of speech in so short a time ; the thing is absolutely impossible." "It is not for me to dispute with you, Gentle-men," the woman meekly replied, her eye glancing at our academical garb; " but I can safely declare that I never heard him speak, nor any child, indeed, of his age." It was a fine placid boy : so far from being disturbed by the interruption, he looked up and smiled. Shelley pressed his fat cheeks with his fingers, we commended his healthy appearance and his equanimity, and the mother was permitted to proceed, probably to her satisfaction, for she would doubtless prefer a less speculative nurse. Shelley sighed deeply as we walked on. " How provokingly close are those new-born babes," he ejaculated ; " but it is not the less certain, notwithstanding their cunning attempts to conceal the truth, that all knowledge is reminiscence : the doctrine is far more ancient than the times of Plato, and as old as the venerable allegory that the Muses are the daughters of Memory ; not one of the nine was ever said to be the child of Invention!"

In consequence of this theory, upon which his active imagination loved to dwell, and which he was delighted to maintain in argument with the few persons qualified to dispute with him on the higher metaphysics, his fondness for children — a fondness innate in generous minds — was augmented and elevated, and the gentle instinct expanded into a profound and philosophical sentiment. The Platonists have been illustrious in all ages, on account of the strength and permanence of their attachments. In Shelley the parental affections were developed at an early period to an unusual extent : it was manifest, therefore, that his heart was formed by nature and by cultivation to derive the most exquisite gratification from the society of his own progeny, or the most poignant anguish from a natural or unnatural bereavement. To strike him here was the cruel admonition which a cursory glance would at once convey to him who might seek where to wound him most severely with a single blow, should he ever provoke the vengeance of an enemy to the active and fearless spirit of liberal investigation and to all solid learning—of a foe to the human race. With respect to the theory of the pre-existence of the soul, it is not wonderful that an ardent votary of the intellectual should love to uphold it in strenuous and protracted disputation, as it places the immortality of the soul in an impregnable castle, and not only secures it an existence independent of the body, as it were, by usage and prescription, but moreover, raising it out of the dirt on tall stilts—elevates it far above the mud of matter. It is not wonderful that a subtle sophist, who esteemed above all riches and terrene honours victory in well-fought debate, should be willing to maintain a dogma that is not only of difficult eversion by those, who, struggling as mere metaphysicians, use no other weapon than unassisted reason, but which one of the most illustrious Fathers of the Church—a man of amazing powers and stupendous erudition, armed with the prodigious resources of the Christian theology, the renowned Origen—was unable to dismiss ; retaining it as not dissonant from his informed reason, and as affording a larger scope for justice in the moral government of the universe.

In addition to his extreme fondness for children, another, and a not less unequivocal, characteristic of a truly philanthropic mind, was eminently and still more remarkably conspicuous in Shelley,—his admiration of men of learning and genius. In truth, the devotion, the reverence, the religion, with which he was kindled towards all the masters of intellect, cannot be described, and must be utterly inconceivable to minds less deeply enamoured with the love of wisdom. The irreverent many cannot comprehend the awe—the careless apathetic worldling cannot imagine the enthusiasm—nor can the tongue that attempts only to speak of things visible to the bodily eye,—express the mighty emotion that inwardly agitated him, when he approached, for the first time, a volume which he believed to be replete with the recondite and mystic philosophy of antiquity : his cheeks glowed, his eyes became bright, his whole frame trembled, and his entire attention was immediately swallowed up in the depths of contemplation. The rapid and vigorous conversion of his soul to intellect can only be compared with the instantaneous ignition and combustion, which dazzle the sight, when a bundle of dry reeds, or other light inflammable substance, is thrown upon a fire already rich with accumulated heat.

The company of persons of merit was delightful to him, and he often spoke with a peculiar warmth of the satisfaction he hoped to derive from the society of the most distinguished literary and scientific characters of the day in England, and the other countries of Europe, when his own attainments would justify him in seeking their acquaintance. He was never weary of recounting the rewards and favours that authors had formerly received ; and he would detail in pathetic language, and with a touching earnestness, the instances of that poverty and neglect, which an iron age assigned as the fitting portion of solid erudition and un-doubted talents. He would contrast the niggard praise and the paltry payments, that the cold and wealthy moderns reluctantly dole out, with the ample and heartfelt commendation, and the noble remuneration, which were freely offered by the more generous but less opulent ancients. He spoke with an animation of gesture and an elevation of voice of him who undertook a long journey, that he might once see the historian Livy ; and he recounted the rich legacies which were bequeathed to Cicero and to Pliny the younger, by testators venerating their abilities and attainments,—his zeal, enthusiastic in the cause of letters, giving an interest and a novelty to the most trite and familiar instances. His dispo-sition being wholly munificent, gentle, and friendly, how generous a patron would he have proved had he ever been in the actual possession of even moderate wealth ! Out of a scanty and somewhat precarious income, inadequate to allow the indulgence of the most ordinary superfluities, and diminished by various casual but unavoidable incumbrances, he was able, by restricting himself to a diet more simple than the fare of the most austere anchorite, and by refusing himself horses and the other gratifications that appear properly to belong to his station, and of which he was in truth very fond, to bestow upon men of letters, whose merits were of too high an order to be rightly estimated by their own genera-tion, donations large indeed, if we consider from how narrow a source they flowed. But to speak of this his signal and truly admirable bounty, save only in the most distant manner, and the most general terms, would be a flagrant violation of that unequalled delicacy with which it was ex-tended to undeserved indigence, accompanied by well founded and most commendable pride. To allude to any particular instance, however ob-scurely and indistinctly, would be unpardonable ; but it would be scarcely less blameable to dismiss the consideration of the character of the benevolent young poet without some imperfect testimony of this rare excellence.

That he gave freely, when the needy scholar asked, or in silent, hope-less poverty seemed to ask, his aid, will be demonstrated most clearly

by relating shortly one example of his generosity, where the applicant
had no pretensions to literary renown, and no claim whatever, except
perhaps honest penury. It is delightful to attempt to delineate from
various points of view a creature of infinite moral beauty,—but one instance must suffice : an ample volume might be composed of such tales,
but one may be selected, because it contains a large admixture of
that ingredient which is essential to the conversion of alms-giving
into the genuine virtue of charity — self-denial. On returning to
town after the long vacation, at the end of October, I found Shelley
at one of the hotels in Covent Garden. Having some business in hand
he was passing a few days there alone. We had taken some mutton
chops hastily at a dark place in one of the minute courts of the
city, at an early hour, and we went forth to walk ; for to walk
at all times, and especially in the evening, was his supreme delight.
The aspect of the fields to the north of Somers-Town, between that
beggarly suburb and Kentish-Town, has been totally changed of late.
Although this district could never be accounted pretty, nor deserving a
high place even amongst suburban scenes, yet the air, or often the wind,
seemed pure and fresh to captives emerging from the smoke of London :
there were certain old elms, much very green grass, quiet cattle feeding,
and groups of noisy children playing with something of the freedom of
the village green. There was, oh blessed thing ! an entire absence of
carriages and of blood-horses ; of the dust and dress and affectation and
fashion of the parks : there were, moreover, old and quaint edifices and
objects which gave character to the scene. Whenever Shelley was imprisoned in London,—for to a poet a close and crowded city must be a dreary
gaol,—his steps would take that direction, unless his residence was too
remote, or he was accompanied by one who chose to guide his walk.
On this occasion I was led thither, as indeed I had anticipated : the
weather was fine, but the autumn was already advanced ; we had not
sauntered long in these fields when the dusky evening closed in, and the
darkness gradually thickened. " How black those trees are," said Shelley, stopping short, and pointing to a row of elms ; " it is so dark the
trees might well be houses, and the turf, pavement,—the eye would sustain
no loss ; it is useless therefore to remain here, let us return." He proposed tea at his hotel, I assented ; and hastily buttoning his coat, he
seized my arm, and set off at his great pace, striding with bent knees
over the fields and through the narrow streets. We were crossing the
New Road, when he said shortly, " I must call for a moment, but it
will not be out of the way at all," and then dragged me suddenly
towards the left. I inquired whither we were bound, and, I believe,
I suggested the postponement of the intended call till the morrow.
He answered, it was not at all out of our way. I was hurried
along rapidly towards the left ; we soon fell into an animated discussion respecting the nature of the virtue of the Romans, which in
some measure beguiled the weary way. Whilst he was talking with
much vehemence and a total disregard of the people who thronged the
streets, he suddenly wheeled about and pushed me through a narrow
door ; to my infinite surprise I found myself in a pawnbroker's shop !
It was in the neighbourhood of Newgate Street; for he had no idea
whatever in practice either of time or space, nor did he in any degree
regard method in the conduct of business. There were several women
in the shop in brown and grey cloaks with squalling children : some of

them were attempting to persuade the children to be quiet, or at least to scream with moderation ; the others were enlarging upon and pointing out the beauties of certain coarse and dirty sheets that lay before them to a man on the other side of the counter.   I bore this substitute for our proposed tea some minutes with tolerable patience, but as the call did not promise to terminate speedily, I said to Shelley, in a whisper, " Is not this almost as bad as the Roman virtue ?" Upon this he approached the pawnbroker : it was long before he could obtain a hearing, and he did not find civility.   The man was unwilling to part with a valuable pledge so soon, or perhaps he hoped to retain it eventually ; or it might be, that the obliquity of his nature disqualified him for respectful beha-viour.   A pawnbroker is frequently an important witness in criminal proceedings : it has happened to me, therefore, afterwards to see many specimens of this kind of banker ; they sometimes appeared not less re-spectable than other tradesmen,, and sometimes I have been forcibly reminded of the first I ever met with, by an equally ill-conditioned fellow. I was so little pleased with the introduction, that I stood aloof in the shop, and did not hear what passed between him and Shelley.   On our way to Covent-Garden, I expressed my surprise and dissatisfaction at our strange visit, and I learned that when he came to London before, in the course of the summer, some old man had related to him a tale of distress,—of a calamity which could only be alleviated by the timely ap-plication of ten pounds ; five of them he drew at once from his pocket, and to raise the other five he had pawned his beautiful solar microscope ! He related this act of beneficence simply and briefly, as if it were a matter of course, and such indeed it was to him.   I was ashamed of my impatience, and we strode along in silence.

It was past ten when we reached the hotel ; some excellent tea and a liberal supply of hot muffins in the coffee-room, now quiet and soli-tary, were the more grateful after the wearisome delay and vast devia-tion.   Shelley often turned his head, and cast eager glances towards the door ; and whenever the waiter replenished our teapot, or approached our box, he was interrogated whether any one had yet called.   At last the desired summons was brought ; Shelley drew forth some bank notes, hurried to the bar, and returned as hastily, bearing in triumph under his arm a mahogany box, followed by the officious waiter, with whose assist-ance he placed it upon the bench by his side.   He viewed it often with evident satisfaction, and sometimes patted it affectionately in the course of calm conversation.   The solar microscope was always a favourite plaything or instrument of scientific inquiry ; whenever he entered a house his first care was to choose some window of a southern aspect, and, if permission could be obtained by prayer or by purchase, straightway to cut a hole through the shutter to receive it.   His regard for his solar microscope was as lasting as it was strong ; for he retained it several years after this adventure, and long after he had parted with all the rest of his philosophical apparatus.

Such is the story of the microscope, and no rightly judging person who hears it will require the further accumulation of proofs of a benevo-lent heart ; nor can I, perhaps, better close these sketches than with that impression of the pure and genial beauty of Shelley's nature which this simple anecdote will bequeath.

☆ ★ ☆

We had read together attentively several of the metaphysical works that were most in vogue at that time, as " Locke on the Human Understanding," and " Hume's Essays," particularly the latter, of which we had made a very careful analysis, as was customary with those who read the Ethics and the other treatises of Aristotle for their degrees.   Shelley had the custody of these papers, which were chiefly in his handwriting, although they were the joint production of both in our common daily studies.   From these, and from a small part of them only, he made up a little book, and had it printed, I believe, in the country, certainly not at Oxford.   His motive was this.   He not only read greedily all the controversial writings on subjects interesting to him, which he could procure, and disputed vehemently in conversation with his friends, but he had several correspondents with whom he kept up the ball of doubt in letters; —of these he received many, so that the arrival of the postman was always an anxious moment with him.   This practice he had learnt from a physician, from whom he had taken instructions in chemistry, and of whose character and talents he often spoke with profound veneration.   It was, indeed, the usual course with men of learning formerly, as their biographies and many volumes of such epistles testify.   The physician was an old man, and a man of the old school; he confined his epistolary discussions to matters of science, and so did his disciple for some time; but when metaphysics usurped the place in his affections that chemistry had before held, the latter gradually fell into disceptations respecting existences still more subtle than gases and the electric fluid. The transition, however, from physics to metaphysics was gradual. Is the electric fluid material? he would ask his correspondent; is light—is the vital principle in vegetables—in brutes—is the human soul? His individual character had proved an obstacle to his inquiries, even whilst they were strictly physical; a refuted or irritated chemist had suddenly concluded a long correspondence by telling his youthful opponent that he would write to his master, and have him well flogged. The discipline of a public school, however salutary in other respects, was not favourable to free and fair discussion; and Shelley began to address inquiries anonymously, or rather, that he might receive an answer, as Philalethes, and the like; but, even at Eton, the postmen do not ordinarily speak Greek—to prevent miscarriages, therefore, it was necessary to adopt a more familiar name, as John Short, or Thomas Long.

When he came to Oxford, he retained and extended his former practice without quitting the convenient disguise of an assumed name. His object in printing the short abstract of some of the doctrines of Hume was to facilitate his epistolary disquisitions. It was a small pill, but it worked powerfully; the mode of operation was this.—He enclosed a copy in a letter, and sent it by the post, stating, with modesty and simplicity, that he had met accidentally with that little tract, which appeared unhappily to be quite unanswerable. Unless the fish was too sluggish to take the bait, an answer of refutation was forwarded to an appointed address in London, and then in a vigorous reply he would fall upon the unwary disputant, and break his bones. The strenuous attack sometimes provoked a rejoinder more carefully prepared, and an animated and protracted debate ensued; the party cited, having put in his answer, was fairly in court, and he might get out of it as he could. The chief difficulty seemed to be to induce the person addressed to acknowledge the jurisdiction, and to plead; and this, Shelley supposed, would be removed by sending, in the first instance, a printed syllabus instead of written arguments. An accident greatly facilitated his object. We had been talking some time before about geometrical demonstration; he was repeating its praises, which he had lately read in some mathematical work, and speaking of its absolute certainty and perfect truth.

I said that this superiority partly arose from the confidence of mathematicians, who were naturally a confident race, and were seldom acquainted with any other science than their own; that they always put a good face upon the matter, detailing their arguments dogmatically and doggedly, as if there was no room for doubt, and concluded, when weary of talking in their positive strain, with Q. E. D.: in which three letters there was so powerful a charm, that there was no instance of any one having ever disputed any argument or proposition to which they were subscribed. He was diverted by this remark and often repeated it, saying, if you ask a friend to dinner, and only put Q. E. D. at the end of the invitation, he cannot refuse to come; and he sometimes wrote these letters at the end of a common note, in order, as he said, to attain to a mathematical certainty. The potent characters were not forgotten when he printed his little syllabus; and their efficacy in rousing his antagonists was quite astonishing.

It is certain that the three obnoxious letters had a fertilizing effect, and raised rich crops of controversy; but it would be unjust to deny, that an honest zeal stimulated divers worthy men to assert the truth against an unknown assailant. The praise of good intention must be conceded; but it is impossible to accord that of powerful execution also to his antagonists: this curious correspondence fully testified the deplorable condition of education at that time. A youth of eighteen was able to confute men who had numbered thrice as many years; to vanquish them on their own ground, although he gallantly fought at a disadvantage by taking the wrong side. His little pamphlet was never offered for sale; it was not addressed to an ordinary reader, but to the metaphysician alone; and it was so short, that it was only designed to point out the line of argument. It was in truth a general issue; a compendious denial of every allegation, in order to put the whole case in proof; it was a formal mode of saying, you affirm so and so, then prove it; and thus was it understood by his more candid and intelligent correspondents. As it was shorter, so was it plainer, and perhaps, in order to provoke discussion, a little bolder, than Hume's Essays,—a book which occupies a conspicuous place in the library of every student. The doctrine, if it deserve the name, was precisely similar; the necessary and inevitable consequence of Locke's philosophy, and of the theory that all knowledge is from without. I will not admit your conclusions, his opponent might answer; then you must deny those of Hume: I deny them; but you must deny those of Locke also; and we will go back together to Plato. Such was the usual course of argument; sometimes, however, he rested on mere denial, holding his adversary to strict proof, and deriving strength from his weakness. The young Platonist argued thus negatively through the love of argument, and because he found a noble joy in the fierce shocks of contending minds; he loved truth, and sought it everywhere, and at all hazards, frankly and boldly, like a man who deserved to find it; but he also loved dearly victory in debate, and warm debate for its own sake. Never was there a more unexceptionable disputant; he was eager beyond the most ardent, but never angry and never personal: he was the only arguer I ever knew who drew every argument from the nature of the thing, and who could never be provoked to descend to personal contentions. He was fully inspired, indeed, with the whole spirit of the true logician; the more obvious and indisputable the proposition which his opponent undertook to maintain, the more complete was the triumph of his art if he could refute and prevent him. To one who was acquainted with the history of our University, with its ancient reputation as the most famous school of logic, it seemed that the genius of the place, after an absence of several generations, had deigned to return at last; the visit, however, as it soon appeared, was ill-timed. The schoolman of old, who occasionally laboured with technical subtleties to prevent the admission of the first principles of belief, could not have been justly charged with the intention of promoting scepticism; his was the age of minute and astute disceptation, it is true, but it was also the epoch of the most firm, resolute, and extensive faith. I have seen a dexterous fencing-master, after warning his pupil to hold his weapon fast, by a few turns of his wrist throw it suddenly on the ground and under his feet; but it cannot be pretended that he neglected to teach the art of self-defence, because he apparently deprived his scholar of that which is essential to the end proposed. To be disarmed is a step in the science of arms, and whoever has undergone it has already put his foot within the threshold; so is it likewise with refutation. In describing briefly the nature of Shelley's epistolary contentions, the recollection of his youth, his zeal, his activity, and particularly of many individual peculiarities, may have tempted me to speak sometimes with a certain levity, notwithstanding the solemn importance of the topics respecting which they were frequently maintained. The impression, that they were conducted on his part, or considered by him, with frivolity, or any unseemly lightness, would, however, be most erroneous; his whole frame of mind was grave, earnest, and anxious, and his deportment was reverential, with an edification reaching beyond the age—an age wanting in reverence; an unlearned age; a young age, for the young lack learning. Hume permits no object of respect to remain; Locke approaches the most awful speculations with the same indifference as if he were about to handle the properties of triangles; the small deference rendered to the most holy things by the able theologian Paley is not the least remarkable of his characteristics. Wiser and better men displayed anciently, together with a more profound erudition, a superior and touching solemnity; the meek seriousness of Shelley was redolent of those good old times before mankind had been despoiled of a main ingredient in the composition of happiness, a well directed veneration.

Whether such disputations were decorous or profitable may be perhaps doubtful; there can be no doubt, however, since the sweet gentleness of Shelley was easily and instantly swayed by the mild influences of friendly admonition, that, had even the least dignified of his elders suggested the propriety of pursuing his metaphysical inquiries with less ardour, his obedience would have been prompt and perfect. Not only had all salutary studies been long neglected in Oxford at that time, and all wholesome discipline was decayed, but the splendid endowments of the University were grossly abused; the resident authorities of the college were too often men of the lowest origin, of mean and sordid souls, destitute of every literary attainment, except that brief and narrow course of reading by which the first degree was attained; the vulgar sons of vulgar fathers, without liberality, and wanting the manners and the sympathies of gentlemen. A total neglect of all learning, and unseemly turbulence, the most monstrous irregularities, open and habitual drunkenness, vice, and violence, were tolerated or encouraged, with the basest sycophancy, that the prospect of perpetual licentiousness might fill the colleges with young men of fortune; whenever the rarely exercised power of coercion was exerted, it demonstrated the utter incapacity of our unworthy rulers by coarseness, ignorance, and injustice. If a few gentlemen were admitted to fellowships, they were always absent; they were not persons of literary pretensions, or distinguished by scholarship; and they, had no more share in the government of the college than the overgrown guardsmen, who, in long white gaiters, bravely protect the precious life of the sovereign against such assailants as the tenth Muse, our good friend, Mrs. Nicholson.

As the term was drawing to a close, and a great part of the books we were reading together still remained unfinished, we had agreed to increase our exertions and to meet at an early hour. It was a fine spring morning on Lady-day, in the year 1811, when I went to Shelley's rooms: he was absent; but before I had collected our books he rushed in. He was terribly agitated. I anxiously inquired what had happened : " I am expelled," he said, as soon as he had recovered himself a little, " I am expelled! I was sent for suddenly a few minutes ago; I went to the common room, where I found our master, and two or three of the fellows. The master produced a copy of the little syllabus, and asked me if I were the author of it. He spoke in a rude, abrupt, and insolent tone. I begged to be informed for what purpose they put the question: No answer was given; but the master loudly and angrily repeated, ' Are you the author of this book?' If I can judge from your manner, I said, you are resolved to punish me, if I should acknowledge that it is my work. If you can prove that it is, produce your evidence; it is neither just nor lawful to interrogate me in such a case and for such a purpose. Such proceedings would become a court of inquisitors, but not free men in a free country. ' Do you choose to deny that this is your composition?' the master reiterated in the same rude and angry voice." Shelley complained much of his violent and ungentlemanlike deportment, saying, " I have experienced tyranny and injustice before, and I well know what vulgar violence is; but I never met with such unworthy treatment. I told him calmly, but firmly, that I was determined not to answer any questions respecting the publication on the table. He immediately repeated his demand; I persisted in my refusal; and he said furiously, ' Then you are expelled; and I desire you will quit the college early to-morrow morning at the latest.' One of the fellows took up two papers, and handed one of them to me; here it is." He produced a regular sentence of expulsion, drawn up in due form, under the seal of the college. Shelley was full of spirit and courage, frank and fearless; but he was likewise shy, unpresuming, and eminently sensitive. I have been with him in many trying situations of his after life, but I never saw him so deeply shocked and so cruelly agitated as on this occasion. A nice sense of honour shrinks from the most distant touch of disgrace— even from the insults of those men whose contumely can bring no shame. He sat on the sofa, repeating, with convulsive vehemence, the words, " Expelled, expelled!" his head shaking with emotion, and his whole frame quivering. The atrocious injustice and its cruel consequences roused the indignation, and moved the compassion, of a friend, who then stood by Shelley. [He has given the following account of his interference :

" So monstrous and so illegal did the outrage seem, that I held it to be impossible that any man, or any body of men, would dare to adhere to it; but, whatever the issue might be, it was a duty to endeavour to the utmost to assist him. I at once stepped forward, therefore, as the advocate of Shelley; such an advocate, perhaps, with respect to judgment, as might be expected at the age of eighteen, but certainly not inferior to the most practised defenders in good will and devotion. I wrote a short note to the master and fellows, in which, as far as I can remember a very hasty composition after a long interval, I briefly expressed my sorrow at the treatment my friend had experienced, and my hope that they would re-consider their sentence; since, by the same course of proceeding, myself, or any other person, might be subjected to the same penalty, and to the imputation of equal guilt. The note was despatched; the conclave was still sitting; and in an instant the porter came to summon me to attend, bearing in his countenance a promise of the reception I was about to find.   The angry and troubled air of men, assembled to commit injustice according to established forms, was then new to me; but a native instinct told me, as soon as I entered the room, that it was an affair of party; that whatever could conciliate the favour of patrons was to be done without scruple; and whatever could tend to impede preferment was to be brushed away without remorse.   The glowing master produced my poor note.   I acknowledged it; and he forthwith put into my hand, not less abruptly, the little syllabus.   ' Did you write this?' he asked, as fiercely as if I alone stood between him and the rich see of Durham.   I attempted, submissively, to point out to him the extreme unfairness of the question; the injustice of punishing Shelley for refusing to answer it; that if it were urged upon me I must offer the like refusal, as I had no doubt every man in college would—every gentleman, indeed, in the University; which, if such a course were adopted with all,—and there could not be any reason why it should be used with one and not with the rest,—would thus be stripped of every member.   I soon perceived that arguments were thrown away upon a man possessing no more intellect or erudition, and far less renown, than that famous ram, since translated to the stars, through grasping whose tail less firmly than was expedient, the sister of Phryxus formerly found a watery grave, and gave her name to the broad Hellespont.

" The other persons present took no part in the conversation : they presumed not to speak, scarcely to breathe, but looked mute subserviency. The few resident fellows, indeed, were but so many incarnations of the spirit of the master, whatever that spirit might be.   When I was silent, the master told me to retire, and to consider whether I was resolved to persist in my refusal.   The proposal was fair enough.   The next day, or the next week, I might have given my final answer—a deliberate answer ; having in the mean time consulted with older and more experienced persons, as to what course was best for myself and for others.   I had scarcely passed the door, however, when I was recalled.   The master again showed me the book, and hastily demanded whether I admitted or denied that I was the author of it.   I answered that I was fully sensible of the many and great inconveniences of being dismissed with disgrace from the University, and I specified some of them, and expressed an humble hope that they would not impose such a mark of discredit upon me without any cause.   I lamented that it was impossible either to admit or to deny the publication,—no man of spirit could submit to do so ;—and that a sense of duty compelled me respectfully to refuse to answer the question which had been proposed.   ' Then you are expelled,' said the master angrily, in a loud, great voice.   A formal sentence, duly signed and sealed, was instantly put into my hand : in what interval the instrument had been drawn up I cannot imagine.   The alleged offence was a contumacious refusal to disavow the imputed publication.   My eye glanced over it, and observing the word *contumaciously*, I said calmly that I did not think that term was justified by my behaviour.   Before I had concluded the remark, the master, lifting up the little syllabus, and then dashing it on the table, and looking sternly at me, said, ' Am I to understand, sir, that you adopt the principles contained in this work?' or some such words ; for, like one red with the suffusion of college port and college ale, the intense heat of anger seemed to deprive him of the power of articulation ; by reason of a rude provincial dialect and thickness of utterance, his speech being at all times indistinct. ' The last question is still more improper than the former,' I replied,—for I felt that the imputation was an insult ; ' and since, by your own act, you have renounced all authority over me, our communication is at an end.' ' I command you to quit my college to-morrow at an early hour.' I bowed and withdrew. I thank God I have never seen that man since : he is gone to his bed, and there let him sleep. Whilst he lived, he ate freely of the scholar's bread, and drank from his cup ; and he was sustained, throughout the whole term of his existence, wholly and most nobly, by those sacred funds that were consecrated by our pious forefathers to the advancement of learning. If the vengeance of the all-patient and long-contemned gods can ever be roused, it will surely be by some such sacrilege ! The favour which he showed to scholars, and his gratitude, have been made manifest If he were still alive, he would doubtless be as little desirous that his zeal should now be remembered as those bigots who had been most active in burning Archbishop Cranmer could have been to publish their officiousness during the reign of Elizabeth."

Busy rumour has ascribed, on what foundation I know not, since an active and searching inquiry has not hitherto been made, the infamy of having denounced Shelley to the pert, meddling tutor of a college of inferior note, a man of an insalubrious and inauspicious aspect. Any paltry fellow can whisper a secret accusation ; but a certain courage, as well as malignity, is required by him who undertakes to give evidence openly against another ; to provoke thereby the displeasure of the accused, of his family and friends ; and to submit his own veracity and his motives to public scrutiny. Hence the illegal and inquisitorial mode of proceeding by interrogation, instead of the lawful and recognized course by the production of witnesses. The disposal of ecclesiastical preferment has long been so reprehensible,—the practice of desecrating institutions that every good man desires to esteem most holy is so inveterate, —that it is needless to add that the secret accuser was rapidly enriched with the most splendid benefices, and finally became a dignitary of the church. The modest prelate did not seek publicity in the charitable and dignified act of deserving ; it is not probable, therefore, that he is anxious at present to invite an examination of the precise nature of his deserts.

The next morning, at eight o'clock, Shelley and his friend set out together for London on the top of a coach ; and with his final departure from the University the reminiscences of his life at Oxford terminate. The narrative of the injurious effects of this cruel, precipitate, unjust, and illegal expulsion upon the entire course of his subsequent life would not be wanting in interest or instruction ; of a period when the scene was changed from the quiet seclusion of academic groves and gardens, and the calm valley of our silvery Isis, to the stormy ocean of that vast and shoreless world, to the utmost violence of which he was, at an early age, suddenly and unnaturally abandoned.

NOTES

p. 62, l. 12: '*aqua regia*': a mixture of nitric and hydrochloric acids, given this name because capable of dissolving 'noble' metals, gold and platinum

p. 64, l. 29: '*Prometheus Vinctus*': *Prometheus Bound*, by Aeschlus

p. 69, l. 22: '...Ray or Linnaeus': John Ray (1627–1705) was an English naturalist who wrote extensively on the classification of plants. Linnaeus was Swedish naturalist Carl Linné (1707–78) whose system of categorizing and naming animals and plants was hugely influential

p. 70, l. 1: 'The prince of Roman eloquence': Cicero

p. 76, l. 12: 'Heaven's exile . . .': not identified.

Thomas Medwin, *The Shelley Papers* (London, 1833)

On February 22nd, 1825, Mary Shelley wrote to Trelawny describing a letter that she had recently received from Medwin. It was 'principally taken up with excuses for having (against my earnest desire) published a very blundering & disagreable memoir of our Shelley in his Conversations' (Bennett, *Letters*, I, p. 469). For all his excuses and apologies, the truth seems to have been that Medwin could hardly write without returning to the influence of his friendship with Shelley. Even his own literary efforts expressed this. His long Orientalist poem – or 'Dramatic Legend', as it called itself – *Ahasuerus, the Wanderer* (1823) was presented as having originated in joint compositions undertaken with Shelley in adolescence, and contained, Medwin told Byron, 'In one of the characters under the name of Julian... a sketch of our poor friend Shelley' (cited in Lovell, *Captain Medwin*, p. 140). His translations of Aeschylus avowedly followed in the wake of Shelley's own. His collection of tales and fictionalised reminiscences, *The Angler in Wales* (1834), exploited his connections with Shelley wherever it could (it used, for instance, Shelley's previously unpublished translation from Dante's *Purgatorio*). There were sound financial reasons for those who had known Byron to publish their supposed recollections, but memories of Shelley were not particularly bankable. Medwin seems to have been driven to publish them by a need for vicarious literary fame.

However, by the time that he wrote the articles that became *The Shelley Papers*, Medwin certainly needed any money that literary journalism might bring him. (For his life before the publication of *Conversations of Lord Byron*, see the headnote in this volume to extracts from that work.) In 1824 he had married a wealthy young widow and had moved with her to Florence. His extravagance, and his foolish speculations in the Italian art market, led to fianancial disaster – and separation from his wife and children. Leaving his debts and his family in Italy to take care of themselves (or to be taken care of by Trelawny), he returned to England. On his arrival, he sold his commission on the half-pay list, and began contributing to the reviews. His long letter defending the *Conversations of Lord Byron* appeared in *The Literary Gazette* in 1832 (February 4th and 11th). Here he conceded for the first time that the author of the vivid cremation scene from that book had in fact been Trelawny. Later the same year his 'Memoir of Shelley' (from which the extracts below are taken) appeared in six weekly installments in *The Atheneum* (July 21st to August 25th, 1832). It was followed in the same journal, with some interruptions until April 20th, 1833, by 'Poems and

Papers': fragments of Shelley's poetry and prose (see Engelberg, p. 200, for the dates of particular installments). These included parts of the essays 'On Love', 'On Life', and 'On a Future State', reviews of Godwin's *Mandeville* and Mary Shelley's *Frankenstein*, and the poems 'Lines Written during the Castlereagh Administration' and 'With a Guitar'. The last of these was addressed to Jane Williams, from whom Medwin obtained his copy. She made sure that her name was omitted from the published text (see Norman, p. 93).

In 1833, the eighteen installments from *The Atheneum* were collected as *The Shelley Papers*, 'many persons having expressed a wish to have them in a separate form', as the book's Advertisement explains. The explanation is obviously self-serving, but the book did appear at a time when critical interest in Shelley's writing was increasing. An odd but telling indication of the growing reputation of his poetry was a motion proposed at the Oxford Union by three delegates from the Cambridge Union in 1829: 'Shelley was a greater poet than Lord Byron'. One of the three Cambridge representatives was Tennyson's friend, Arthur Hallam; he had brought from Italy a copy of *Adonais*, printed in Pisa, and had it reprinted in Cambridge that same year. At around this time Shelley was being celebrated not only by his friend Leigh Hunt in *Lord Byron and Some of His Contemporaries* (1828), but also in Walter Savage Landor's *Imaginary Conversations*, published in the same year. For the first time, a vogue for Shelley's poetry was beginning. In 1830, there was a collection of *The Beauties of Percy Bysshe Shelley* (it included 'a Revised Edition of Queen Mab Free from All the Objectionable Passages') which went through three editions by the end of the year. The reviewers had begun treating Shelley's beliefs as pardonable eccentricities, and, to a remarkable extent, had begun praising his poetry. In the same year in which Medwin commenced his 'Memoir', Hunt felt safe to publish *The Masque of Anarchy* for the first time. The anonymous reviewer in *The Atheneum* declared that this most political of poems showed that Shelley's poetic powers transcended politics (see *The Atheneum*, No. 262, 3 November, 1832).

Medwin's new memoir was, therefore, part of an upsurge of interest in Shelley, as well as testimony to his own continuing preoccupation with his cousin. Indeed, his explaining away of Shelley's enthusiasms was in tune with the new trend amongst commentators. Shelley's visions were those seen with 'a poet's eye' (*Shelley Papers*, p. 97). 'Pure and moral himself', he believed that 'no other ties were necessary than the restraints imposed by a consciousness of right and wrong implanted in our natures'. In other words, he was led into strange opinions by his unworldly (but 'poetic') goodness. Yet Medwin's account is also 'personal' – indeed, more personal in tone than anything that has gone before. This is not just a matter of Medwin writing about himself, though the author's own appearances in the narrative are emphasised. It is also a matter of beginning to deal with some of the more tender parts of the poet's history. In particular, Shelley's love-life is discussed, albeit with an odd turn. His first marriage, to Harriet Westbrook, is given a perfunctory treatment that will contrast with the account in Medwin's later *Life of Percy Bysshe Shelley* (1847), and Shelley is represented as having been somehow bewildered into the relationship. His disappointed passion for his cousin Harriet Grove, however, is accorded great importance. Out of this youthful amour Medwin supposes that much poetry came. We are told about Harriet Shelley's suicide, but, unsurprisingly, Medwin is entirely evasive about her husband's relationship with Mary Godwin. Indeed, Mary is notable by her absence from the narrative. Nor can Medwin bring himself to acknowledge that he is recasting his 1824 account. He only implicitly concedes the fiction of his witnessing of Shelley's cremation: 'I have already, as taken from the mouth of Mr. Trelawney, given a description of the funeral ceremony, and my finding Byron in a high fever, on his return from the sad obsequies, and have nothing to add to that account' (*Shelley Papers*, p. 77). In the 1847 *Life*, he would have to make another attempt at self-correction.

Shelley, like Byron, knew early what it was to love : almost all the great poets have. After twenty-five years, I still remember Harriet G., and when I call to mind all the women I have ever seen and admired, I know of none that surpassed, few that could compare with her in beauty. I think of her as of some picture of Raphael's, or as one of Shakspeare's women. Shelley and Miss G. were born in the same year. There was a resemblance, as is often the case in cousins, between them, such as Byron describes as existing between Manfred and Astarte, or, as Shelley himself, in a fragment, says—

They were two cousins almost like to twins,

*   *   *   *   *   *

And so they grew together like two flowers
Upon one stem, which the same beams and showers
Lull or awaken in their purple prime.

If two persons were ever designed for each other, these seemed to be so. His novel of ' Zastrozzi,' a very wonderful work for a boy of sixteen, embodies much of the intensity of this passion that devoured him; and some of the chapters were, he told me, written by the lady herself. Shelley's mishap at Oxford was a blight to all his hopes, the rock on which all his happiness split;—he had the heart-rending misery of seeing her he adored wedded to another. Save for that expulsion (which I had almost called an unfortunate one, but that, as far as the world is concerned, the epithet would have been misapplied), Shelley would probably have become a member for some close borough, a good acting magistrate, and an excellent country 'squire. It is my firm belief, that he never wholly shook off this early attachment, that it was long the canker of his life, even if he ever really loved a second time.

☆ ★ ☆

In looking back to his first marriage, it is surprising, not that it should have ended in a separation, but that he should have continued to drag for
more than three years the matrimonial chain, every
link of which was a protraction of torture. That
separation, for which there were other and more
serious grounds, into which I shall not enter, took
place by mutual consent, and, considering himself
free, he resolved to go abroad. His health, always

delicate, was impaired by the misery he had undergone, and the quantity of that beverage, other than
a Lethean one to him, laudanum, which he had
taken.   He required change of scene, and a milder
climate ; and on the 28th July, 1814, commenced
a continental tour.   He crossed the Channel in an
open boat, and had a very narrow escape of being
upset in a sudden squall.   Passing a few days in
Paris, he received a small remittance ; and after
talking over with his party, and rejecting many
plans, fixed on one eccentric enough — to walk
through France—went to the Marché des Herbes,
bought an ass, and thus started for Charenton :
there, finding the quadruped too weak to carry his
portmanteau, he made the purchase of a mule, and
not without many adventures arrived with this singular *equipage* at Troyes.

The desolation and ruin that the Cossacks left
everywhere behind them in their pestilential march
—the distress of the inhabitants, whose houses had

been so lately burned, their cattle killed, and their all destroyed, made a deep impression on Shelley's feeling mind, and gave a sting to his detestation of war and despotism.

Further pedestrianism being rendered impossible by a sprained ancle, the remainder of the journey to Neuchatel was performed *par voiture*. Lucerne was the next canton visited: coasting its romantic lake up to Brunen, the château was hired for a week. But finding he had only 28*l.* left, and no chance of further remittances till December, he resolved with that small sum to return home by the Reuss and the Rhine. Shelley and his party took the *coche d'eau* for Loffenburgh: thence to Mumph the passage was made in a narrow, long flat-bottomed machine, consisting of pieces of deal nailed together. " The river is rapid, and sped swiftly, breaking as it passed over rocks just covered by the water. It was a sight of some dread to see the frail boat winding along the eddies of the rocks, which it was death to touch, and where the slightest inclination on one side would instantly have overset it." However, this punt brought them in safety to Basle, where, hiring a boat for Mayence, they bade adieu to Switzerland; and landed in England from Rotterdam on the 13th August, having travelled 800 miles at an expense of less than 30*l.* Shelley used to describe with an enthusiasm that was infectious, the rapturous enjoyment this voyage down the Rhine was to him;—to dilate with all the fire of poetic inspiration, on the rapidity of their descent of that torrent-like river—winding now along banks of vines, or greenest pastures—now rushing past craggy heights surmounted by feudal castles.

This was one of the favourite topics in which he delighted to intoxicate his imagination; and, with a prodigality, like that of Nature in some tropical island, to lavish a world of wealth, as though his store was inexhaustible as hers.

The next eighteen months after his return were

passed almost exclusively in London, where he had to suffer all the horrors of poverty. It was at this time, I imagine, that he walked the hospitals, and studied medicine, not with any intention of practising it as a profession, but with a view of alleviating the sufferings of humanity. His knowledge of anatomy was very limited; but he made himself a tolerable botanist. I doubt, however, whether Shelley had not too much imagination to make any great proficiency in the abstract sciences : nature and education both designed him for a poet.

☆ ★ ☆

Shelley was at Bath in November 1817, when an event occurred which was destined to darken the remainder of his existence ; or, in his own words, written about this period, when for him

> Black despair,
> The shadow of a starless night, was thrown
> Over the world.

This event, upon which I could wish to throw a veil, was the death of his wife under the most distressing circumstances. Her fate was a dreadful misfortune, to him who survived, and her who perished. It is impossible to acquit Shelley of all blame in this calamity. From the knowledge of her character, and her unfitness for self-government, he should have kept an eye over her conduct. But if he was blameable, her relations were still more so; and, having confided her to their care, he might consider, with many others similarly circumstanced, that his responsibility was at an end. That he did not do so, his compunction, which brought on a temporary derangement, proves; and yet was it not most barbarous in a reviewer to gangrene the wounds which his sensitive spirit kept ever open? How pathetically does he, in a dirge not unworthy of Shakspeare, addressed to whom I know not, give vent to his agonized heart:

> That time is dead for ever, child—
> *Drowned*, frozen, dead for ever;
>   We look on the past,
>   And stare aghast,
> At the spectres, wailing, pale and ghast,
> Of hopes that thou and I beguiled
>   To death on Life's dark river.

"Até does not die childless," says the Greek dramatist. A scarcely less misfortune, consequent on this catastrophe, was the barbarous decree of the Court of Chancery, unhappily since made a precedent, by which he was deprived of his children, had them torn from him and consigned to strangers.

The grounds upon which this act of oppression

and cruelty, only worthy of the most uncivilized
nations, was founded,—

Trial

I think they call it,—

was decided against him upon the evidence, if such
it can be called, of a printed copy of ' Queen
Mab,' which, in his preface to ' Alastor,' he disclaimed any intention of publishing. It is said
that he was called upon, by the court, to recant
the opinions contained in that work. Shelley was
the last man in existence to recant any opinion
from fear: and a fiat worse than death was the
consequence — sundering all the dearest ties of
humanity.

Byron told me, that (well knowing Shelley could
not exist without sympathy) it was by his persuasion that Shelley married again. None who
have the happiness of knowing Mrs. Shelley can
wonder at that step. But in 1812, a year and a
half after his first marriage, that he continued to

think with Plato on the subject of wedlock is clear, from a letter addressed to Sir James Lawrence, who had sent him his ' History of the Nairs.' Shelley says, " I abhor seduction as much as I adore love ; and if I have conformed to the usages of the world on the score of matrimony, it is that disgrace always attaches to the weaker sex." An irresistible argument.*

His short residence at Marlow has been already described. There he led a quiet, retired, domestic life, and has left behind him a character for benevolence and charity, that still endears him to its inhabitants.

* Has a woman obeyed the impulse of unerring nature, society declares war against her—pitiless and unerring war. She must be the tame slave ; she must make no reprisals : theirs is the right of persecution, hers the duty of endurance. She lives a life of infamy. The loud and bitter laugh of scorn scares her from all return. She dies of long and lingering disease ; yet *she* is in fault. *She* is the criminal—*she* the froward, the untameable child ;—and society, forsooth, the pure and virtuous matron, who casts her as an abortion from her undefiled bosom.—*Shelley.*

He became about this time acquainted with
Keats; and Shelley told me that it was a friendly
rivalry between them, which gave rise to ' Endymion' and the ' Revolt of Islam,'—two poems
scarcely to be named in the same sentence.
Shelley was too classical—had too much good taste
—to have fallen into the sickly affectation—the
obsoletas scribendi formas of that perverse and
limited school.† The ' Revolt of Islam' must be

---

† The following note, by the Editor of the *Athenæum*, was
appended to this passage on its publication in that paper :—
" Nothing is more ridiculous, than a running commentary,
wherein an editor apologizes for, or dissents from, the opinions
of a writer in his own paper. Occasions, however, may arise
to excuse, if not to justify, such disclaimer; and for self-satis-
faction we enter our protest on this occasion. We go as far
as Captain Medwin in admiration of Shelley; but as far as
Shelley—" infallible," says the Captain, " in his judgment of
the works of others"—in admiration of Keats. Shelley was a
worshipper of Truth—Keats of Beauty; Shelley had the greater
power—Keats the finer imagination : both were single-hearted,
sincere, admirable men. When we look into the world,—nay,
not to judge others, when we look into our own hearts, and see
how certainly manhood shakes hands with worldliness, we
should despair, if such men did not occasionally appear among

looked upon as the greatest effort of any individual mind, (whatever may be its defects,) in one at the

us. Shelley and Keats were equal enthusiasts—had the same hopes of the moral improvement of society—of the certain influence of knowledge—and of the ultimate triumph of truth; —and Shelley, who lived longest, carried all the generous feelings of youth into manhood; age enlarged, not narrowed his sympathies; and learning bowed down his humanity to feel its brotherhood with the humblest of his fellow-creatures. If not judged by creeds and conventional opinions, Shelley must be considered as a moral teacher both by precept and example : he scattered the seed of truth, so it appeared to him, every where, and upon all occasions,—confident that, however disregarded, however long it might lie buried, it would not perish, but spring up hereafter in the sunshine of welcome, and its golden fruitage be garnered by grateful men. Keats had naturally much less of this political philosophy; but he had neither less resolution, less hope of, or less good-will towards man. Lord Byron's opinion, that he was killed by the reviewers, is wholly ridiculous; though his epitaph, and the angry feelings of his friends, might seem to countenance it. Keats died of hereditary consumption, and was fast sinking before either *Blackwood* or the *Quarterly* poured out their malignant venom. Even then it came but as a mildew upon his generous nature, injuring the leaves and blossoms, but leaving untouched the heart within, the courage to dare and to suffer. Keats (we speak of him in health and vigour,) had a resolution, not only physical but moral, greater than any man we ever knew : it was unshakable by everything but his affections. We are not inclined to stretch this note into an essay,

same period of life. I do not forget Milton, or Chatterton, or Pope, when I say this. It occupied him only six months. The dedicating lines lose nothing in comparison with Byron's to Ianthe; and the structure of his Spenserian stanzas, in harmony and the varied flow of the versification, may serve as a model for all succeeding writers in that metre.

Early in the spring of 1818, various reasons induced Shelley again to quit England, with scarcely a hope or wish to revisit it. The breach between himself and his relatives had been made irreparable. He was become *fatherless*—he was highly unpopular from the publicity given to the trial— from the attacks of the reviewing churchmen on his works; and his health was gradually becoming

and shall not therefore touch on the ' Endymion' further than to say, that Captain Medwin cannot produce anything in the ' Revolt of Islam' superior to the Hymn to Pan ; nor in the English language anything written by any poet at the same age with which it may not stand in honourable comparison."

worse. The vegetable system which he followed, as to diet, did not agree with his constitution, and he was finally obliged to abandon it. That he was a Pythagorean from principle, is proved by the very luminous synopsis of all the arguments in its favour, contained in a note appended to ' Queen Mab.' He was of opinion, and I agree with him and the disciples of that school, that abstinence from animal food subtilizes and clears the intellectual faculties. For all the sensualities of the table Shelley had an ineffable contempt, and, like Newton, used sometimes to inquire if he had dined —a natural question from a Berkleyist.

But to follow him in his travels—a more interesting topic. He passed rapidly through France and Switzerland, and, crossing the Mont Cenis into Italy, paid a visit to Lord Byron at Venice, where he made a considerable stay.

Under the names of Julian and Maddalo, written at Rome some months afterwards, Shelley paints himself and Byron in that city. The sketch is highly valuable. He says of Byron, at this time, " He is cheerful, frank, and witty : his more serious conversation a sort of intoxication; men are held by it as a spell":—of himself, that he " was attached to that philosophical sect that assert the power of man over his own mind, and the immense improvements of which, by the extinction of certain moral superstitions, human society may be made susceptible." I shall enter more at large hereafter on Shelley's particular theories, though they are somewhat subtle and difficult of analysis.

Venice was a place peculiarly adapted to the studious life Shelley loved to lead.

> The town is silent—one may write
> Or read in gondolas by day or night,
> Unseen, uninterrupted. Books are there—
> Pictures, and casts from all the statues fair,
> That are twin-born with poetry ; and all
> We seek in towns ; with little to recall
> Regrets for the green country.

In the autumn we find Shelley at Naples. Fortune did not seem tired of persecuting him, for he
became the innocent actor in a tragedy here, more
extraordinary than any to be found in the pages
of romance. The story, as he related it to myself
and Byron, would furnish perfect materials for a
novel in three volumes, and cannot be condensed
into a few sentences, marvellous as the scenes of
that drama were. Events occur daily, and have
happened to myself, far more incredible than any
which the most disordered fancy can conjure up,
casting " a shade of falsehood" on the records of
what are called reality. Certain it is, that Shelley,
as may be judged from his ' Lines written in
Despondency,' must have been most miserable at
Naples. No one could have poured forth those
affecting stanzas, but with a mind, as he says in
the ' Cenci,' hovering on the devouring edge of
darkness. His departure from Naples was, he said,
precipitated by this event; and he passed the en-

suing winter at Rome. There is something in-spiring in the very atmosphere of Rome. Is it fanciful, that being encircled by images of beauty —that in contemplating works of beauty such as Rome and the Vatican only can boast—that by gazing on the scattered limbs of that mighty co-lossus, whose shadow eclipsed the world, — we should catch a portion of the sublime—become a portion of that around us?

☆ ★ ☆

It is to be lamented that no bust or portrait
exists of Shelley, though the infinite versatility
and play of his features would have baffled either
sculpture or painting. His frame was a mere tene-
ment for spirit, and in every gesture and lineament
showed that intellectual beauty which animated
him. There was in him a spirit which seemed to
defy time, and suffering, and misfortune. He was
twenty-nine when he died, but he might have been
taken for nineteen. His features were small; the
upper part not strictly regular. The lower had
a Grecian contour. He did not look so tall as
he was, his shoulders being a little bent by study
and ill health. Like Socrates, he united the
gentleness of the lamb with the wisdom of the
serpent—the playfulness of the boy with the pro-

foundness of the philosopher. In argument he was irresistible, always calm and unruffled; and in eloquence surpassed all men I have ever conversed with. Byron was so sensible of his inability to cope with him, that he always avoided coming to any trial of their strength; for Shelley was what Byron could not be, a close, logical and subtle reasoner, much of which he owed to Plato, whose writings he used to call the model of a prose style.

He was not likely to have lived long. His health had been impaired by what he had undergone, and by the immoderate use he at one time made of laudanum. He was, besides, narrow-chested, and subject to a complaint which, from day to day, might have cut him off. Its tortures were excruciating, but, during his worst spasms, I never saw him peevish or out of humour—indeed, as an Italian said to me, he was *veramente un angelo*.

> But thou art fled,
> Like some fair exhalation,—
> The brave, the gentle, and the beautiful,
> The child of grace and genius :
> Thou canst no longer know or love the shapes
> Of this phantasmal scene, who have to thee
> Been purest ministers ; who are, alas !
> Now thou art not.

These affecting lines would have furnished his most appropriate epitaph. I have never been able to read them without applying them to Shelley, or his tribute to the memory of Keats, without, under the name of Adonais, impersonating the companion of my youth. There was, unhappily, too much similarity in the destinies of Keats and Shelley: both were victims to persecution—both were marked out for the envenomed shafts of invidious critics—and both now sleep together in a foreign land.   Peace to their manes !

NOTES

p. 93, l. 3: 'Harriet G.': this is Harriet Grove, who was Shelley's cousin. In 1809, when Shelley was sixteen and she a year older, they began a friendship and a correspondence, and he addressed poems to her. At the end of this year, however, she became engaged to a gentleman farmer who lived near her home in Wiltshire and her relationship with Shelley came to an end.

p. 93, ll. 11–12: 'Manfred and Astarte': Manfred is the protagonist of Byron's 'Dramatic Poem' of the same name, published, shortly after it was completed, in June 1817. Astarte was the Phoenician goddess of love and appears as a 'Phantom' in Act II of *Manfred*, where she speaks the protagonist's doom.

p. 93, ll. 14–17: 'They were two cousins...': from Shelley's 'Fiordispina', an incomplete poem first published in the 1824 *Posthumous Poems*

p. 100, ll. 5–7: 'Black despair...': from the Dedication (to Mary Shelley) of *The Revolt of Islam* (stanza VI), published in 1818. The same lines had first appeared in this poem's first incarnation as *Laon and Cythna*, published in 1817, but then withdrawn from sale and heavily revised

p. 101, ll. 8–14: 'That time is dead...': the first stanza of a two stanza poem by Shelley, published by Mary Shelley as 'Lines' in *Posthumous Poems* (1824), but entitled in manuscript 'Nov. 5 1817'

p. 101, ll. 15–16: 'the Greek dramatist': Aeschylus

p. 102, ll. 3–4: 'Trial/ I think they call it...': from Shelley's *Rosalind and Helen* (ll. 866–7), first published in 1819

p. 104, footnote: 'The editor of the *Atheneum*': Charles Wentworth Dilke, who was also the owner of this periodical

p. 111, ll. 1–2: 'no bust or portrait exist of Shelley': in fact, a portrait of Shelley had been painted in Italy in 1819 by Amelia Curran. (It was not, however, completed until after Shelley's death.) Eventually, it was obtained by Mary Shelley, and was the basis of later engravings. It is now in the National Portrait Gallery in London

p. 113, ll. 1–8: 'But thout art fled...': from Shelley's *Alastor* (l. 686 onwards), first published in 1816

Mary Shelley, Preface and notes to *Essays, Letters from Abroad, Translations and Fragments, by Percy Bysshe Shelley. Edited by Mrs. Shelley* 2 vols (London, 1840)

Any reader of Mary Shelley's surviving letters from the 1830s will recognize that the publication of her husband's writings remained her aim and her preoccupation, despite her father-in-law's intervention to block her previous editorial efforts (see the headnote to *Posthumous Poems of Percy Bysshe Shelley* in this volume). If anything, this ambition became more compelling as, with the slow growth of Shelley's poetic reputation, unauthorized editions of his work began to appear (for a description of them, see Taylor, pp. 11–33). (Mary Shelley had herself secretly contributed to one of these, the Galignani edition of 1829: see the headnote to *Posthumous Poems*). Yet Sir Timothy Shelley, on whom she still relied for financial support, remained utterly opposed to such publication. Given both her concern during this period with the education as a gentleman of her son, Percy, and the insufficiency of her earnings as a writer of novels, reviews, and short biographies, it seemed to her that she had to tread carefully – and await Sir Timothy's death.

Mary Shelley had this eventuality in mind when she wrote to the publisher Edward Moxon in January 1834 in reply to his enquiries about the prospects for a proper edition of Shelley's poems.

> Family reasons prevent my undertaking the republication of them at present. When these no longer exist (& it is probable that they will not endure any very long time) – it is my intention to endeavour to arrange to republish them – with the addition of some letters and prose pieces in my possession. If it were then thought best to add a life – though I should decline writing it myself – I should wish to elect the person I should wish to undertake the task (Bennett, *Letters*, II, p. 198).

She added, 'when I am free to follow my own wishes I shall be most happy to enter into any arrangement with you for their execution'. Yet, of course, Shelley's father lived on. 'It is a hard world – & there are some Immortals in it', she was to reflect acidly in a letter to Marianne Hunt in 1840 (Bennett, II, p. 345). Her father-in-law was a 'Strulbrugg' (sic) (a bitter reference to the Struldbrugs, grotesque immortal creatures that Gulliver meets in Part III of Swift's *Gulliver's Travels*). So, a year after that first letter to Moxon, she is beginning to entertain thoughts of just the edition that she had said was impossible.

The evidence comes in a letter to Maria Gisborne of February 1835. Mary Shelley has had an offer of £600 for 'an edition of Shelley's works with life & notes', an offer that we know to have come from Moxon (Bennett, *Letters*, II, p. 221). Though 'the *life* is out of the question', she is contemplating the publication of some of Shelley's letters (and indeed asking Maria Gisborne if her own correspondence with Shelley might be made available). 'You know how I shrink from all *private* detail for the public – but Shelley's letters are beautifully written, & every thing *private* could be omitted'. Although she still said that such an edition 'cannot be arranged yet at least', Moxon's offer remained in her head – not least, one would imagine because of the large sum of money involved. We do not know every move that led to her decision to attempt publication, but we do know that, in August 1838, she wrote to John Gregson, Sir Timothy Shelley's lawyer and her usual go-between in her communications with him, asking Gregson to apply for permission to publish Shelley's poetry. She pointed out that there had been many pirated editions, and that Sir Timothy's injunction 'has not prevented the publication, but only prevented me from receiving any benefit from it' (Bennett, II, p. 298). 'There is now a question of another edition, which if I were allowed to carry on myself would be very advantageous to me. I wish therefore to learn whether I might'.

Gregson wrote to Sir Timothy Shelley, quoting Mary Shelley's letter and supporting her application. Sir Timothy agreed, provided that no memoir were published with the poems (Ingpen, II, pp. 618–9). Soon Mary Shelley was negotiating with Moxon, agreeing to £200 for an edition of 2,000, and an additional £500 for the copyright (Bennett, *Letters*, II, pp. 300–1). The first volume of the four-volume *Poetical Works* appeared in January 1839, the short lapse in time since Sir Timothy gave permission indicating that Mary Shelley had long since been working on the text. As is well known, she got around the ban on a memoir by including memories and descriptions of Shelley in her notes to the edition (see the discussion in the Introduction to this volume). Having established this precedent, it is not surprising that she was soon suggesting to Moxon the publication of a collection of 'Letters and other prose essays' (letter of 2 May, 1839, in Bennett, II, p. 315). After some flustered gathering of material in the possession of some of Shelley's former friends, in particular Leigh Hunt, who was her main advisor, she put together the two-volume collection that was published in November 1839 (although its title page says '1840').

Rather as its awkward title suggests, *Essays, Letters from Abroad, Translations and Fragments* is a fairly miscellaneous collection. In her Preface, from which the first two of the three extracts below are taken, Mary Shelley explains that what holds it all together is just what Sir Timothy Shelley wanted kept from the public: a sense, if not quite of biography, at least of the poet's personality. These volumes have been published, says Mary Shelley's Preface, to satisfy readers who 'desire to know the man' (p. v): 'turn to these pages to gather proof of sincerity, and to become acquainted with the form that such gentle sympathies and lofty aspirations wore in private life' (p. vi). The Preface itself is a survey of the pieces contained in the collection which finds in each one evidence of Shelley's poetic and spiritual elevation. The commentary on his 'Defence of Poetry', which opens the collection, is representative of its celebration of Shelley's idealism. The essay, says Mary Shelley, teaches 'a young poet' that 'his best claim on the applause of mankind, results from his being one more in the holy brotherhood, whose vocation it is to divest life of its material grossness and stooping tendencies, and to animate with that power of turning all things to the beautiful and good, which is the spirit of poetry' (p. vii). The most embarrassment is caused by Shelley's 'Essay on a Future State', which prompts his widow to a discussion of his supposedly irreligious views. This is given in the first of the extracts below. When she discusses the letters to herself that she prints, she reaches the highest pitch of her celebration of Shelley. This can be found in the second of the extracts given.

The third and final extract below features, albeit as a lengthy footnote to one of Shelley's letters, extracts from the journal of Edward Williams, who drowned with Shelley. The journal was actually aboard the *Don Juan* when it sank, and was discovered when the boat was raised by fishing boats two months after the accident. It was bought by Captain Daniel Roberts, the friend of Trelawny who had built the *Don Juan*, and left with Leigh Hunt. Mary Shelley took charge of it and, after transcribing portions, sent it to Jane Williams. It was kept in her family, until one of her grandsons left it to the British Musem. Mary Shelley's transcription is accurate (only punctuation is much changed), but her choices of passages is highly selective. She excludes not only entries concerned only with the Williamses, but also, for instance, Williams's account of Shelley telling Claire of the death of her daughter, Allegra. In 1951, a full and carefully annotated edition of the journal was produced by Frederick L. Jones.

The " Essay on a Future State" is also unhappily a fragment. Shelley observes, on one occasion, " man is not a being of reason only, but of imaginations and affections." In this portion of his Essay he gives us only that view of a future state which is to be derived from reasoning and analogy. It is not to be supposed that a mind so full of vast ideas concerning the universe, endowed with such subtle discrimination with regard to the various modes in which this does or may appear to our eyes, with a lively fancy and ardent and expansive feelings, should be content with a mere logical view of that which even in religion is a mystery and a wonder. I cannot pretend to supply the deficiency, nor say what Shelley's views were—they were vague, certainly ;

yet as certainly regarded the country beyond the grave as one by no means foreign to our interests and hopes. Considering his individual mind as a unit divided from a mighty whole, to which it was united by restless sympathies and an eager desire for knowledge, he assuredly believed that hereafter, as now, he would form a portion of that whole— and a portion less imperfect, less suffering, than the shackles inseparable from humanity impose on all who live beneath the moon. To me, death appears to be the gate of life; but my hopes of a hereafter would be pale and drooping, did I not expect to find that most perfect and beloved specimen of humanity on the other shore ; and my belief is that spiritual improvement in this life prepares the way to a higher existence. Traces of such a faith are found in several passages of Shelley's works. In one of the letters of the second volume he says, " The destiny of man can scarcely be so degraded, that he was born only to die." And again, in a journal, I find these feelings recorded, with regard to a danger we incurred together at sea. " I had time in that moment to reflect and even to reason on death ; it was rather a thing of discomfort and disappointment than terror to me. We should never be separated; but in death we might not know and feel our union as now. I hope—but my hopes are not unmixed with fear for what will befal this inestimable spirit when we appear to die." A mystic ideality tinged these speculations in Shelley's mind; certain stanzas in the poem of "The Sensitive Plant," express, in some degree, the almost inexpressible idea, not that we die into another state, when this state is no longer, from some reason, unapparent as well as apparent, accordant with our being—but that those who rise above the ordinary nature of man, fade from before our imperfect organs; they remain in their "love, beauty, and delight," in a world congenial to them—we, clogged by "error, ignorance, and strife," see them not, till we are fitted by purification and improvement for their higher state.* For myself, no religious

---

*"But in this life
Of terror, ignorance, and strife,
Where nothing is, but all things seem,
And we the shadows of the dream,

It is a modest creed, and yet
Pleasant, if one considers it,
To own that death, itself must be,
Like all the rest, a mockery.

That garden sweet, that lady fair,
And all sweet shapes, and odours there,

doctrine, nor philosophical precept, can shake the
faith that a mind so original, so delicately and
beautifully moulded, as Shelley's, so endowed with
wondrous powers and eagle-eyed genius—so good,
so pure, would never be shattered and dispersed by
the Creator; but that the qualities and consciousness that formed him, are not only indestructible
in themselves, but in the form under which they
were united here, and that to become worthy of
him is to assure the bliss of a reunion.

In truth, have never passed away;
'Tis we, 'tis ours are changed – not they.

For love, and beauty, and delight,
There is no death, nor change; their might
Exceeds our organs, which endure
No light, being themselves obscure."

☆ ★ ☆

I have added such letters as, during our brief separations in Italy, were addressed to myself; precious relics of love, kindness, gentleness, and wisdom. I have but one fault to find with them, or with Shelley, in my union with him. His inexpressible tenderness of disposition made him delight in giving pleasure, and, urged by this feeling, he praised too much. Nor were his endeavours to exalt his correspondent in her own eyes founded on this feeling only. He had never read " Wilhelm Meister," but I have heard him say that he regulated his conduct towards his friends by a maxim which I found afterwards in the pages of Goethe—" When we take people merely as they are, we make them worse ; when we treat them as if they were what they should be, we improve them as far as they can be improved." This rule may perhaps admit of dispute, and it may be argued that truth and frankness produce better fruits than the most generous deceit. But ·when we consider the difficulty of keeping our best virtues free from self-blindness and self-love, and recollect the intolerance and fault-finding that usually blots social intercourse; and compare such with the degree of forbearance and imaginative sympathy, so to speak, which such a system necessitates, we must think highly of the generosity and self-abnegation of the man who regulated his conduct undeviatingly by it.

Can anything be more beautiful than these letters? They are adorned by simplicity, tenderness, and generosity, combined with manly views, and acute observation. His practical opinions may be found here. His indignant detestation of political oppression did not prevent him from deprecating the smallest approach to similar crimes on the part of his own party, and he abjured revenge and retaliation, while he strenuously advocated reform. He felt assured that there would be a change for the better in our institutions; he feared bloodshed, he feared the ruin of many. Wedded as he was to the cause of public good, he would have hailed the changes that since his time have so signally ameliorated our institutions and opinions, each acting on the other, and which still, we may hope, are proceeding towards the establishment of that liberty and toleration which he worshipped. " The thing to fear," he observes, "will be, that the change should proceed too fast—it must be gradual to be secure."

I do not conceal that I am far from satisfied with the tone in which the criticisms on Shelley are written. Some among these writers praise the poetry with enthusiasm, and even discrimination ; but none understand the man. I hope these volumes will set him in a juster point of view. If it be alleged in praise of Goethe that he was an *artist* as well as a poet ; that his principles of composition, his theories of wisdom and virtue, and the ends of existence, rested on a noble and secure basis ; not less does that praise belong to Shelley. His Defence of Poetry is alone sufficient to prove that his views were, in every respect, congruous and complete ; his faith in good firm, his respect for his fellow-creatures unimpaired by the wrongs he suffered. Every word of his letters displays that modesty, that forbearance, and mingled meekness and resolution that, in my mind, form the perfection of man. " Gentle, brave, and generous," he describes the Poet in Alastor : such he was himself, beyond any man I have ever known. To these admirable qualities were added, his genius; his keen insight into human motive—as his theory of morals, which, based on a knowledge of his kind, was perspicuous, subtle, comprehensive, and just; the pure and lofty enthusiasm with which he regarded the improvement of his own species. He had but one defect—which was his leaving his life incomplete by an early death. O that the serener hopes of maturity, the happier contentment of mid-life, had descended on his dear head, to calm the turbulence of youthful impetuosity — that he had lived to see his country advance towards freedom, and to enrich the world with his own virtues and genius in their completion of experience and power! When I think that such things might have been, and of my own share in such good and happiness; the pang occasioned by his loss can never pass away—and I gain resignation only by believing that he was spared much suffering, and that he has passed into a sphere of being, better adapted to his inexpressible tenderness, his generous sympathies, and his richly gifted mind. That, free from the physical pain to which he was a martyr, and unshackled by the fleshly bars and imperfect senses which hedged him in on earth, he enjoys beauty, and good, and love there, where those to whom he was united on earth by various ties of affection, sympathy, and admiration, may hope to join him.

☆ ★ ☆

LETTER LXIII.

To Mrs. SHELLEY.

(AT SPEZZIA.)

[*Lerici, Sunday, April 28th*, 1822.]

DEAREST MARY,

I AM this moment arrived at Lerici, where I am necessarily detained, waiting the furniture, which left Pisa last night at midnight; and as the sea has been calm, and the wind fair, I may expect them every moment. It would not do to leave affairs here in an *impiccio*, great as is my anxiety to see you.—How are you, my best love? How have you sustained the trials of the journey? Answer me this question, and how my little babe and C * * * are.

Now to business:—Is the Magni House taken?

if not, pray occupy yourself instantly in finishing, the affair, even if you are obliged to go to Sarzana, and send a messenger to me to tell me of your success. I, of course, cannot leave Lerici, to which place the boats, (for we were obliged to take two,) are directed. But *you* can come over in the same boat that brings this letter, and return in the evening.

I ought to say that I do not think that there is accommodation for you all at this inn; and that, even if there were, you would be better off at Spezzia; but if the Magni House is taken, then there is no possible reason why you should not take a row over in the boat that will bring this—but don't keep the men long. I am anxious to hear from you on every account.*

Ever yours,
S.

* I insert a few extracts from the Journal of Williams, as affording a picture of Shelley's habits during these last months of his life. How full he was of hope, life and love, when lost to us for ever !

" *Sunday, April* 28*th.*

" Fine.   Arrive at Lerici at 1 o'clock—the harbour-master called. Not a house to be had.   On our telling him we had brought our furniture, his face lengthened considerably, for he informed us that the dogana would amount to £300 English, at least.   Dined, and resolved on sending our things back without unlading—in fact, found ourselves in a devil of a mess.   S. wrote to Mary, whom we heard was at Spezzia.

" *Monday,* 29*th.*

" Cloudy.   Accompanied the harbour-master to the chief of the

LETTER LXIV.

To HORATIO SMITH, Esq.

(VERSAILLES.)

Lerici, May, 1822.

MY DEAR SMITH,

IT is some time since I have heard from you; are you still at Versailles? Do you still cling

customs at Spezzia. Found him exceedingly polite, and willing to do all that lay in his power to assist us. He will, therefore, take on himself to allow the furniture to come on shore when the boats arrive, and then consider our house as a sort of depôt, until further leave from the Genoa government. Returned to Lerici somewhat calmed. Heard from Mary at Sarzana, that she had concluded for Casa Magni—but for ourselves no hope.

" *Wednesday, May* 1*st.*

"Cloudy, with rain. Came to Casa Magni after breakfast; the Shelleys having contrived to give us rooms. Without them, heaven knows what we should have done. Employed all day putting the things away. All comfortably settled by four. Passed the evening in talking over our folly and our troubles.

" *Thursday, May* 2*d.*

" Cloudy, with intervals of rain. Went out with Shelley in the boat—fish on the rocks—bad sport. Went in the evening after some wild ducks—saw nothing but sublime scenery, to which the grandeur of a storm greatly contributed.

" *Friday, May* 3*d.*

" Fine. The captain of the port despatched a vessel for Shelley's boat. Went to Lerici with S., being obliged to market there; the servant having returned from Sarzana without being able to procure anything.

" *Saturday, May* 4*th.*

" Fine. Went fishing with Shelley. No sport. Loitered away the whole day. In the evening tried the rocks again, and had no less than thirty baits taken off by the small fish. Returned late

to France, and prefer the arts and conveniences of that over-civilised country to the beautiful nature

—a heavy swell getting up. I think if there are no tides in the Mediterranean, that there are strong currents, on which the moon, both at the full and at the change, has a very powerful effect; the swell this evening is evidently caused by her influence, for it is quite calm at sea.

" *Sunday, May 5th.*

" Fine. Kept awake the whole night by a heavy swell, which made a noise on the beach like the discharge of heavy artillery. Tried with Shelley to launch the small flat-bottomed boat through the surf; we succeeded in pushing it through, but shipped a sea on attempting to land. Walk to Lerici along the beach, by a winding path on the mountain's side. Delightful evening—the scenery most sublime.

" *Monday, May 6th.*

" Fine. Some heavy drops of rain fell to-day, without a cloud being visible. Made a sketch of the western side of the bay. Read a little. Walked with Jane up the mountain.

After tea walking with Shelley on the terrace, and observing the effect of moonshine on the waters, he complained of being unusually nervous, and stopping short, he grasped me violently by the arm, and stared stedfastly on the white surf that broke upon the beach under our feet. Observing him sensibly affected, I demanded of him if he were in pain ? But he only answered, by saying, ' There it is again— there !' He recovered after some time, and declared that he saw, as plainly as he then saw me, a naked child, (*the child of a friend who had lately died,*) rise from the sea, and clap its hands as in joy, smiling at him. This was a trance that it required some reasoning and philosophy entirely to awaken him from, so forcibly had the vision operated on his mind. Our conversation, which had been at first rather melancholy, led to this; and my confirming his sensations, by confessing that I had felt the same, gave greater activity to his ever-wandering and lively imagination.

" *Sunday, May 12th.*

" Cloudy and threatening weather. Wrote during the morning. Mr.

and mighty remains of Italy? As to me, like Anacreon's swallow, I have left my Nile, and have

Maglian, (*harbour-master at Lerici*), called after dinner, and while walking with him on the terrace, we discovered a strange sail coming round the point of Porto Venere, which proved at length to be Shelley's boat. She had left Genoa on Thursday, but had been driven back by prevailing bad winds. A Mr. Heslop, and two English seamen brought her round, and they speak most highly of her performances. She does, indeed, excite my surprise and admiration. Shelley and I walked to Lerici, and made a stretch off the land to try her, and I find she fetches whatever she looks at. In short, we have now a perfect plaything for the summer.

" *Monday, May* 13*th.*

" Rain during night in torrents—a heavy gale of wind from SW. and a surf running heavier than ever; at 4 gale unabated, violent squalls. Walked to Lerici with Shelley and went on board. Called on M. Maglian ; and found him anxiously awaiting the moment of a third child's birth. In the evening an electric arch forming in the clouds announces a heavy thunder storm, if the wind lulls. Distant thunder—gale increases—a circle of foam surrounds the bay—dark, rainy, and tempestuous, with flashes of lightning at intervals, which give us no hope of better weather. The learned in these things say, that it generally lasts three days when once it commences as this has done. We all feel as if we were on board ship—and the roaring of the sea brings this idea to us even in our beds.

" *Tuesday, May* 14*th.*

" Clear weather, and the breeze greatly moderated, contrary to all the expectations and the prophecies of these would-be sailors—these weather-wise landsmen. While dressing this morning, I saw the boat, under easy sail, bearing on and off land. At 9 we took her down, under top-sails and flying jib, to Spezzia ; and, after tacking round some of the craft there, returned to Lerici in an hour and a half—a distance, they say, of four leagues. On our return, we were hailed by a servant of Count S——, a minister of the Emperor of Austria, who sent desiring to have a sail; but before he could get on board, the wind had lulled into a perfect calm, and we only got into the swell, and made him sick.

taken up my summer quarters here, in a lonely house close by the sea-side, surrounded by the soft

" *Wednesday, May* 15*th.*

"Fine and fresh breeze in puffs from the land. Jane and Mary consent to take a sail. Run down to Porto Venere and beat back at 1 o'clock. The boat sailed like a witch. After the late gale, the water is covered with purple nautili, or as the sailors call them, ' Portuguese men-of-war.' After dinner, Jane accompanied us to the point of the Magra ; and the boat beat back in wonderful style.

" *Saturday, May* 18*th.*

"Fine fresh breeze. Sailed with Shelley to the outer island, and find that there is another small one beyond, which we have named the Sirens' rock. This name was chosen in consequence of hearing, at the time we were beating to windward to weather it, a sort of murmuring, which, as if by magic, seemed to proceed from all parts of our boat, now on the sea, now here, now there. At length we found that a very small rope (or cord rather) had been fastened to steady the peak when the boat was at anchor, and being drawn extremely tight with the weight of the sail, it vibrated as the wind freshened. Being on the other tack as we approached, it ceased, and again as we stood off it recommenced its song. The Sirens' island was well named ; for standing in close to observe it, from a strong current setting towards it, the boat was actually attracted so close, that we had only time to tack, and save ourselves from its alluring voice.

" *Wednesday, May* 22*d.*

" Fine, after a threatening night. After breakfast Shelley and I amused ourselves with trying to make a boat of canvas and reeds, as light and as small as possible—she is to be eight and a half feet long, and four and a half broad.

" *Sunday, May* 26*th.*

" Cloudy. Rose at six, and went with Shelley and Maglian to Massa. The landing-place, or rather the beach, which is about three miles from the town, affords no kind of shelter, but where there is a continued sea running. A little to the left of the second gun-battery,

and sublime scenery of the gulf of Spezzia. I
do not write; I have lived too long near Lord

is a shelf running parallel to the beach, at the termination of which
five feet water may be had.   This shelf is indicated by the shortness
and frequency of the surf, and the deep water by a partial cessation of
it.   It is necessary before any effort is made to work her in—to send
a strong sternfast on shore for this purpose, as the current of the
Magra sets forcibly to the eastward, and sweeps her suddenly into the
surf beyond.   We dined at Massa, and left it again at ten minutes past
four, with a strong westerly wind straight in our teeth.   This wind,
(the Ponente as it is called) always sends a damp vapour from the sea,
which gathers into watery clouds on the mountain tops, and generally
sinks with the sun, but strengthens as he declines.   To the landing-
place it is said to be fifteen miles to Lerici.   We left the latter place
at a little past eight and arrived at eleven, and returned in seven
hours.

" Thursday, June 6th.

" Calm.   Left Villa Magni, at five, on our way to Via Reggio.   At
eight the wind sprung up, baffling in all directions but the right one.
At eleven we could steer our course; but at one it fell calm, and left
us like a log on the water, but four miles to windward of Massa.   We
remained there till six; the thunder-clouds gathering on the mountains around, and threatening to burst in squalls; heat excessive.   At
seven rowed into Massa beach—but on attempting to land we were
opposed by the guard, who told us that the head person of the fort (of
two rusty guns) being at Festa, that, as he was not able to read, we
must wait till the former arrived.   Not willing to put up with such
treatment, Shelley told him at his peril to detain us, when the fellow
brought down two old muskets, and we prepared our pistols, which he
no sooner saw we were determined to use, than he called our servant
to the beach, and desiring him to hold the paper about a yard from him,
he suffered two gentlemen who were bathing near the place to explain
who and what we were.   Upon this, the fellow's tone changed from
presumption to the most cowardly fawning, and we proceeded to
Massa unmolested.   Slept at Massa, about three miles inland.

Byron, and the sun has extinguished the glow-worm; for I cannot hope, with St. John, that " *the light came into the world, and the world knew it not.*"

> " *Friday, June 7th.*

" Left Massa at half-past five—a dead calm, the atmosphere hot and oppressive. At eight a breeze sprung up, which enabled us to lie up to Magra Point. Beat round the point and reached home at half-past two.

> " *Wednesday, June 12th.*

" Launched the little boat, which answered our wishes and expectations. She is 86 lbs. English weight, and stows easily on board. Sailed in the evening, but were becalmed in the offing, and left there with a long ground swell, which made Jane little better than dead. Hoisted out our little boat and brought her on shore. Her landing attended by the whole village.

> " *Thursday, June 13th.*

" Fine. At nine, saw a vessel between the straits of Porto Venere. like a man-of-war brig. She proved to be the Bolivar, with Roberts and Trelawny on board, who are taking her round to Livorno. On meeting them we were saluted by six guns. Sailed together to try the vessels—in speed no chance with her, but I think we keep as good a wind. She is the most beautiful craft 1 ever saw, and will do more for her size. She costs Lord Byron £750 clear off and ready for sea, with provisions and conveniences of every kind.

> " *Wednesday, June 19th.*

" Fine. The swell continues, and I am now the more persuaded that the moon influences the tides here, particularly the new moon, on the first week before she makes her appearance. Took the ballast out and hauled the boat on the beach. Cleaned and greased her.

> " *Thursday, June 20th.*

" Fine. Shelley hears from Hunt that he is arrived at Genoa : having sailed from England on the 13th May.

> " *Saturday, June 22d.*

" Calm. Heat overpowering, but in the shade refreshed by the sea breeze. At seven launched our boat, with all her ballast in. She floats three inches lighter than before. This difference is caused, I imagine, by her planks having dried while on shore.

" *Thursday, June 27th.*

" Fine. The heat increases daily, and prayers are offering for rain. At Parma, it is now so excessive that the labourers are forbidden to work in the fields after ten and before five, fearful of an epidemic."

John Dix, *Pen and Ink Sketches of Poets, Preachers, and Politicians* (London, 1846)

This 'Personal Notice' of Shelley appears to be an unusual mixture of the factual and the fictional: factual, in that it is likely that it is based on a real incident; fictional, in that its author is unlikely to have witnessed what he here describes. Indeed, at least one contemporary reviewer noticed that this story of Shelley's angry attempts to get help and shelter for a sick young woman whom he had found on Hampstead Heath was similar to a recollection already published by Leigh Hunt. This reviewer, writing in *The Atheneum* of 5 September 1846, pointed out remarkable similarities between the two accounts of 'Shelley's Hampstead Adventure', and preferred the earlier version. This had appeared in *The Literary Examiner* on 23 August 1823, under the heading 'On the Suburbs of Genoa and the Country about London'. It was anonymous, but was written by Leigh Hunt, and was to be included, practically verbatim, in his *Autobiography*, published in 1850 (see the headnote to extracts from this work in this volume). So, although Dix's memoir has a ring of truth, it is probably a truth that he purloined.

This is all the more probable given the little that we know about Dix. A Bristol surgeon with a hankering to mix with literati, his early forays into print brought accusations of fraudulence. In 1837 he published a *Life of Chatterton* which included a portrait of the poet that Dix claimed to have found in a shop in Bristol. Reviewers believed that he knew it to be a fake (see *DNB* entry). Later he published a 'true' account of the inquest on Chatterton's body which he also claimed to have discovered, and which was also widely believed to be his own invention. Sometimes writing under the pseudonym 'John Ross', sometimes, as here, anonymously, he published several small volumes of reminiscences recording his encounters with (usually minor) literary celebrities, although they also included accounts of meetings with Wordsworth, Coleridge and Southey. The latter two are often mentioned as his companions on visits and outings. Frequently the characters whom he recalled were dead by the time that his recollections were published; his distance from his 'memories' of these meetings was the greater as he had emigrated to America in 1846, the year in which the text below was published.

Dix did know Leigh Hunt. A closely observed description of him is given in Dix's *Pen and Ink Sketches of Eminent English Literary Personages. By a Cosmopolitan* (1850) (pp. 30–1). It may be that Dix derived the story of Shelley's intervention on behalf of the young woman directly from Hunt, rather than from the earlier article. Indeed, he may not have been aware that a version had been published. The anecdote belongs with the other stories of Shelley's generosity that his friends, especially Hunt, liked to tell. It also belongs with all the other somewhat condescending Victorian re-interpretations of the poet's youthful idealism – all the more so, as Dix found it necessary to imagine himself actually witnessing Shelley behaving like a philanthropic 'madman'.

MR. DE QUINCY, in his notes on " Gilfillan's Gallery of Literary Portraits, "says of Percy Bysshe Shelley— " Everything was romantic in his short career, everything wore a tragic interest.   From his childhood he moved through a series of afflictions; always craving for love, loving and seeking to be loved, always he was destined to reap hatred from those with whom life had connected him."   Perhaps the following reminiscence of Shelley may bear out Mr. De Quincy's remarks, so far as the term " romantic" is concerned.

In the last chapter, I have alluded to a Sunday evening interview with Samuel Taylor Coleridge. After quitting his residence, I had crossed the fine fields between Highgate and Hampstead to the latter place, when just entering on the Heath, at rather a late hour, I was startled by a sort of disturbance among a few persons at the door of a large house. Drawing near, I perceived what seemed the lifeless body of a woman, by the imperfect light of one lantern, upheld in a half-sitting posture, with lolling head, by a tall young man, evidently no vulgar brawler by his speech, but in a highly excited state, who seemed disposed to force an entrance with his senseless charge, which two or three men-servants resisted. There was a voice, or more than one, almost screaming from within,—the tall stranger's tones were as high without; all were too busy to have satisfied any inquiry; and in the midst of uproar, the sound of wheels was heard—it was the carriage of the master of the mansion returning home. To him, who seemed astonished at the scene, the friend of the dead or dying woman turned, and detained him on the steps of the carriage, before he could set foot on the ground, pointing at the same time to the female figure. The servants, however, quickly explaining the cause of the turmoil; angry words passed, and he was no nearer to his benevolent object—the introducing his burthen (which he had brought on his back from Heaven knows where,) into the house. Some wine, and restoratives, and volatile essences, and smelling-bottles, were sent out from the dwelling, and I was gratified to find the " suspended animation" of the sufferer itself happily suspended so far as to admit the entrance of a whole glass of wine, her deglutition seeming to me better " than could be expected." It was a young woman in draggled plight, but her features were hardly visible where I stood.

Her humane but unreflecting friend had found her in
a fit, or fainting from illness, and insisted, on the
score of humanity, on the admission *for the night* of
this poor woman into the strange gentleman's house;
so I was informed afterwards.   He forgot that he
himself, being unknown, the inmates might justly
fear that it was a *ruse* to rob the house, concocted
between some " Jack Sheppard" of the day and his
lady ; or even if he could have proved his own respectability, he could not answer for hers.   The air
was no bad aid to recovery from syncope, and every
relief but a lodging was afforded, as I have shown.
This did not content PERCY BYSSHE SHELLEY, for
he it was ; but he vociferated a philippic against the
selfishness of the aristocracy ; he almost wept ; he
stood prophesying downfall to the unfeeling higher
orders ! a servile war ! a second edition, in England,
of the bloody tragedy of the French revolution, and
I know not what more ; the gentleman being at all
this very indignant, and the servants insolently bantering him.   Indeed, one could not well wonder at
this, for his gestures and deportment were like those
of a madman.

Meanwhile, his female *protegé*, finding attention
directed from herself to the parties quarrelling, very
quietly adjusted her drapery, seemingly making up
her mind that no more relief was likely to be forth-
coming ; and I fancied that her tones, when she made
some passing remark, were of the harsh, hoarse,
unfeminine kind, which is soon acquired by those

wretched women who perambulate London streets
after nightfall, in cold and damp weather, when on the
very brink of starvation.

I believe she proved to be one of those characters,
or an impostor, or both—she did not appear to be
drunk, as the servants would have it she was. It was
not until a week afterwards, I heard from a literary
friend living on Hampstead Heath, that this was
Shelley. I know not how he got rid of his reviving
companion, for I left the spot in the midst of his
oration. It was a strong practical illustration of
Shelley's theoretical monomania of philanthropy—
that fine, but preposterous excess of humanity, that
almost drove him melancholy mad over the condition
of man. He wished to make a new world where men
should be angels, and died too soon to learn that he
must take the world as he found it, and perhaps, by
such patient reconciliation to its wretchedness and
errors, he would have found it very tolerable at least.

Just as he desired to force into a quiet household,
the members of which were about to retire to rest, a
suspicious looking stranger who might have plundered
it, he passionately longed to introduce his own darling
theories into society, running all hazards of mischief
incurred by the violent experiment. But his very
error, his ardent desire to better the lot of man, was
surely more Christian in spirit (infidel though he was,)
than the furious zeal of intolerance in those " who
profess and call themselves Christians," which grows
complacent over the sufferings of those who differ

from their infallible selves, even about a dogma—
(perhaps a dogma seeming once false and foolish
even to themselves)—than that horrid diabolical spirit
which dared to pollute a newspaper published in
Christian London with that inhuman yell of pleasure,
over the melancholy end of the most gentle, generous,
highly gifted, *brotherly*-natured being on earth, however mistaken in his noble dream of human perfectibility. These remarks especially refer to a paragraph
that appeared on the occasion of his being drowned·
" Shelley the atheist is drowned at Pisa; he knows
now whether there is a hell or no." Multiplied
examples of such religious zeal would go further to
overturn Christianity in a nation, than all the mournful misgivings, clouds, and shadows of the soul, that
haunted Shelley, Byron, and numbers beside, could
they be daily put forth in all the newspapers of that
nation.

A sort of melancholy beyond that of the poetic temperament seemed to pursue Shelley all his life. His
appearance and manners were very eccentric, though
polished and subdued, except in excited moments.
He went to Charles Richards, the printer in St. Martin's
Lane, when quite young, about the printing a little
volume of Keats' first poems. (I have a copy given
me by Richards.) The printer told me, that he had
never had so strange a visitor. He was gaunt, and
had peculiar starts and gestures, and a way of fixing
his eyes, and his whole attitude for a good while,
like the abstracted apathy of a musing madman.

Thomas Medwin, *The Life of Percy Bysshe Shelley* (London, 1847)

A short time after the publication of his *Shelley Papers* in 1833 (see previous headnote in this volume), Medwin was already collecting materials for a more substantial biography. In 1835 he was in Marlow, interviewing those who had met Shelley when he had stayed there in 1817 (see Lovell, *Captain Medwin*, pp. 282–3). He left for Germany two years later, and thoughts of a Shelley biography must have given way to kinds of writing that his impecuniousness forced on him: between 1837 and 1847 he wrote tales and sketches for English periodicals, and in 1840 became German correspondent for *The Atheneum*. In 1842 he published a novel, *Lady Singleton*. By this time he had begun a relationship with Caroline de Crespigny, an Englishwoman living in Germany. She was the daughter of the Bishop of Norwich and a minor poet. She was also married, though separated from her husband who was in a debtor's prison. Medwin's biographer, Ernest Lovell, notes that in both his novel and his *Life of Shelley* 'he penned bitter and violent outbursts against the state of the divorce laws' (*Captain Medwin*, p. 308).

In 1845, while living in Heidelberg, Medwin began attempting to track down some of Shelley's correspondence, plans for a biography clearly having revived. In the Autumn of that year, he returned to England, and in May 1846 he approached Mary Shelley for help with his proposed *Life*. In her reply, she described herself as 'surprised and pained' to learn of his intentions (Bennett, *Letters*, III, p. 284). Even twenty-four years after Shelley's death (and, it should be noted, two years after Sir Timothy Shelley's death had freed her from her promises to suppress biographical details) she believed that 'the time has not yet come to recount the events of my husband's life'. She told Medwin that the memory of Shelley – 'an angel among his fellow mortals' – had been sufficiently vindicated by her edition of his work, and that a biography 'would wound and injure the living'. 'In these publishing, inquisitive, scandal-mongering days, one feels called upon for a double exercise of delicacy, forbearance – and reserve'. She was sure, she said, that Medwin would shrink from 'dragging private names and private life before the world'.

He showed no such inclination to shrink. 'You tell me that my letter has surpised & pained you. – Why it should pain you I am at a loss to guess, & had thought that it was pretty generally known that I had long been engaged in this work' (Bennett, *Letters*, III, p. 285). He continued to write to Mary

Shelley, pressing her for information. She did not reply, even when his pressure edged into blackmail. In one letter he told her, 'I have found in the Record Office & made extracts of the Proceedings in Chancery regarding Shelley's children which I have deemed an indispensible passage in his Life' (ibid, p. 287). This 'indispensible passage' would include, of course, discussion of the reasons for Harriet Shelley's suicide, and arguments about Shelley's parental unsuitability. Yet, although he saw that these were delicate matters, he could not possibly just suppress his account: 'The book occupied me 8 Months & I have taken an expensive journey (have an expensive journey back) to bring it out & have now disposed of it for £250 – You are too reasonable to ask me poor as I am to make this great sacrifice'. He would be willing to give her the manuscript and promise never to write again about Shelley, but only if she would 'make me some indemnity for the losses I should sustain'. 'As we are going to press immediately, let me have a reply by return of post'. She enclosed his letter in one of her own to Jane Williams Hogg, commenting, 'I think I told you I did not answer his last – nor of course shall I this' (ibid, p. 286).

Medwin's *Life of Percy Bysshe Shelley* appeared in late August or early September 1847. When she saw it advertised in July, Mary Shelley wrote to Leigh Hunt saying that she was sure that it would be 'a most blackguard Publication' and asking him to use his influence 'to prevent *any notice whatever* being taken of it in the Newspapers' (ibid, p. 319). However, she had decided that it would probably not be 'as scandalous as he threatened'. 'Whatever it may be, I shall not read it' (ibid, p. 320). Nor, apparently, did she. Yet, for all Medwin's intrusiveness, his account of what were potentially the most embarrassing parts of Shelley's life was less troubling than she might have expected. On the subject of Harriet Shelley's suicide, for instance, he is keener than he ever was in the *Shelley Papers* to exculpate Shelley entirely (see the third of the extracts below). Though he does now dwell on Shelley's first marriage, it is represented as, from the beginning, a '*mesalliance*' (*Life of Percy Bysshe Shelley*, I, p. 165). The battle for custody of his children does feature – 'a continual canker on the mind of Shelley' (ibid, I, p. 207) – but without inclusion of the arguments that were used to deprive Shelley of custody. And though 'the present Mrs. Shelley, the daughter of Godwin and Mary Wollstonecraft' is mentioned, she appears only after Harriet Shelley's death has been dealt with, travelling to France with Shelley, in the company of 'another lady' (ibid, I, p. 213). He later mentions 'Lord Byron's *liason* with Miss Clara C – ' (ibid, I, p. 280), but is keen to say that 'the Shelleys' were, 'for a long time', not 'privy to it' (ibid, I, p. 283).

As ever, Medwin tries to establish his authority as a biographer by invoking his boyhood friendship with Shelley. He possesses 'data absolutely requisite for tracing Shelley's genius from its first germs up to its maturity, and forming an impartial judgement of his character – data which no one but myself could have supplied, inasmuch as I knew him from childhood' (ibid, I, p. v). In his Preface, Medwin is his usual mixture of humility and boastfulness: he is aware of his 'unworthiness to touch the hem of Shelley's garment', but tells us that he was 'the first to turn the tide of obloquy', so that readers could know the true Shelley (ibid, I, p. viii). To know all, as he claims to do, is to forgive all. 'How painfully interesting is his Life! With so many weaknesses – with so much to pardon – so much to pity – so much to love'. To know the boy who 'loved fairies, genii, giants, and monsters' (see below) is to forgive the idealistic visionary.

The *Life* was Medwin's last word on Shelley – but he planned it otherwise. In 1862, he was back in England and was evidently revising the book (Lovell, *Captain Medwin*, pp. 327–8). He was still at work on this when he died in August 1869. No new edition of *The Life of Percy Bysshe Shelley* appeared.

Youthful feelings are not deep, but the impression of this scene long left a sting behind it ; perhaps Shelley, in brooding over the prediction as to his incapacity for writing Latin verses, then resolved to falsify it, for he afterwards, as will appear by two specimens which I give in their proper place, became a great proficient in the art.

He passed among his schoolfellows as a strange and unsocial being, for when a holiday relieved us from our tasks, and the other boys were engaged in such sports as the narrow limits of our prison-court allowed, Shelley, who entered into none of them, would pace backwards and forwards—I think I see him now—along the southern wall, indulging in various vague and undefined ideas, the chaotic elements, if I may say so, of what afterwards produced so beautiful a, world. I very early learned to penetrate into this soul sublime—why may I not say divine, for what is there that comes nearer to God than genius in the heart of a child ? I, too, was the only one at the school with whom he could communicate his sufferings, or exchange ideas: I was, indeed, some years his senior, and he was grateful to me for so often singling him out for a companion; for it is well known that it is considered in some degree a *condescension* for boys to make intimates of those in a lower form than themselves. Then we used to walk together up and down his favourite spot, and there he would outpour his sorrows to me, with observations far beyond his years, and which, according to his after ideas, seemed to have sprung from an antenatal life. I have often thought that he had these walks of ours in mind, when, in describing an antique group, he says, " Look, the figures are walking with a sauntering and idle pace, and talking to each other as they walk, as you may have seen a younger and an elder boy at school, walking in some grassy spot of the play-ground, with that tender friendship for each other which the age inspires." If Shelley abominated one task more than another it was a dancing lesson. At a Ball at Willis's rooms, where, among other pupils of Sala, I made one, an aunt of mine, to whom the

Letter No. 1, in the Appendix, was addressed, asked the dancing master why Bysshe was not present, to which he replied in his broken English, " Mon Dieu, madam, what should he do here ? Master Shelley will not learn any ting—he is so *gauche*." In fact, he contrived to abscond as often as possible from the dancing lessons, and when forced to attend, suffered inexpressibly.

Half-year after half-year passed away, and in spite of his seeming neglect of his tasks, he soon surpassed all his competitors, for his memory was so tenacious that he never forgot a word once turned up in his dictionary. He was very fond of reading, and greedily devoured all the books which were brought to school after the holidays ; these were mostly *blue* books. Who does not know what blue books mean ? but if there should be any one ignorant enough not to know what those dear darling volumes, so designated from their covers, contain, be it known, that they are or were to be bought for sixpence, and embodied stories of haunted castles, bandits, murderers, and other grim personages—a most exciting and interesting sort of food for boys' minds; among those of a larger calibre was one which I have never seen since, but which I still remember with a *recouché* delight. It was "Peter Wilkins." How much Shelley wished for a winged wife and little winged cherubs of children!

But this stock was very soon exhausted. As there was no school library, we soon resorted, "under the rose," to a low circulating one in the town (Brentford), and here the treasures at first seemed inexhaustible. Novels at this time, (I speak of 1803) in three goodly volumes, such as we owe to the great Wizard of the North, were unknown. Richardson, Fielding, and Smollett, formed the staple of the collec-tion. But these authors were little to Shel-ley's taste. Anne Ratcliffe's works pleased him most, particularly the Italian, but the Rosa-Matilda school, especially a strange, wild romance, entitled "Zofloya, or the Moor," a Monk-Lewisy production, where his Satanic Majesty, as in Faust, plays the chief part, enraptured him. The two novels he afterwards

wrote, entitled " Zastrozzi" and the " Rosicrucian," were modelled after this ghastly production, all of which I now remember, is, that the
principal character is an incarnatian of the devil,
but who, unlike the Monk, (then a prohibited
book, but afterwards an especial favourite with
Shelley) instead of tempting a man and turning him into a likeness of himself, enters into a
woman called Olympia, who poisons her husband homœopathically, and ends by being carried
off very melodramatically in blue flames to the
place of dolor.

" Accursed," said Schiller, " the folly of our
nurses, who distort the imagination with frightful ghost stories, and impress ghastly pictures
of executions on our weak brains, so that involuntary shudderings seize the limbs of a man,
making them rattle in frosty agony," &c. " But
who knows," he adds, " if these traces of early
education be ineffaceable in us ?" Schiller
was, however, himself much addicted to this
sort of reading. It is said of Collins that he
employed his mind chiefly upon works of fiction

and subjects of fancy, and by indulging some
peculiar habits of thought, was universally delighted with those flights of imagination which
pass the bounds of nature, and to which the
mind is reconciled only by a passive acquiescence
in popular tradition. He loved fairies, genii,
giants, and monsters; he delighted to rove
through the meanders of enchantment, to gaze
on the magnificence of golden palaces, to repose
by the waterfalls of Elysian gardens. Milton,
too, in early life, lived in a similar dream-land,
was fond of high romance and gothic diableries;
and it would seem that such contemplations furnish a fit *pabulum* for the development of poetical genius.

This constant dwelling on the marvellous,
had considerable influence on Shelley's imagination, nor is it to be wondered, that at that age
he entertained a belief in apparitions, and the
power of evoking them, to which he alludes frequently in his afterworks, as in Alastor:

> By forcing some lone ghost,
> My messenger, to render up the tale
> Of what we are ;

and in an earlier effusion :

> Oh, there are genii of the air,
> And genii of the evening breeze,
> And gentle ghosts, with eyes as fair
> As star-beams among twilight trees ;

and again in the Hymn to Intellectual Beauty :

> While yet a boy I sought for ghosts, and sped
> Through many a listening chamber, cave and ruin,
> And starlight wood, with fearful steps pursuing
> Hopes of high talk with the departed dead,
> I called on poisonous names with which our youth is
>   fed—
> I was not heard—I saw them not.

After supping on the horrors of the Minerva press, he was subject to strange, and sometimes frightful dreams, and was haunted by apparitions that bore all the semblance of reality. We did not sleep in the same dormitory, but I shall never forget one moonlight night seeing Shelley walk into my room. He was in a state of somnambulism. His eyes were open, and he advanced with slow steps to the window, which, it being the height of summer, was open. I got out of bed, seized him with my arm, and waked him—I was not then aware of the danger of suddenly rousing the sleep-walker. He was excessively agitated, and after leading him back with some difficulty to his couch, I sat by him for some time, a witness to the severe erethism of his nerves, which the sudden shock produced.

This was the only occasion, however, to my knowledge, that a similar event occurred at school, but I remember that he was severely punished for this involuntary transgression. If, however, he ceased at that time to somnambulize, he was given to waking dreams, a sort of lethargy and abstraction that became habitual to him, and after the *accès* was over, his eyes flashed, his lips quivered, his voice was tremulous with emotion, a sort of ecstacy came over him, and he talked more like a spirit or an angel than a human being.

☆ ★ ☆

The next morning at eight o'clock, Shelley and Mr. H., who had been involved in the same fate, set out together for London on the top of the coach ; and with his final departure from the university, the reminiscences of his life at Oxford terminate.

The narration of the injurious effects of this cruel, precipitate, unjust, and illegal expulsion, upon the entire course of his subsequent life, will not be wanting in interest or instruction ; of a period, when the scene was changed from the quiet seclusion of academic groves and gardens, and the calm valley of the silvery Isis, to the stormy ocean of that vast and shoreless world, and to the utmost violence of which, he was, at an early age, suddenly and unnaturally abandoned.

I remember, as if it occurred yesterday, his knocking at my door in Garden Court, in the Temple, at four o'clock in the morning, the second day after his expulsion. I think I hear his cracked voice, with his well-known pipe,—

" Medwin, let me in, I am expelled;" here followed a sort of loud, half-hysteric laugh, and a repetition of the words—" I am expelled," with the addition of, " for Atheism." Though greatly shocked, I was not much surprised at the news, having been led to augur such a close to his collegiate career, from the Syllabus and The Posthumous Works of Peg Nicholson, and the bold avowal of his scepticism. My apprehensions, too, of the consequences of this unhappy event, from my knowledge of Sir Timothy's character, were soon confirmed ; nor was his partner in misfortune doomed to a milder fate. Their fathers refused to receive them under their roofs. Like the old men in Terence, they compared notes, and hardened each other's hearts. This unmitigable hatred was continued down to the deaths of both. One had not the power of carrying his worldly resentment beyond the grave, but the other not only never forgave, or I believe ever would see his eldest son, (for such he was, and presumptive heir to a large fortune) but cut him off, speaking after the manner of the Roman law, with a shilling.

During Shelley's ostracism, he and his friend took a lodging together, where I visited them, living as best they could. Good arises out of evil. Both owe, perhaps, to this expulsion, their celebrity ; one has risen to an eminence as a lawyer, which he might never have attained, and the other has made himself a name which will go down to posterity with those of Milton and Byron.

At this time Shelley was ever in a dreamy state, and he told me he was in the habit of noting down his dreams. The first day, he said, they amounted to a page, the next to two, the third to several, till at last they constituted the greater part of his existence ; realising Calderon's *Sueno e Sueno*. One morning he told me he was satisfied of the existence of two sorts of dreams, the Phrenic and the Psychic ; and that he had witnessed a singular phenomenon, proving that the mind and the soul were separate and differ-

ent entities—that it had more than once happened to him to have a dream, which the mind
was pleasantly and actively developing ; in the
midst of which, it was broken off by a dream
within a dream—a dream of the soul, to which the
mind was not privy ; but that from the effect it
produced—the start of horror with which he
waked, must have been terrific. It is no wonder
that, making a pursuit of dreams, he should have
left some as a catalogue of the phenomena of
dreams, as connecting sleeping and waking.

" I distinctly remember," he says, " dreaming
several times, between the intervals of two or
three years, the same precise dream. It was
not so much what is ordinarily called a dream :
The single image, unconnected with all other
images, of a youth who was educated at the same
school with myself, presented itself in sleep.
Even now, after a lapse of many years, I can
never hear the name of this youth, without the
three places where I dreamed of him presenting
themselves distinctly to my mind." And again,

" in dreams, images acquire associations peculiar to dreaming; so that the idea of a particular house, when it occurs a second time in dreams, will have relation with the idea of the same house in the first time, of a nature entirely different from that which the house excites when seen or thought of in relation to waking ideas."

His systematising of dreams, and encouraging, if I may so say, the habit of dreaming, by this journal, which he then kept, revived in him his old somnambulism. As an instance of this, being in Leicester Square one morning at five o'clock, I was attracted by a group of boys collected round a well-dressed person lying near the rails. On coming up to them, my curiosity being excited, I descried Shelley, who had unconsciously spent a part of the night *sub dio*. He could give me no account of how he got there.

We took during the spring frequent walks in the Parks, and on the banks of the Serpentine. He was fond of that classical recreation, as it appears by a fragment from some comic drama of

Æschylus, of making "ducks and drakes," counting with the utmost glee the number of bounds, as the flat stones flew skimming over the surface of the water; nor was he less delighted with floating down the wind, paper boats, in the constructing of which, habit had given him a wonderful skill. He took as great interest in the sailing of his frail vessels as a ship-builder may do in that of his vessels—and when one escaped the dangers of the winds and waves, and reached in safety the opposite shore, he would run round to hail the safe termination of its voyage. Mr. H. gives a very pleasant account of Shelley's fondness for this sort of navigation, and on one occasion, wearied with standing shivering on the bank of the canal, said, " ' Shelley, there is no use in talking to you, you are the Demiurgus of Plato.' He instantly caught up the whole flotilla he was preparing, and bounding homewards with mighty strides, laughed aloud,—laughed like a giant, as he used to say."

☆ ★ ☆

In looking back to this marriage of Shelley's
with an individual neither adapted to his con-
ditionin life, nor fitted for his companionship by
accomplishments or manners, it is surprising,
not that it should have ended in a separation,

but that for so long a time, (for time is not to be calculated by years,) he should have continued to drag on a chain, every link of which was a protraction of torture.

It was not without mature deliberation, and a conviction common to both, of their utter incapacity of rendering the married state bearable to each other, that they came to a resolve, which, the cold, formal English world, with its conventionalities, under any circumstances short of legally proved infidelity, stamps as a dereliction of duty on the side of the man. Ours is the only country where the yoke of marriage, when it is an iron one, weighs down and crushes those who have once thrown it over their necks. It may be compared to the leaden mantle in the Inferno. It is true that the Roman Catholic religion in some countries, such as Italy and France, except by the express permission, rarely obtained, (though it was in the case of the Countess Guiccioli,) of the Pope, does not allow divorces ; but separations, tantamount to them, constantly take place by mutual agreement, without placing the parties in a false position as regards society. Spain has emancipated herself from the inextricability of the chain. In Poland and Russia remarriages are of daily occurrence. But let us look into Protestant lands, for we are yet Protestants, and we shall find that in most of the states in Germany, nothing is easier than to dissolve the tie. The marriage laws in Prussia are very liberal. In Norway the parties cannot be disunited under three years. In Sweden one year's notice suffices. But with us, not even confirmed insanity is sufficient to dissolve a marriage! Our laws admit of but one ground for divorces, and who with any fine feeling would like to drag through the mire of public infamy, her who had once been dear to him— the mother, perhaps, of his children ? How long will our statute-book continue to uphold this barbarous and unnatural law, on the very doubtful plea, according to Dr. Wheatley and others, that marriage is of divine institution—a law a disgrace to our civilization, the source of more miseries than all " that flesh is heir to ?"

Ill-omened and most unfortunate, indeed, was the union !   He had joined himself to one utterly incapable of estimating his talents—one destitute of all delicacy of feeling, who made his existence

> " A blight and a curse ;"

one who had " a heart, hard and cold,"

> " Like weight of icy stone,
> That crushed and withered his."

It is in his own writings, and from them his life may be drawn as in a mirror, that the best insight is to be found of the character of the first Mrs. Shelley.   He calls her

> " A mate with feigned sighs,
> Who fled in the April hour."

In the bitterness of his soul, he exclaims :

> " Alas ! that love should be a blight and snare
> To those who seek all sympathies in one ;
> Such one I sought in vain,—then black despair,
> The shadow of a starless night, was thrown
> Over the world in which I moved alone."

And we find her in the Epipsychidion thus alle-
gorised :

" Then one whose voice was venomed melody
    Sate by a well, under blue nightshade-bowers.
    Her touch was as electric poison—flame
    Out of her looks into my vitals came,
    And from her living cheeks and bosom flew
    A killing air that pierced like honeydew
    Into the core of my green heart, and lay
    Upon its leaves, until as *hair grown grey*
    On a young brow, they hid its unblown prime
    With ruins of unseasonable time."

The beautiful fragment on Love which appeared
originally in the Athenæum, and may be found
among the Prose Works, proves with what a
lacerated heart he poured out his love, in aspi-
ration for an object who could sympathise
with his ; and how pathetically does he paint his
yearning after such a being, when he says :—

" I know not the internal constitution of other
men. I see that in some external attributes
they resemble me ; but when misled by that
appearance, I have thought to appeal to something in common, and unburthen my inmost

soul, I have found my language misunderstood, like one in a desert and savage land. The more opportunities they have afforded me for experience, the wider has appeared the interval between us, and to a greater distance have the points of sympathy been withdrawn. With a spirit ill fitted to sustain such proofs, trembling and feeble through its tenderness, I have everywhere sought sympathy, and found only repulse and disappointment." And after a description of what he did seek for in this union, he adds, " Sterne says, that if he were in a desert, he would love some cypress." No sooner is this want or power dead, than man becomes the living sepulchre of himself, and what yet survives is the mere wreck of what he was."

The disappointed hopes that gave birth to this eloquence of passion, may be more than conjectured. To love, to be beloved, became an insatiable famine of his nature, which the wide circle of the universe, comprehending beings of such inexhaustible variety and stupendous magnitudo of excellence, appeared too narrow and confined to satiate.

It was with the recollection of these withered feelings, that he afterwards, in his desolation, thus apostrophised a wild swan that rose from a morass in the wilderness :—

" *Thou* hast a home,
Beautiful bird ! thou voyagest to thine home !
Where thy sweet mate will twine her downy neck
With thine, and welcome thy return with eyes
Bright in the lustre of their own fond joy."

The example of the most surpassing spirits that have ever appeared, Dante, Shakspeare, and Milton, proves that poets have been most unfortunate in their matrimonial choice, not, as Moore would endeavour to establish, because such are little fitted for the wedded state, but because in the condition of society, which Shelley characterises as " a mixture of feudal savageness and imperfect civilisation," women are unequally educated, and are hence on an inequality with men, and unable to form a just estimate

of their genius, or to make allowances for those
eccentricities of genius, those deviations from the
standard of common minds which they have set
up.

Mr. Moore is a married man, and as such his
opinion is worth quoting, though I cannot agree
with him in his deductions, that poets should
never marry. He says, that " those who have
often felt in themselves a call to matrimony,
have kept aloof from such ties, and the exercise
of the softer duties and rewards of *being amiable*
reserved themselves for the high and hazardous
chances of being great." He adds, that " to
follow poetry, one must forget father and mother,
and cling to it alone ;" and he compares marriage to " the wormwood star, whose light
filled the waters on which it fell, with bitterness."

But if a poetical temperament unfits *man*kind
from entering into the married state, and if
those who possess it are to be debarred from
those sympathies which are the only leaven in

the dull dough of mortality,—if they are to be
made responsible for all the misery of which
such unions are often the fertile source, it would,
in his view, be only fair to consider that poetesses
are to be visited with a similar measure of reproach ; and, alas ! how many of the female
writers of this and former days, have found marriage anything but a bed of roses ! Charlotte
Smith, L. E. L., Mrs. Hemans, Mrs. Norton,
stand at the head of the long catalogue with us.
In America, Mrs. Butler and Mrs. Sigourney.
In Germany, beginning with the Karschin, their
name is legion. In France, two examples suffice
—De Stael and George Sand. Were they alone
to blame ? Who will venture to cast the first
stone at them ? Surely not Mr. Moore, who is
too *gallant*, and too fond of the sex, to raise a
whisper against their good fame ? Lady Byron
also is a poetess,—good, bad, or indifferent,—
and on the principle, that acids neutralise each
other, that remarkable case ought, on the principle of the homœopathic system, to have proved

an exception to the general rule, instead of being the rule itself.

The last name calls up a whole Iliad of woes. Yes, true it is, and "pity 'tis, 'tis true," that two other poets must be added to the number of the unfortunates,—two the greatest of our times, Shelley and Byron. The world has long given up troubling itself about the causes of the domestic differences of "the three gods of poetry," as they soon will about those of the two last; ceasing, ere long, to canvass Byron's feverish existence, to speculate on his intrigues, or to think about Lady Byron or the first Mrs. Shelley, more than it now does la Signora Dante, Mrs. Shakspeare, or Mrs. Milton. But there was this difference in the destinies of the two poet-friends : Byron was separated from Lady Byron, by Lady Byron, against his will, after a short trial,—less than twelve months ; Shelley and his wife parted by mutual consent, after a much longer test of the incompatibility of their tempers, and incapacity to render the duration

of their union anything but an intolerable
tyranny ; and it must not be forgotten, too, that
isolation from society made them perfectly acquainted with each other's dispositions and
habits and pursuits.   In both cases the world
ranged itself on the weaker side ; but if Byron
had his measure of reproach and defamation,
Shelley was persecuted with a more exceeding
amount of obloquy, driven from his native land,
placed under a ban by his friends and relations,
and considered, as he says, " a rare prodigy of
crime and pollution."   It is true that a tragic
circumstance arose out of his separation, over
which I could have wished, were it possible, to
draw a veil ; but as that may not be, and though
by an anachronism, as I shall have no further
occasion to mention the first Mrs. Shelley, now
advert to it.—She cut off her days by suicide.

De Quincey, speaking of this dreadful event,
says, " It is one chief misery of a beautiful young
woman separated from her natural protector, that
her desolate situation attracts and stimulates the

calumnies of the malicious. Stung by these calumnies," he adds, " and oppressed, as I have understood, by the loneliness of her abode, she threw herself into a pond and was drowned." Now it must be remembered that the separation took place in the beginning of 1813, and that the catastrophe occurred nearly three years afterwards,—a long period for her to have brooded over her wrongs or misfortunes before they produced such frightful effects. Her fate was a dreadful misfortune to her who perished, and him who survived.

I have said in the " Shelley Papers," that it is impossible to acquit Shelley of all blame in this calamity. From his knowledge of her character, he must have been aware, as has been said by another, " that she was an individual unadapted to an exposure to principles of action, which if even pregnant with danger when of self-organisation, are doubly so when communicated to minds altogether unfit for their reception ;" and he should have kept an eye over her conduct.

But I have since had reason, from undoubted authority, to change this opinion. On their separation, he delivered her back into the hands of her father and eldest sister. He told them almost in these words, that "his wife and himself had never loved each other; that to continue to drag on the chain, would only be a protraction of torture to both, and that as they could not legally extricate themselves from the Gordian knot, they had mutually determined to cut it. That he wished her all happiness, and should endeavour by sympathy with another, to seek it himself. He added, that having received no fortune with her, and her father being in easy circumstances, he was not at the moment able to make her the allowance he could wish; that the sum he then gave her, was all he could command; that as the child was an infant, he should for a time leave it in their hands, and care; but should at a more advanced age, claim it; and they parted on good terms, though not without reproaches and harsh language from the father.

Little or no blame as to the melancholy catastrophe that succeeded, could therefore be imputed to Shelley; *that* must fall on her relations, who with the knowledge of her character
and conduct, by advice, or other measures, ought
to have watched over both. Having once
confided her to their superintendence, he might
consider, with many others similarly circumstanced, that his responsibility was over. That
he did not do so, his compunction, which brought
on a temporary derangement, proves. De Quincey,
in speaking of this circumstance, to which I alluded in a memoir of Shelley, says that the mention of it arose from a wish to gratify a fugitive
curiosity in strangers ; and adds, that it appears
from the peace of mind which Shelley is reported
afterwards to have recovered for a time, that he
could not have had to reproach himself with any
harshness or neglect as contributing to the
shocking catastrophe. Without any compunc-
tious visitings, however, morbidly sensitive as
he was, well might it painfully excite him. Such

a fate as hers, could not be contemplated even by
the most indifferent stranger, without a deep sympathy; much more must the shock have come
home to the feelings of one so intimately connected with her.

☆ ★ ☆

A singular circumstance occurred to Shelley,
which, after his death, I talked over with Lord
Byron at Pisa—for he was equally acquainted
with the story, as told to us mutually, and
which he more than once made a subject of conversation with me.

The night before his departure from London,
in 1814, he received a visit from a married lady,
young, handsome, and of noble connections, and
whose disappearance from the world of fashion,
in which she moved, may furnish to those curious
in such inquiries a clue to her identity.

The force of love could not go further, when

a person so richly endowed, as he described her, could so far forget the delicacy of her sex, and the regard due to the character of woman, as to make the following confession :—" I have long known you in your Queen Mab. In the empassioned tenderness of your picture of Ianthe, I have read and understood the heart that inspired it. In your uncompromising passion for liberty— your universal and disinterested benevolence— your aspiring after the amelioration of the state of mankind, and the happiness of your species, and more than all, in your sentiments respecting the equality of conditions, and the unfettered union between the sexes,—your virtues, removed from all selfish considerations, and a total disregard of opinion, have made you in my eyes the *beau ideal* of what I have long sought for in vain. I long for the realisation of my day and night dream. I come, after many vain and useless struggles with myself, to tell you that I have renounced my husband, my name, my family and friends ; and have resolved, after mature deliberation, to follow you through the world, to attach my fortune, which is considerable, to yours, in spite of all the obloquy that be cast on me."

Shelley was at that moment, on the eve, as I have said, of parting from England with one to whom he was devotedly attached ;—none but a perfect gentleman, (and none, as admitted by Byron, surpassed him in the qualities of one,) could have succeeded in acting with a high-born and high-bred woman, a becoming part in such an arduous scene. He could not but feel deep gratitude—admiration without bounds, for that enthusiastic and noble-minded person ; who had not shrunk from a confession—a confession hard indeed for her to have made—an avowal of a love that must have cost her so many struggles to have clothed in words.

I shall not endeavour to throw the whole of this interview into dialogue, or to paint the language in which he extricated himself from the painful task of relieving both, by the explanation of his engagement ; or in what terms he endeavoured to infuse a balm into her wounded soul, to soothe her hurt pride,—I had almost said, hurt affection.

Shelley detailed to me at much length, and with more than his accustomed eloquence, their parting ; and though I do not pretend to remember his exact words, their purport has not es- caped me.

She said she had listened to his explanation with patience ; she ought to listen to it with re- signation.   The pride of a woman—the pride of a —————————, might have revolted to acknow- ledge, much more to feel, that she loved in vain ; she said she might conceal all that she endured —might have died under the blow she had re- ceived—-that death-blow to her heart, and all its hopes, or might spurn him from her with dis- dain, chase him from her presence with rage, or call to her aid revenge, that cicatrice to a wounded spirit ; but that she would rise superior to such littleness.   Had she been base—very base—she should no longer have esteemed him,—that she

believed herself worthy of him, and would not
prove she was otherwise, by leaving on his memory a feeling towards her of contempt. You are
rich, she added, in resources; comfort at least by
your pity a heart torn by your indifference;
lend me some aid to endure the trial you have
brought upon me—the greatest it is allotted to
one of us to endure—blighted hopes—a life of
loneliness—withered affections.

" Cold indeed would have been my heart," said
Shelley to her, " if I should ever cease to acknowledge with gratitude, the flattering, the undeserved preference you have so nobly confessed to
me; the first, the richest gift a woman can
bestow—the only one worth having. Adieu, may
God protect, support, and bless you! Your
image will never cease to be associated in my
mind with all that is noble, pure, generous,
and lovely. Adieu."

Thus they parted; but this meeting, instead of extinguishing, only seemed to fan the
flame in the bosom of the *Incognita.* This in-

fatuated lady followed him to the Continent.
He had given her a clue to his place of destination, Geneva. She traced him to Secheron—
used to watch him with her glass in his water
parties on the lake. On his return to England,
he thought she had long forgotten him ; but her
constancy was untired. During his journey to
Rome and Naples, she once lodged with him at
the same hotel, *en route*, and finally arrived at
the latter city the same day as himself.

He must have been more or less than man,
to have been unmoved by the devotedness of this
unfortunate and infatuated lady. At Naples, he
told me that they met, and when he learnt
from her all those particulars of her wanderings,
of which he had been previously ignorant ; and
at Naples—she died.

Mrs. Shelley, who was unacquainted with all
those circumstances, in a note to the poems
written at Naples, describes what Shelley suffered during this winter, which she attributes
solely to physical causes, but which had a far

deeper root. " Constant and poignant physical sufferings," she says, "exhausted him, and though he preserved the appearance of cheerfulness, and often enjoyed our wanderings in the environs of Naples, and our excursions on its sunny sea, yet many hours were passed when his thoughts, shadowed by illness, became gloomy, and then he escaped to solitude, and in verses which *he hid from me, from fear of wounding me*, poured forth morbid, but too natural bursts of discontent and sadness ;" and she adds, " *that it was difficult to imagine that any melancholy he shewed, was aught but the effect of the constant pain to which he was a martyr.*"

Had she been able to disentangle the threads of the mystery, she would have attributed his feelings to more than purely physicial causes. Among the verses which she had probably never seen till they appeared in print, was " The Invocation to Misery," an idea taken from Shakspeare—Making Love to Misery, betokening his soul lacerated to rawness by the tragic event.

above detailed—the death of his unknown adorer.
The state of his mind must indeed have been
bordering on madness—hanging on the devouring edge of mental darkness, when he could give
utterance to those wonderful lines :—

> "Hasten to the bridal bed !
> Underneath the grave 'tis spread !
> In darkness may our love be hid,
> Oblivion be our coverlid !
> We may rest, and none forbid.
>
> Kiss me ! Oh ! thy lips are cold !
> Round my neck thine arms enfold,
> They are *soft*—yet chill and dead,
> And thy tears upon my heart,
> *Burn like points of frozen lead.*"

The epithet *soft* in the last stanza, and *burn
like points of frozen lead*, surpass in the subli-
mity of horror, anything in our own, or any
other language.

* ★ ☆

I found one of the great remedies for my bodily
sufferings this winter, in Shelley's reading.   No
one ever gave such emphasis to poetry.   His
voice, it is true, was a cracked soprano, but in
the variety of its tones, and the intensity of
feeling which he displayed in the finest passages,
produced an effect almost electric.   He had just
completed the Witch of Atlas, which in lyrical
harmony and fancy, must be considered as a
masterpiece.   It may be called, if you will, an
ignis fatuus of the imagination, and was objected to by Mrs. Shelley as such,—a censure that
hurt Shelley, and called forth his lines to her, in
which he compares it with Peter Bell, which according to Wordsworth, cost him nineteen years
in composing and retouching—Shelley's Witch
of Atlas, not so many hours. How well does he,

in these exculpatory verses, characterise the difference between her and Ruth, or Lucy, the first " in a light vest of flowing metre," and Peter, " proud as a dandy with his stays hanging on his wiry limbs, a dress,

Like King Lear's looped and windowed raggedness."

Shelley used to chuckle, with his peculiar hysterical cachination, over this Nursery Tale of Wordsworth's, and to repeat the stanza which forms the motto of his own Peter Bell, with tears running down his laughing eyes, as he gave utterance to,—

> This is Hell, and in this smother,
> All are damnable and damned,
> Each one damning, damns the other,
> They are damned by one another,
> By no other are they damned.

No one was more sensible to the merits of Wordsworth than himself, but he no longer, as proved by his sonnet, looked upon him as his ideal. He was still an enthusiastic admirer

MEDWIN: LIFE OF SHELLEY 183

of his early productions, and particularly of
his inimitable lines in blank verse to his
sister, which satiate with excess of sweetness ;
but these, he said, were written in the golden
time of his genius, and he held with Byron,
as Nursery Rhymes, the Idiot Boy, and many
others. The Excursion I never heard him mention ; and he thought that Wordsworth had left
no perfect specimen of an Ode,—that he always
broke down when he attempted one. Collins he
thought a cold, artificial writer ; and of all the
Odes in our language, he most preferred Coleridge's on the French Revolution, beginning,
" Ye Clouds," which he used to thunder out with
marvellous energy, as well as the Ancient Mariner.

Leigh Hunt, *The Autobiography of Leigh Hunt; with Reminiscences of Friends and Contemporaries* 3 vols (London, 1850)

When Leigh Hunt composed his *Autobiography*, he was a different writer from the hard-up father of a young family (he had seven children) whom the publisher Colburn had once pressured into turning a would-be autobiography into a book centred on Byron (see the headnotes to Leigh Hunt, *Lord Byron and Some of His Contemporaries* in both this volume and in C. Hart, *Byron*). Not only was his *Autobiography* written with some of the reflectiveness of age (Hunt was by this time in his mid-sixties), but also with the belated mellowness that came with his achievement of modest financial security. On Sir Timothy Shelley's death in 1844, Sir Percy Shelley, Mary Shelley's son, honoured his father's wish to settle an income (£120 per annum) on Hunt, and in 1847 he was granted a civil list pension of £200 per annum. He was established as a Victorian man of letters, and was over the keen money worries by which he and, perhaps even more, his wife Marianne had been dominated for most of their married life. At last, reflectiveness was in order.

During the 1830s and early 1840s, Hunt had scraped a living from his literary essays, his plays (although some of these never reached the stage), and his editorial work. The latter included *Imagination and Fancy; or Selections from the English Poets. Illustrative of those First Requisites of Their Art*, published in 1844, which reprinted highlights of Shelley's poetry, and most of all of verse from *The Cenci* (which had, of course, been dedicated to Hunt). Throughout this period he found himself borrowing money – often, it would seem, to pay off earlier debts. His correspondence with Mary Shelley, in particular, is full of the talk of money, and often of her regrets that she can hardly help him until her father-in-law dies. (Though she did clearly give the Hunts some money: a letter to Marianne Hunt of 21 November 1843, for example, speaks of the impossibility of raising funds 'on a post-orbit on Sir Tim's life', yet adds that at Christmas 'you will have £10 as usual' (Bennett, *Letters*, III, 106).) While Mary Shelley was sympathetic in her responses to Hunt and his wife (it was often the latter who actually wrote the begging letters), it is clear from her correspondence with Claire Clairmont that their endless requests for assistance did sometimes nettle her.

However, it is striking that when Mary Shelley embarked on the publication of Shelley's poetry and prose, it was Leigh Hunt to whom she seemed to turn for encouragement and advice. Their correspondence was only intermittent, but in 1839 and 1840, when she was editing Shelley's work, she wrote more letters to Hunt than to anyone else. Soon after Shelley's death, she indicated that she considered Hunt the best possible biographer of her husband, and it is clear that, despite the difficulties of their relationship, he kept his status in her eyes as Shelley's best advocate. We might think her confidence borne out by the extracts below, in which Hunt combines robust exoneration (Shelley's courtship of Mary Godwin was 'in the spirit of Milton's doctrines' – Milton having argued for allowing married couples to agree to separate) with subtle untruths (he says that Shelley separated from Harriet 'after the birth of two children', when in fact he had left her while she was pregnant with their son, Charles). Hunt's Shelley is a young man caused pain by his sympathies for others, so he retells the story of his helping an ailing young woman whom he has found one winter's night on Hampstead Heath (see headnote to J. Dix, *Pen and Ink Sketches of Poets, Preachers, and Politicians*, in this volume). Comparison with the first extract from *Lord Byron and Some of His Contemporaries* (pp. 36–40) will show that he also relies on some of his own earlier material. All is dedicated to making clear that, as he says in the concluding passage below on the poet's character, Shelley aroused consternation or antagonism only because he was a 'spirit' too good for this world.

Had he now behaved himself pardonably in the eyes of the conventional in those days (for it is wonderful in how short a time honest discussion may be advanced by a court at once correct and un-bigoted, and a succession of calmly progressing ministries ; and all classes are now beginning to suffer the wisdom of every species of abuse to be doubted), Shelley would have gone to London with the resolution of sowing his wild oats, and becoming a decent

member of society; that is to say, he would have
seduced a few maid-servants, or at least haunted the
lobbies, and then bestowed the remnant of his constitution upon some young lady of his own rank in
life, and settled into a proper church-and-king man
of the old leaven, perhaps a member of the Society for
the Suppression of Vice.   This used to be the proper
routine, and gave one a right to be didactic.   Alas!
Shelley did not do so; and bitterly had he to repent,
not that he did not do it, but that he married while
yet a stripling, and that the wife whom he took was
not of a nature to appreciate his understanding, or,
perhaps, to come from contact with it uninjured in
what she had of her own.   They separated by mutual
consent, after the birth of two children.   To this
measure his enemies would hardly have demurred;
especially as the marriage was disapproved by the
husband's family, and the lady was of inferior rank.
It might have been regarded even as something like
making amends.   But to one thing they would
strongly have objected.   He proceeded, in the spirit
of Milton's doctrines, to pay his court to another
lady.   I wish I could pursue the story in the same
tone; but now came the greatest pang of his life.
He was residing at Bath, when news came to him
that his wife had destroyed herself.   It was a heavy
blow to him; and he never forgot it.   For a time, it
tore his being to pieces; nor is there a doubt, that,

however deeply he was accustomed to reason on the nature and causes of evil, and on the steps necessary to be taken for opposing it, he was not without remorse for having no better exercised his judgment with regard to the degree of intellect he had allied himself with, and for having given rise to a premature independence of conduct in one unequal to the task.   The lady was greatly to be pitied; so was the survivor.   Let the collegiate refusers of argument, and the conventional sowers of their wild oats, with myriads of unhappy women behind them, rise up in judgment against him!   Honester men will not be hindered from doing justice to sincerity wherever they find it; nor be induced to blast the memory of a man of genius and benevolence, for one painful passage in his life, which he might have avoided, had he been no better than his calumniators.

On the death of this unfortunate lady, Shelley married the daughter of Mr. Godwin, and resided at Great Marlow in Buckinghamshire, where my family and myself paid him a visit, and where he was a blessing to the poor.   His charity, though liberal, was not weak.   He inquired personally into the circumstances of his petitioners; visited the sick in their beds (for he had gone the round of the hospitals on purpose to be able to practise on occasion), and kept a regular list of industrious poor, whom he assisted with small sums to make up their accounts.

Here he wrote the *Revolt of Islam,* and *A Proposal for putting Reform to the Vote through the Country.* He offered to give a tenth part of his income for a year towards the advancement of the project. He used to sit in a study adorned with casts, as large as life, of the Vatican Apollo and the celestial Venus. Between whiles he would walk in the garden, or take strolls about the country, or a sail in a boat, a diversion of which he was passionately fond. Flowers, or the sight of a happy face, or the hearing of a congenial remark, would make his eyes sparkle with delight. At other times he would suddenly droop into an aspect of dejection, particularly when a wretched face passed him, or when he saw the miserable-looking children of a lace-making village near him, or when he thought of his own children, of whom he had been deprived by the Court of Chancery. He once said to me during a walk in the Strand, " Look at all these worn and miserable faces that pass us, and tell me what is to be thought of the world they appear in ? " I said, " Ah, but these faces are not all worn with grief. You must take the wear and tear of pleasure into the account ; of secret joys as well as sorrows ; of merry-makings, and sittings-up at night." He owned that there was truth in the remark. This was the sort of consolation which I was in the habit of giving him, and for which he was thankful, because I was sincere.

As to his children, the reader perhaps is not aware, that in this country of England, so justly called free on many accounts, and so proud of its " Englishman's castle,"—of the house, which nothing can violate,—a man's offspring can be taken from him to-morrow, who holds a different opinion from the Lord Chancellor in faith and morals. Hume's, if he had any, might have been taken. Gibbon's might have been taken. The virtuous Condorcet, if he had been an Englishman and a father, would have stood no chance. Plato, for his *Republic*, would have stood as little; and Mademoiselle de Gournay might have been torn from the arms of her adopted father Montaigne, convicted beyond redemption of seeing farther than the walls of the Court of Chancery. That such things are not done often, I believe: that they may be done oftener than people suspect, I believe also; for they are transacted with closed doors, and the details are forbidden to transpire.

Queen Mab, Shelley's earliest poetical production, written before he was out of his teens, and regretted by him as a crude production, was published without his consent. Yet he was convicted from it of holding the opinion which his teachers at the University had not thought fit to reason him out of. He was also charged with not being of the received opinions with regard to the intercourse of the sexes; and his children, a girl and boy, were taken from him. They were transferred to the care of a clergyman of the Church of England. The circumstance deeply affected Shelley : so much so, that he never afterwards dared to trust himself with mentioning their names in my hearing, though I had stood at his side throughout the business; probably for that reason.* Shelley's manner of life suffered greatly in its repute from this circumstance. He was said to be keeping a scraglio at Marlow; and his friends partook of the scandal. This keeper of a seraglio, who, in fact, was extremely difficult to please in such matters, and who had no idea of love unconnected with sentiment, passed his days like a hermit. He rose early in the morning, walked and read before breakfast, took that meal sparingly, wrote and studied the greater part of the morning, walked and read again, dined on vegetables (for he took neither meat nor wine), conversed

---

* The boy is since dead; and Shelley's son by his second wife, the daughter of Godwin, has succeeded to the baronetcy. It seldom falls to the lot of a son to have illustrious descent so heaped upon him; his mother a woman of talents, his father a man of genius, his grandfather, Godwin, a writer secure of immortality; his grandmother, Godwin's wife, the celebrated Mary Wollstonecraft : and on the side of his father's ancestors he partakes of the blood of the intellectual as well as patrician family of the Sackvilles. But, what is most of all, his own intelligent and liberal nature makes him worthy of all this lustre.

with his friends (to whom his house was ever open), again walked out, and usually finished with reading to his wife till ten o'clock, when he went to bed. This was his daily existence. His book was generally Plato, or Homer, or one of the Greek tragedians, or the Bible, in which last he took a great, though peculiar, and often admiring interest. One of his favourite parts was the book of Job. The writings attributed to Solomon he thought too Epicurean, in the modern sense of the word; and in his notions of St. Paul, he agreed with the writer of the work entitled *Not Paul but Jesus.* For his Christianity, in the proper sense of the word, he went to the gospel of St. James, and to the Sermon on the Mount by Christ himself, for whose truly divine spirit he entertained the greatest reverence. There was nothing which embittered his enemies against him more than the knowledge of this fact. His want of faith, indeed, in the letter, and his exceeding faith in the spirit, of Christianity, formed a comment, the one on the other, very formidable to those who choose to forget what scripture itself observes on that point.*

As an instance of Shelley's extraordinary generosity, a friend of his, a man of letters, enjoyed from him at that period a pension of a hundred a year, though he had but a thousand of his own; and he

---

* " For the letter killeth, but the spirit giveth life."

continued to enjoy it till fortune rendered it superfluous. But the princeliness of his disposition was
seen most in his behaviour to another friend, the
writer of this memoir, who is proud to relate, that
with money raised by an effort, Shelley once made
him a present of fourteen hundred pounds, to extricate him from debt. I was not extricated, for
I had not yet learned to be careful : but the
shame of not being so, after such generosity, and
the pain which my friend afterwards underwent
when I was in trouble and he was helpless, were the
first causes of my thinking of money-matters to any
purpose. His last sixpence was ever at my service,
had I chosen to share it. In a poetical epistle written
some years afterwards, and published in the volume
of *Posthumous Poems,* Shelley, in alluding to his
friend's circumstances, which for the second time
were then straitened, only made an affectionate lamen-
tation that he himself was poor ; never once hinting
that he had already drained his purse for his friend.

To return to Hampstead.—Shelley often came
there to see me, sometimes to stop for several days.
He delighted in the natural broken ground, and in
the fresh air of the place, especially when the wind
set in from the north-west, which used to give him
an intoxication of animal spirits. Here also he swam
his paper boats on the ponds, and delighted to play
with my children, particularly with my eldest boy,

the seriousness of whose imagination, and his sus-
ceptibility of a "grim" impression (a favourite epithet
of Shelley's), highly interested him. He would play
at "frightful creatures" with him, from which the
other would snatch "a fearful joy," only begging him
occasionally "not to do the horn," which was a way
that Shelley had of screwing up his hair in front, to
imitate a weapon of that sort. This was the boy
(now a man of forty, and himself a fine writer) to
whom Lamb took such a liking on similar accounts,
and addressed some charming verses as his "favourite
child." I have already mentioned him during my imprisonment.

As an instance of Shelley's playfulness when he
was in good spirits, he was once going to town with
me in the Hampstead stage, when our only companion was an old lady, who sat silent and still after
the English fashion. Shelley was fond of quoting a
passage from *Richard the Second*, in the commencement of which the king, in the indulgence of his
misery, exclaims—

"For Heaven's sake, let us sit upon the ground,
    And tell sad stories of the death of kings.

Shelley, who had been moved into the ebullition by
something objectionable which he thought he saw
in the face of our companion, startled her into a
look of the most ludicrous astonishment, by suddenly
calling this passage to mind, and in his enthusiastic

tone of voice, addressing me by name with the first two lines. "Hunt!" he exclaimed,—

> " For Heaven's sake, let us sit upon the ground,
> And tell sad stories of the death of kings."

The old lady looked on the coach-floor, as if expecting to see us take our seats accordingly.

But here follows a graver and more characteristic anecdote. Shelley was not only anxious for the good of mankind in general. We have seen what he proposed on the subject of Reform in Parliament, and he was always very desirous of the national welfare. It was a moot point when he entered your room, whether he would begin with some half-pleasant, half-pensive joke, or quote something Greek, or ask some question about public affairs. He once came upon me at Hampstead, when I had not seen him for some time; and after grasping my hands into both his, in his usual fervent manner, he sat down, and looked at me very earnestly, with a deep, though not melancholy, interest in his face. We were sitting with our knees to the fire, to which we had been getting nearer and nearer, in the comfort of finding ourselves together. The pleasure of seeing him was my only feeling at the moment; and the air of domesticity about us was so complete, that I thought he was going to speak of some family matter, either his or my own, when he asked me, at the close of an intensity of pause, what was "the amount of the National Debt."

I used to rally him on the apparent inconsequentiality of his manner upon those occasions, and he was always ready to carry on the jest, because he said that my laughter did not hinder my being in earnest.

But here follows a crowning anecdote, into which I shall close my recollections of him at this period. We shall meet him again in Italy, and there, alas! I shall have to relate events graver still.

I was returning home one night to Hampstead after the opera. As I approached the door, I heard strange and alarming shrieks, mixed with the voice of a man. The next day, it was reported by the gossips that Mr. Shelley, no Christian (for it was he who was there), had brought some "very strange female" into the house, no better, of course, than she ought to be. The real Christian had puzzled them. Shelley, in coming to our house that night, had found a woman lying near the top of the hill, in fits. It was a fierce winter night, with snow upon the ground; and winter loses nothing of its fierceness at Hampstead. My friend, always the promptest as well as most pitying on these occasions, knocked at the first houses he could reach, in order to have the woman taken in. The invariable answer was, that they could not do it. He asked for an outhouse to put.

her in, while he went for a doctor. Impossible! In vain he assured them she was no impostor. They would not dispute the point with him; but doors were closed, and windows were shut down. Had he lit upon worthy Mr. Park, the philologist, he would assuredly have come, in spite of his Calvinism. But he lived too far off. Had he lit upon my friend, Armitage Brown, who lived on another side of the heath; or on his friend and neighbour, Dilke; they would, either of them, have jumped up from amidst their books or their bed-clothes, and have gone out with him. But the paucity of Christians is astonishing, considering the number of them. Time flies; the poor woman is in convulsions; her son, a young man, lamenting over her. At last my friend sees a carriage driving up to a house at a little distance. The knock is given; the warm door opens; servants and lights pour forth. Now, thought he, is the time. He puts on his best address, which anybody might recognise for that of the highest gentleman as well as of an interesting individual, and plants himself in the way of an elderly person, who is stepping out of the carriage with his family. He tells his story. They only press on the faster. " Will you go and see her?" " No, sir; there's no necessity for that sort of thing, depend on it. Impostors swarm everywhere: the thing cannot be done; sir, your conduct is extraordinary." " Sir," cried Shelley, assuming a very different manner, and forcing the flourishing householder to stop out of astonishment, " I am sorry to say that *your* conduct is *not* extraordinary; and if my own seems to amaze you, I will tell you something which may amaze you a little more, and I hope will frighten you. It is such men as you who madden the spirits and the patience of the poor and wretched; and if ever a convulsion comes in this country (which is very probable), recollect what I tell you :—you will have your house, that you refuse to put the miserable woman into, burnt over your head." " God bless me, sir! Dear me, sir!" exclaimed the poor frightened man, and fluttered into his mansion. The woman was then brought to our house, which was at some distance, and down a bleak path; and Shelley and her son were obliged to hold her till the doctor could arrive. It appeared that she had been attending this son in London, on a criminal charge made against him, the agitation of which had thrown her into the fits on her return. The doctor said that she would have perished, had she lain there a short time longer. The next day my friend sent mother and son comfortably home to Hendon, where they were known, and whence they returned him thanks full of gratitude.

* ★ *

The remains of Shelley and Mr. Williams were burnt after the good ancient fashion, and gathered into coffers. Those of Mr. Williams were subsequently taken to England. Shelley's were interred at Rome, in the Protestant burial-ground, the place which he had so touchingly described in recording its reception of Keats. The ceremony of the burning was alike beautiful and distressing. Trelawney, who had been the chief person concerned in ascertaining the fate of his friends, completed his kindness by taking the most active part on this last mournful occasion. He and his friend Captain Shenley were first upon the ground, attended by proper assistants. Lord Byron and myself arrived shortly afterwards. His lordship got out of his carriage, but wandered away from the spectacle, and did not see it. I remained inside the carriage, now looking on, now drawing back with feelings that were not to be witnessed.

None of the mourners, however, refused themselves the little comfort of supposing, that lovers of books and antiquity, like Shelley and his companion, Shelley in particular with his Greek enthusiasm, would not have been sorry to foresee this part of their fate. The mortal part of him, too, was saved from corruption; not the least extraordinary part of his history. Among the materials for burning, as many of the gracefuller and more classical articles as could be procured—frankincense, wine, &c.—were not forgotten; and to these Keats's volume was added. The beauty of the flame arising from the funeral pile was extraordinary. The weather was beautifully fine. The Mediterranean, now soft and lucid, kissed the shore as if to make peace with it. The yellow sand and blue sky were intensely contrasted with one another : marble mountains touched the air with coolness; and the flame of the fire bore away towards heaven in vigorous amplitude, waving and quivering with a brightness of inconceivable beauty. It seemed as though it contained the glassy essence of vitality. You might have expected a seraphic countenance to look out of it, turning once more before it departed, to thank the friends that had done their duty.

Yet see how extremes can appear to meet even on occasions the most overwhelming; nay, even by reason of them; for as cold can perform the effect of fire, and burn us, so can despair put on the monstrous aspect of mirth. On returning from one of our visits to this sea-shore, we dined and drank; I mean, Lord Byron and myself;—dined little, and drank too much. Lord Byron had not shone that even in his cups, which usually brought out his best qualities. As to myself, I had bordered upon

emotions which I have never suffered myself to indulge, and which, foolishly as well as impatiently,
render calamity, as somebody termed it, " an affront,
and not a misfortune." The barouche drove rapidly
through the forest of Pisa. We sang, we laughed,
we shouted. I even felt a gaiety the more shocking, because it was real and a relief. What the
coachman thought of us, God knows ; but he helped
to make up a ghastly trio. He was a good-tempered
fellow, and an affectionate husband and father ; yet
he had the reputation of having offered his master to
kill a man. I wish to have no such waking dream
again. It was worthy of a German ballad.

Shelley, when he died, was in his thirtieth year.
His figure was tall and slight, and his constitution
consumptive. He was subject to violent spasmodic
pains, which would sometimes force him to lie on the
ground till they were over ; but he had always a
kind word to give to those about him, when his
pangs allowed him to speak. In this organization, as
well as in some other respects, he resembled the German poet, Schiller. Though well-turned, his shoulders
were bent a little, owing to premature thought and
trouble. The same causes had touched his hair with
grey ; and though his habits of temperance and exercise gave him a remarkable degree of strength, it
is not supposed that he could have lived many years.
He used to say that he had lived three times as

long as the calendar gave out; which he would prove, between jest and earnest, by some remarks on Time,

"That would have puzzled that stout Stagyrite."

Like the Stagyrite's, his voice was high and weak. His eyes were large and animated, with a dash of wildness in them; his face small, but well-shaped, particularly the mouth and chin, the turn of which was very sensitive and graceful. His complexion was naturally fair and delicate, with a colour in the cheeks. He had brown hair, which, though tinged with grey, surmounted his face well, being in considerable quantity, and tending to a curl. His side-face upon the whole was deficient in strength, and his features would not have told well in a bust; but when fronting and looking at you attentively, his aspect had a certain seraphical character that would have suited a portrait of John the Baptist, or the angel whom Milton describes as holding a reed "tipt with fire." Nor would the most religious mind, had it known him, have objected to the comparison; for, with all his scepticism, Shelley's disposition was truly said to have been anything but irreligious. A person of much eminence for piety in our times has well observed, that the greatest want of religious feeling is not to be found among the greatest infidels, but among those who never think of religion except as a matter of course. The leading feature of Shelley's character may be said to have been a natural piety. He was pious towards nature, towards his friends, towards the whole human race, towards the meanest insect of the forest. He did himself an injustice with the public, in using the popular name of the Supreme Being inconsiderately. He identified it solely with the most vulgar and tyrannical notions of a God made after the worst human fashion ; and did not sufficiently reflect, that it was often used by a juster devotion to express a sense of the great Mover of the universe. An impatience in contradicting worldly and pernicious notions of a supernatural power, led his own aspirations to be misconstrued ; for though, in the severity of his dialectics, and particularly in moments of despondency, he sometimes appeared to be hopeless of what he most desired—and though he justly thought that a Divine Being would prefer the increase of benevolence and good before any praise, or even recognition of himself (a reflection worth thinking of by the intolerant), yet there was in reality no belief to which he clung with more fondness than that of some great pervading " Spirit of Intellectual Beauty ;" as may be seen in his aspirations on that subject. He assented warmly to an opinion which I expressed in the cathedral at Pisa, while the organ was playing, that a truly divine religion might yet be established, if charity were really made the principle of it, instead of faith.

Music affected him deeply. He had also a delicate perception of the beauties of sculpture. It is not one of the least evidences of his conscientious turn of mind, that, with the inclination and the power to surround himself in Italy with all the graces of life, he made no sort of attempt that way; finding other use for his money, and not always satisfied with himself for indulging even in the luxury of a boat. When he bought elegancies of any kind, it was to give away. Boating was his great amusement. He loved the mixture of action and repose which he found in it; and delighted to fancy himself gliding away to Utopian isles, and bowers of enchantment. But he would give up any pleasure to do a deed of kindness. Indeed, he may be said to have made the whole comfort of his life a sacrifice to what he thought the wants of society.

Temperament and early circumstances conspired to make him a reformer, at a time of life when few begin to think for themselves; and it was his misfortune, as far as immediate reputation was concerned, that he was thrown upon society with a precipitancy and vehemence, which rather startled them with fear for themselves, than allowed them to become sensible of the love and zeal that impelled him. He was like a spirit that had darted out of its orb, and found itself in another world. I used to tell him that he had come from the planet Mercury. When I heard of the catastrophe that overtook him, it seemed as if this spirit, not sufficiently constituted like the rest of the world, to obtain their sympathy, yet gifted with a double portion of love for all living things, had been found dead in a solitary corner of the earth, its wings stiffened, its warm heart cold; the relics of a misunderstood nature, slain by the ungenial elements.

NOTE

p. 201, l. 3: 'That would have puzzled that stout Stagyrite': a misquoted line from 'Written at Cambridge', by Charles Lamb. He had written of 'Truths, which . . . half had staggere'd that stout Stagirite'. The 'Stagirite' is Aristotle.

Thomas Jefferson Hogg, *The Life of Percy Bysshe Shelley* (London, 1858)

The Dedication of Hogg's biography of Shelley proclaims not only the work's aims, but also the identity of its sponsor. It is dedicated to Lady Jane Shelley, the wife of Sir Percy Shelley, the poet's son. It was she, writes Hogg, 'at whose request the delicate and difficult task was undertaken of giving a full and authentic account of a life innocent and imaginative' – the life of 'THE DIVINE POET'. Lady Shelley had married Sir Percy in 1848, and had committed herself to preserving and celebrating Shelley's memory (see the headnote in this volume to her *Shelley Memorials*). In 1855 she summoned Hogg to the family home that her husband had bought after their marriage, Boscombe Manor, near Bournemouth. Hogg was to be given access to the Shelley manuscripts, especially letters, in their possession in order that he produce a proper biography of the poet. This would be an authoritative rebuttal of Medwin's *Life*, but was also made necessary by the many forgeries of Shelley's (and Byron's) correspondence that appeared in the 1850s (some of which Sir Percy and Lady Shelley themselves purchased: see Norman, pp. 191–2). When Tennyson's friend Francis Palgrave recognized one of Shelley's supposed letters to Godwin, published in a volume with an introduction by Browning, as having been copied from an article about Florentine art written by his father in 1840, speculation about Shelley's correspondence became public (Norman, p. 190). This meant that Shelley's private life was again under scrutiny. Hogg, the former radical who was now not only a respectable lawyer but also an Anglican and a Tory, was judged to be the right person to produce the authorized, incontestable account of Shelley's life and relationships.

   In a sense, Hogg was all too well qualified to write about Shelley. His own involvement in the poet's life before he left England for Italy led him to slant his account and falsify his documents in ways that have seemed both daring and shameful to scholars. For all Shelley's memoirists, both his marriages were tender topics. For Hogg, matters were all the more difficult given his own relationships with first Harriet Shelley and then Mary Godwin. Hogg had rushed to join Shelley and Harriet when they eloped to Edinburgh to marry in August 1811, and stayed with the couple for the month or so they spent in Scotland after their marriage. In October 1811 the three of them travelled to York, where Hogg was studying law. After ten days, Shelley, who was preoccupied by financial difficulties, left his wife and Hogg in order to travel to Sussex to persuade his family to restore the allowance that was being witheld from him. In his absence, Hogg made unreciprocated advances to Harriet, who told Shelley when he returned to York at the end of October. After a traumatic 'interview' between Shelley and Hogg, the Shelleys hurriedly left York in the company of Eliza Westbrook, Harriet's sister, without telling Hogg (see Holmes, pp. 89–93, for a succinct account of the episode). They moved temporarily to Keswick, in the Lake District. In his *Life*, Hogg explains that 'their whole souls' were 'possessed by the Genius of the Lakes' and that the Shelleys' rushed departure was a consequence of their reading Wordsworth's 'picturesque' descriptions of the area. He says that they 'strongly urged' him to accompany them (in fact they left him a note pretending that they had travelled to Richmond), but that he had had to forsake their company for his 'professional duties' (*The Life of Percy Bysshe Shelley*, II, pp. 9–10). Soon 'a passionate exchange of letters' took place between Shelley and Hogg (Holmes, p. 91). It was a correspondence that Hogg was only able to use in the *Life* by dint of some imaginative doctoring.

'You know the implicit faith I had in him, the unalterableness of my attachment, the exalted thoughts I entertained of his excellence. Can you then conceive that he would have attempted to *seduce my wife*, that he should have chosen the very time for this attempt when I most confided in him, when I least doubted him'. Thus Shelley wrote to his friend Elizabeth Hitchener shortly after his arrival in Keswick (Jones, *Letters*, I, p. 168). 'Virtue has lost one of its defenders – vice has gained a proselyte. The thought makes me shudder' (ibid, p. 169). In the letters that he sent to Hogg, Shelley can be heard grappling rather awkwardly with his own attachment to what he calls 'the Godwinian plan' (ibid, p. 184), but what we might call the ideal of 'free love'. 'You have been led by false reasoning, or as I conjecture more probable, real feeling, into a great & terrible mistake', Shelley wrote to his friend (ibid, p. 167). Certainly Hogg had mistaken Harriet's feelings, and, in the course of their heated correspondence, Shelley clutched at this in his attempts to explain his own feelings: 'I am not jealous. – Heaven knows that if the possession of Harriet's person, or the attainment of her love was all that intervened between our meeting again tomorrow, willingly would I return to York, aye willingly, to be happy thus to prove my friendship' (ibid, p. 184). Harriet, however, remained, he said, 'prejudiced' against such a possibility.

All this was concealed in Hogg's *Life*. Hogg did what he could with the letters that he received from Shelley; by a labour of cutting and rewriting he managed to produce a correspondence passionate only in the friendship that Shelley professes for him. Some of the genuine material, however, must have seemed to him to have been too good for omission, for he made one of Shelley's more feverish letters into a 'Fragment of a Novel' by changing

Harriet's name to 'Charlotte' and claiming that it was part of Shelley's projected sequel to Goethe's *The Sorrows of Young Werther* (Hogg, *Life*, II, p. 56). (Some of Hogg's other adaptations are described in Cameron, III, pp. 24–34.) 'I knew Shelley more intimately than any man', is Hogg's claim (see the fourth of the extracts below). The publication of a good deal of previously unknown correspondence was necessary evidence for this claim (and material with which his volumes might trump Medwin). Yet Hogg had his own reputation to worry about. He had faced problems with the use of correspondence from the earliest phases of his friendship with Shelley. In the first volume of the *Life* letters were censored in order to mute the antireligious enthusiasm of his youth and entirely to conceal his epistolary courtship of Shelley's sister Elizabeth (whom he had never met). As K.N. Cameron observes in his discussion of this censorship, Hogg was concerned to depict himself as 'the rational, sophisticated young man of the world trying to direct the eccentric footsteps of his poet friend' (Cameron, II, p. 669).

An attachment to Harriet is evident in the *Life*, even if Hogg's readers would have known nothing of the truth of it. She is constantly 'the good Harriet' (eg *Life*, II, p. 265); he frequently expresses his admiration and sympathy for her. It is her sister Eliza – 'lovely yet spiteful' (ibid, p. 371) – who is to be blamed for any strains in the Shelleys' marriage. Harriet is nervous and has a preoccupation with suicide which is seen to pre-date her separation from her husband, but she receives much more sympathetic treatment than Lady Jane Shelley appears to have bargained for. Hogg was not to be given the opportunity to describe her death. Volume II of his biography ends with Shelley meeting Mary Godwin (see below), only a few pages after it has described the Shelleys happily together in their 'paradise in Bracknell' (ibid, p. 530). The account is clearly awkward for Hogg, who wanders off into the story of an 'innocent' adolescent 'adventure' of his own with a girl whom he encountered reading William Godwin's memoir of Mary Godwin's mother, Mary Wollstonecraft. It is where his biography had to end, for, when they had read it, Sir Percy and Lady Jane Shelley demanded the return of all documents, effectively preventing the composition of the further two volumes that Hogg's title page had promised. In a letter to Leigh Hunt shortly after the book's publication in April 1858, Sir Percy Shelley called it 'the most disgusting book that can be conceived' (cited in Norman, p. 198).

Hogg therefore never had to deal with Shelley's adultery, or his own relationship with Mary when she was living with Shelley and Claire Clairmont in London in 1815. The correspondence between Hogg and Mary at this time chronicles an intimacy that often sounds like that of lovers (nicknames and enclosed locks of hair), although there is no evidence of a sexual relationship (Mary was heavily pregnant at the time). The intimacy was evidently encouraged by Shelley (see Bennett, *Letters*, I, pp. 6–16). It is difficult, of course, not to notice how readily Hogg was drawn to any woman who was drawn to Shelley, and not to suspect that his eventual relationship with Jane Williams had something to do with her earlier closeness to the poet. It is notable also that, no doubt to the horror of Shelley's son and his wife, Hogg's incomplete biography relishes Shelley's attractiveness to women: 'Bysshe, as has been asserted already, and will be declared again and again, was invariably an especial favourite of the fair sex; he was cherished as the apple of beauty's eye' (*Life*, II, p. 275). Perhaps there was not such a contradiction between Hogg's breathy celebration of 'the Divine Poet' and his hopes for sexual relationships with the women who loved him.

PREFACE.

───•───

"What are they, if they knew their calling high,
  But crushed perfumes exhaling to the sky ;
  Or weeping clouds, that but awhile are seen,
  Yet keep the earth, they haste to, bright and green !"

" THIS is a motto befitting all the illustrious unhappy. But it is too presumptuous an one for me
to use, though it bears some affinity to the strange
world I fabricate about me, and to the destiny I
conceive to be marked out for me. By his works
Shelley has raised himself to that well deserved
height, that must make him the wonder and glory
of future ages. But his private life would remain
unknown, and many of his most excellent qualities
sleep with his beloved ashes, if I did not fulfil the
task of recording them. His life was in every way
romantic, and to have been united to him, and to
have been the partner of his fortunes for eight

years, has imbued my thoughts and existence with romance ; it is, indeed, only by help of this feeling, and the indulgence that I give to it, that I can in any way endure the prolongation of life marked out for me in the eternal decrees. Strip my situation of its adventitious colours, and what is it ? Alas ! in the drear visitings of cold reality, in moments of torpid despair, I but too truly feel what it is. I am one cut off in the prime of life from hope, enjoyment, and prosperity. The prospect was smiling, but I am in a desert ; the rock on which I built my hopes has crumbled away ; my bark of refuge is wrecked, while the universal flood from out of the opened windows of Heaven is emptying its tempests upon me. But I extricate myself from these ideas, and arranging myself in the majesty of the imagination, I give other, and, in very truth, truer names to the circumstances around me. I was the chosen mate of a celestial spirit. He has left me, and I am here to learn wisdom until I am fitted to join him in his native sky. I was the mother of lovely children ; they are gone to attend him in his beautiful mansion ; yet, in pity, they have left one behind them to adorn my loneliness. Methinks my calling is high ; I am to justify his ways ; I am to make him beloved to all posterity.

My goal is fixed. The prize waves in the air, and I am ready for the course. Who are the spectators? Sits umpire Love, and all the virtues attend him. There Wisdom and Self-approbation sit enthroned, and the wise and good of all ages throng around. These are to be my future companions, and I must work hard to make myself worthy of so illustrious a company. Thus I would make my misery my crown; my solitude, my select society of worthies; my tears, the ambrosia conferring immortality; my eternal regrets, the nectar to inebriate me, until I arrive at the divine impulse, which is to inspire my tale. I am a priestess, dedicated to his glorification by my sufferings; the bride of the dead, my daily sacrifice is brought to his temple, and under the shadow of his memory I watch each sun to its decline."

* * * * *

"I shall write his Life, and thus occupy myself in the only manner from which I can derive consolation. It will be a task that may bring some balm. What, though I weep? What, though each letter costs a tear? All is better than inaction—not forgetfulness—that never is, but an inactivity of remembrance. Well, I shall commence my task; commemorate the virtues of the only creature on

earth worth loving or living for, and then, may be,
I may join him; moonshine may be united to her
planet, and wander no more, a sad reflection of all
she loved on earth. And you, my own boy, I am
about to begin a task which, if you live, will be an
invaluable treasure in after-times. I must collect
my materials; and then, in the commemoration of
the divine virtues of your father, I shall fulfil the
only act of pleasure there remains for me, and be
ready to follow you, my child, if you should leave
me, my task being accomplished."

*   *   *   *   *

"One of Shelley's characteristics was, that although he had a passion for the reformation of
mankind, and though he sacrificed both himself and
his possessions to the general and individual view
of this question, yet he was never a dupe; his pene-
tration was wonderful; he read a man's character in
his look, his gesture, his phraseology, and I never
knew him mistaken. I would rely on his judgment
of a character, as on omniscience, and most certainly was never deceived, when others might think
that the ingratitude and treachery which he often
encountered, might have disappointed him. It did
not, for he expected it. He acted from the fixed
principle of endeavouring to benefit and improve

each person with whom he had communion; and his chief method to achieve the latter was to make the person satisfied with himself. He was right: the constant benevolence of manner and action to which this system gave rise, and from which he never deviated, except on the most pressing necessity of self-defence; this amenity of manner awoke an enthusiasm of love, that of force amended and exalted his friends; and that mind must have been cold and depraved which did not experience this necessary result from his sensibility united to his urbanity."

So far Mrs. Shelley has written, but not farther, except a few scraps, which have been inserted at the commencement of this work. The following letter will best explain the motives and the necessity of her silence, and will fully justify it:—

41, PARK STREET, *Dec.* 11, 1838.

DEAR JEFFERSON,

J—— has told you, I suppose, that I am about to publish an Edition of Shelley's Poems. She says, you have not a " Queen Mab." Yet have you not? Did not Shelley give you one—one of the first printed? If you will lend it me, I shall be so very much obliged; and I will return it safely when the book is printed.

Will you lend me your "Alastor" also? It will not go to the printer; I shall only correct the press from it.

Sir Timothy forbids Biography, under a threat of stopping the supplies. What could I do then? How could I live? And my poor boy! But I mean to write a few Notes appertaining to the history of the Poems. If you have any of Shelley's letters, mentioning his poetry, and would communicate them, I should be glad, and thank you.

I am ever truly yours,

MARY W. S.

To T. J. H., Temple.

The Notes appeared, together with the "Poetical Works of Percy Bysshe Shelley," not long after the date of this letter. They are exceedingly valuable, and have been read with interest and delight. Be silent, or starve! The prohibition is certainly hard: harder than all things; harder than all hard things; harder than all hard things put together, and hardened into one superlatively hard thing. The poor widowed dove was forbidden to lament her lost mate; the consolation of bewailing and celebrating him was denied her on pain of

death. The brother poets have told us, that
Philomela was treated with barbarous cruelty, yet
perpetual silence was not enjoined ; and every
returning summer we hear the nightingale re-ite-
rating anew her plaintive, love-lorn sorrows in
woods and groves. But we must restrain our
indignation. Let us be just. The author of the
injunction did not know how severe it was. He
never felt as an enthusiastic biographer feels ; he
never glowed with generous desire to vindicate
aspersed, but unsullied, honour, to maintain the
just claims of transcendant genius. So that a man
had an abundant share of the creature comforts, or
at least a competent maintenance, he had all that
could be wished for ; everything else was sentiment, illusion, affectation : such, no doubt, was his
honest and intimate conviction. Thus, a certain
would-be Junius—a person as incapable of
writing the celebrated work which he laboured to
father upon himself, as was the proud jackdaw of
producing peacocks' feathers,—is reported to have
said to his daughter, as she stood weeping by her
mother's coffin : " Come, come, screw her down,
screw her down ; let us have no snivelling here ! "
It might be unfair to assert that the fellow was a
brute ; he was, probably, only a man destitute of

the ordinary feelings of humanity, who was really unable to comprehend how so trivial a matter as the death of a beloved parent could be the cause to a child of unaffected grief, of genuine, gushing tears. If the bereaved lady—illustrious in her parentage, illustrious in herself and in her works, and most illustrious through her union with the divine Poet—had been permitted to complete the narrative which she had begun, she would have given to the world a precious volume, a book more golden than gold. During the eight years that she was the partner of his fortunes, her account of a life, in every way romantic, would have been inestimable. To esteem or to extol the genius and character of Shelley too highly is impossible; consequently, even her partiality and affection, however excessive, could never have offended against truth and verisimilitude. The earlier, and perhaps the more interesting, portion of a wild and wondrous tale could only have been told by her at second-hand from the relations of others. It was my good fortune to see much of Shelley,—to know more of him, indeed, on the whole, than any one; and, therefore, I have constantly been pointed at as "the person best qualified for such an undertaking."

* ★ ☆

ONE morning, a few days after I made Shelley's acquaintance, I was at his rooms, and we were reading together, two Etonians called on him, as they were wont to do; they remained a short time conversing with him.

"Do you mean to be an Atheist here, too, Shelley?" one of them inquired.

"No!" he answered, "certainly not. There is no motive for it; there would be no use in it; they are very civil to us here; they never interfere with us; it is not like Eton."

To this they both assented. When his visitors were gone, I asked him what they meant. He told me that at Eton he had been called Shelley the Atheist; and he explained to me the true signification of the epithet. This is the substance of his explanation :—

All persons who are familiar with public schools, are well aware that there is a set of nicknames, many of them denoting offices, as the Pope, the

Bishop, the Major, the General, the Governor, and the like, and these are commonly filled by successive generations. At Eton, but at no other school, that I ever heard of, they had the name and office of Atheist; but this usually was not full, it demanded extraordinary daring to attain to it; it was commonly in commission, as it were, and the youths of the greatest hardihood might be considered as boys commissioners for executing the office of Lord High Atheist.

Shelley's predecessor had filled the office some years before his time; he also was called Blank the Atheist, we must say, for I have forgotten his name. The act of Atheism, in virtue of which he obtained the title, was gross, flagrant, and downright.

A huge bunch of grapes, richly gilded, hung in front of " The Christopher," as the sign, or in aid of the sign, of the inn. This the profane young wretch took down one dark winter's night, and suspended at the door of the head-master of his day. In the morning, when he rushed out in the twilight to go to chapel, being habitually too late, and always in a hurry, he ran full butt against the bunch of grapes, which was at least as big as himself, a little man. From this it is evident that the word Atheist was used by the learned at Eton, not in a modern, but in an ancient and classical sense, meaning an Antitheist, rather than an Atheist; for an opposer and contemner of the gods, not one who denies their existence.

Capaneus, Salmoneus, the Cyclops, and the other strong spirits of the olden time, were termed ἄθεοι, because they insulted and defied their deities; not because they doubted, or denied, that they existed.

The gods of Eton were the authorities of the school; nobody ever denied the existence of Old Keate, but many a lad of pluck did everything in his power to torment the old boy; and amongst these Shelley was conspicuous; he held the fulminating Jove in scorn, and despised his birchen thunderbolts.

It was for contumaciously setting the old tree on fire, of which we have spoken, that he first obtained the full title of Shelley the Atheist, which he held and enjoyed so long as he remained at school.

Two or three Eton boys called another day, and begged their former schoolfellow to curse his father and the king, as he used occasionally to do at school. Shelley refused, and for some time persisted in his refusal, saying that he had left it off; but as they continued to urge him, by reason of their importunity he suddenly broke out, and delivered, with vehemence and animation, a string of execrations, greatly resembling in its absurdity a papal anathema; the fulmination soon terminated in a hearty laugh, in which we all joined. When we were alone, I said :

" Why, you young reprobate, who in the world taught you to curse your father—your own father ? "

" My grandfather, Sir Bysshe, partly ; but principally my friend, Dr. Lind, at Eton. When anything goes wrong at Field Place, my father does nothing but swear all day long afterwards. Whenever I have gone with my father to visit Sir Bysshe, he always received him with a tremendous oath, and continued to heap curses upon his head so long as he remained in the room."

Sir Bysshe being Ogygian, gouty, and bed-ridden, the poor old baronet had become excessively testy and irritable ; and a request for money instantly aggravated and inflamed every symptom, moved his choler, and stirred up his bile, impelling him irresistibly to alleviate his sufferings by the roundest oaths.

The grandson gave me some choice specimens of his grandfather's male and nervous eloquence in that peculiar department of oratory. Dr. Lind communicated to Shelley a taste for chemistry and chemical experiments, as has been before stated ; the mild, the amiable, the gentle Dr. Lind, also taught his young pupil how to deal damnation round the land.

Shelley invariably spoke with respect, regard, and

gratitude of Dr. Lind, and of the injuries which the Doctor had received, whatever they might be, with indignant sympathy. He used to go to tea with the meek and benevolent physician at Eton ; and after tea they used to curse King George the Third, for the Doctor had really been, or firmly believed that he had been, cruelly wronged by that pious and domestic, but obstinate and impracticable, monarch.

After a light and digestible repast of tea—made by the daughter, or niece, of the Doctor, with a proper regard, doubtless, for the nervous system, and of bread and butter prepared upon sanatory principles, the butter being thinly superinduced upon bread, the stalest that could be procured, or of the same bread lightly toasted, and to be taken without any condiment—the execrations began.

After the salubrious meal, the good old Doctor proceeded solemnly to launch the greater excommunication against the father of his people, who, he thought, had acted like a step-father to himself, and the rest joined in the condemnatory rite : in what precise form of words Miss Lind chimed in, I never heard. From cursing the father of his people, it was an easy and natural transition to curse his own natural father.

The diræ, as they were recited before me once, and once only, were of a peculiar character, differing much from ordinary execrations, and they operated, if at all, demoniacally, by devoting their object to the evil spirits and infernal gods; whatever else might be the effect of these curses, they certainly did not shorten life, either in the case of the excommunicated monarch, or of his liege man, old Timotheus. The denunciations at Oxford were plainly a joke; of the estimable, but angry Doctor's vehement scolding, without having heard him, it would be unfair to form any judgment. Shelley had a decided inclination for magic, demonology, incantations, raising the dead, evoking spirits and devils, seeing ghosts, and chatting familiarly with apparitions, which led him to interesting reading, and curious and amusing investigations; it is probable that he picked up, or improved, these medieval fancies at the physician's sober board. One thing at least is certain, the denial of the existence of gods, and devils, and spirits, if it was to be found in him at all, was only to be found in his words and arguments; practically, his turn of mind was towards superstition, by no means towards irreligion and materialism.

* ★ ☆

Shelley went every morning himself, before breakfast, to the post-office for his letters, of which he
received a prodigious number; and he used to
bring back with him splendid plates of virgin honey.
I never saw such fine honeycombs before or since,
and it was delicious. Shelley was for the most part
indifferent to food, to all meats and drinks, but he
relished this honey surprisingly: so much did he
enjoy it, that he was almost offended when I said,
exquisite though it was, it was a shame to eat it.;
wantonly to destroy, merely to flatter the palate,
so beautiful and so wonderful a structure, was

as barbarous as it would be to devour roses and lilies. It was far too great a marvel to be eaten; it should only be looked at, kept entire, to be admired. It approaches cannibalism to feed on it; indeed, it is too like eating Harriet! I think you would eat Harriet herself!

" So I would, if she were as good to eat, and I could replace her as easily!"

" Oh! fie, Bysshe!" the young lady exclaimed, who inclined somewhat to my heresy, feasting her eyes with the honeycomb, and declaring it was quite a pity to eat it: this the greedy poet said was tiresome.

> " The sound of the church-going bell
> These valleys and rocks never heard."

Since the Reformation they had never heard it; and in this particular Presbyterian Edinburgh, so far advanced in enlightened wisdom, secular and ecclesiastical, afforded us a strong contrast to our poor, ignorant, benighted Popish Oxford.

After breakfast on Sunday, a verbal announcement was made to us by our landlord himself: " They are drawing nigh unto the kirk!"

On looking from the windows, we saw the grave Presbyterians, with downcast looks, like conscience-stricken sinners, slowly crawling towards their place of gathering. We were admonished—

for Shelley said, one Sunday, " Let us go and take a walk "—that it was not lawful to go forth to walk purposely and avowedly on the Sabbath, a day of rest and worship ; but if a man happen to find himself in the streets casually, he may walk a little with perfect innocence, only it is altogether unlawful to go out from his door with the mind of taking a walk of pure pleasure.

After this serious and edifying warning we sometimes casually found ourselves without the house on a Sunday, and walked about a little, as we believed, innocently.

We were taking such a harmless stroll, by mere accident, in Princes Street; Bysshe laughed aloud, with a fiendish laugh, at some remark of mine.

"You must not laugh openly, in that fashion, young man," an ill-looking, ill-conditioned fellow said to him. " If you do, you will most certainly be convened !"

"What is that?" asked Shelley, rather displeased, at the rude interpellation.

"Why; if you laugh aloud in the public streets and ways on the Christian Sabbath, you will be cast into prison, and eventually banished from Scotland."

The observance of the Sabbath in North Britain, as I have been credibly informed, has been, since the year of the comet, like the manufacture of hats in England, decidedly improved, both articles being now much lighter, and less oppressive.

I once asked the way to some place in Edinburgh of a staid old gentlewoman: "I am going the same road in part, and I will attend you."

We proceeded leisurely along together; she con-versed gravely, but affably: How do you like this; how that; "How do you like our public worship?"

"I have not assisted at it yet."

"Oh! but you must; you must go and hear Dr. Mac Quisquis; he is a fine preacher; an accomplished divine; he wrestles most powerfully with Satan, every Sabbath morn!"

I promised my obliging conductress to go and witness these spiritual struggles with a ghostly enemy; but I could not redeem a pledge somewhat rashly given, for I did not know in what arena this powerful gymnast fought. I did not even catch the name of the accomplished divine. One Sabbath morn, however, when we were again advised that they were drawing nigh unto the Kirk, Shelley and myself boldly resolved to draw nigh also; the lovely Harriet would not accompany us, alleging, and with some probability, that the wearisome perform-ances would give her a head-ache. We joined the scattered bands, which increased in number as we advanced, creeping with them for a considerable distance. We reached a place of worship, and entered it with the rest; it was plain, spacious, and gloomy. We suffered ourselves rather incautiously to be planted side by side, on a bench in the middle of the devout assembly, so that escape was impossible. There was singing, in which all, or almost all, the congregation joined; it was loud, and discordant, and protracted. There was praying, there was . preaching,—both extemporaneous. We prayed for all sorts and conditions of men, more particularly for our enemies. The preacher discoursed at a prodigious length, repeating many times things that were not worthy to be said once, and threatening us much with the everlasting punishments, which, solemnly and confidently, he declared were in store for us. I never saw Shelley so dejected, so desponding, so despairing; he looked like the picture of perfect wretchedness; the poor fellow sighed piteously, as if his heart would break. If they thought that he was conscience-stricken, and that his vast sorrow was for his sins, all, who observed him, must have been delighted with him, as with one filled with the comfortable assurance of eternal perdition. No one present could possibly have comprehended the real nature of his acute sufferings,—could have sympathized in the anguish and agony of a creature of the most poetic temperament that ever was bestowed, for his weal or his woe, upon any human being, at feeling himself in the most unpoetic position in which he could possibly be placed. At last, after expectations many times disappointed of an approaching deliverance, and having been repeatedly deceived by glimpses of an impending discharge, and having long endured that sickness of heart caused by hopes deferred, the tedious worship actually terminated.

We were eagerly pressing forward to get out of our prison, and out of the devout crowd, but a man in authority pushed us aside :

"Make way for the Lord Provost and the Bellies!"

We stood on one side for a while, that the civic dignitaries might pass. My friend asked, in a whisper, what in the world the man meant ? I informed him that a Provost is a Mayor, and that a Belly (Baillie) is Scotch for an Alderman.

It was a consolation to the poor sufferer to laugh once more. It had seemed to him in his captivity that his healthful function had ceased for ever.

We made the best of our way homewards, and at a brisker pace than the rude apostle of the north, John Knox, would have approved of, discussing the wonderful advantages of a ritual, and their comfortless, inhuman church music.

Acknowledging the superiority of our chapels, churches, and cathedral in Oxford, and the vast benefits of written sermons, after having just had painful experience how tedious a thing it was to listen to an extemporaneous discourse; and, moreover, how distressing for the hearer to have to sit and wonder what monstrous extravagance, what stupid and preposterous absurdity the heavy orator, with no succour at hand, would utter next.

The malicious Harriet laughed at our sufferings, and made herself merry with the deep dejection of her husband.

We were never tempted to enter the Kirk again. Satan must very shortly prevail, if he could only be kept under, by our presence, at such powerful wrestlings!

Yet were we, poor Oxford scholars, predestined to undergo another trial of the same kind, but less severe, and far more brief,—sharp, though short. It was notified to us one Sunday evening, as we were sitting together after dinner, that "They are drawing nigh unto the Catechist,—children and domestics must attend."

We had discovered that little Christie was going, and as we already knew something of her temporal concerns, ("oh! the kittle!") we were curious to learn a little about her spiritual condition. Accordingly, we followed her at a distance.

At the first notification, Bysshe, to my surprise, exclaimed, "Let us go!"

Harriet sought to dissuade him, and earnestly, as if she thought we were going to a place where he would probably have his throat cut. But persuasion availed not. We followed the slow advance of children and domestics still more slowly, and entered a roomy building, gloomy and unadorned, like a Kirk. A man in rusty black apparel, of a mean and somewhat sinister aspect, was standing in the middle of the floor; children and domestics were standing round him; we remained in a corner.

"Wha was Adam?" he suddenly and loudly asked.

Nobody answered. He appeared to be much displeased at their silence; and after a while he repeated the question, in a louder voice,

"Wha was Adam?"

Still no answer. The name is so common in these anti-episcopalian regions. Did he ask after Adam Black, Willie Adam, or Adam, late of Eden, the protoplast; he did not limit his question, but put it in the most general terms. Nobody answered it.

The indignation of the Catechist waxing hot, in a still louder and very angry tone he broke forth with,—

"Wha's the Deel?"

This was too much; Shelley burst into a shrieking laugh, and rushed wildly out of doors. I slowly followed him, thinking seriously of Elders, Presbyteries, and Kirk Synods. However, nothing came of it; we were not cast into prison.

Shelley and his future had travelled from London to Edinburgh by the mail, without stopping. A young Scotch advocate was their companion in the coach for part of the way; he was an agreeable, obliging person. Shelley confided to him the object of his journey, and asked his advice.

The young lawyer told the young poet how to get married. They followed his directions, and were married on their arrival in Edinburgh,—how, or where, I never heard. Harriet had some marriage lines, which she sent to her father. I never saw them.

* ★ ☆

It has been represented by reckless or ill-informed biographers that Harriet was illiterate, and therefore she was not a fit companion for Shelley. This representation is not correct; she had been well-educated; and as the coffee-house people could not have taught her more than they knew themselves, which was little or nothing, she must have received her education at school; and she was unquestionably a credit to the establishment.

Drawing she had never learned, at least she gave no indications of taste or skill in that department; her proficiency in music was moderate, and she seemed to have no very decided natural talent for it; her accomplishments were slight, but with regard to acquirements of higher importance, for her years, she was exceedingly well read. I have seldom, if ever, met with a girl who had read so much as she had, or who had so strong an inclination for reading. I never once saw a Bible, a prayer book, or any devotional work, in her hand; I never heard her utter a syllable on the subject of religion, either to signify assent or dissent, approbation, or censure, or doubt; Eucharis, or Egeria, or Antiope, could not have appeared more entirely uninstructed than herself in such matters. I never heard her say that she had been at church, or ever once visited any place of worship; never, in my hearing, did she criticise any sermon, as is so common with the generality of young ladies, or express admiration of, or curiosity concerning, a popular preacher. Her music was wholly secular; of the existence of sacred music she seemed to be unconscious, and never to have heard the illustrious name of Handel. Her reading was not of a frivolous description; she did not like light, still less trifling, ephemeral productions. Morality was her favourite theme; she found most pleasure in works of a high ethical tone. Telemachus and Belisarius were her chosen companions, and other compositions of the same leaven, but of less celebrity.

She was fond of reading aloud; and she read remarkably well, very correctly, and with a clear, distinct, agreeable voice, and often emphatically. She was never weary of this exercise, never fatigued; she never ceased of her own accord, and left off reading only on some interruption. She has read to me for hours and hours; whenever we were alone together, she took up a book and began to read, or more commonly read aloud from the work, whatever it might be, which she was reading to herself. If anybody entered the room she ceased to read aloud, but recommenced the moment he retired. I was grateful for her kindness; she has read to me grave and excellent books innumerable. If some few of these were a little wearisome, on the whole I

profited greatly by her lectures. I have sometimes
certainly wished for rather less of the trite moral
discourses of Idomeneus and Justinian, which are
so abundant in her two favourite authors, and a
little more of something less in the nature of
truisms; but I never showed any signs of impatience. In truth, the good girl liked a piece of
resistance, a solid tome, where a hungry reader
might read and come again. I have sometimes
presumed to ask her to read some particular work,
but never to object to anything which she herself
proposed. If it was agreeable to listen to her, it
was not less agreeable to look at her: she was
always pretty, always bright, always blooming;
smart, usually plain in her neatness; without a
spot, without a wrinkle, not a hair out of its place.
The ladies said of her, that she always looked as if
she had just that moment stepped out of a glass-
case; and so indeed she did. And they inquired,
how that could be? The answer was obvious;
she passed her whole life in reading aloud, and
when that was not permitted, in reading to herself,
and invariably works of a calm, soothing, tran-
quillising, sedative tendency; and in such an existence there could be nothing to stain, to spot, to
heat, to tumble, to cause any the slightest disorder
of the hair or dress. Hers was the most distinct
utterance I ever heard; I do not believe that I lost

a single word of the thousands of pages which she
read to me. Of course I never dared to yield to
sleep, even when the virtuous Idomeneus was giving
wise laws to Crete, and therefore I am now alive to
write our simple story.

The more drowsy Bysshe would sometimes drop
off: his innocent slumbers gave serious offence, and
his neglect was fiercely resented; he was stigmatised,
as an inattentive wretch.

A distinct articulation is pleasing, but by no
means common. Another young lady was so good
as to read to me for several years; but I never
heard a single word she said. However, I cherished
the hope, that some day or other I might at least
hear one word, as a reward for my patience; but I
was disappointed, and the poor girl has long ceased
to read and to breathe.

☆ ★ ☆

THE arrival of Bysshe was acknowledged by Harriet, but it was plain that he had been superseded; Eliza once or twice betrayed a faint consciousness of his presence, as if the lamp of her life had been faintly glimmering in its socket, which fortunately it was not; that was all the notice she took of her sister's husband. His course, therefore, was plain; his peace might have been assured; whether his happiness would ever have been great, may well be doubted. It was absolutely necessary to declare peremptorily, "Either Eliza goes, or I go;" and instantly to act upon the declaration. This so necessary course the poor fellow did not take; and it is certain that the Divine Poet could not have taken it, for with super-human strength, weakness less than human was strangely blended; accordingly, from the days of the blessed advent, our destinies were entirely changed. The house lay, as it were, under an interdict; all our accustomed occupations were suspended; study was forbidden; reading was injurious—to read aloud might terminate fatally; to go abroad was death, to stay at home the grave! Bysshe became nothing; I, of course, very much less than nothing—a negative quantity of a very high figure.

Harriet still existed, it was true; but her existence was to be in future a seraphic life, a beatific vision, to be passed exclusively in the assiduous contemplation of Eliza's infinite perfections.

That all this was very well meant, very disinterested, kind, benevolent, sisterly, it would be unjust to deny, or even to doubt; but it was all the more pernicious on that account.

Before the angelic visit, we had never heard of Harriet's nerves, we had never once suspected that such organs existed; now we heard of little else. "Dearest Harriet, you must not do that; think of your nerves; only consider, dearest, the state of your nerves; Harriet, dear, you must not eat this; you are not going to drink that, surely; whatever will become of your poor nerves? Gracious heaven! What would Miss Warne say?"

Miss Warne was the highest sanction; her name was often invoked, and her judgment appealed to. "What will Miss Warne say?" That single, simple, but momentous question set every other question at rest.

Who was Miss Warne? I inquired of the now nervous Harriet. She informed me, that she stood in the same relation to some coffee-house or hotel in London, as the lovely Eliza; she was a daughter of the house; a mature virgin also, quite ripe, perhaps rather too mellow; a prim old maid indeed, an old frump, she said; there was nothing particular about her in any way; but Eliza had the highest opinion of Miss Warne; she had been long her bosom friend!

Eliza was vigilant, keeping a sharp look-out after the nerves; yet was she frequently off duty; her time was chiefly spent in her bed-room. What does that dear Eliza do alone in her bed-room? Does she read? No.—Does she work? Never.—Does she write? No.—What does she do, then?

Harriet came quite close to me, and answered in a whisper, lest peradventure her sister should hear her, with the serious air of one who communicates some profound and weighty secret, "She brushes her hair!" The coarse black hair was glossy, no doubt; but to give daily sixteen hours out of four-and-twenty to it, was certainly to bestow much time on a crop. Yet it was by no means impossible, that whilst she plied her hair-brush, she was revolving in her mind dearest Harriet's best interests; or seriously reflecting upon what Miss Warne would say.

The poor Poet was overwhelmed by the affectionate invasion; he lay prostrated and helpless, under the insupportable pressure of our domiciliary visit; but the good Harriet knew how, school-girl like, and contrary to her sisterly allegiance, sometimes to take advantage, by stealth, of dear Eliza's absence. " Come quite close to me, and I will read to you. I must not speak loud, lest I should disturb poor Eliza."

Sometimes she could escape for a short walk before dinner. One day, whilst the guardian angel kept on brushing, we brushed off, and wandered to the river. We stood on the high centre of the old Roman bridge; there was a mighty flood; father Ouse had overflowed his banks, carrying away with him timber and what not.

" Is it not an interesting, a surprising sight ? "

" Yes, it is very wonderful. But, dear Harriet, how nicely that dearest Eliza would spin down the river! How sweetly she would turn round and round, like that log of wood! And, gracious heaven, what would Miss Warne say ? "

She turned her pretty face away, and laughed—

as a slave laughs, who is beginning to grow weary of an intolerable yoke.

In York, an old English city, Harriet's beauty attracted the eyes of all beholders, in walking through its narrow streets; her cheeks were suffused with the blush of modesty, which made her still more engaging, more bright and radiant; and then the good girl bashfully drew down her veil. Her charms did not appear to be equally captivating in the Northern metropolis: I went abroad with her there more frequently, but nobody ever noticed her; she was short, and slightly and delicately formed; not raw-boned enough for the Scottish market.

When I first knew Shelley, he was alike indifferent to all works of art. He learned afterwards to admire statues, and then, at a still later period, pictures; but he never had any feeling for the wonders of architecture; even our majestic cathedrals were viewed with indifference. I took him into York Minster several times, but to no purpose; it was thrown away, entirely lost upon him. The insensible Harriet appeared to feel its beauty, until her admiration of the sublime structure was proscribed and forbidden by authority.

One day, when we were going together to the Minster, Eliza intervened, and instead of interdicting our walk, to our surprise said, that she would

go with us, and inflicted upon us her comfortless
company. She had heard of the celebrated window
at the end of the north transept, called "The Five
Sisters," because five ladies had given it to the
church: the stained glass in each of the five bays
had been copied from a pattern in needlework
embroidered by one of the five lady sisters. On
entering the Minster, she at once inquired for
"The Five Sisters;" the window was pointed out
to her. "Lord! What stiff, ugly, old-fashioned,
formal patterns! Gracious heaven! What would
Miss Warne say? Harriet!" After this solemn
censure and condemnation, inasmuch as the two
irrefragable tapsters disapproved of the tapestry, as
being ill suited for an urn-rug, the docile and
obedient Harriet dutifully forbore to admire the
glorious edifice.

"What is your opinion of suicide? Did you
never think of destroying yourself?" It was a
puzzling question indeed, for the thought had never
entered my head.

"What do you think of matricide; of high trea-
son; of rick-burning? Did you never think of
killing any one; of murdering your mother; of
setting stack-yards on fire?" I had never contemplated the commission of any of these crimes, and I
should scarcely have been more astonished if I had
been interrogated concerning my dispositions and

inclinations with respect to them, than I was when, early in our acquaintance, the good Harriet asked me, " What do you think of suicide ? "

She often discoursed of her purpose of killing herself some day or other, and at great length, in a calm, resolute manner.   She told me that at school, where she was very unhappy, as she said, but I could never discover why she was so, for she was treated with much kindness and exceedingly well instructed, she had conceived and contrived sundry attempts and purposes of destroying herself.   It is possible that her sister had assured her that she was very unhappy, and had supported the assurance by the incontrovertible opinion of Miss Warne, and of course Harriet became firmly convinced of her utter wretchedness.   She got up in the night, she said, sometimes with a fixed intention of making away with herself—in what manner she did not unfold—and bade a long farewell to the world, looked out of the window, taking leave of the bright moon and of all sublunary things, and then, it should seem, got into bed again and went quietly to sleep, and rose in the morning and wrote neatly upon her slate, in the school-room at Clapham, the admirable ordinances of Idomeneus and Numa Pompilius as sedately as before.

She spoke of self-murder serenely before strangers; and at a dinner party I have heard her describe her feelings, opinions, and intentions with respect to suicide with prolix earnestness; and she looked so calm, so tranquil, so blooming, and so handsome, that the astonished guests smiled. She once, in particular—I well remember the strange scene and the astonishment of the harmless company—at a Pythagorean dinner in the house of a medical philosopher, scattered dismay amongst a quiet party of vegetable-eaters, persons who would not slay a shrimp, or extinguish animal life in embryo by eating an egg, by asking, whether they did not feel sometimes strongly inclined to kill themselves.

The poor girl's monomania of self-destruction, which we long looked upon as a vain fancy, a baseless delusion, an inconsequent hallucination of the mind, amused us occasionally for some years; eventually it proved a sad reality, and drew forth many bitter tears.

We have sometimes consoled ourselves by cherishing the belief, that if none of those contingencies had happened, to the influence of which a rash act has, with mistaken confidence, been ascribed, the morbid predisposition might have produced the same melancholy result. But he who anticipates ill discharges the duty of a faithful biographer.

☆ ★ ☆

The whole soul of my ardent and imaginative young friend was inflamed at this period of his life, by a glowing desire to witness and to promote the improvement and progress of civil society. He had translated an essay, or treatise, of some French philosopher, on the Perfectibility of the Human Species; and he read his translation aloud to me, as well as the writings of other authors on the same fanciful subject. A state of things was fast approaching, we were assured, in which mankind, having become perfectly virtuous, the sanction of laws, as well as all binding contracts and agreements, would no longer be required. It would be fortunate and happy, indeed, if the accession of this complete change and entire amelioration were true, or even probable. A man might then lend ten or fifty thousand pounds to a friend, or even to any stranger, at four per cent., or on any other terms, without the trouble and delay of executing mortgages, or bonds, or other securities; without the wearisome investigation of intricate titles; without the dull, tedious, and expensive formalities of lawyers. And so it would be with all other transactions whatever, no other safeguard than that of triumphant and universally prevailing virtue ought ever to be looked for. Marriage, of course, would be on the same easy, but secure, footing as all other agreements. So far as it is a civil contract, this might very well be, if all men and all women were perfectly true,

honourable, and virtuous. Nobody affected to believe
that such a condition of affairs actually existed ; but
that it would soon arrive, some well-meaning persons
confidently asserted, and seemed to credit it.   I met
with certain of the advocates of the coming perfectibility, worthy, but somewhat credulous people : the men
discoursed of its influence over all human affairs, the
women treated it principally with reference to those
matters which most nearly concern themselves.   I
listened to observations and conversations which to
me, doubting of the blessed advent, were laughable.

One example will suffice : I went to drink coffee
and tea, to listen to conversation more or less
instructive, and to music, and to enjoy all such
innocent recreations as are not inconsistent with
perfectibility, at the handsome house of a very
hospitable and agreeable perfectible.   In the course
of the evening a lady stole into the room, and took
her seat on a solitary sofa opposite ; she was a most
lovely creature, in every respect, and I expressed
my admiration of her in no measured terms to the
lady of the house, with whom I was conversing, as I
had supposed, in confidence, and under the belief
that what I had said was to go no farther.   After a
little while, the lady of the house crossed the room,
sat down by the side of her lovely guest, and
conversed earnestly with her, both the ladies occasionally looking at me.   Afterwards, a signal was
made that I was to approach ; I obeyed it.   The

lady of the house then told the fair stranger, word
for word, all that I had said about her, pausing from
time to time, and asking me if I had not said so. It
was impossible to deny it. "Well, sir," said the
stranger lady, with a certain gracious gravity, when
she had heard all my praises, and I had confirmed
them, "your homage is accepted, and when the perfectibility of the human race is accomplished, you
shall be made happy." " Thank you, Madam," I answered, somewhat impertinently, I fear; "and when
the Millennium commences, we will go and reside
in the New Jerusalem; we will hire a handsome
first-floor in a commodious house, hollowed out of
one huge emerald, and live together in it!" She
frowned at this harmless jest, but made no reply.
I did not think that so rare a beauty could have
looked so black, and withdrew in manifest anger.

A few days after our conversation, she related
what I had said to Bysshe, adding, "Your friend is
a very strange person indeed; it is quite plain that
he does not believe in the perfectibility of the human
race. How unaccountable! and indeed he seems to
make it the sole business of his life to scoff at
everything!"

"How could you think of living with her in a
house carved out of an emerald?" He inquired with
his saddest look and in his most plaintive voice,
when he told me this.

I answered, "We read in the Book of Revelation

that each of the twelve gates of the New Jerusalem was a pearl, and one foundation of the walls was a topaz, another an amethyst, and so on; and conse-quently it did not seem too much to expect that when the number of the elect has been accomplished, and what she promised me is to take place, I might easily hire such apocalyptic apartments for us to live in together, as I proposed to her."

He looked grave, and said mournfully, "You laugh at everything! I am convinced that there can be no entire regeneration of mankind until laughter is put down!"

On that point at least we were agreed.

The poetic temperament is naturally melancholy, the poet's airy realms being thickly peopled by ima-ginary sorrows; and Shelley's natural melancholy had been confirmed and increased by manifold crosses, vexations, and disappointments; yet occa-sionally he could be merry, notwithstanding the strong aversion for laughter and ridicule which he habitually and vehemently expressed. He could indulge in a mirthful sally; he could play joyous, funny pranks, and could relate or even act them over again, in a vivacious manner, and with a keen relish and agreeable recollections of his own mis-chievous raillery. His frolics were ever peculiar and characteristic; their nature will be best explained and illustrated by an example:

One summer's evening he had to travel a short

distance in his own country, in the county of Sussex ;—such, if I mistake not, for I know the adventure only from Bysshe's account of it, was the scene of his whimsical exploit. He set out on foot, expecting that the stage would soon overtake him. He had not proceeded far when the heavy coach came up. There was no room outside, but the six inside seats were unoccupied; he got in, and the vehicle rumbled along the dusty road. For a little while it was all very well, but the heavy stage coach stopped suddenly, and a heavy old woman came in to him, reddened with heat, steaming and running down with perspiration. She took her place in the middle seat, like a huge ass between a pair of enormous panniers; for, on one side was a mighty basket, crammed full of mellow apples, and on the other a like basket, equally well filled with large onions. The odour of the apples and the onions, and the aspect of the heated, melting, smoking old woman, were intolerable to the delicate, sensitive young poet. He bore it, at first, patiently, then impatiently, at last he could endure it no longer ; so, starting up, he seated himself on the floor of the coach, and, fixing his tearful, woeful eyes upon her, he addressed his companion thus, in thrilling accents :

> " For heaven's sake, let us sit upon the ground,
> And tell sad stories of the death of kings !

> How some have been deposed, some slain in war,
> Some haunted by the ghosts they dispossessed ;
> Some poisoned by their wives; some sleeping killed,
> All murthered ! "

" Oh, dear !" exclaimed the terrified old woman. "Dear ! dear ! Oh, Lord ! Oh, Lord!"

But when he shrieked out the two last words, "All murthered !" she ran to the window in an agony, and, thrusting out her head, cried :

" Oh, guard, guard ! stop ! Oh, guard, guard, guard ! let me out!"

The door was opened, she alighted immediately with her strong-smelling wares, and through the united wit of two great poets, that of Shakspeare and his own, he was permitted to finish his journey alone.

He was proud of this achievement, and delighted in it long afterwards.

" Show us, Bysshe, how you got rid of the old woman in Sussex."

He sprang wildly on his feet, and, taking his seat on the floor, with a melancholy air, and in a piteous voice, cried out :

> " For heaven's sake, let us sit upon the ground !"

When he had given out the words, "All murthered!" with a fiendish yell, he started up, threw open the window, and began to call, " Guard! guard!" often, to the astonishment of persons passing by, whose temperament was less poetic, and less excitable than his own.

So moving were the woes of the gentle Richard Plantagenet, told by the great dramatist, and declaimed by another poet, second to him, at least in time! So drastic was their effect!

Quitting the Swan of Avon, and the Swan of the Arun, and of Warnham mere, we will return for a moment to the lovely and indignant lady.

Some months after the huge emerald had proved to be a stone of offence and a stumbling-block in the way to her good graces, I met her alone in Orchard Street; she was exceedingly handsome by daylight, but less handsome than she had appeared by candlelight; the tell-tale summer's sun showed brown or yellow hues. It struck me that the emerald mansion would not be becoming to her complexion; it would be preferable to reside in a ruby, or a topaz. She received me graciously, shaking hands cordially; and we walked round Portman Square together. To say the truth, I met her again soon after my first disaster, and, as a Christian, I desired to live and to die in peace with her. Accordingly, when she was quite alone, I ventured to creep up to her, and, sitting down softly by her side, humbly to address her. I said nothing of her transcendent beauty, which had been the cause of my original discomfiture, and had brought down upon my head the odious and opprobrious appellation of a scoffer; nor of the progress of mankind towards perfection, of which I doubted; but I spoke of indifferent subjects only; of chess, of cards, of quadrille. At first, certainly, she was somewhat crusty, treating me as an Infidel ought always to be treated, but she softened by degrees.

"Well! Have you made it up?" the lady of the house asked, as she walked past us, and saw us conversing together in a friendly manner.

"We never had anything to make up," answered the lovely lady, obligingly; "we never had any quarrel!"

She spoke much of Shelley, and in such terms that, had we been old and bitter enemies, we should have been at once reconciled. She spoke also of him whilst we were walking round the square, and with so great warmth, admiration, and enthusiasm, that the yellow tints on her skin rapidly and completely disappeared, and I thought she would look perfectly charming even in the emerald messuage.

"I was talking about him with a female friend the other day, that he is so modest, so reserved, so pure, so virtuous,

'A clear, immaculate, and silver fountain!'

and we were saying what terrible havoc he would make, if he were at all rakish!"

"If he were less modest, he would be less attractive, and therefore less dangerous."

"Yes, it would be so. But that did not occur to us."

"I wonder it did not, for it is sufficiently obvious."

"Have you seen him lately?"

"Have you?"

There were many mutual inquiries.

"Does he not visit you then?"

"I wish he did; I would gladly, oh, so gladly, give half of all I possess, if he were an habitual, I will add even an occasional visitor! Cannot you bring him to me? Will you?"

"I will try."

"You said you wish to learn quadrille; we will teach you. My mother, my sister, and myself have lived much in Spain, where alone they understand the game: quadrille is well played there. If you can excuse our not playing for money, which we never do, we will play with you whenever you choose."

"To learn so difficult a game as quadrille demands much leisure, and I have none."

"That is a pity, for it is well worth learning! However, you will come and see me?"

"It must be after my return to London, because

I am going into the country to-morrow, for some months."

" Whenever you please; but bring him with you."

In one respect only is the long vacation too long; on every other account I have invariably found it too short. The absence from London is so long, that it causes a disruption of studies, pursuits, and acquaintances; of acquaintances that might have ripened into valuable friendships.

When I returned to town in November, the recollection of my obliging instructress in quadrille had faded, and Bysshe and myself were so ungrateful as to forget the lovely perfectible! The precise nature of the perfect felicity which was promised to the elect, and was to be enjoyed by them, when the perfectibility of the human species was accomplished, I never discovered. It certainly was not that kind of felicity that one would at first infer from the lax, ambiguous manner of talking in use among zealous votaries. It was something etherial, spiritualised, transcendent, remote from the gratifications of the senses, and the grossness of mortal frailty,—a certain celestial joy. In truth, my curiosity did not stimulate me to inquire minutely into the conditions of a state of society, in which I did not myself believe.

☆ ★ ☆

Shelley fed much on pulse at different periods, and for a long time together, but never in a pet; on the contrary, through a calm, deliberate choice, and a sincere conviction of the propriety and superior salubrity of such food. His letters inform us, that he had occasionally restricted himself in great measure, if not entirely, to a vegetable diet. What first suggested to him the abstinence from flesh does not anywhere appear; whether his own feelings and reflections, or the advice of others given orally, or in books. It was not until the spring of the year 1813 that he entered upon a full and exact course of vegetable diet. His Pythagorean, or Brahminical, existence, and his intimate association with the amiable and accomplished votaries of a Return to Nature, was perhaps the prettiest and most pleasing portion of his poetical, philosophical, and lovely life. His nutriment had ever been, and always was, simple; consisting, as has been already mentioned, principally of bread eaten by itself, or with some very slight and frugal condiment. Spirituous liquors he never tasted; beer, rarely. He never called for, purchased, or drew, wine for his own drinking; but if it came in his way, and the company was not disagreeable to him, he would sit at table a while after dinner, and take two or three glasses of any white wine, uniformly selecting the weakest. I will not be hard upon him, and say that he absolutely disliked port wine—what Oxford man ever did?—but he had unpleasant associations with it. The sight of port wine reminded him of his father, who loved it dearly, and drank it freely; not to any reprehensible excess, but as a country gentleman and a justice of the peace ought to drink it.

I have often thought, and I have now and then even hinted, that if he could only bring himself to drink a bottle of choice port with his father, to sit sociably with him for an hour or two, and patiently to hear the old squire extol his wine and himself, they would get on much better together, and many serious difficulties and inconveniences would be avoided. But it was all in vain; my efforts as a peace-maker were thrown away. The alliance was impracticable—impossible. It may be very well to pour oil and wine into wounds, they may heal; but it is useless to stir the two liquors together, they will never mix.

Poor Bysshe was doomed to encounter many of those severe trials which wring the heart and wring it so hard. As the happiest period of his life was that spent at Oxford, so also was it the jolliest. He partook of the Oxonian potation, negus, with a real relish, and drank it freely, like a true and studious Academic, as he was.

After reading for many hours, and walking for many hours, during the livelong day, indeed, the peripatetic student could not but enjoy his supper; and after supper—for the Genius of the place would admit of no denial, or excuse—two tumblers of hot negus, each containing two full glasses of sherry, followed quietly and in order, as the silent planets pursue their nightly courses. He did this then, did it freely, and thought no evil—in mental blind-ness. Afterwards, his eyes were opened. For I have reminded him of it; proposing, once in a way, a recurrence to old habits. But the child of light wondered how he could have been guilty of such a piece of odious and disgusting sensuality, sometimes adding, " I ought to have been shot for it ! "

Sobriety was the exception, not the rule, at our very learned and most orthodox University. The college servants at Oxford were good, but muzzy, as the best servants often are, with an abiding and perennial muzziness, being constantly inspired with the soft inspiration of strong, sound ale, which flowed copiously from the buttery. When the ascetic young poet returned to Nature, alcohol in every shape—even in the subdued shape of negus—was strictly prohibited.

If his diet, fluid and solid, was cool, not less cool was his dress. I never remember to have seen Bysshe in a great coat or cloak, even in the coldest weather. He wore his waistcoat much or entirely open ; sometimes there was an ellipsis of his waistcoat ; it was not expressed, but understood. Unless he was compelled to cover it by main force, he had his throat bare ; the neckcloth being cast aside, lost, over the hills and far away, and the collar of his shirt unbuttoned. In the street or road he reluctantly wore a hat, but in fields and gardens his little round head had no other covering than his long, wild, ragged locks.

The poor, imaginative, creative head was plunged several times a-day into a basonful of cold water, which he invariably filled brimful, in order to throw as much water as possible on his feet and the floor. That the dripping locks might dry, he thrust, ever and anon, the fingers of both hands through them, and set them on end—

" With hair upstaring then, like reeds, not hair."

However, the abstinence from wraps, from great-coats and cloaks, was a characteristic of the age as well as of the individual. In the last of his notes on " Queen Mab," as a commentary on the lines—

" No longer now
He slays the lamb, that looks him in the face,
And horribly devours his mangled flesh,"

the author has set forth his views on the subject of vegetable diet; it would be presumptuous, therefore, for another to discuss it; if it were not so indeed, most assuredly I am altogether inadequate to the task; and it is needless to reprint here what is in the hands of every reader. My impression is, that the matter contained in this long note was published originally in a separate, independent form. Whether I ever received a copy of the little work, if there was any such work, I do not remember; it is certain that I cannot lay my hand upon it at present. For some months, for some years, I was in the thick of it, for I lived much with a select and most estimable society of persons, who had returned to nature, and of course I heard much discussion on the topic of vegetable diet. I never presumed to take a part myself in their arguments, for two reasons : first, because I heard quite enough of the matter, to say the least, without entering into the controversy; secondly, and principally, because I did not understand it, and was not qualified to arrive at a sound conclusion. That some persons may be competent to determine the question, I do not deny; I will only affirm, that I never was so fortunate as to fall in with even one of them. I did more than discuss, I conformed; not through faith, but for good fellowship, and because it was an agreeable experiment, if that can be called an experiment by which nothing is to be tried or discovered; perhaps I should rather say, that it was an agreeable change. Solomon says, and he says wisely : " Better is a dinner of herbs where love is, than a stalled ox and hatred therewith." My kind friends asserted, and they were wise in their generation,—whether also in their choice of diet, I cannot decide,—that a dinner of herbs, a vegetable dinner, is better than roast beef and love and friendship therewith. Certainly their vegetable dinners were delightful; elegant and excellent repasts; looking only to the table and the viands placed upon it, and not to those who sat round it

" In solemn troops and sweet societies."

Flesh, fowl, fish, game, never appeared ; nor eggs bodily in their individual capacity, nor butter in the gross : the two latter articles were admitted into cookery, it is true, but as sparingly as possible, and their presence was provisional, interlocutory, under protest, as culinary aids not approved of, and soon to be dispensed with. The injunction extended to shell-fish. John Horne Tooke proposed shrimps and treacle to one of the fathers of the church vegetant here on earth; the treacle might have been accepted, but every individual shrimp would have been black-balled. We had soups in great variety, that seemed the more delicate from the absence of meat. There were vegetables of every kind, the finest and best of the kind, dressed with care and skill; either plainly or stewed, and otherwise artfully and scientifically arranged and disguised. Puddings, tarts, confections, sweets, abounded. Cheese was under the ban,—anathematized, excommunicate. Milk and cream might not be taken unreservedly; however, they were allowed to form ingredients in puddings, and to be poured sparingly into tea, as an indulgence to the weakness of neophytes, tender plants. Fruits of every description were welcomed,—hailed rapturously, received with plaudits, as if the goddess, Nature, herself stood bodily before her votaries. We luxuriated, ran riot in tea and coffee, and sought variety occasionally in cocoa and chocolate. Bread and butter and buttered toast were eschewed; but bread-cakes, plain seed-cakes, were liberally divided amongst the faithful.

☆ ★ ☆

Lord Ellenborough had come to Guildhall to get a verdict at all hazards. He was rolling about on the bench like a stormy sea, that seemed somehow to desire to calm itself. His head was tossed up and down as a cockboat in the surf; like the white buoy on the bar amidst the breakers. He was clumsily courteous to the jury, to the defendants, to everybody; roughly bland in an awkward fashion, like a pet bear, and freely rejecting immaterial evidence with conspicuous impartiality. The appearance of the defendants certainly was not prepossessing. The three first-named seemed to be at home, but the noble and gallant admiral was ill at ease; it was quite plain that he did not like to be thus aground, stranded, but heartily wished himself afloat again. As regards Lord Cochrane, at least, it was not a creditable proceeding, I confess, although I drew the information myself; but to discuss the matter here would be inopportune, even if its interest had not long since passed away. On the level floor of the old court of King's Bench it was impossible to hear, or to see, with advantage. The old courts at Guildhall were disgraceful to the administration of justice and to the city of London. To eat and drink and job away their funds, not to erect suitable buildings for public purposes, was in those days esteemed the paramount, the sole duty of a municipal corporation.

I stood in the court for an hour or two, amongst the crowd on the floor, and then withdrew; my fellow-pupil remained. I contrived to gather from the bench that I should leave the affair in very good hands; that my criminal information was pretty safe. In Cheapside I fell in with Shelley : I spoke to him of the trial that was depending. He rarely took an interest in such matters, and he expressed no curiosity as to the result. We walked westward, through Newgate Street. When we reached Skinner Street, he said "I must speak with God- win; come in, I will not detain you long."

I followed him through the shop, which was the only entrance, and up-stairs. We entered a room on the first floor; it was shaped like a quadrant. In the arc were windows ; in one radius a fire-place, and in the other a door, and shelves with many old books. William Godwin was not at home. Bysshe strode about the room, causing the crazy floor of the ill-built, unowned dwelling-house to shake and tremble under his impatient footsteps. He ap- peared to be displeased at not finding the fountain of Political Justice. "Where is Godwin ? " he asked me several times, as if I knew. I did not know, and, to say the truth, I did not care. He continued his uneasy promenade; and I stood reading the names of old English authors on the backs of the venerable volumes, when the door was partially and softly opened. A thrilling voice called " Shelley ! " A thrilling voice answered, " Mary ! " And he darted out of the room, like an arrow from the bow of the far-shooting king. A very young female, fair and fair-haired, pale indeed, and with a piercing look, wearing a frock of tartan, an unusual dress in London at that time, had called him out of the room. He was absent a very short time—a minute or two; and then returned, " Godwin is out; there is no use in waiting." So we continued our walk along Holborn.

" Who was that, pray ? " I asked; " a daughter?' " Yes."

" A daughter of William Godwin ? " " The daughter of Godwin and Mary."

NOTES

p. 209: '"This is a motto ..."': Hogg begins his *Life* with a fragment of a projected biography of Shelley by Mary Shelley. This was one of the manuscripts lent to him by Lady Jane Shelley

p. 220, l. 13: 'Ogygian': of great age (after the mythical King Ogyges)

p. 224: 'The sound of the church-going bell ...': from William Cowper's 'Verses', supposed to be written by Alexander Selkirk

p. 232, l. 23: 'Eucharis, or Egeria, or Antiope': nymphs in classical mythology

pp. 248–9: 'For heaven's sake ...': *Richard II*, III. ii

p. 251: 'A clear, immaculate, and silver fountain': *Richard II*, V. ii: 'clear' is a misquotation of 'sheer' in Shakespeare's text

p. 257: 'With hair upstaring ...', *The Tempest*, I. ii

E. J. Trelawny, *Recollections of the Last Days of Shelley and Byron* (London, 1858)

On February 9th, 1822, Mary Shelley wrote from Pisa to her friend Maria Gisborne in London to tell her about her 'Colony' in Italy. One recently arrived member was 'Trelawny – a kind of half Arab Englishman', whom Mary Shelley described as 'a strange web which I am endeavouring to unravel' (Bennett, *Letters*, I, p. 218).

> I would fain learn if generosity is united to impetuousness – Nobility of spirit to his assumption of singularity & independence – he is six feet high – raven black hair which curls thickly and shortly like a Moors dark, grey – expressive eyes – overhanging brows upturned lips & a smile which expresses good nature and kindheartedness – his shoulders are high like an Orientalist – his voice is monotonous yet emphatic & his language as he relates the events of his life energetic & simple – whether the tale be one of blood & horror or of irrisistable comedy. His company is delightful …

Trelawny had travelled to Pisa at the invitation of Williams and Medwin, whom he had met in Geneva in 1820. We cannot know quite what 'events of his life' Trelawny so energetically related, but it is likely that they were close to the exotic inventions of his 'autobiography', *Adventures of a Younger Son*, which was published in 1831. This would briefly earn him renown as the Byronic adventurer that he so much wished to be. A quarter of a century later, his *Recollections* made him famous for the second time in his life.

The true story of Trelawny's early life is not told in his *Adventures*, which mixes some facts with some vivid fictions of daring, battle, and a tragic love affair with an African princess – the latter ending, like Shelley's life, with a funeral pyre at the edge of the ocean. However, he had had adventures. He had joined the Royal Navy at the age of thirteen, perhaps in order to escape his harsh military father, and was at sea for most of the next seven years. Wounded in an invasion of Java, he was invalided out of the service in 1812. He married in 1813, but discovered that his wife was conducting an affair with a fellow boarder in their lodging house. Soon after the birth of their second daughter, she eloped with her lover, and Trelawny entered into divorce proceedings that occupied him for several years. After a final act of divorce was obtained in 1819, Trelawny, leaving one daughter with his former wife and the other with remarkably cooperative friends, moved to France with his mother and sisters, and thence, supported by an allowance from his father, on to Switzerland, where he met Williams and Medwin and read *Queen Mab*. The *Recollections* begins with his encounter with this poem, shown to him by 'a young bookseller at Lausanne' (*Recollections*, p. 1). It also tells, perhaps reliably, how Medwin's account of the poem's author stirred Trelawny with thoughts of Italy: 'Medwin was the chief medium that impressed us with a desire to know Shelley; he had known him from childhood; he talked of nothing but the inspired boy, his virtues and his sufferings, so that, irrespective of his genius, we all longed to know him' (ibid, p. 10).

When he joined the Pisa circle, Trelawny soon became friendly with both Byron and Shelley. For the former, he helped build and sail the *Bolivar* (Shelley described him to Hunt as 'a wild but kind hearted sea-man': Jones, *Letters*, II, p. 439). For the latter, he was to make the famous funeral arrangements described below – after the publication of his *Recollections*, he became renowned as the man who had snatched Shelley's heart from the flames. Whatever the truth of this part of his story, he did certainly arrange the burial of Shelley's ashes in the Protestant Cemetary in Rome and the erection of a gravestone with Leigh Hunt's suggested epitaph ('COR COR-DIUM') and his own addition of lines from *The Tempest* ('Nothing of him that doth fade . . .'). He also took the opportunity to buy the plot adjoining Shelley's grave – where his own ashes were indeed eventually buried (see St Clair, *Trelawny*, p. 197).

Trelawny also claimed his place in the Byron legend by accompanying him to Greece to join the struggle for Greek independence. He was, as it were, witness to the two most romantic deaths of the literary era. It is clear that he had intended to make a book out of his friendship with Shelley long before 1858. He had written from Florence to Mary Shelley in 1829 saying that he was writing a memoir of Shelley, and asking for her help (which she politely refused to give) (see Bennett, II, pp. 82–3). Indeed, the following advertisement appeared in the *New Monthly Magazine* for November 1830: 'A Memoir of the Life of the Poet Shelley during his residence in Italy will shortly appear from the pen of his friend, Captain Trelawny' (St Clair, *Trelawny*, p. 133). But no such book appeared. Instead he produced only his *Adventures of a Younger Son*, which Mary Shelley helped to correct and find a publisher for. It was apparently she who was responsible for the title; Trelawny had wanted to call it simply *A Man's Life* (see Reiman, p. 60). At around this time he appears to have proposed to Mary Shelley, having earlier offered himself to Claire Clairmont (Reiman, p. 63).

During the 1730s he spent time in America, cohabited with a married woman, Augusta Goring, and when she obtained a divorce in 1841, married her and moved to rural Monmouthshire. The couple had three children, but in 1857 the marriage broke up, apparently because Trelawny had installed his mistress in the house. Augusta left for Italy, Trelawny's house and farm were sold, and he moved to London with his mistress. It was at this time, and with his own return to metropolitan life, that he produced his *Recollections*. He may also have been stimulated by Lady Jane Shelley's schemes for a biography, for she had asked him for his assistance. He refused to cooperate with her, and instead wrote to Daniel Roberts and Claire Clairmont for reminiscences of Shelley for his own book. His final product constantly contrasts Shelley and Byron – and constantly to Shelley's credit. Byron shrinks by Shelley's side. 'In fact, his pride and vanity mastered him, and he made no effort to control their dominion ... Shelley had a far loftier spirit. His pride was spiritual ... Whilst men tried to force him down to their level, he toiled to draw their minds upwards' (*Recollections*, p. 67). The illustrative anecdote, given below, of his discovery of Shelley musing in the pine woods outside Pisa is typical of his representation of the poet. And because the book really purports to be 'recollected' – a text in which Trelawny is always present – the memoirist never has to stoop to examine the past of this poetic dreamer.

For Trelawny's later life, see the headnote to *Records of Shelley, Byron and the Author*, in this volume.

Swiftly gliding in, blushing like a girl, a tall thin stripling held out both his hands; and although I could hardly believe as I looked at his flushed, feminine, and artless face that it could be the Poet, I returned his warm pressure. After the ordinary greetings and courtesies he sat down and listened. I was silent from astonishment: was it possible this mild-looking, beardless boy, could be the veritable monster at war with all the world? —excommunicated by the Fathers of the Church, deprived of his civil rights by the fiat of a grim Lord Chancellor, discarded by every member of his family, and denounced by the rival sages of our literature as the founder of a Satanic school? I could not believe it; it must be a hoax. He was habited like a boy, in a black jacket and trowsers, which he seemed to have outgrown, or his tailor, as is the custom, had most shamefully stinted him in his "sizings." Mrs. Williams saw my embarrassment, and to relieve me asked Shelley what book he had in his hand? His face brightened, and he answered briskly.

"Calderon's Magico Prodigioso, I am translating some passages in it."

"Oh, read it to us!"

Shoved off from the shore of common-place incidents that could not interest him, and fairly launched on a theme that did, he instantly became oblivious of everything but the book in his hand. The masterly manner in which he analysed the genius of the author, his lucid interpretation of the story, and the ease with which he translated into our language the most subtle and imaginative passages of the Spanish poet, were marvellous, as was his command of the two languages. After this touch of his quality I no longer doubted his identity; a dead silence ensued; looking up, I asked,

" Where is he ? "

Mrs. Williams said, " Who ? Shelley ? Oh, he comes and goes like a spirit, no one knows when or where."

Presently he re-appeared with Mrs. Shelley. She brought us back from the ideal world Shelley had left us in, to the real one, welcomed me to Italy, and asked me the news of London and Paris, the new books, operas, and bonnets, marriages, murders, and other marvels. The Poet vanished, and tea appeared. Mary Woolstoncraft (the authoress), the wife of William Godwin, died in 1797, in giving birth to their only child, Mary, married to the poet Shelley; so that at the time I am speaking of Mrs. Shelley was twenty-seven. Such a rare pedigree of genius was enough to interest me in her, irrespective of her own merits as an authoress. The most striking feature in her face was her calm, grey eyes; she was rather under the English standard of woman's height, very fair and light-haired, witty, social, and animated in the society of friends, though mournful in solitude; like Shelley, though in a minor degree, she had the power of expressing her thoughts in varied and appropriate words, derived from familiarity with the works of our vigorous old writers. Neither of them used obsolete or foreign words. This command of our language struck me the more as contrasted with the scanty vocabulary used by ladies in society, in which a score of poor hackneyed phrases suffice to express all that is felt or considered proper to reveal.

☆ ★ ☆

To know an author, personally, is too often but
to destroy the illusion created by his works; if
you withdraw the veil of your idol's sanctuary, and
see him in his night-cap, you discover a querulous
old crone, a sour pedant, a supercilious coxcomb,
a servile tuft-hunter, a saucy snob, or, at best,
an ordinary mortal. Instead of the high-minded
seeker after truth and abstract knowledge, with
a nature too refined to bear the vulgarities of life,
as we had imagined, we find him full of egotism
and vanity, and eternally fretting and fuming about
trifles. As a general rule, therefore, it is wise to
avoid writers whose works amuse or delight you, for
when you see them they will delight you no more.
Shelley was a grand exception to this rule. To
form a just idea of his poetry, you should have
witnessed his daily life; his words and actions best
illustrated his writings. If his glorious conception
of Gods and men constituted an atheist, I am afraid
all that listened were little better. Sometimes he
would run through a great work on science, con-
dense the author's laboured exposition, and by
substituting simple words for the jargon of the
schools, make the most abstruse subject trans-

parent. The cynic Byron acknowledged him to be the best and ablest man he had ever known. The truth was, Shelley loved everything better than himself. Self-preservation is, they say, the first law of nature, with him it was the last; and the only pain he ever gave his friends arose from the utter indifference with which he treated everything concerning himself. I was bathing one day in a deep pool in the Arno, and astonished the Poet by performing a series of aquatic gymnastics, which I had learnt from the natives of the South Seas. On my coming out, whilst dressing, Shelley said, mournfully,

" Why can't I swim, it seems so very easy ? "

I answered, " Because you think you can't. If you determine, you will; take a header off this bank, and when you rise turn on your back, you will float like a duck; but you must reverse the arch in your spine, for it's now bent the wrong way."

He doffed his jacket and trowsers, kicked off his shoes and socks, and plunged in; and there he lay stretched out on the bottom like a conger eel, not making the least effort or struggle to save himself. He would have been drowned if I had not instantly fished him out. When he recovered his breath, he said :

"I always find the bottom of the well, and they say Truth lies there. In another minute I should have found it, and you would have found an empty shell. It is an easy way of getting rid of the body."

"What would Mrs. Shelley have said to me if I had gone back with your empty cage?"

"Don't tell Mary—not a word!" he rejoined, and then continued, "It's a great temptation; in another minute I might have been in another planet."

"But as you always find the bottom," I observed, "you might have sunk 'deeper than did ever plummet sound.'"

"I am quite easy on that subject," said the Bard. "Death is the veil, which those who live call life : they sleep, and it is lifted. Intelligence should be imperishable; the art of printing has made it so in this planet."

"Do you believe in the immortality of the spirit?"

He continued, "Certainly not; how can I? We know nothing; we have no evidence; we cannot express our inmost thoughts. They are incomprehensible even to ourselves."

"Why," I asked, "do you call yourself an atheist? it annihilates you in this world."

"It is a word of abuse to stop discussion, a painted devil to frighten the foolish, a threat to intimidate the wise and good. I used it to express my abhorrence of superstition; I took up the word, as a knight took up a gauntlet, in defiance of injustice. The delusions of Christianity are fatal to genius and originality: they limit thought."

Shelley's thirst for knowledge was unquenchable. He set to work on a book, or a pyramid of books; his eyes glistening with an energy as fierce as that of the most sordid gold-digger who works at a rock of quartz, crushing his way through all impediments, no grain of the pure ore escaping his eager scrutiny. I called on him one morning at ten, he was in his study with a German folio open, resting on the broad marble mantel-piece, over an old-fashioned fire-place, and with a dictionary in his hand. He always read standing if possible. He had promised over night to go with me, but now begged me to let him off. I then rode to Leghorn, eleven or twelve

miles distant, and passed the day there; on returning at six in the evening to dine with Mrs. Shelley
and the Williams's, as I had engaged to do, I went
into the Poet's room and found him exactly in the
position in which I had left him in the morning,
but looking pale and exhausted.

"Well," I said, "have you found it?"

Shutting the book and going to the window, he
replied, "No, I have lost it:" with a deep sigh: "'I
have lost a day.'"

"Cheer up, my lad, and come to dinner."

Putting his long fingers through his masses of
wild tangled hair, he answered faintly, "You go,
I have dined—late eating don't do for me."

"What is this?" I asked as I was going out of
the room, pointing to one of his bookshelves with
a plate containing bread and cold meat on it.

"That,"—colouring,—"why that must be my
dinner. It's very foolish; I thought I had
eaten it."

Saying I was determined that he should for once
have a regular meal, I lugged him into the dining-
room, but he brought a book with him and read
more than he ate. He seldom ate at stated periods,

but only when hungry—and then like the birds, if he saw something edible lying about,—but the cupboards of literary ladies are like Mother Hubbard's, bare. His drink was water, or tea if he could get it, bread was literally his staff of life; other things he thought superfluous. An Italian who knew his way of life, not believing it possible that any human being would live as Shelley did, unless compelled by poverty, was astonished when he was told the amount of his income, and thought he was defrauded or grossly ignorant of the value of money. He, therefore, made a proposition which much amused the Poet, that he, the friendly Italian, would undertake for ten thousand crowns a-year to keep Shelley like a grand Seigneur, to provide his table with luxuries, his house with attendants, a carriage and opera box for my lady, besides adorning his person after the most approved Parisian style. Mrs. Shelley's toilette was not included in the wily Italian's estimates. The fact was, Shelley stinted himself to bare necessaries, and then often lavished the money, saved by unprecedented self-denial, on selfish fellows who denied themselves nothing; such as the great philosopher had in his eye, when he said, "It is the nature of extreme self-lovers, as they will set a house on fire, an' it were only to roast their own eggs."

Byron on our voyage to Greece, talking of England, after commenting on his own wrongs, said, "And Shelley, too, the best and most benevolent of men; they hooted him out of his country like a mad-dog, for questioning a dogma. Man is the same rancorous beast now that he was from the beginning, and if the Christ they profess to worship re-appeared, they would again crucify him."

✳ ✱ ✳

As I mused upon his sagacity and my own stupidity, the braying of a brother jackass startled me. He was followed by an old man picking up pine cones. I asked him if he had seen a stranger ?

"L'Inglese malincolico haunts the wood maledetta. I will show you his nest."

As we advanced, the ground swelled into mounds and hollows. By-and-by the old fellow pointed with his stick to a hat, books, and loose papers lying about, and then to a deep pool of dark glimmering water, saying " Eccolo ! " I thought he meant that Shelley was in or under the water. The careless, not to say impatient, way in which the Poet bore his burden of life, caused a vague dread amongst his family and friends that he, might lose or cast it away at any moment.

The strong light streamed through the opening of the trees. One of the pines, undermined by the water, had fallen into it. Under its lee, and nearly hidden, sat the Poet, gazing on the dark mirror beneath, so lost in his bardish reverie that he did not hear my approach. There the trees were stunted and bent, and their crowns

were shorn like friars by the sea breezes, excepting
a cluster of three, under which Shelley's traps were
lying; these overtopped the rest.   To avoid startling
the Poet out of his dream, I squatted under the
lofty trees, and opened his books.   One was a
volume of his favourite Greek dramatist, Sophocles,—the same that I found in his pocket after
his death—and the other was a volume of Shakespeare.   I then hailed him, and, turning his head,
he answered faintly,

"Hollo, come in."

"Is this your study?" I asked.

"Yes," he answered, "and these trees are my
books—they tell no lies.   You are sitting on the
stool of inspiration," he exclaimed.   "In those three
pines the weird sisters are imprisoned, and this,"
pointing to the water, "is their cauldron of black
broth.   The Pythian priestesses uttered their ora-
cles from below—now they are muttered from above.
Listen to the solemn music in the pine-tops—don't
you hear the mournful murmurings of the sea?
Sometimes they rave and roar, shriek and howl, like
a rabble of priests.   In a tempest, when a ship sinks,
they catch the despairing groans of the drowning

mariners. Their chorus is the eternal wailing of wretched men."

"They, like the world," I observed, "seem to take no note of wretched women. The sighs and wailing you talk about are not those of wretched men afar off, but are breathed by a woman near at hand— not from the pine-tops, but by a forsaken lady."

"What do you mean?" he asked.

"Why, that an hour or two ago I left your wife, Mary Shelley, at the entrance of this grove, in despair at not finding you."

He started up, snatched up his scattered books and papers, thrust them into his hat and jacket pockets, sighing "Poor Mary! her's is a sad fate. Come along; she can't bear solitude, nor I society —the quick coupled with the dead."

He glided along with his usual swiftness, for nothing could make him pause for an instant when he had an object in view, until he had attained it. On hearing our voices, Mrs. Shelley joined us; her clear gray eyes and thoughtful brow expressing the love she could not speak. To stop Shelley's self-reproaches, or to hide her own emotions, she began in a bantering tone, chiding and coaxing him:

" What a wild-goose you are, Percy; if my thoughts
have strayed from my book, it was to the opera,
and my new dress from Florence—and especially
the ivy wreath so much admired for my hair, and
not to you, you silly fellow ! When I left home, my
satin slippers had not arrived. These are serious
matters to gentlewomen, enough to ruffle the
serenest tempered. As to you and your ungallant
companion, I had forgotten that such things are;
but as it is the ridiculous custom to have men at
balls and operas, I must take you with me, though,
from your uncouth ways, you will be taken for
Valentine and he for Orson."

Shelley, like other students, would, when the
spell that bound his faculties was broken, shut his
books, and indulge in the wildest flights of mirth
and folly. As this is a sport all can join in, we
talked·and laughed, and shrieked, and shouted, as
we emerged from under the shadows of the melancholy pines and their nodding plumes, into the now
cool purple twilight and open country. The cheerful
and graceful peasant girls, returning home from the
vineyards and olive groves, stopped to look at us.
The old man I had met in the morning gathering

pine cones, passed hurriedly by with his donkey, giving Shelley a wide berth, and evidently thinking that the melancholy Englishman had now become a raving maniac. Sancho says, " Blessings on the man who invented sleep ;" the man who invented laughing deserves no less.

The day I found Shelley in the pine forest he was writing verses on a guitar. I picked up a fragment, but could only make out the first two lines :—

> " Ariel, to Miranda take
> This slave of music.'

It was a frightful scrawl; words smeared out with his finger, and one upon the other, over and over in tiers, and all run together in most "admired disorder;" it might have been taken for a sketch of a marsh overgrown with bulrushes, and the blots for wild ducks; such a dashed off daub as self-conceited artists mistake for a manifestation of genius. On my observing this to him, he answered,

" When my brain gets heated with thought, it soon boils, and throws off images and words faster than I can skim them off. In the morning, when cooled down, out of the rude sketch as you justly call it, I shall attempt a drawing. If you ask me why I publish what few or none will care to read, it is that the spirits I have raised haunt me until they are sent to the devil of a printer. All authors are anxious to breech their bantlings."

* * *

On Monday, the 8th of July, 1822, I went with Shelley to his bankers, and then to a store. It was past one P.M. when, we went on board our respective boats,—Shelley and Williams to return to their home in the Gulf of Spezzia; I in the 'Bolivar,' to accompany them into the offing. When we were under weigh, the guard-boat boarded us to overhaul our papers. I had not got my port clearance, the captain of the port having refused to give it to the mate, as I had often gone out without. The officer of the Health Office consequently threatened me with forty days' quarantine. It was hopeless to think of detaining my friends. Williams had been for days fretting and fuming to be off; they had no time to spare, it was past two o'clock, and there was very little wind.

Sullenly and reluctantly I re-anchored, furled my sails, and with a ship's glass watched the progress of my friends' boat. My Genoese mate observed,—"They should have sailed this morning at three or four A.M., instead of three, P.M. They are standing too much in shore; the current will set them there."

I said, "They will soon have the land-breeze."

"May-be," continued the mate, "she will soon have too much breeze; that gaff top-sail is foolish in a boat with no deck and no sailor on board." Then pointing to the S.W., "Look at those black lines and the dirty rags hanging on them out of the sky—they are a warning; look at the smoke on the water; the devil is brewing mischief."

There was a sea-fog, in which Shelley's boat was soon after enveloped, and we saw nothing more of her.

Although the sun was obscured by mists, it was oppressively sultry. There was not a breath of air in the harbour. The heaviness of the atmosphere and an unwonted stillness benumbed my senses. I went down into the cabin and sank into a slumber. I was roused up by a noise over-head and went on deck. The men were getting up a chain cable to let go another anchor. There was a general stir amongst the shipping; shifting berths, getting down yards and masts, veering out cables, hauling in of hawsers, letting go anchors, hailing from the ships and quays, boats sculling rapidly to and fro. It was almost dark, although only half-past six o'clock. The sea was of the colour, and looked as solid and smooth as a sheet of lead, and covered with an oily scum. Gusts of wind swept over without ruffling it, and big drops of rain fell on its surface, rebounding, as if they could not penetrate it. There was a commotion in the air, made up of many threatening sounds, coming upon us from the sea. Fishing-craft and coasting-vessels under bare poles rushed by us in shoals, running foul of the ships in the harbour. As yet the din and hubbub was that made by men, but their shrill pipings were suddenly silenced by the crashing voice of a thunder squall that burst right over our heads. For some time no other sounds were to be heard than the thunder, wind, and rain. When the fury of the storm, which did not last for more than twenty minutes, had abated, and the horizon was in some degree cleared,

I looked to seaward anxiously, in the hope of descrying Shelley's boat, amongst the many small craft scattered about. I watched every speck that loomed on the horizon, thinking that they would have borne up on their return to the port, as all the other boats that had gone out in the same direction had done.

I sent our Genoese mate on board some of the returning craft to make inquiries, but they all professed not to have seen the English boat. So remorselessly are the quarantine laws enforced in Italy, that, when at sea, if you render assistance to a vessel in distress, or rescue a drowning stranger, on returning to port you are condemned to a long and rigorous quarantine of fourteen or more days. The consequence is, should one vessel see another in peril, or even run it down by accident, she hastens on her course, and by general accord, not a word is said or reported on the subject. But to resume my tale. I did not leave the 'Bolivar' until dark. During the night it was gusty and showery, and the lightning flashed along the coast: at daylight I returned on board, and resumed my examinations of the crews of the various boats which

had returned to the port during the night. They
either knew nothing, or would say nothing. My
Genoese, with the quick eye of a sailor, pointed out,
on board a fishing-boat, an English-made oar, that
he thought he had seen in Shelley's boat, but the
entire crew swore by all the saints in the calendar
that this was not so. Another day was passed in
horrid suspense. On the morning of the third day I
rode to Pisa. Byron had returned to the Lanfranchi
Palace. I hoped to find a letter from the Villa
Magni: there was none. I told my fears to Hunt, and
then went upstairs to Byron. When I told him, his lip
quivered, and his voice faltered as he questioned me.
I sent a courier to Leghorn to despatch the 'Bolivar,'
to cruise along the coast, whilst I mounted my
horse and rode in the same direction. I also despatched a courier along the coast to go as far as
Nice. On my arrival at Via Reggio I heard that a
punt, a water-keg, and some bottles had been found
on the beach. These things I recognised as having
been in Shelley's boat when he left Leghorn.
Nothing more was found for seven or eight days,
during which time of painful suspense I patrolled
the coast with the coast-guard, stimulating them to

keep a good look-out by the promise of a reward.
It was not until many days after this that my worst
fears were confirmed. Two bodies were found on
the shore,—one near Via Reggio, which I went and
examined. The face and hands, and parts of the
body not protected by the dress, were fleshless.
The tall slight figure, the jacket, the volume of
Sophocles in one pocket, and Keats's poems in
the other, doubled back, as if the reader, in the
act of reading, had hastily thrust it away, were
all too familiar to me to leave a doubt on my
mind that this mutilated corpse was any other than
Shelley's. The other body was washed on shore
three miles distant from Shelley's, near the tower of
Migliarino, at the Bocca Lericcio. I went there at
once. This corpse was much more mutilated; it
had no other covering than,—the shreds of a shirt,
and that partly drawn over the head, as if the
wearer had been in the act of taking it off,—a black
silk handkerchief, tied sailor-fashion round the
neck,—socks,—and one boot, indicating also that
he had attempted to strip. The flesh, sinews, and
muscles hung about in rags, like the shirt, exposing
the ribs and bones. I had brought with me from

Shelley's house a boot of Williams's, and this exactly matched the one the corpse had on. That, and the handkerchief, satisfied me that it was the body of Shelley's comrade. Williams was the only one of the three who could swim, and it is probable he was the last survivor. It is likewise possible, as he had a watch and money, and was better dressed than the others, that his body might have been plundered when found. Shelley always declared that in case of wreck he would vanish instantly, and not imperil valuable lives by permitting others to aid in saving his, which he looked upon as valueless. It was not until three weeks after the wreck of the boat that a third body was found—four miles from the other two. This I concluded to be that of the sailor boy, Charles Vivian, although it was a mere skeleton, and impossible to be identified. It was buried in the sand, above the reach of the waves. I mounted my horse, and rode to the Gulf of Spezzia, put up my horse, and walked until I caught sight of the lone house on the sea-shore in which Shelley and Williams had dwelt, and where their widows still lived. Hitherto in my frequent visits—in the absence of direct evidence to the contrary. I had buoyed up their spirits by maintaining that it was not impossible but that the friends still lived; now I had to extinguish the last hope of these forlorn women. I had ridden fast, to prevent any ruder messenger from bursting in upon them. As I stood on the threshold of their house, the bearer, or rather confirmer, of news which would rack every fibre of their quivering frames to the utmost, I paused, and, looking at the sea, my memory reverted to our joyous parting only a few days before.

The two families, then, had all been in the verandah, overhanging a sea so clear and calm that every star was reflected on the water, as if it had been a mirror; the young mothers singing some merry tune, with the accompaniment of a guitar. Shelley's shrill laugh—I heard it still—rang in my ears, with Williams's friendly hail, the general *buona notte* of all the joyous party, and the earnest entreaty to me to return as soon as possible, and not to forget the commissions they had severally given me. I was in a small boat beneath them, slowly rowing myself on board the ' Bolivar,' at anchor in the bay, loath to part from what I verily believed to have been at that time the most united, and happiest, set of human beings in the whole world. And now by the blow of an idle puff of wind the scene was changed. Such is human happiness.

My reverie was broken by a shriek from the nurse Caterina, as, crossing the hall, she saw me in the doorway. After asking her a few questions, I went up the stairs, and, unannounced, entered the room. I neither spoke, nor did they question me. Mrs. Shelley's large grey eyes were fixed on my face. I turned away. Unable to bear this horrid silence, with a convulsive effort she exclaimed—

" Is there no hope ? "

I did not answer, but left the room, and sent the servant with the children to them. The next day I prevailed on them to return with me to Pisa. The misery of that night and the journey of the next day, and of many days and nights that followed, I can neither describe nor forget. It was ultimately determined by those most interested, that Shelley's remains should be removed from where they lay, and conveyed to Rome, to be interred near the bodies of his child, and of his friend Keats, with a suitable monument, and that Williams's remains should be taken to England. To do this, in their then far advanced state of decomposition, and to obviate the obstacles offered by the quarantine laws, the ancient custom of burning and reducing the body to ashes was suggested. I wrote to our minister at Florence, Dawkins, on the subject, and solicited his friendly intercession with the Lucchese and Florentine governments, that I might be furnished with authority to accomplish our purpose.

The following was his answer:—

DEAR SIR,

An order was sent yesterday from hence to the Governor of Via Reggio, to deliver up the remains of Mr. Shelley to you, or any person empowered by you to receive them.

I said they were to be removed to Leghorn for interment, but that need not bind you. If they go by sea, the governor will give you the papers necessary to insure their admittance elsewhere. If they travel by land, they must be accompanied by a guard as far as the frontier,—a precaution always taken to prevent the possibility of infection. Quick-lime has been thrown into the graves, as is usual in similar cases.

With respect to the removal of the other corpse, I can tell you nothing till I hear from Florence. I applied for the order as soon as I received your letter, and I expect an answer to my letter by to-morrow's post.

I am very sensible of Lord Byron's kindness, and should have called upon him when I passed through Pisa, had he been anybody but Lord Byron. Do not mention trouble; I am here to take as much as my countrymen think proper to give me; and all I ask in return is fair play and good humour, which I am sure I shall always find in the S. S. S.

Believe me, dear sir,

Yours very faithfully,

W. DAWKINS.

Such were his subsequent influence and energy, that he ultimately overcame all the obstacles and repugnance of the Italians to sanction such an unprecedented proceeding in their territories.

CHAPTER XII.

———◆———

All things that we love and cherish,
Like ourselves, must fade and perish ;
Such is our rude mortal lot,
Love itself would, did they not.

Shelley.

I GOT a furnace made at Leghorn, of iron-bars and strong sheet-iron, supported on a stand, and laid in a stock of fuel, and such things as were said to be used by Shelley's much loved Hellenes on their funeral pyres.

On the 13th of August, 1822, I went on board the 'Bolivar,' with an English acquaintance, having written to Byron and Hunt to say I would send them word when everything was ready, as they wished to be present. I had previously engaged two large feluccas, with drags and tackling, to go before, and endeavour to find the place where Shelley's boat had foundered; the captain of one of the feluccas having asserted that he was out in the fatal squall, and had seen Shelley's boat go

down off Via Reggio, with all sail set. With light
and fitful breezes we were eleven hours reaching our
destination—the tower of Migliarino, at the Bocca
Lericcio, in the Tuscan States. There was a
village there, and about two miles from that place
Williams was buried. So I anchored, landed,
called on the officer in command, a major, and
told him my object in coming, of which he was
already apprised by his own government. He
assured me I should have every aid from him. As
it was too late in the day to commence operations,
we went to the only inn in the place, and I wrote
to Byron to be with us next day at noon. The
major sent my letter to Pisa by a dragoon, and made
arrangements for the next day. In the morning he
was with us early, and gave me a note from Byron,
to say he would join us as near noon as he could.
At ten we went on board the commandant's boat,
with a squad of soldiers in working dresses, armed
with mattocks and spades, an officer of the quarantine service, and some of his crew. They had their
peculiar tools, so fashioned as to do their work without coming into personal contact with things that
might be infectious—long handled tongs, nippers,

poles with iron hooks and spikes, and divers others that gave one a lively idea of the implements of torture devised by the holy inquisitors. Thus freighted, we started, my own boat following with the furnace, and the things I had brought from Leghorn. We pulled along the shore for some distance, and landed at a line of strong posts and railings which projected into the sea—forming the boundary dividing the Tuscan and Lucchese States. We walked along the shore to the grave, where Byron and Hunt soon joined us : they, too, had an officer and soldiers from the tower of Migliarino, an officer of the Health Office, and some dismounted dragoons, so we were surrounded by soldiers, but they kept the ground clear, and readily lent their aid. There was a considerable gathering of spectators from the neighbourhood, and many ladies richly dressed were amongst them. The spot where the body lay was marked by the gnarled root of a pine tree.

A rude hut, built of young pine-tree stems, and wattled with their branches, to keep the sun and rain out, and thatched with reeds, stood on the beach to shelter the look-out man on duty. A few yards from this was the grave, which we commenced opening—the Gulf of Spezzia and Leghorn at equal distances of twenty-two miles from us. As to fuel I might have saved myself the trouble, of bringing any, for there was an ample supply of broken spars and planks cast on the shore from wrecks, besides the fallen and decaying timber in a stunted pine forest close at hand. The soldiers collected fuel whilst I erected the furnace, and then the men of the Health Office set to work, shovelling away the sand which covered the body, while we gathered round, watching anxiously. The first indication of their having found the body, was the appearance of the end of a black silk handkerchief—I grubbed this out with a stick, for we were not allowed to touch anything with our hands—then some shreds of linen were met with, and a boot with the bone of the leg and the foot in it. On the removal of a layer of brushwood, all that now remained of my lost friend was exposed—a shapeless mass of bones and flesh. The limbs separated from the trunk on being touched.

"Is that a human body?" exclaimed Byron; "why it's more like the carcase of a sheep, or any other animal, than a man: this is a satire on our pride and folly."

I pointed to the letters E. E. W. on the black silk handkerchief.

Byron looking on, muttered, " The entrails of a worm hold together longer than the potter's clay, of which man is made. Hold! let me see the jaw," he added, as they were removing the skull, " I can recognise any one by the teeth, with whom I have talked. I always watch the lips and mouth : they tell what the tongue and eyes try to conceal."

I had a boot of Williams's with me ; it exactly corresponded with the one found in the grave. The remains were removed piecemeal into the furnace.

" Don't repeat this with me," said Byron; " let my carcase rot where it falls."

The funereal pyre was now ready ; I applied the fire, and the materials being dry and resinous the pine-wood burnt furiously, and drove us back. It was hot enough before, there was no breath of air, and the loose sand scorched our feet. As soon as the flames became clear, and allowed us to approach, we threw frankincense and salt into the furnace, and poured a flask of wine and oil over the body. The Greek oration was omitted, for we had lost our Hellenic bard. It was now so insufferably hot that the officers and soldiers were all seeking shade.

"Let us try the strength of these waters that drowned our friends," said Byron, with his usual audacity. "How far out do you think they were when their boat sank?"

"If you don't wish to be put into the furnace, you had better not try; you are not in condition."

He stripped, and went into the water, and so did I and my companion. Before we got a mile out, Byron was sick, and persuaded to return to the shore. My companion, too, was seized with cramp, and reached the land by my aid. At four o'clock the funereal pyre burnt low, and when we uncovered the furnace, nothing remained in it but dark-coloured ashes, with fragments of the larger bones. Poles were now put under the red-hot furnace, and it was gradually cooled in the sea. I gathered together the human ashes, and placed them in a small oak-box, bearing an inscription on a brass plate, screwed it down, and placed it in Byron's carriage. He returned with Hunt to Pisa, promising to be with us on the following day at Via Reggio. I returned with my party in the same way we came, and supped and slept at the inn. On the following morning we went on board the same boats, with the same things and party, and rowed down the little river near Via Reggio to the sea, pulled along the coast towards Massa, then landed, and began our preparations as before.

Three white wands had been stuck in the sand to mark the Poet's grave, but as they were at some distance from each other, we had to cut a trench thirty yards in length, in the line of the sticks, to ascertain the exact spot, and it was nearly an hour before we came upon the grave.

In the mean time Byron and Leigh Hunt arrived in the carriage, attended by soldiers, and the Health Officer, as before. The lonely and grand scenery that surrounded us so exactly harmonised with Shelley's genius, that I could imagine his spirit soaring over us. The sea, with the islands of Gorgona, Capraji, and Elba, was before us; old battlemented watch-towers stretched along the coast, backed by the marble-crested Apennines glistening in the sun, picturesque from their diversified outlines, and not a human dwelling was in sight. As I thought of the delight Shelley felt in such scenes of loneliness and grandeur whilst living, I felt we were no better than a herd of wolves or a pack of wild dogs, in tearing out his battered and naked body from the pure yellow sand that lay so lightly over it, to drag him back to the light of day; but the dead have no voice, nor had I power to check the sacrilege—the work went on silently in the deep and unresisting sand; not a word was spoken, for the Italians have a touch of sentiment, and their feelings are easily excited into sympathy. Even Byron was silent and thoughtful. We were startled and drawn together by a dull hollow sound that followed the blow of a mattock; the iron had struck a skull, and the body was soon uncovered. Lime had been strewn on it; this, or decomposition, had the effect of staining it of a dark and ghastly indigo colour. Byron asked me to preserve the skull for him; but remembering that he had formerly used one as a drinking-cup, I was determined Shelley's should not be so profaned. The limbs did not separate from the trunk, as in the case of Williams's body, so that the corpse was removed entire into the furnace. I had taken the precaution of having more and larger pieces of timber, in consequence of my experience of the day before of the difficulty of consuming a corpse in the open air with our apparatus. After the fire was well kindled we repeated the ceremony of the previous day; and more wine was poured over Shelley's dead body than he had consumed during his life. This with the oil and salt made the yellow flames glisten and quiver. The heat from the sun and fire was so intense that the atmosphere was tremulous and wavy. The corpse fell open and the heart was laid bare. The frontal bone of the skull, where it had been struck with the mattock, fell off; and, as the back of the head rested on the red-hot bottom bars of the furnace, the brains literally seethed, bubbled, and boiled as in a cauldron, for a very long time.

Byron could not face this scene, he withdrew to the beach and swam off to the 'Bolivar.' Leigh Hunt remained in the carriage. The fire was so fierce as to produce a white heat on the iron, and to reduce its contents to grey ashes. The only portions that were not consumed were some fragments of bones, the jaw, and the skull, but what surprised us all, was that the heart remained entire.

In snatching this relic from the fiery furnace, my hand was severely burnt; and had any one seen me do the act I should have been put into quarantine.

After cooling the iron machine in the sea, I collected the human ashes and placed them in a box, which I took on board the 'Bolivar.' Byron and Hunt retraced their steps to their home, and the officers and soldiers returned to their quarters. I liberally rewarded the men for the admirable manner in which they behaved during the two days they had been with us.

As I undertook and executed this novel ceremony, I have been thus tediously minute in describing it.

Byron's idle talk during the exhumation of Williams's remains, did not proceed from want of feeling, but from his anxiety to conceal what he felt from others. When confined to his bed and racked by spasms, which threatened his life, I have heard him talk in a much more un-orthodox fashion, the instant he could muster breath to banter. He had been taught during his town-life, that any exhibition of sympathy or feeling was maudlin and unmanly, and that the appearance of daring and indifference, denoted blood and high breeding.

* * *

Shelley came of a long-lived race, and, barring accidents, there was no reason why he should not have emulated his forefathers in attaining a ripe age. He had no other complaint than occasional spasms, and these were probably caused by the excessive and almost unremitting strain on his mental powers, the solitude of his life, and his long fasts, which were not intentional, but proceeded from the abstraction and forgetfulness of himself and his wife. If food was near him, he ate it,—if not, he fasted, and it was after long fasts that he suffered from spasms. He was tall, slim, and bent from eternally poring over books; this habit had contracted his chest. His limbs were well proportioned, strong and bony—his head was very small —and his features were expressive of great sensibility, and decidedly feminine. There was nothing about him outwardly to attract notice, except his extraordinarily juvenile appearance. At twentynine, he still retained on his tanned and freckled cheeks, the fresh look of a boy—although his long wild locks were coming into blossom, as a polite hairdresser once said to me, whilst cutting mine.

It was not until he spoke that you could discern anything uncommon in him—but the first sentence he uttered, when excited by his subject, riveted your attention. The light from his very soul streamed from his eyes, and every mental emotion of which the human mind is susceptible, was expressed in his pliant and ever-changing features. He left the conviction on the minds of his audience, that however great he was as a Poet, he was greater as an orator. There was another and most rare peculiarity in Shelley,—his intellectual faculties completely mastered his material nature, and hence he unhesitatingly acted up to his own theories, if they only demanded sacrifices on his part,—it was where they implicated others that he forbore. Mrs. Shelley has observed, " Many have suggested and advocated far greater innovations in our political and social system than Shelley ; but he alone practised those he approved of as just."

Godwin observed to me,—"that Byron must occasionally have said good things, though not

capable, as Shelley was, of keeping up a long conversation or argument; and that Shelley must
have been of great use to Byron, as from the commencement of their intimacy at Geneva, he could
trace an entirely new vein of thought emanating
from Shelley, which ran through Byron's subsequent works, and was so peculiar that it could not
have arisen from any other source." This was
true. Byron was but superficial on points on which
Shelley was most profound—and the latter's capacity for study, the depth of his thoughts as well
as their boldness, and his superior scholarship,
supplied the former with exactly what he wanted :
and thus a portion of Shelley's aspirations were
infused into Byron's mind. Ready as Shelley
always was with his purse or person to assist
others, his purse had a limit, but his mental
wealth seemed to have none ; for not only to
Byron, but to any one disposed to try his hand
at literature, Shelley was ever ready to give any
amount of mental labour. Every detail of the life
of a man of genius is interesting, and Shelley's was
so pre-eminently, as his life harmonised with his
spiritual theories. He fearlessly laid bare those

mysterious feelings and impulses, of which few dare to speak, but in a form so purified from earthy matter that the most sensitive reader is never shocked. Shelley says of his own writings in the preface to the Cenci,—" they are little else than visions which impersonate my own apprehensions of the beautiful and the just,—they are dreams of what ought to be, or may be." Whilst he lived, his works fell still-born from the press—he never complained of the world's neglect, or expressed any other feeling than surprise at the rancorous abuse wasted on an author who had no readers. "But for them," he said, laughing, "I should be utterly unknown." "But for them," I observed, "Williams and I should never have crossed the Alps in chase of you. Our curiosity as sportsmen, was excited to see and have a shot at so strange a monster as they represented you to be."

NOTES

p. 277, l. 4: 'our voyage to Greece': Trelawny travelled to Greece with Byron to fight for its liberation from Turkish rule (see headnote). This comment was therefore made after Shelley's death
p. 281, l. 13: Valentine and Orson: characters in an early French romance. Orson is a wild man reared by bears; Valentine is the knight who attempts to tame him

Thomas Love Peacock, 'Memoirs of Percy Bysshe Shelley', in *Fraser's Magazine*, June, 1858

Thomas Love Peacock was always Shelley's most sceptical, and even satirical, friend and admirer. The two men met through the bookseller Thomas Hookham in 1812, when Shelley was twenty and Peacock twenty-seven. A strong bond was forged when Peacock aided Shelley and Mary Godwin on their return from the Continent in 1814, helping them to elude bailiffs and survive financially at a time when other friends and relations, disapproving of their elopement, would not offer support. He and Shelley became particularly intimate in 1815, when Shelley and Mary moved to Bishopsgate, near where Peacock lived in Marlow. The first of Peacock's prose satires, *Headlong Hall*, was composed at this time and seems in part to derive from his intellectual disputes with Shelley (see Butler, pp. 41–57). The friendship became even closer in 1817, when, after Harriet's suicide and Shelley's marriage to Mary, the couple moved to Marlow and established a literary circle with themselves and Peacock at its centre. Peacock's *Nightmare Abbey*, published in 1818, which satirizes a protagonist, Scythrop, who much resembles Shelley, draws on the friendship that they enjoyed at this time. It was characteristic of Peacock to turn this into the material of (sometimes affectionate) satire, and to do so in such a way as to strengthen rather than corrode the relationship. ('I am delighted with Nightmare Abbey. I think Scythrop a character admirably conceived & executed', wrote Shelley from Italy in June 1819: Jones, *Letters*, II, p. 98).

When Shelley met him, Peacock had a modest private income which allowed him to live the life of a man of letters, publishing poetry and indulging his enthusiasm for classical learning (in which pursuit he much influenced Shelley: see Butler, pp. 103–9 and passim). In 1819, after the Shelleys had left for Italy, he joined the East India Company, for which he worked as an administrator until his retirement, and moved to London. While Shelley was in Italy, the correspondence between the two men preserved the mixture of candour and dispute that always characterised their friendship. It is significant, for instance, both that Shelley's famous *Defence of Poetry* was composed as a rejoinder to Peacock's 'The Four Ages of Poetry' (1820), and that, at the same time, Peacock was entrusted with the correction of proofs of *Prometheus Unbound*. With Peacock, Shelley discovered a kind of friendly antagonism absent from all his other relationships save, perhaps, that with Byron. After Shelley's death and Mary Shelley's return to England, Peacock continued to play a quietly influential role. He was an executor of Shelley's estate and often negotiated with Sir Timothy Shelley and his lawyers on Mary Shelley's behalf. His relationship with his friend's widow does not, however, seem to have been warm, although Mary Shelley was friendly with Peacock's much loved daughter, Mary Ellen. In the years when he worked at East India House he also had to bring up his son and two daughters alone, as his wife Jane, whom he had married in 1819, had a breakdown in 1826 from which she never recovered. He kept up with a small circle of intellectual friends and wrote for periodicals and reviews, especially about opera. His temperamental scepticism and his hostility to Christianity drew him to Utilitarians like Bentham, with whom he often dined, and James Mill, under whom he worked at the East India Company. Yet, as ever, his intellectual interests were expressed via satire rather than allegiance, in this case in *Crotchet Castle* (1831).

Peacock was neither a professional writer nor one fired by literary or intellectual idealism. It is unsurprising, therefore, that he went through periods when he wrote little and published less – in particular during the 1840s. Biographers can usually only speculate about the reasons for his silences and his spurts of productivity – it is clear to all that he most readily made writing out of dialogue (which is the form in which almost all his satire is cast), and that he needed the fuel of friendly dispute. It is also clear that his renewed literary output of the 1850s must have had something to do simply with his retirement from the East India Company. He returned to satire with *Gryll Grange* (1860), published (like his 'Memoirs of Percy Bysshe Shelley') in instalments in *Fraser's Magazine*, and, with his first public comments on Shelley, he turned to a genre that he had always deprecated: biography – that pandering to what he calls, on the first page of his Shelley 'Memoirs', the 'appetite for gossip about notorieties'. Yet, as Marilyn Butler says, his 'Memoirs' 'are in origin anti-biography, an effort to correct the falsifications in the recent wave of Shelleyana, and they give away as little as Peacock can contrive' (Butler, p. 6). It is important, therefore, that his account be read in its original instalments: the first part, from which the extracts below are taken, appeared in June 1858 and must have been composed only shortly before it was published. It is couched as a kind of review of Hogg's *Life*, Trelawny's *Recollections*, and a third recent account, *Shelley and His Writings* (1858), this time by someone who had not known Shelley, Charles Middleton. It contradicts some of Hogg's judgements, in particular. Yet although Peacock certainly gives an anti-idealistic account of Shelley – a description of a poet who is prone to self-delusion and even hallucination – he does not at this stage enter into controversies about either of Shelley's marriages. Indeed, Peacock held back from such discussion until, as he expected, the two final volumes of Hogg's biography appeared. In the event, of course, the second half of Hogg's work was never to be produced (see the headnote to Hogg's *Life of Percy Bysshe Shelley* in this volume). Instead, Peacock was to be faced with Lady Jane Shelley's *Shelley Memorials*, published in 1859, and the second instalment of his own 'Memoirs', which appeared in *Fraser's* in January 1860, was to contest this new account (see the headnote to 'Memoirs of Shelley', January 1860, in this volume).

FRASER'S MAGAZINE.

JUNE, 1858.

MEMOIRS OF PERCY BYSSHE SHELLEY.*

'Rousseau, ne recevant aucun auteur, remercie Madame —— de ses bontés, et la prie de ne plus venir chez lui.'

ROUSSEAU had a great aversion to visitors of all classes, but especially to literary visitors, feeling sure that they would print something about him. A lady who had long persisted in calling on him, one day published a *brochure*, and sent him a copy. He rejoiced in the opportunity which brought her under his rule of exclusion, and terminated their intercourse by the above *billet-doux*.

Rousseau's rule bids fair to become general with all who wish to keep in the *secretum iter et fallentis semita vitæ*, and not to become materials for general gossip. For not only is a departed author of any note considered a fair subject to be dissected at the tea-table of the reading public, but all his friends and connexions, however quiet and retiring and unobtrusive may have been the general tenor of their lives, must be served up with him. It is the old village scandal on a larger scale; and as in these days of universal locomotion people know nothing of their neighbours, they prefer tittle-tattle about notorieties to the retailing of whispers about the Jenkinses and Tomkinses of the vicinity.

This appetite for gossip about notorieties being once created in the 'reading public,' there will be always found persons to minister to it; and among the volunteers of this service, those who are best informed and who most valued the departed will probably not be the foremost. Then come biographies abounding with errors; and then, as matter of defence perhaps, comes on the part of friends a tardy and more authentic narrative. This is at best, as Mr. Hogg describes it, a 'difficult and delicate task.' But it is always a matter of choice and discretion. No man is bound to write the life of another. No man who does so is bound to tell the public all he knows. On the contrary, he is bound to keep to himself whatever may injure the interests or hurt the feelings of the living, especially when the latter have in no way injured or calumniated the dead, and are not necessarily brought before the tribunal of public opinion in the character of either plaintiffs or defendants. Neither if there be in the life of the subject of the biography any event which he himself would willingly have blotted from the tablet of his own memory, can it possibly be the duty of a survivor to drag it into daylight. If such an event be the cardinal point of a life; if to conceal it or to misrepresent it would be to render the whole narrative incomplete, incoherent, unsatisfactory alike to the honour of the dead and the feelings of the living; then, as there is no moral compulsion to speak of the matter at all, it is better to let the whole story slumber in silence.

Having lived some years in very familiar intimacy with the subject of these memoirs; having had as good opportunities as any, and better than most persons now living, to observe and appreciate his great genius, extensive acquirements, cordial friendships, disinterested devotion to the well-being of the few with whom he lived in domestic intercourse, and ardent endeavours by private charity and public advo-

---

* *Shelley and his Writings.* By Charles S. Middleton. London: Newby. 1856.
   Recollections of the Last Days of Shelley and Byron. By E. J. Trelawney. London: Moxon. 1858.
   The Life of Percy Bysshe Shelley. By Thomas Jefferson Hogg. In Four Volumes. Vols. 1 and 2. London: Moxon. 1858.

cacy to ameliorate the condition of the many who pass their days in unremunerating toil; having been named his executor conjointly with Lord Byron, whose death, occurring before that of Shelley's father, when the son's will came into effect, left me alone in that capacity; having lived after his death in the same cordial intimacy with his widow, her family, and one or two at least of his surviving friends, I have been considered to have some peculiar advantages for writing his life, and have often been requested to do so; but for the reasons above given I have always refused.

Wordsworth says to the Cuckoo:

O blithe new-comer! I have heard,
I hear thee, and rejoice.
O Cuckoo! shall I call thee Bird,
Or but a wandering Voice?

*   *   *

Thrice welcome, darling of the Spring!
Even yet thou art to me
No bird, but an invisible thing,
A voice, a mystery.

Shelley was fond of repeating these verses, and perhaps they were not forgotten in his poem 'To a Skylark:'—

Hail to thee, blithe spirit!
Bird thou never wert,
That from heaven, or near it,
Pourest thy full heart,
In profuse strains of unpremeditated art.

*   *   *   *

The pale purple even
Melts around thy flight:
Like a star of heaven,
In the broad daylight,
Thou art unseen, but yet I hear thy shrill delight.

Now, I could have wished that, like Wordsworth's Cuckoo, he had been allowed to remain a voice and

a mystery: that, like his own Sky-lark, he had been left unseen in his congenial region,

Above the smoke and stir of this
dim spot
Which men call earth,

and that he had been only heard in the splendour of his song. But since it is not to be so, since so much has been, and so much more will probably be, written about him, the motives which deterred me from originating a substantive work on the subject, do not restrict me from commenting on what has been published by others, and from correcting errors, if such should appear to me to occur, in the narratives which I may pass under review.

I have placed the works at the head of this article in the order in which they were published. I have no acquaintance with Mr. Middleton. Mr. Trelawney and Mr. Hogg I may call my friends.

Mr. Middleton's work is chiefly a compilation from previous publications, with some very little original matter, curiously obtained.

Mr. Trelawney's work relates only to the later days of Mr. Shelley's life in Italy.

Mr. Hogg's work is the result of his own personal knowledge, and of some inedited letters and other documents, either addressed to himself or placed at his disposal by Sir Percy Shelley and his lady. It is to consist of four volumes, of which the two just published bring down the narrative to the period immediately preceding Shelley's separation from his first wife. At that point I shall terminate this first part of my proposed review.

☆ ★ ☆

To the circumstances of Shelley's first marriage I find no evidence but in my own recollection of what he told me respecting it. He often spoke to me of it; and with all allowance for the degree in which his imagination coloured events, I see no improbability in the narration.

Harriet Westbrook, he said, was a schoolfellow of one of his sisters ; and when, after his expulsion from Oxford, he was in London, without money, his father having refused him all assistance, this sister had requested her fair schoolfellow to be the medium of conveying to him such small sums as she and her sisters could afford to send, and other little presents which they thought would be acceptable. Under these circumstances the ministry of the young and beautiful girl presented itself like that of a guardian angel, and there was a charm about their intercourse which he readily persuaded himself could not be exhausted in the duration of life.

The result was that in August, 1811, they eloped to Scotland, and were married in Edinburgh.* Their journey had absorbed their stock of money. They took a lodging, and Shelley immediately told the landlord who they were, what they had come for, and the exhaustion of their resources, and asked him if he would take them in, and advance them money to get married and to carry them on till they could get a remittance. This the man agreed to do, on condition that Shelley would treat him and his friends to a supper in honour of the occasion. It was arranged accordingly ; but the man was more obtrusive and officious than Shelley was disposed to tolerate. The marriage was concluded, and in the evening Shelley and his bride were alone together, when the man tapped at their door. Shelley opened it, and the landlord said to him—' It is customary here at weddings for the guests to come in, in the middle of the night, and wash the bride with whisky.' ' I immediately,' said Shelley, ' caught up my brace of pistols, and pointing them both at him, said to him,—I have had enough of your impertinence ; if you give me any more of it I will blow your brains out ;' on which he ran or rather tumbled down stairs, and I bolted the doors.'

The custom of washing the bride with whisky is more likely to have been so made known to him than to have been imagined by him.

Leaving Edinburgh, the young couple led for some time a wandering life. At the lakes they were kindly received by the Duke of Norfolk, and by others through his influence. They then went to Ireland, landed at Cork, visited the lakes of Killarney, and stayed some time in Dublin, where Shelley became a warm repealer and emancipator. They then went to the Isle of Man, then to Nant Gwillt† in

* Not at Gretna Green, as stated by Captain Medwin.

† Nant Gwillt, the Wild Brook, flows into the Elan (a tributary of the Wye), about five miles above Rhayader. Above the confluence, each stream runs in a rocky channel through a deep narrow valley. In each of these valleys is or was a spacious mansion, named from the respective streams. Cwm Elan House was the seat of Mr. Grove, whom Shelley had visited there before his marriage in 1811. Nant Gwillt House, when Shelley lived in it in 1812, was inhabited by a farmer, who let some of the best rooms in lodgings. At a subsequent period I stayed a day in Rhayader, for the sake of seeing this spot. It is a scene of singular beauty.

Radnorshire, then to Lymouth near Barnstaple,* then came for a short time to London ; then went to reside in a furnished house belonging to Mr. Maddocks at Tanyrallt,† near Tremadoc, in Caernarvonshire. Their residence at this place was made chiefly remarkable by an imaginary attack on his life, which was followed by their immediately leaving Wales.

Mr. Hogg inserts several letters relative to this romance of a night : the following extract from one of Harriet Shelley's, dated from Dublin, March 12th, 1813, will give a sufficient idea of it :—

'Mr. Shelley promised you a recital of the horrible events that caused us to leave Wales. I have undertaken the task, as I wish to spare him, in the present nervous state of his health, everything that can recall to his mind the horrors of that night, which I will relate.

On the night of the 26th February we retired to bed between ten and eleven o'clock. We had been in bed about half an hour, when Mr. S—— heard a noise proceeding from one of the parlours. He immediately went down stairs with two pistols which he had loaded that night, expecting to have occasion for them. He went into the billiard-room, when he heard footsteps retreating ; he followed into another little room, which was called an office. He there saw a man in the act of quitting the room through a glass window which opened into the shrubbery ; the man fired at Mr. S——, which he avoided. Bysshe then fired, but it flashed in the pan. The man then knocked Bysshe down, and they struggled on the ground. Bysshe then fired his second pistol, which he thought wounded him in the shoulder, as he uttered a shriek and got up, when he said these words— 'By God, I will be revenged. I will murder your wife, and will ravish your sister ! By God, I will be revenged !' He then fled, as we hoped for the night. Our servants were not gone to bed, but were just going when this horrible affair happened. This was about eleven o'clock. We all assembled in the parlour, where we remained for two hours. Mr. S—— then advised us to retire, thinking it was impossible he would make a second attack. We left Bysshe and our man-servant—who had only

arrived that day, and who knew nothing of the house—to sit up. I had been in bed three hours when I heard a pistol go off. I immediately ran down stairs, when I perceived that Bysshe's flannel gown had been shot through, and the window curtain. Bysshe had sent Daniel to see what hour it was, when he heard a noise at the window ; he went there, and a man thrust his arm through the glass and fired at him. Thank heaven ! the ball went through his gown and he remained unhurt. Mr. S—— happened to stand side-ways ; had he stood fronting, the ball must have killed him. Bysshe fired his pistol, but it would not go off ; he then aimed a blow at him with an old sword which we found in the house. The assassin attempted to get the sword from him, and just as he was pulling it away Dan rushed into the room, when he made his escape. This was at four in the morning. It had been a most dreadful night ; the wind was as loud as thunder, and the rain descended in torrents. Nothing has been heard of him ; and we have every reason to believe it was no stranger, as there is a man . . . . who, the next morning, went and told the shopkeepers that it was a tale of Mr. Shelley's to impose upon them, that he might leave the country without paying his bills. This they believed, and none of them attempted to do anything towards his discovery. We left Tanyrallt on Sunday.'

Mr. Hogg subjoins :—

Persons acquainted with the localities and with the circumstances, and who had carefully investigated the matter, were unanimous in the opinion that no such attack was ever made.

I may state more particularly the result of the investigation to which Mr. Hogg alludes. I was in North Wales in the summer of 1813, and heard the matter much talked of. Persons who had examined the premises on the following morning had found that the grass of the lawn appeared to have been much trampled and rolled on, but there were no footmarks on the wet ground, except between the beaten spot and the window ; and the impression of the ball on the wainscot showed that the pistol had been fired towards the window, and not from it. This appeared

---

* He had introduced himself by letter to Mr. Godwin, and they carried on a correspondence some time before they met. Mr. Godwin, after many pressing invitations, went to Lymouth on an intended visit, but when he arrived the birds had flown.   † *Tan-yr-allt*—Under the precipice.

conclusive as to the whole series of operations having taken place from within. The mental phenomena in which this sort of semi-delusion originated will be better illustrated by one which occurred at a later period, and which, though less tragical in its appearances, was more circumstantial in its development, and more perseveringly adhered to. It will not come within the scope of this article.

I saw Shelley for the first time in 1812, just before he went to Tanyrallt. I saw him again once or twice before I went to North Wales in 1813. On my return he was residing at Bracknell, and invited me to visit him there. This I did, and found him with his wife Harriet, her sister Eliza, and his newly-born daughter Ianthe.

Mr. Hogg says:—

This accession to his family did not appear to afford him any gratification, or to create an interest. He never spoke of this child to me, and to this hour I never set eyes on her.

Mr. Hogg is mistaken about Shelley's feelings as to his first child. He was extremely fond of it, and would walk up and down a room with it in his arms for a long time together, singing to it a monotonous melody of his own making, which ran on the repetition of a word of his own making. His song was 'Yáhmani, Yáhmani, Yáhmani, Yáhmani.'* It did not please me, but, what was more important, it pleased the child, and lulled it when it was fretful. Shelley was extremely fond of his children. He was pre-eminently an affectionate father. But to this first-born there were accompaniments which did not please him. The child had a wet-nurse whom he did not like, and was much looked after by his wife's sister, whom he intensely disliked. I have often thought that if Harriet had nursed her own child, and if this sister had not lived with them, the link of their married love would not have been so readily broken. But of this here-

after, when we come to speak of the separation.

At Bracknell, Shelley was surrounded by a numerous society, all in a great measure of his own opinions in relation to religion and politics, and the larger portion of them in relation to vegetable diet. But they wore their rue with a difference. Every one of them adopting some of the articles of the faith of their general church, had each nevertheless some predominant crotchet of his or her own, which left a number of open questions for earnest and not always temperate discussion. I was sometimes irreverent enough to laugh at the fervour with which opinions utterly unconducive to any practical result were battled for as matters of the highest importance to the well-being of mankind; Harriet Shelley was always ready to laugh with me, and we thereby both lost caste with some of the more hot-headed of the party. Mr. Hogg was not there during my visit, but he knew the whole of the persons there assembled, and has given some account of them under their initials, which for all public purposes are as well as their names.

The person among them best worth remembering was the gentleman whom Mr. Hogg calls J. F. N., of whom he relates some anecdotes. I will add one or two from my own experience. He was an estimable man and an agreeable companion, and he was not the less amusing that he was the absolute impersonation of a single theory, or rather of two single theories rolled into one. He held that all diseases and all aberrations, moral and physical, had their origin in the use of animal food and of fermented and spirituous liquors; that the universal adoption of a diet of roots, fruits, and distilled† water, would restore the golden age of universal health, purity, and peace; that this most ancient and sublime morality was mystically inculcated in the most

* The tune was the uniform repetition of three notes, not very true in their intervals. The nearest resemblance to it will be found in the second, third, and fourth of a minor key: B C D, for example, on the key of A natural: a crotchet and two quavers.

† He held that water in its natural state was full of noxious impurities, which were only to be got rid of by distillation.

ancient Zodiac, which was that of Dendera; that this Zodiac was divided into two hemispheres, the upper hemisphere being the realm of Oromazes or the principle of good, the lower that of Ahrimanes or the principle of evil; that each of these hemispheres was again divided into two compartments, and that the four lines of division radiating from the centre were the prototype of the Christian cross. The two compartments of Oromazes were those of Uranus or Brahma the Creator, and of Saturn or Veishnu the Preserver. The two compartments of Ahrimanes were those of Jupiter or Seva the Destroyer, and of Apollo or Krishna the Restorer. The great moral doctrine was thus symbolized in the Zodiacal signs:—In the first compartment, Taurus the Bull, having in the ancient Zodiac a torch in his mouth, was the type of eternal light. Cancer the Crab was the type of celestial matter, sleeping under the all-covering water, on which Brahma floated in a lotus-flower for millions of ages. From the union, typified by Gemini, of light and celestial matter, issued in the second compartment Leo, Primogenial Love, mounted on the back of a Lion, who produced the pure and perfect nature of things in Virgo, and Libra the Balance denoted the coincidence of the ecliptic with the equator, and the equality of man's happy existence. In the third compartment, the first entrance of evil into the system was typified by the change of celestial into terrestrial matter—Cancer into Scorpio. Under this evil influence man became a hunter, Sagittarius the Archer, and pursued the wild animals, typified by Capricorn. Then, with animal food and cookery, came death into the world, and all our woe. But in the fourth compartment, Dhanwantari or Æsculapius, Aquarius the Waterman, arose from the sea, typified by Pisces the Fish, with a jug of pure water and a bunch of fruit, and brought back the period of universal happiness under Aries, the Ram, whose benignant ascendancy was the golden fleece of the Argonauts, and the true talisman of Oromazes.

He saw the Zodiac in everything. I was walking with him one day on a common near Bracknell, when we came on a public-house which had the sign of the Horse-shoes. They were four on the sign, and he immediately determined that this number had been handed down from remote antiquity as representative of the compartments of the Zodiac. He stepped into the public-house, and said to the landlord, ' Your sign is the Horse-shoes ?'—'Yes, sir.' 'This sign has always four Horse-shoes ?' —'Why mostly, sir.' 'Not always?' —'I think I have seen three.' 'I cannot divide the Zodiac into three. But it is mostly four. Do you know why it is mostly four ?'—'Why, sir, I suppose because a horse has four legs.' He bounced out in great indignation, and as soon as I joined him, he said to me, ' Did you ever see such a fool ?'

I have also very agreeable reminiscences of Mrs. B. and her daughter Cornelia. Of these ladies Shelley says (Hogg, ii. 515):—

I have begun to learn Italian again. Cornelia assists me in this language. Did I not once tell you that I thought her cold and reserved ? She is the reverse of this, as she is the reverse of everything bad. She inherits all the divinity of her mother.

Mr. Hogg 'could never learn why Shelley called Mrs. B. Meimouné.' In fact he called her, not Meimouné, but Maimuna, from Southey's *Thalaba*:—

Her face was as a damsel's face,
And yet her hair was grey.

She was a young-looking woman for her age, and her hair was as white as snow.

About the end of 1813, Shelley was troubled by one of his most extraordinary delusions. He fancied that a fat old woman who sat opposite to him in a mail coach was afflicted with elephantiasis, that the disease was infectious and incurable, and that he had caught it from her. He was continually on the watch for its symptoms; his legs were to swell to the size of an elephant's, and his skin was to be crumpled over like goose-skin. He would draw the skin of his own hands, arms, and neck very tight, and if he discovered any deviation from smoothness, he would seize the person next to him, and endeavour by a corresponding pressure to see if any corresponding deviation

existed. He often startled young
ladies in an evening party by this
singular process, which was as instantaneous as a flash of lightning.
His friends took various methods of
dispelling the delusion. I quoted
to him the words of Lucretius:—

Est elephas morbus, qui propter flumina
  Nili
Gignitur Ægypto in media, neque præ-
  terea usquam.

He said these verses were the
greatest comfort he had. When he
found that, as the days rolled on,
his legs retained their proportion,
and his skin its smoothness, the delusion died away.

I have something more to say
belonging to this year 1813, but
it will come better in connexion
with the events of the succeeding
year. In the meantime I will
mention one or two traits of character in which chronology is unim-
portant.

It is to be remarked that, with
the exception of the clergyman from
whom he received his first instructions, the Reverend Mr. Edwards,
of Horsham, Shelley never came,
directly or indirectly, under any
authority, public or private, for
which he entertained, or had much
cause to entertain, any degree of
respect. His own father, the
Brentford schoolmaster, the head
master of Eton, the Master and
Fellows of his college at Oxford, the
Lord Chancellor Eldon, all succes-
sively presented themselves to him
in the light of tyrants and oppres-
sors. It was perhaps from the
recollection of his early preceptor
that he felt a sort of poetical regard
for country clergymen, and was
always pleased when he fell in with
one who had a sympathy with him
in classical literature, and was
willing to pass sub silentio the de-
bateable ground between them. But
such an one was of rare occurrence.
This recollection may also have
influenced his feeling under the
following transitory impulse.

He had many schemes of life.
Amongst them all, the most singular
that ever crossed his mind was that
of entering the church. Whether
he had ever thought of it before, or
whether it only arose on the moment, I cannot say: the latter is
most probable; but I well remember

the occasion. We were walking in
the early summer through a village
where there was a good vicarage
house, with a nice garden, and the
front wall of the vicarage was covered
with corchorus in full flower, a plant
less common then than it has since become. He stood some time admiring
the vicarage wall. The extreme
quietness of the scene, the pleasant
pathway through the village churchyard, and the brightness of the
summer morning, apparently con-
curred to produce the impression
under which he suddenly said to
me,—'I feel strongly inclined to
enter the church.' 'What,' I said,
'to become a clergyman, with your
ideas of the faith?' 'Assent to the
supernatural part of it,' he said, 'is
merely technical. Of the moral
doctrines of Christianity I am a
more decided disciple than many of
its more ostentatious professors.
And consider for a moment how
much good a good clergyman may
do. In his teaching as a scholar
and a moralist; in his example as a
gentleman and a man of regular
life; in the consolation of his personal intercourse and of his charity
among the poor, to whom he may
often prove a most beneficent friend
when they have no other to comfort
them. It is an admirable institution that admits the possibility
of diffusing such men over the surface of the land. And am I to deprive myself of the advantages of
this admirable institution because
there are certain technicalities to
which I cannot give my adhesion,
but which I need not bring promi-
nently forward?' I told him I
thought he would find more restraint in the office than would suit
his aspirations. He walked on some
time thoughtfully, then started
another subject, and never returned
to that of entering the church.

He was especially fond of the
novels of Brown—Charles Brockden
Brown, the American, who died at
the age of twenty-nine.

The first of these novels was
Wieland. Wieland's father passed
much of his time alone in a summer-
house, where he died of spontaneous
combustion. This summer-house
made a great impression on Shelley,
and in looking for a country house
he always examined if he could find

such a summer-house, or a place to erect one.

The second was *Ormond*. The heroine of this novel, Constantia Dudley, held one of the highest places, if not the very highest place, in Shelley's idealities of female character.

The third was *Edgar Huntly; or, the Sleep-walker*. In this his imagination was strangely captivated by the picture of Clitheroe in his sleep digging a grave under a tree.

The fourth was *Arthur Mervyn*: chiefly remarkable for the powerful description of the yellow fever in Philadelphia and the adjacent country, a subject previously treated in *Ormond*. No descriptions of pestilence surpass these of Brown. The transfer of the hero's affections from a simple peasant-girl to a rich Jewess, displeased Shelley extremely, and he could only account for it on the ground that it was the only way in which Brown could bring his story to an uncomfortable conclusion. The three preceding tales had ended tragically.

These four tales were unquestionably works of great genius, and were remarkable for the way in which natural causes were made to produce the semblance of supernatural effects. The superstitious terror of romance could scarcely be more strongly excited than by the perusal of *Wieland*.

Brown wrote two other novels, *Jane Talbot* and *Philip Stanley*, in which he abandoned this system, and confined himself to the common business of life. They had little comparative success.

Brown's four novels, Schiller's *Robbers*, and Goethe's *Faust*, were, of all the works with which he was familiar, those which took the deepest root in his mind, and had the strongest influence in the formation of his character. He was an assiduous student of the great classical poets, and among these his favourite heroines were Nausicaa and Antigone. I do not remember that he greatly admired any of our old English poets, excepting Shakspeare and Milton. He devotedly admired Wordsworth and Coleridge, and in a minor degree Southey: these had great influence on his style, and Coleridge especially on his imagination; but admiration is one thing and assimilation is another; and nothing so blended itself with the structure of his interior mind as the creations of Brown. Nothing stood so clearly before his thoughts as a perfect combination of the purely ideal and possibly real, as Constantia Dudley.

He was particularly pleased with Wordsworth's Stanzas written in a pocket copy of Thomson's *Castle of Indolence*. He said the fifth of these stanzas always reminded him of me. I told him the four first stanzas were in many respects applicable to him. He said: 'It was a remarkable instance of Wordsworth's insight into nature, that he should have made intimate friends of two imaginary characters so essentially dissimilar, and yet severally so true to the actual characters of two friends, in a poem written long before they were known to each other, and while they were both boys, and totally unknown to him.'

The delight of Wordsworth's first personage in the gardens of the happy castle, the restless spirit that drove him to wander, the exhaustion with which he returned and abandoned himself to repose, might all in these stanzas have been sketched to the life from Shelley. The end of the fourth stanza is especially apposite:—

> Great wonder to our gentle tribe it was
> Whenever from our valley he withdrew;
> For happier soul no living creature has
> Than he had, being here the long day through.
> Some thought he was a lover, and did woo:
> *Some thought far worse of him, and judged him wrong:*
> *But verse was what he had been wedded to;*
> *And his own mind did like a tempest strong*
> *Come to him thus, and drive the weary wight along.*

He often repeated to me, as applicable to himself, a somewhat similar passage from *Childe Harold*:—

> ——- On the sea
> The boldest steer but where their ports invite :
> But there are wanderers o'er Eternity,
> Whose bark drives on and on, and anchor'd ne'er shall be.

His vegetable diet entered for something into his restlessness. When he was fixed in a place he adhered to this diet consistently and conscientiously, but it certainly did not agree with him; it made him weak and nervous, and exaggerated the sensitiveness of his imagination. Then arose those thick-coming fancies which almost invariably preceded his change of place. While he was living from inn to inn he was obliged to live, as he said, 'on what he could get;' that is to say, like other people. When he got well under this process he gave all the credit to locomotion, and held himself to have thus benefited, not in consequence of his change of regimen, but in spite of it. Once, when I was living in the country, I received a note from him wishing me to call on him in London. I did so, and found him ill in bed. He said, 'You are looking well. I suppose you go on in your old way, living on animal food and fermented liquor?' I answered in the affirmative. 'And here,' he said, 'you see a vegetable feeder overcome by disease.' I said 'Perhaps the diet is the cause.' This he would by no means allow; but it was not long before he was again posting through some yet unvisited wilds, and recovering his health as usual, by living 'on what he could get.'

He had a prejudice against theatres which I took some pains to overcome. I induced him one evening to accompany me to a representation of the *School for Scandal*. When, after the scenes which exhibited Charles Surface in his jollity, the scene returned, in the fourth act, to Joseph's library, Shelley said to me,—'I see the purpose of this comedy. It is to associate virtue with bottles and glasses, and villany with books.' I had great difficulty to make him stay to the end. He often talked of 'the withering and perverting spirit of comedy.' I do not think he ever went to another. But I remember his absorbed attention to Miss O'Neill's performance of Bianca in *Fazio*, and it is evident to me that she was always in his thoughts when he drew the character of Beatrice in the *Cenci*.

In the season of 1817, I persuaded him to accompany me to the opera. The performance was *Don Giovanni*. Before it commenced he asked me if the opera was comic or tragic. I said it was composite,—more comedy than tragedy. After the killing of the Commendatore, he said, 'Do you call this comedy?' By degrees he became absorbed in the music and action. I asked him what he thought of Ambrogetti? He said, 'He seems to be the very wretch he personates.' The opera was followed by a ballet, in which Mdlle. Milanie was the principal *danseuse*. He was enchanted with this lady; said he had never imagined such grace of motion; and the impression was permanent, for in a letter he afterwards wrote to me from Milan he said, 'They have no Mdlle. Milanie here.'

From this time till he finally left England he was an assiduous frequenter of the Italian Opera. He delighted in the music of Mozart, and especially in the *Nozze di Figaro*, which was performed several times in the early part of 1818.

With the exception of *Fazio*, I do not remember his having been pleased with any performance at an English theatre. Indeed I do not remember his having been present at any but the two above mentioned. I tried in vain to reconcile him to comedy. I repeated to him one day, as an admirable specimen of diction and imagery, Michael Perez's soliloquy in his miserable lodgings, from *Rule a Wife and Have a Wife*. When I came to the passage :

> There's an old woman that's now grown to marble,
> Dried in this brick-kiln : and she sits i' the chimney
> (Which is but three tiles, raised like a house of cards),
> The true proportion of an old smoked Sibyl.
> There is a young thing, too, that Nature meant

For a maid-servant, but 'tis now a monster :
She has a husk about her like a chestnut,
With laziness, and living under the line here :
And these two make a hollow sound together,
Like frogs, or winds between two doors that murmur.

He said, ' There is comedy in its perfection. Society grinds down poor wretches into the dust of abject poverty, till they are scarcely recognisable as human beings ; and then, instead of being treated as what they really are, subjects of the deepest pity, they are brought forward as grotesque monstrosities to be laughed at.' I said, ' You must admit the fineness of the expression.' ' It is true,' he answered; ' but the finer it is the worse it is, with such a perversion of sentiment.'

I postpone, as I have intimated, till after the appearance of Mr. Hogg's third and fourth volumes, the details of the circumstances which preceded Shelley's separation from his first wife, and those of the separation itself.

There never was a case which more strongly illustrated the truth of Payne Knight's observation, that ' the same kind of marriage, which usually ends a comedy, as usually begins a tragedy.'*

T. L. PEACOCK.

NOTES

p. 311, ll. 15–16: '*secretum iter et fallentis semita vitae*': Horace, *Epistles*, I, xviii, line 103. It means 'a secluded journey along the path of an unnoticed life'

p. 315, l. 36: 'the gentleman whom Hogg calls J.F.N.': this was Dr. John Newton, naturist and Zoroastrian, whom Shelley met through William Godwin. It was with Newton's sister-in-law, Mrs. Boinville, that Shelley and Harriet stayed in Bracknell in 1813

p. 316, l. 23: 'Mrs. B.': Mrs. Boinville (see previous note). She had recently been widowed at the time that she befriended the Shelleys

p. 317, l. 7: 'Est elephantas morbus...': Lucretius, *De Rerum Natura*, VI, lines 1114–5. They translate as, 'It is elephantiasis, which occurs midway along the River Nile in Egypt, *and nowhere else*'

p. 319, ll. 1–4: 'On the sea...': *Childe Harold's Pilgrimage*, Canto III, stanza LXX (lines 667–70)

Lady Jane Shelley (ed.), *Shelley Memorials: From Authentic Sources* (1859)

Lady Jane Shelley, wife of Shelley's son Sir Percy Shelley, is the one author of passages in this anthology who never met Shelley – but then she wrote as a family representative rather than as an individual. The title page of her volume of *Memorials* declares it to have been 'Edited by Lady Shelley'. The reader was asked to believe that she was not the inventor of a narrative, but merely the publisher of evidence ('From Authentic Sources'). The book was presented as an authorised collection of data about the poet – a family document, rather than the creation of a particular writer. And there was some truth in this. Sir Percy Shelley, who had inherited the baronetcy from his grandfather in 1844, was certainly concerned about his father's reputation, and had indicated his dissatisfaction with the version of Shelley's life given by his old university friend Thomas Jefferson Hogg – a version that he had himself sponsored (see headnote in this volume to Hogg, *The Life of Percy Bysshe Shelley*). Yet, equally certainly, Sir Percy did not have the wherewithal to produce his own account ('no aim – no exertion – no ambition', admitted his otherwise doting mother in a letter to Claire Clairmont: Bennett, *Letters*, III, p. 83). He reserved his energies mostly for yachting and amateur dramatics, and trusted to his wife to build a proper version of the Shelley legend.

Sir Percy Shelley was Lady Shelley's second husband. Born Jane Gibson, she had married the Hon. Charles St. John in 1841. He had died less than three years later, leaving her comfortably off. ('She has a fortune of £15,000 which will lighten our odious mortgages', commented Mary Shelley, though it is clear that she had other reasons for thinking the marriage a good one – she said that she 'never knew any one so good, true & affectionate': ibid, III, p. 342). She and Sir Percy were married in June 1848, a year after they first met. Lady Shelley brought to the marriage an enthusiasm for Shelley's poetry that had kindled before she met his son and an admiration for his widow that seems to have stood the test of acquaintance: 'She was a Shelleyan already' (Norman, p. 178). In her old age, it was her first meeting with Mary Shelley rather than with Sir Percy Shelley that she fondly recalled (see Rolleston, pp. 25–9). In her new marital home, Boscombe Manor, near Bournemouth, she made a shrine to the poet's memory – a special room where she kept not only manuscripts but also other relics of the poet: pictures, possessions, locks of hair. She referred to it as 'my sanctum' (Rolleston, p. 69). Those who were trusted were allowed to view it; a few had their own effects included in the collection. (There was a portrait of Trelawny and some of his hair: see St Clair, *Trelawny*, pp. 172–3 for an account of the creation of the Boscombe shrine). Lady Shelley was always committed to fashioning Shelley's 'poetic' reputation. 'Victorian idealization' is Richard Holmes's phrase, echoing other modern commentators (Holmes, p. xi). The business of Hogg's *Life*, where a trusted Shelleyan had still failed to produce the desired story of the poet's trials and triumphs, persuaded Lady Shelley that even more careful control had to be exercised over the materials out of which biography might be made.

Shelley Memorials was the beginning of a campaign that lasted almost four decades (Lady Shelley died in 1899, eleven years after her husband). It involved the selection of a few scholars and enthusiasts who, through the last decades of the nineteenth century, would help establish Shelley as an unworldly, much misunderstood and sinned-against saint. It also involved the highly selective use – and suppression – of the Boscombe collection of Shelley's manuscripts, access to which Lady Shelley strictly controlled. (See Norman, ch. XII, for a description of the control that she exercised.) The first of the all-too-willing Shelleyans whom she recruited was Richard Garnett, an assistant in the library at the British Museum and eventually, like his father before him, keeper of printed books. Garnett, already in his twenties a considerable scholar, helped produce the *Memorials*, and was to continue to be associated with the family's shaping of the poet's reputation. (In 1862 he edited *Relics of Shelley*, the family's publication of previously unpublished poems held in its manuscript collection: see Everest, *Poems of Shelley*, Introduction, p. xvii.) He would help make an account in which Shelley was to be made to fit a new age. In his own day, the poet had been forced to seem rebellious. 'In the present day, when a brighter morn seems breaking on the future; when another spirit is breathing over us; when vengeance is departing from our laws, and love is gradually creeping in; when freedom of inquiry is becoming at once a social and a legal right; when the fierce voices of hatred, which burst in Shelley's time on the man bold enough to question the received notions of Church and State orthodoxy, have ceased, or are faintly heard; when a protecting hand is extended over the toil of women and children...', it is not surprising that there is a 'throbbing interest' in Shelley's life (*Shelley Memorials*, pp. 18–19). We might call truly 'Victorian' not so much this text's evasiveness as its announcement of a poet and thinker posthumously vindicated by progressive humanity.

Yet, as will be seen below, evasiveness, amounting to deception, there certainly was. Lady Shelley baldly asserted that Harriet Shelley's suicide had nothing to do with Shelley's own conduct. She also structured her chapters so that Harriet's death was followed by a description of 'the society and sympathy of the Godwins', as if Shelley only became intimate with the

Godwins after his wife's death. The lifelong pledge of allegiance to Shelley given by Lady Shelley's mother-in-law sounds like solace for his undeserved troubles and not like adultery. By telling of Shelley's marriage to Mary in December 1816 (*Memorials*, p. 72) at a point in the book that is safely distant from his separation from Harriet (dated 1813 – in fact it was 1814) and her suicide (which is carefully undated), by omitting the birth of Mary's first child, by leaving Claire Clairmont out of the story altogether, various embarrassments are avoided in ways that seem entirely calculating. *Shelley Memorials* was dedicated to celebrating not only Shelley, but also Mary Shelley (who had died eight years before it appeared). Indeed, Lady Shelley's 'official' biography draws to a close with some of Mary Shelley's grieving correspondence in the aftermath of Shelley's death, and twenty pages of extracts from her 'Private Journal'. It is an account that is determined to rebut the 'calumnies heaped upon Shelley by his unscrupulous detractors' (ibid, p. 160), but that one is unable to bring itself to detail those 'calumnies'.

PREFACE BY THE EDITOR.

HAD it been left entirely to the uninfluenced wishes of Sir Percy Shelley and myself, we should have preferred that the publication of the materials for a life of Shelley which we possess should have been postponed to a later period of our lives; but, as we had recently noticed, both in French and English magazines, many papers on Shelley, all taking for their text Captain Medwin's Life of the Poet (a book full of errors), and as other biographies had been issued, written by those who had no means of ascertaining the truth, we were anxious that the numerous misstatements which had gone forth should be corrected.

For this purpose, we placed the documents in our possession at the disposal of a gentleman whose literary habits and early knowledge of the poet seemed to point him out as the most fitting person for bringing them to the notice of the public. It was clearly understood, however, that our wishes and feelings should be consulted in all the details.

We saw the book for the first time when it was given to the world. It was impossible to imagine beforehand that from such materials a book could have been produced which has astonished and shocked those who have the greatest right to form an opinion on the character of Shelley; and it was with the most painful feelings of dismay that we perused what we could only look upon as a fantastic caricature, going forth to the public with my apparent sanction,—for it was dedicated to myself.

Our feelings of duty to the memory of Shelley left us no other alternative than to withdraw the materials which we had originally entrusted to his early friend, and which we could not but consider had been strangely misused; and to take upon ourselves the task of laying them before the public, connected only by as slight a thread of narrative as would suffice to make them intelligible to the reader.

I have condensed as much as possible the details of the early period of Shelley's life, for I am aware that a great many of them have already appeared in print. The repetition of some, however, was considered advisable, since it is very probable that this volume will be read by many who have not seen, nor are likely to see, any other work giving an account of the writings and actions of Shelley.

I little expected that this task would devolve on me;

and I am fully sensible how unequal I am to its proper fulfilment. To give a truthful statement of long-distorted facts, and to clear away the mist in which the misrepresentations of foes and professed friends have obscured the memory of Shelley, have been my only objects. My labours have been greatly assisted by the help of an intimate and valued friend of Mrs. Shelley, and by Mr. Edmund Ollier, whose father (the publisher of Shelley's works) at once freely offered me the use of some most interesting letters written to himself. I regret to say that this gentleman died while the present work was passing through the printer's hands.

It is needless to say that the authenticity of all the documents contained in this volume is beyond question; but the public would do well to receive with the utmost caution all letters purporting to be by Shelley, which have not some indisputable warrant.*

The art of forging letters purporting to be relics of men of literary celebrity, and therefore apparently possessing a commercial value, has been brought to a rare perfection by those who have made Mr. Shelley's handwriting the object of their imitation. Within the last

---

* Those printed in the work to which allusion has already been made have never, for the most part, been seen by any other person than the author of that work; and the erasures which he has already made in them, together with the arrangement of their paragraphs, render them of doubtful value, however authentic may be the originals which that gentleman asserts he possesses.

fourteen years, on no less than three occasions, have forged letters been presented to our family for purchase. In December, 1851, Sir Percy Shelley and the late Mr. Moxon bought several letters, all of which proved to be forgeries, though, on the most careful inspection, we could scarcely detect any difference between these and the originals; for some were exact copies of documents in our possession. The water-mark on the paper was generally, though not always, the mark appropriate to the date; and the amount of ingenuity exercised was most extraordinary. Mr. Moxon published what he had bought in a small volume, but recalled the work shortly afterwards, on discovering that some of the letters had been manufactured from articles in magazines and reviews, written long after Shelley's death.

The letter to Lord Ellenborough has never before been published; but I regard it as too extraordinary a production for a youth of eighteen to feel myself justified in suppressing it.

The fragmentary Essay on Christianity, published at the end of this volume, was found amongst Shelley's papers in the imperfect state in which it is now produced.

Boscombe, June 22nd, 1859.

☆ ★ ☆

The Miss Shelleys were at that period at school at Brompton, and among the pupils was a very handsome girl named Harriet Westbrook. To her (as her parents resided in London) was consigned the task of conveying the little sums of money to Shelley, on whose susceptible fancy she dawned as a celestial being, illumining the dingy lodgings he inhabited. During the young lady's holidays, Shelley was a constant and welcome visitor at the house of her father; and, on Harriet's recovery from a slight indisposition, the young poet was chosen to escort her back to school. About the same time, he went for a few days to Field Place, and during this visit came to an amicable arrangement with his father. In consideration of a new settlement of the property, Sir Timothy agreed to make him an allowance of 200*l.* a year, and his son was to be at liberty to live where he pleased.

On leaving Field Place, he went to his cousin, Mr. T. Grove, who resided at a country house near Rhayader, in Radnorshire; whence, summoned by the pressing appeals of the Miss Westbrooks, he hastily returned to London, and eloped with Harriet.

From Shelley's own account, and from other sources of information which have since transpired, this unfortunate marriage seems to have been thus brought about:

To the wild eloquence of the enthusiast, who claimed

it as his mission to regenerate the world, and to give it freedom from the shackles which had been too long endured, and which barred its progress to indefinite perfectibility, Harriet had in their many interviews in London bent a well-pleased ear; and when the day came for her return to her Brompton seminary, these new lights seemed to her mind to have a practical bearing on the forms and discipline of her boarding-school. She therefore petitioned her father to be allowed to remain at home. On his refusal, she wrote to Shelley; and, in a sad and evil hour for both, this girl, " who had thrown herself upon his protection," and " with whom he was not in love,"* became his wife.

From London, the young pair (whose united ages amounted to thirty-five years, Harriet being sixteen, and Shelley nineteen) went to Edinburgh, and thence to York. During their residence in the latter town, a new inmate was added to their circle in the person of the elder Miss Westbrook—a visitor whose presence was in many respects unfortunate. From strength of character and disparity of years (for she was much older than Harriet), she exercised a strong influence over her sister; and this influence was used without much discretion, and with little inclination to smooth the difficulties or promote the happiness of the young couple.

Keswick was the next resting-place to which the Shelleys were tempted by the beauty of the scenery and the cheapness of the necessaries of life, which gave some

---

* These expressions are quoted from some published letters of Shelley's, the authenticity of which I am not able to guarantee.

hope that their scanty income might suffice for their moderate wants. While residing here, the then Duke of Norfolk, who owned a large extent of land in the neighbourhood, greatly interested himself in Shelley and his girl wife, introduced them to the neighbouring gentry, directed his agents to furnish their house with necessary accommodations, and interceded (but in vain) with the elder Mr. Shelley. The young poet became speedily acquainted with Robert Southey, Thomas De Quincey, and other eminent writers then resident in the north. With Southey he was particularly intimate for a time, despite the diametrical opposition of their creeds. It was in the year 1811, also—but previous to his marriage —that Shelley sought and obtained the friendship of Leigh Hunt, whose noble-spirited political writings in the *Examiner* had moved the highest admiration of the youthful enthusiast. While the latter was yet unknown to the journalist, he had proposed to him, in a letter, a scheme for forming an association of Liberals, with a view to resisting the spread of despotic principles; and this was followed by Shelley's self-introduction. The friendship of the two writers was only broken by death.

☆ ★ ☆

Shelley was now in severe pecuniary distress; for he received nothing from his father beyond the stipulated 200*l*. a year, and he had not found it possible to raise money on his future expectations. For the purpose of economy he retired to a small cottage in Berkshire, which bore the lofty title of High Elms, and where, in the society of a few friends, varied by frequent visits to London, some months glided by happily and quietly.

During this summer, Shelley paid a visit to Field Place, and his reception there is graphically told by a friend of the family (Captain Kennedy), who was then staying in the house :—

" At this time I had not seen Shelley; but the servants, especially the old butler, Laker, had spoken of him to me. He seemed to have won the hearts of the whole household. Mrs. Shelley often spoke to me of her son; her heart yearned after him with all the fondness of a mother's love. It was during the absence of his father and the three youngest children that the natural desire of a mother to see her son induced her to propose that he should pay her a short visit. At this time he resided somewhere in the country with his first wife and their only child, Ianthe. He walked from his house until within a very few miles of Field Place, when a farmer gave him a seat in his travelling cart. As he passed along, the farmer, ignorant of the quality of his companion, amused Bysshe with descriptions of the country and its inhabitants. When Field Place came in sight, he told whose seat it was ; and, as the most remarkable incident connected with the family, that young Master Shelley seldom went to church. He arrived at Field Place exceedingly fatigued. I came there the following morning to meet him. I found him with his mother and his two elder sisters in a small room off the drawing-room, which they had named Confusion Hall.

" He received me with frankness and kindliness, as if he had known me from childhood, and at once won my heart. I fancy I see him now, as he sat by the window, and hear his voice, the tones of which impressed me with his sincerity and simplicity. His resemblance to his sister Elizabeth was as striking as if they had been twins. His eyes were most expressive, his complexion beautifully fair, his features exquisitely fine ; his hair was dark, and no peculiar attention to its arrangement was manifest. In person he was slender and gentlemanlike, but inclined to stoop ; his gait was decidedly not military. The general appearance indicated great delicacy of constitution. One would at once pronounce of him that he was something different from other men. There was an earnestness in his manner, and such perfect gentleness of breeding, and freedom from everything artificial, as charmed every one. I never met a man who so immediately won upon me.

" The generosity of his disposition and utter unselfishness imposed upon him the necessity of strict self-denial in personal comforts.   Consequently, he was obliged to be most economical in his dress.   He one day asked us how we liked his coat, the only one he had brought with him.   We said it was very nice ; it looked as if new.   ' Well,' said he, ' it is an old black coat which I have had done up, and smartened with metal buttons and a velvet collar.'

" As it was not desirable that Bysshe's presence in the country should be known, we arranged that, walking out, he should wear my scarlet uniform, and that I should assume his outer garments.   So he donned the soldier's dress, and sallied forth.   His head was so remarkably small that, though mine be not large, the cap came down over his eyes, the peak resting on his nose, and it had to be stuffed before it would fit him.   His hat just stuck on the crown of my head.   He certainly looked like anything but a soldier.   The metamorphosis was very amusing; he enjoyed it much, and made himself perfectly at home in his unwonted garb.   We gave him the name of Captain Jones, under which name we used to talk of him after his departure; but, with all our care, Bysshe's visit could not be kept a secret.

" I chanced to mention the name of Sir James Macintosh, of whom he expressed the highest admiration.   He told me Sir James was intimate with Godwin, to whom, he said, he owed everything; from whose book, _Political Justice_, he had derived all that was valuable in knowledge and virtue.   He discoursed with eloquence and enthusiasm; but his views seemed to me exquisitely metaphysical, and by no means clear, precise, or decided. He told me that he had already read the Bible four times. He was then only twenty years old.* He spoke of the Supreme Being as of infinite mercy and benevolence. He disclosed no fixed views of spiritual things; all seemed wild and fanciful. He said that he once thought the surrounding atmosphere was peopled with the spirits of the departed. He reasoned and spoke as a perfect gentleman, and treated my arguments, boy as I was (I had lately completed my sixteenth year), with as much consideration and respect as if I had been his equal in ability and attainments.

" Shelley was one of the most sensitive of human beings; he had a horror of taking life, and looked upon it as a crime. He read poetry with great emphasis and solemnity; one evening he read aloud to us a translation of one of Goethe's poems, and at this day I think I hear him. In music he seemed to delight, as a medium of association; the tunes which had been favourites in boyhood charmed him. There was one, which he played several times on the piano with one hand, which seemed to absorb him : it was an exceedingly simple air, which, I understand, his earliest love (Harriet Grove) was wont to play for him. He soon left us, and I never saw him afterwards; but I can never forget him. It was his last visit to Field Place. He was an amiable, gentle being."

Towards the close of 1813, estrangements, which for some time had been slowly growing between

---

* As this was in the summer of 1813, Shelley must have been nearly, if not quite, twenty-one.—ED.

Mr. and Mrs. Shelley came to a crisis.   Separation ensued; and Mrs. Shelley returned to her father's house. Here she gave birth to her second child—a son, who died in 1826.

The occurrences of this painful epoch in Shelley's life, and of the causes which led to them, I am spared from relating.   In Mary Shelley's own words:—" This is not the time to relate the truth; and I should reject any colouring of the truth.   No account of these events has ever been given at all approaching reality in their details, either as regards himself or others; nor shall I further allude to them than to remark that the errors of action committed by a man as noble and generous as Shelley, may, as far as he only is concerned, be fearlessly avowed by those who loved him, in the firm conviction that, were they judged impartially, his character would stand in fairer and brighter light than that of any contemporary."

Of those remaining who were intimate with Shelley at this time, each has given us a different version of this sad event, coloured by his own views and personal feelings.   Evidently Shelley confided to none of these friends. We, who bear his name, and are of his family, have in our possession papers written by his own hand, which in after years may make the story of his life complete, and which few now living, except Shelley's own children, have ever perused.

One mistake which has gone forth to the world, we feel ourselves called upon positively to contradict.

Harriet's death has sometimes been ascribed to Shelley.

This is entirely false.   There was no immediate connection whatever between her tragic end and any conduct on the part of her husband.   It is true, however,
that it was a permanent source of the deepest sorrow
to him ; for never during all his after life did the dark
shade depart which had fallen on his gentle and sensitive
nature from the self-sought grave of the companion
of his early youth.

☆ ★ ☆

To the family of Godwin, Shelley had, from the
period of his self-introduction at Keswick, been an
object of interest ; and the acquaintanceship which had
sprung up between them during the poet's occasional
visits to London had grown into a cordial friendship.
It was in the society and sympathy of the Godwins
that Shelley sought and found some relief in his present
sorrow.   He was still extremely young.   His anguish,
his isolation, his difference from other men, his gifts of
genius and eloquent enthusiasm, made a deep impression
on Godwin's daughter Mary, now a girl of sixteen, who
had been accustomed to hear Shelley spoken of as
something rare and strange.   To her, as they met
one eventful day in St. Pancras Churchyard, by her
mother's grave, Bysshe, in burning words, poured forth
the tale of his wild past—how he had suffered, how he
had been misled, and how, if supported by her love,
he hoped in future years to enrol his name with the
wise and good who had done battle for their fellow-

men, and been true through all adverse storms to the cause of humanity.

Unhesitatingly, she placed her hand in his, and linked her fortune with his own; and most truthfully, as the remaining portions of these Memorials will prove, was the pledge of both redeemed.

The theories in which the daughter of the authors of *Political Justice* and of the *Rights of Woman* had been educated, spared her from any conflict between her duty and her affection. For she was the child of parents whose writings had had for their object to prove that marriage was one among the many institutions which a new era in the history of mankind was about to sweep away. By her father, whom she loved—by the writings of her mother, whom she had been taught to venerate— these doctrines had been rendered familiar to her mind. It was, therefore, natural that she should listen to the dictates of her own heart, and willingly unite her fate with one who was so worthy of her love.

☆ ★ ☆

From Shelley to Mr. Ollier.

" Dear Sir,   *Pisa, Nov. 11th,* 1821.

" I send you the drama of *Hellas*, relying on your
assurance that you will be good enough to pay immediate attention
to my literary requests.   What little interest this poem may ever
excite, depends upon its immediate publication; I entreat you,
therefore, to have the goodness to send the MS. instantly to a
printer, and the moment you get a proof despatch it to me by the
post.   The whole might be sent at once.   Lord Byron has his
poem sent to him in this manner, and I cannot see that the
inferiority in the composition of a poem can affect the powers of
a printer in the matter of despatch, &c.   If any passages should
alarm you in the notes, you are at liberty to suppress them; the
poem contains nothing of a tendency to danger.

" Do not forget my other questions.   I am especially curious to
hear the fate of *Adonais*.   I confess I should be surprised if *that*
poem were born to an immortality of oblivion.

" Within a few days I may have to write to you on a subject of
greater interest.   Meanwhile, I rely on your kindness for carrying
my present request into immediate effect.

" Dear Sir,
" Your very faithful servant,
" Percy B. Shelley.

" I need not impress on you the propriety of giving a speedy
answer to Mrs. S.'s proposal.   Her volumes are now ready for the
press.   The *Ode to Napoleon* to print at the end."

The calumnies heaped upon Shelley by his unscrupulous detractors often gave him great pain.   In writing
to Mr. Ollier, on the 11th of June, 1821, he says:—
" I hear that the abuse against me exceeds all bounds.
Pray, if you see any one article particularly outrageous,
send it me.   As yet, I have laughed; but woe to these
scoundrels if they should once make me lose my
temper!   I have discovered that my calumniator in the

Quarterly Review was the Rev. Mr. Milman. Priests have their privilege."

Malicious reports seemed to track him wherever he went; and one of these is the subject of some letters which will be found below. Mrs. Shelley writes in her journal, under date August 4th:—" Shelley is gone to see Lord Byron at Ravenna. This is his [Shelley's] birthday: seven years are now gone—what changes! We now appear tranquil; yet who knows what wind ——but I will not prognosticate evil; we have had enough of it. When we arrived in Italy; I said, all is well, if it were permanent. It was more passing than an Italian twilight. I now say the same: may it be a Polar day!—yet that, too, has an end." They had passed a very pleasant summer, having both derived great enjoyment from frequently going to see some friends living at the village of Pugnano. They reached that place by the canal, "which, fed by the Serchio, was, though an artificial, a full and picturesque stream, making its way under verdant banks sheltered by trees that dipped their boughs into the murmuring waters. By day, multitudes of ephemera darted to and fro on the surface; at night, the fireflies came out among the shrubs on the banks: the cicale at noon-day kept up their hum; the aziola cooed in the quiet evening."* Yet, as Mrs. Shelley prognosticated in her diary, their happiness was soon to be dashed. Shelley writes from Ravenna on August 7th:—

---

* Notes to the Poems.

" My DEAREST MARY,

" I ARRIVED last night at ten o'clock, and sat up talking with Lord Byron until five o'clock this morning. I then went to sleep, and now awake at eleven, and, having despatched my breakfast as quick as possible, mean to devote the interval until twelve, when the post departs, to you. . . . .

" Lord Byron has told me of a circumstance that shocks me exceedingly, because it exhibits a degree of desperate and wicked malice for which I am at a loss to account. When I hear such things, my patience and my philosophy are put to a severe proof, whilst I refrain from seeking out some obscure hiding-place, where the countenance of man may never meet me more.

*   *   *   *   *

" Imagine my despair of good; imagine how it is possible that one of so weak and sensitive a nature as mine can run further the gauntlet through this hellish society of men. *You* should write to the Hoppners a letter refuting the charge, in case you believe and know, and can prove that it is false; stating the grounds and proofs of your belief. I need not dictate what you should say; nor, I hope, inspire you with warmth to rebut a charge which you only effectually *can* rebut."

To this letter, Mrs. Shelley thus replied :—

" My DEAR SHELLEY,

" SHOCKED beyond all measure as I was, I instantly wrote the inclosed. If the task be not too dreadful, pray copy it for me. I cannot.

" Read that part of your letter which contains the accusation. I tried, but I could not write it. I think I could as soon have died. I send also Elise's last letter : enclose it or not, as you think best.

" I wrote to you with far different feelings last night, beloved friend. Our bark is indeed 'tempest-tost;' but love me, as you have ever done, and God preserve my child to me, and our enemies shall not be too much for us. Consider well if Florence be a fit residence for us. I love, I own, to face danger ; but I would not be imprudent.

"Pray get my letter to Mrs. H. copied, for a thousand reasons. Adieu, dearest! Take care of yourself—all yet is well. The shock for me is over, and I now despise the slander; but it must not pass uncontradicted. I sincerely thank Lord Byron for his kind unbelief.

"Affectionately yours,

"M. W. S."

"*Friday.*

"Do not think me imprudent in mentioning C.'s illness at Naples. It is well to meet facts. They are as cunning as wicked. I have read over my letter: it is written in haste; but it were as well that the first burst of feeling should be expressed. No letters."

From Shelley to Mrs. Shelley.

" *Thursday, Ravenna.*

"I HAVE received your letter with that to Mrs. Hoppner. I do not wonder, my dearest friend, that you should have been moved. I was at first, but speedily regained the indifference which the opinion of anything or anybody, except our own consciences, amply merits, and day by day shall more receive from me. I have not recopied your letter—such a measure would destroy its authenticity—but have given it to Lord Byron, who has engaged to send it, with his own comments, to the Hoppners.

"People do not hesitate, it seems, to make themselves panders and accomplices to slander; for the Hoppners had exacted from Lord Byron that these accusations should be concealed from *me*. Lord Byron is not a man to keep a secret, good or bad; but, in openly confessing that he has not done so, he must observe a certain delicacy, and therefore wished to send the letter himself; and indeed this adds weight to your representations.

"Have you seen the article in the *Literary Gazette* on me? They evidently allude to some story of this kind. However cautious the Hoppners have been in preventing the calumniated person from asserting his justification, you know too much of the world not to be certain that this was the utmost limit of their caution. So much for nothing.

*   *   *   *   *

" My greatest comfort would be utterly to desert all human society. I would retire with you and our children to a solitary island in the sea; would build a boat, and shut upon my retreat the floodgates of the world. I would read no reviews, and talk with no authors. If I dared trust my imagination, it would tell me that there are one or two chosen companions, besides yourself, whom I should desire. But to this I would not listen. Where two or three are gathered together, the devil is among them; and good, far more than evil, impulses—love, far more than hatred—has been to me, except as you have been its object, the source of all sorts of mischief. So, on this plan, I would be *alone*, and would devote, either to oblivion or to future generations, the over-flowings of a mind which, timely withdrawn from the contagion, should be kept fit for no baser object. But this it does not appear that we shall do.

" The other side of the alternative (for a medium ought not to be adopted) is to form for ourselves a society of our own class, as much as possible, in intellect or in feelings; and to connect ourselves with the interests of that society. Our roots never struck so deeply as at Pisa, and the transplanted tree flourishes not. People who lead the lives which we led until last winter, are like a family of Wahabee Arabs pitching their tent in the middle of London. We must do one thing or the other: for yourself—for our child—for our existence. The calumnies, the sources of which are probably deeper than we perceive, have ultimately for object the depriving us of the means of security and subsistence. You will easily perceive the gradations by which calumny proceeds to pretext, pretext to persecution, and persecution to the ban of fire and water. It is for this—and not because this or that fool, or the whole court of fools curse and rail—that calumny is worth refuting or chastising."

But from these painful details let us pass to other subjects.

Thomas Love Peacock, 'Memoirs of Percy Bysshe Shelley. Part II', *Fraser's Magazine*, January, 1860 and March, 1862

Having been drawn unwillingly into his first (1858) article on Shelley in *Fraser's Magazine*, Peacock found himself further provoked the next year by Lady Shelley's *Shelley Memorials* and drawn to defend Harriet Shelley in accents of frosty anger. 'Some of Shelley's friends have spoken and written of Harriet as if to vindicate him it were necessary to disparage her', he wrote (see the first of the passages below). Medwin and Hogg had both been guilty of this, but perhaps only ignorantly. (Hogg had indeed spoken up for Harriet, if condescendingly.) Lady Shelley, however, had been more thoughtfully dishonest, and Part II of Peacock's 'Memoirs', the article that he had projected as a review of the completion of Hogg's biography, became a nettled reply to the Shelley family's official version of events. Above all, it was written, as Peacock says in the opening of the 1860 article, 'under the necessity of dissenting from Lady Shelley respecting the facts of the separation of Shelley and Harriet' (see below).

Peacock's sense of this 'necessity' stems not only from the loyalty to Harriet that he here expresses, but also from his idea of Shelley's 'genius'. As is clear from his conclusion to his 1860 article (the second of the extracts below), he thought of Shelley as an inspired idealist who did not live long enough to experience necessary disillusion. If Shelley's principles had allowed him to act in ways that caused misery, not least to himself, then it was important to say so. Thus Peacock's surprisingly sympathetic explanation of Lord Eldon's refusal to allow Shelley custody of his children by Harriet after her death. In Peacock's version, this was not the outraged reflex of an establishment shocked by Shelley's writing, but a rational response to one who believed that marital responsibilities could be set aside at pleasure. Peacock had himself been an advocate of free love in his youth, and when his own daughter Mary Ellen deserted her husband, George Meredith, for the painter Henry Wallis in the 1850s he seemed to condone her actions and enjoy a friendly relationship with her illicit partner (see Butler, pp. 7–10). He had no inclination to flinch from the facts of Shelley's desertion of his wife for Mary Godwin. He was a moralist only in his willingness to detect contrasts between ideals and realities – a tendency that had always shown, not least in his satires, and that was the more marked now that he was in his seventies and recalling events from almost half a century earlier.

Part II of Peacock's 'Memoir' stung the Shelley family into a response. *Macmillan's Magazine* of June, 1860, featured an article by Richard Garnett which commented on Peacock's 'statements respecting Shelley's first wife' (see headnote to Lady Shelley's *Shelley Memorials* in this volume for Garnett's involvement).

> According to these, the transaction was not preceded by long-continued unhappiness, neither was it an amicable agreement effected in virtue of a mutual understanding. The time cannot be distant when these assertions must be refuted by the publication of documents hitherto witheld, and Shelley's family have doubted whether it be worth while to anticipate it. Pending their decision, I may be allowed to state most explicitly that the evidence to which they would in such a case appeal, and to the nature of which I feel fully competent to speak, most decidedly contradicts the allegations of Mr. Peacock (from 'Shelley in Pall Mall', in *Macmillan's Magazine*, June, 1860, p. 100).

This provoked, in turn, Peacock's 'Supplementary Notice', which appeared in *Fraser's Magazine* in March, 1862, and which is given in the third of the extracts below. In reply to its confidently brandished dates, vagueness about which had been one of the necessary devices of the *Shelley Memorials*, Garnett was hastily to add a section to his 1862 *Relics of Shelley*: 'Shelley, Harriet Shelley, and Mr. T. L. Peacock' (Garnett, *Relics*, pp. 147–74). Here he asserted (correctly) that correspondence in the possession of the Shelley family showed Shelley to have taken an 'affectionate interest' in Harriet's welfare after their separation, and to have been concerned to make proper financial provision for her (ibid, p. 149). Garnett also declared that Peacock was absolutely wrong to 'accuse Mary of having caused an estrangement' between the poet and his wife (ibid, p. 154). Shelley, he said, had been disappointed in Harriet before he was ever drawn to Mary Godwin, giving as evidence a letter from Shelley to Hogg in which he appears to regard his wife with 'disgust and horror' (ibid, p. 153). The letter was genuine, but Shelley was referring not to Harriet, but to Eliza Westbrook (whose name was conveniently omitted).

Under Lady Shelley's supervision, Shelleyans would continue to assert that Shelley's 'domestic infelicity' (ibid, p. 154) preceded his attachment to Mary Godwin, implying that Harriet had been unfaithful to her husband before he turned from her. Peacock's 'Supplementary Notice' was his last blow against Lady Shelley and her allies. He died in 1866. A final injustice was done to him when Richard Garnett was given the responsibility of writing his entry in the *Dictionary of National Biography*. Here, amongst generous comments on Peacock's valuable committee work for the East India Company, passing mention is made of his 'reminiscences of Shelley': 'Shelley's admirers were annoyed at their apparent coldness, and not without reason'. Garnett also wrote the *DNB* entries on Shelley, Mary Shelley, Claire Clairmont, Polidori, Trelawny and Hogg. The work of the Shelleyans went on.

MEMOIRS OF PERCY BYSSHE SHELLEY.

PART II.*

Y Gwir yn erbyn y Byd.
The Truth against the World.
Bardic Maxim.

MR. HOGG'S third and fourth volumes not having appeared, and the materials with which Sir Percy and Lady Shelley had supplied him having been resumed by them, and so much of them as it was thought desirable to publish having been edited by Lady Shelley,† with a connecting thread of narrative, I shall assume that I am now in possession of all the external information likely to be available towards the completion of my memoir; and I shall proceed to complete it accordingly, subject to the contingent addition of a postscript, if any subsequent publication should render it necessary.

Lady Shelley says in her preface:

We saw the book (Mr. Hogg's) for the first time when it was given to the world. It was impossible to imagine beforehand that from such materials a book could have been produced which has astonished and shocked those who have the greatest right to form an opinion on the character of Shelley; and it was with the most painful feelings of dismay that we perused what we could only look upon as a fantastic caricature, going forth to the public with my apparent sanction,—for it was dedicated to myself.

Our feelings of duty to the memory of Shelley left us no other alternative than to withdraw the materials which we had originally intrusted to his early friend, and which we could not but consider had been strangely misused; and to take upon ourselves the task of laying them before the public, connected only by as slight a thread of narrative as would suffice to make them intelligible to the reader.

I am very sorry, in the outset of this notice, to be under the necessity of dissenting from Lady Shelley respecting the facts of the separation of Shelley and Harriet. Captain Medwin represented this separation to have taken place by

mutual consent. Mr. Leigh Hunt and Mr. Middleton adopted this statement; and in every notice I have seen of it in print it has been received as an established truth.

Lady Shelley says—

Towards the close of 1813 estrangements, which for some time had been slowly growing between Mr. and Mrs. Shelley, came to a crisis. Separation ensued, and Mrs. Shelley returned to her father's house. Here she gave birth to her second child—a son, who died in 1826.

The occurrences of this painful epoch in Shelley's life, and of the causes which led to them, I am spared from relating. In Mary Shelley's own words—' This is not the time to relate the truth; and I should reject any colouring of the truth. No account of these events has ever been given at all approaching reality in their details, either as regards himself or others; nor shall I further allude to them than to remark that the errors of action committed by a man as noble and generous as Shelley, may, as far as he only is concerned, be fearlessly avowed by those who loved him, in the firm conviction that, were they judged impartially, his character would stand in fairer and brighter light than that of any contemporary.'

Of those remaining who were intimate with Shelley at this time, each has given us a different version of this sad event, coloured by his own views or personal feelings. Evidently Shelley confided to none of these friends. We, who bear his name, and are of his family, have in our possession papers written by his own hand, which in after years may make the story of his life complete; and which few now living, except Shelley's own children, have ever perused.

One mistake, which has gone forth to the world, we feel ourselves called upon positively to contradict.

Harriet's death has sometimes been ascribed to Shelley. This is entirely false. There was no immediate connexion

---

* Part I. appeared in this Magazine for June, 1858.

† *Shelley Memorials.* From Authentic Sources.   Edited by Lady Shelley. London: Smith and Elder. 1859.

whatever between her tragic end and any conduct on the part of her husband. It is true, however, that it was a permanent source of the deepest sorrow to him; for never during all his after-life did the dark shade depart which had fallen on his gentle and sensitive nature from the self-sought grave of the companion of his early youth.

This passage ends the sixth chapter. The seventh begins thus—

To the family of Godwin, Shelley had, from the period of his self-introduction at Keswick, been an object of interest; and the acquaintanceship which had sprung up between them during the poet's occasional visits to London had grown into a cordial friendship. It was in the society and sympathy of the Godwins that Shelley sought and found some relief in his present sorrow. He was still extremely young. His anguish, his isolation, his difference from other men, his gifts of genius and eloquent enthusiasm, made a deep impression on Godwin's daughter Mary, now a girl of sixteen, who had been accustomed to hear Shelley spoken of as something rare and strange. To her, as they met one eventful day in St. Pancras' churchyard, by her mother's grave, Bysshe, in burning words, poured forth the tale of his wild past—how he had suffered, how he had been misled; and how, if supported by her love, he hoped in future years to enrol his name with the wise and good who had done battle for their fellow-men, and been true through all adverse storms to the cause of humanity.

Unhesitatingly she placed her hand in his, and linked her fortune with his own; and most truthfully, as the remaining portion of these *Memorials* will prove, was the pledge of both redeemed.

I ascribe it to inexperience of authorship, that the sequence of words does not, in these passages, coincide with the sequence of facts: for in the order of words, the present sorrow would appear to be the death of Harriet. This however occurred two years and a half after the separation; and the union of his fate with Mary Godwin was simultaneous with it. Respecting this separation, whatever degree of confidence Shelley may have placed in his several friends, there are some facts which speak for themselves and admit of no misunderstanding.

The Scotch marriage had taken

place in August, 1811. In a letter which he wrote to a female friend sixteen months later (Dec. 10, 1812), he had said :—

How is Harriet a fine lady ? You indirectly accuse her in your letter of this offence—to me the most unpardonable of all. The ease and simplicity of her habits, the unassuming plainness of her address, the uncalculated connexion of her thought and speech, have ever formed in my eyes her greatest charms : and none of these are compatible with fashionable life, or the attempted assumption of its vulgar and noisy *éclat*. You have a prejudice to contend with in making me a convert to this last opinion of yours, which, so long as I have a living and daily witness to its futility before me, I fear will be insurmountable.—*Memorials*, p.44.

Thus there had been no estrangement to the end of 1812. My own memory sufficiently attests that there was none in 1813.

From Bracknell, in the autumn of 1813, Shelley went to the Cumberland lakes ; then to Edinburgh. In Edinburgh he became acquainted with a young Brazilian named Baptista, who had gone there to study medicine by his father's desire, and not from any vocation to the science, which he cordially abominated, as being all hypothesis, without the fraction of a basis of certainty to rest on. They corresponded after Shelley left Edinburgh, and subsequently renewed their intimacy in London. He was a frank, warm-hearted, very gentlemanly young man. He was a great enthusiast, and sympathized earnestly in all Shelley's views, even to the adoption of vegetable diet. He made some progress in a translation of *Queen Mab* into Portuguese. He showed me a sonnet, which he intended to prefix to his translation. It began—

Sublime Shelley, cantor di verdade !

and ended—

Surja *Queen Mab* a restaurar o mundo.

I have forgotten the intermediate lines. But he died early, of a disease of the lungs. This climate did not suit him, and he exposed himself to it incautiously.

Shelley returned to London shortly before Christmas, then took a furnished house for two or three months at Windsor, visiting London occasionally. In March, 1814, he married Harriet a second time, according to the following certificate:—

MARRIAGES IN MARCH 1814.

164. Percy Bysshe Shelley and Harriet Shelley (formerly Harriet Westbrook, Spinster, a Minor), both of this Parish, were re-married in this Church by Licence (the parties having been already married to each other according to the Rites and Ceremonies of the Church of Scotland), in order to obviate all doubts that have arisen, or shall or may arise, touching or concerning the validity of the aforesaid Marriage (by and with the consent of John Westbrook, the natural and lawful father of the said Minor), this Twenty-fourth day of March, in the Year 1814.   By me,

EDWARD WILLIAMS, *Curate.*

This Marriage was solemnized between us { PERCY BYSSHE SHELLEY, HARRIET SHELLEY, formerly Harriet Westbrook.

In the presence of { JOHN WESTBROOK, JOHN STANLEY.

The above is a true extract from the Register Book of Marriages belonging to the Parish of Saint George, Hanover-square; extracted thence this eleventh day of April, 1859.—By me,   H. WEIGHTMAN, *Curate.*

It is, therefore, not correct to say that 'estrangements which had been slowly growing came to a crisis towards the close of 1813.' The date of the above certificate is conclusive on the point. The second marriage could not have taken place under such circumstances. Divorce would have been better for both parties, and the dissolution of the first marriage could have been easily obtained in Scotland.

There was no estrangement, no shadow of a thought of separation, till Shelley became acquainted, not long after the second marriage, with the lady who was subsequently his second wife.

The separation did not take place by mutual consent. I cannot think that Shelley ever so represented it. He never did so to me: and the account which Harriet herself gave me of the entire proceeding was decidedly contradictory of any such supposition.

He might well have said, after first seeing Mary Wollstonecraft Godwin, '*Ut vidi! ut perii!*' Nothing that I ever read in tale or history could present a more striking image of a sudden, violent, irresistible, uncontrollable passion, than that under which I found him labouring when, at his request, I went up from the country to call on him in London. Between his old feelings towards Harriet, *from whom he was not then separated*, and his new passion for Mary, he showed in his looks, in his gestures, in his speech, the state of a mind 'suffering, like a little kingdom, the nature of an insurrection.' His eyes were bloodshot, his hair and dress disordered. He caught up a bottle of laudanum, and said : 'I never part from this.'*

* In a letter to Mr. Trelawny, dated June 18th, 1822, Shelley says :—'You of course enter into society at Leghorn. Should you meet with any scientific person capable of preparing the *Prussic Acid, or Essential Oil of Bitter Almonds*, I should regard it as a great kindness if you could procure me a small quantity. It requires the greatest caution in preparation, and ought to be highly concentrated. I would give any price for this medicine. You remember we talked of it the other night, and we both expressed a wish to possess it. My wish was serious, and sprung from the desire of avoiding needless suffering. I need not tell you I have no intention of suicide at present; but I confess it would be a comfort to me to hold in my possession that golden key to the chamber of perpetual rest. The *Prussic Acid* is used in medicine in infinitely minute doses ; but that preparation is weak, and has not the concentration necessary to medicine all ills infallibly. A single drop, even less, is a dose, and it acts by paralysis.'—*Trelawny*, pp. 100, 101.

I believe that up to this time he had never travelled without pistols for defence, nor without laudanum as a refuge from intolerable pain. His physical suffering was often very severe ; and this last letter must have been written under the anticipation that it might become incurable, and unendurable to a degree from which he wished to be permanently provided with the means of escape.

He added : ' I am always repeating to myself your lines from Sophocles:

Man's happiest lot is not to be :
And when we tread life's thorny steep,
Most blest are they, who earliest free
Descend to death's eternal sleep.'

Again, he said more calmly: ' Every one who knows me must know that the partner of my life should be one who can feel poetry and understand philosophy. Harriet is a noble animal, but she can do neither.' I said, ' It always appeared to me that you were very fond of Harriet.' Without affirming or denying this, he answered : ' But you did not know how I hated her sister.'

The term 'noble animal' he applied to his wife, in conversation with another friend now living, intimating that the nobleness which he thus ascribed to her would induce her to acquiesce in the inevitable transfer of his affections to their new shrine. She did not so acquiesce, and he cut the Gordian knot of the difficulty by leaving England with Miss Godwin on the 28th of July, 1814.

Shortly after this I received a letter from Harriet, wishing to see me. I called on her at her father's house in Chapel-street, Grosvenor-square. She then gave me her own account of the transaction, which, as I have said, decidedly contradicted the supposition of anything like separation by mutual consent. She at the same time gave me a description, by no means flattering, of Shelley's new love, whom I had not then seen. I said, ' If you have described her correctly, what could he see in her ?' ' Nothing,' she said, ' but that her name was Mary, and not only Mary, but Mary Wollstonecraft.'

The lady had nevertheless great personal and intellectual attractions, though it is not to be wondered at that Harriet could not see them.

I feel it due to the memory of Harriet to state my most decided conviction that her conduct as a wife was as pure, as true, as absolutely faultless, as that of any who for such conduct are held most in honour.

Mr. Hogg says : ' Shelley told me his friend Robert Southey once said to him, "A man ought to be able to live with any woman. You see that I can, and so ought you. It comes to pretty much the same thing, I apprehend. There is no great choice or difference."'—*Hogg :* vol. i. p. 423. *Any woman,* I suspect, must have been said with some qualification. But such an one as either of them had first chosen, Southey saw no reason to change.

Shelley gave me some account of an interview he had had with Southey. It was after his return from his first visit to Switzerland, in the autumn of 1814. I forget whether it was in town or country; but it was in Southey's study, in which was suspended a portrait of Mary Wollstonecraft. Whether Southey had been in love with this lady, is more than I know. That he had devotedly admired her is clear from his *Epistle to Amos Cottle,* prefixed to the latter's *Icelandic Poetry* (1797); in which, after describing the scenery of Norway, he says :—

Scenes like these
Have almost lived before me, when I
    gazed
Upon their fair resemblance traced by
    him,
Who sung the banished man of Ardebeil ;
Or to the eye of Fancy held by her,
Who among women left no equal mind
When from this world she passed ; and I
    could weep
To think that she is to the grave gone
    down!

Where a note names Mary Wollstonecraft, the allusion being to her *Letters from Norway.*

Shelley had previously known Southey, and wished to renew or continue friendly relations; but Southey was repulsive. He pointed to the picture, and expressed his bitter regret that the daughter of that angelic woman should have been so misled. It was most probably on this occasion that he made the remark cited by Mr. Hogg: his admiration of Mary Wollstonecraft may have given force to the observation : and as he had known Harriet, he might have thought that, in his view of the matter, she was all that a husband could wish for.

Few are now living who remember Harriet Shelley. I remember her well, and will describe her to the best of my recollection. She had a good figure, light, active, and graceful. Her features were regular and well proportioned. Her hair was light brown, and dressed with taste and simplicity. In her dress she was truly *simplex munditiis*. Her complexion was beautifully transparent; the tint of the blush rose shining through the lily. The tone of her voice was pleasant; her speech the essence of frankness and cordiality; her spirits always cheerful; her laugh spontaneous, hearty, and joyous. She was well educated. She read agreeably and intelligently. She wrote only letters, but she wrote them well. Her manners were good; and her whole aspect and demeanour such manifest emanations of pure and truthful nature, that to be once in her company was to know her thoroughly. She was fond of her husband, and accommodated herself in every way to his tastes. If they mixed in society, she adorned it; if they lived in retirement, she was satisfied; if they travelled, she enjoyed the change of scene.

That Shelley's second wife was intellectually better suited to him than his first, no one who knew them both will deny; and that a man, who lived so totally out of the ordinary world and in a world of ideas, needed such an ever-present sympathy more than the general run of men, must also be admitted; but Southey, who did not want an intellectual wife, and was contented with his own, may well have thought that Shelley had equal reason to seek no change.

After leaving England, in 1814, the newly-affianced lovers took a tour on the Continent. He wrote to me several letters from Switzerland, which were subsequently published, together with a *Six Weeks' Tour*, written in the form of a journal by the lady with whom his fate was thenceforward indissolubly bound. I was introduced to her on their return.

The rest of 1814 they passed chiefly in London. Perhaps this winter was the most solitary period of Shelley's life. I often passed an evening with him at his lodgings, and I do not recollect ever meeting any one there, excepting Mr. Hogg. Some of his few friends of the preceding year had certainly at that time fallen off from him. At the same time he was short of money, and was trying to raise some on his expectations, from 'Jews and their fellow-Christians,' as Lord Byron says. One day, as we were walking together on the banks of the Surrey Canal, and discoursing of Wordsworth, and quoting some of his verses, Shelley suddenly said to me: 'Do you think Wordsworth could have written such poetry, if he had ever had dealings with money-lenders?' His own example, however, proved that the association had not injured his poetical faculties.

The canal in question was a favourite walk with us. The Croydon Canal branched off from it, and passed very soon into wooded scenery. The Croydon Canal is extinct, and has given place to the, I hope, more useful, but certainly less picturesque, railway. Whether the Surrey exists, I do not know. He had a passion for sailing paper-boats, which he indulged on this canal, and on the Serpentine river. The best spot he had ever found for it, was a large pool of transparent water, on a heath above Bracknell, with determined borders free from weeds, which admitted of launching the miniature craft on the windward, and running round to receive it on the leeward, side. On the Serpentine, he would sometimes launch a boat constructed with more than usual care, and freighted with halfpence. He delighted to do this in the presence of boys, who would run round to meet it, and when it landed in safety, and the boys scrambled for their prize, he had difficulty in restraining himself from shouting as loudly as they did. The river was not suitable to this amusement, nor even Virginia Water, on which he sometimes practised it; but the lake was too large to allow of meeting the landing. I sympathized with him in this taste: I had it before I knew him: I am not sure that I did not originate it with him; for which I should scarcely receive the thanks of my friend, Mr. Hogg, who never took any pleasure in it, and cordially abominated it, when, as frequently happened, on a cold winter day, in a walk from Bishopgate over Bagshot Heath, we came on a pool of water, which Shelley would not part from till he had rigged out a flotilla from any unfortunate letters he happened to have in his pocket. Whatever may be thought of this amusement for grown gentlemen, it was at least innocent amusement, and not mixed up with any 'sorrow of the meanest thing that feels.'*

In the summer of 1815, Shelley took a furnished house at Bishopgate, the eastern entrance of Windsor Park, where he resided till the summer of 1816. At this time he had, by the sacrifice of a portion of his expectations, purchased an annuity of £1000 a-year from his father, who had previously allowed him £200.

I was then living at Marlow, and frequently walked over to pass a few days with him. At the end of August, 1815, we made an excursion on the Thames to Lechlade, in Gloucestershire, and as much higher as there was water to float our skiff. It was a dry season, and we did not get much beyond Inglesham Weir, which was not then, as now, an immovable structure, but the wreck of a movable weir, which had been subservient to the navigation, when the river had been, as it had long ceased to be, navigable to Cricklade. A solitary sluice was hanging by a chain, swinging in the wind and creaking dismally. Our voyage terminated at a spot where the cattle stood entirely across the stream, with the water scarcely covering their hoofs. We started from, and returned to, Old Windsor, and our excursion occupied about ten days. This was, I think, the origin of Shelley's taste for boating, which he retained to the end of his life. On our way up, at Oxford, he was so much out of order that he feared being obliged to return. He had been living chiefly on tea and bread and butter, drinking occasionally a sort of spurious lemonade, made of some powder in a box, which, as he was reading at the time the Tale of a Tub, he called *the powder of pimperlimpimp*. He consulted a doctor, who may have done him some good, but it was not apparent. I told him ' if he would allow me to prescribe for him, I would set him to rights.' He asked, ' What would be your prescription?' I said, ' Three mutton chops, well peppered.' He said, ' Do you really think so?' I said, ' I am sure of it.' He took the prescription; the success was obvious and immediate. He lived in my way for the rest of our expedition, rowed vigorously, was cheerful, merry, overflowing with animal spirits, and had certainly one week of thorough enjoyment of life. We passed two nights in a comfortable inn at Lechlade, and his lines, 'A Summer Evening on the Thames at Lechlade,' were written then and there. Mrs. Shelley (the second, who always bore his name), who was with us, made a diary of the little trip, which I suppose is lost.

The whole of the winter 1815-16, was passed quietly at Bishopgate. Mr. Hogg often walked down from London; and, I, as before, walked over from Marlow. This winter was, as Mr. Hogg expressed it, a mere Atticism. Our studies were exclusively Greek. To the best of my recollection, we were, through-

---

* This lesson, shepherd, let us two divide,
　Taught both by what she[1] shows and what conceals,
　Never to blend our pleasure or our pride
　With sorrow of the meanest thing that feels.
　　　　　　　　　　Wordsworth, *Hartleap Well.*

---

[1] Nature.

out the whole period, his only visitors. One or two persons called on him ; but they were not to his mind, and were not encouraged to reappear. The only exception was a physician whom he had called in ; the Quaker, Dr. Pope, of Staines. This worthy old gentleman came more than once, not as a doctor, but a friend. He liked to discuss theology with Shelley. Shelley at first avoided the discussion, saying his opinions would not be to the Doctor's taste ; but the Doctor answered, 'I like to hear thee talk, friend Shelley ; I see thee art very deep.'

At this time Shelley wrote his *Alastor*. He was at a loss for a title, and I proposed that which he adopted : *Alastor; or, the Spirit of Solitude.* The Greek word Ἀλάστωρ is an evil genius, κακοδαίμων, though the sense of the two words is somewhat different, as in the Φανεὶς Ἀλάστωρ ἢ κακὸς δαίμων ποϑέν, of Æschylus. The poem treated the spirit of solitude as a spirit of evil. I mention the true meaning of the word, because many have supposed *Alastor* to be the name of the hero of the poem.

He published this, with some minor poems, in the course of the winter.

In the early summer of 1816, the spirit of restlessness again came over him, and resulted in a second visit to the Continent. The change of scene was preceded, as more than once before, by a mysterious communication from a person seen only by himself, warning him of immediate personal perils to be incurred by him if he did not instantly depart.

I was alone at Bishopgate, with him and Mrs. Shelley, when the visitation alluded to occurred. About the middle of the day, intending to take a walk, I went into the hall for my hat. His was there, and mine was not. I could not imagine what had become of it ; but as I could not walk without it, I returned to the library. After some time had elapsed, Mrs. Shelley came in, and gave me an account which she had just received from himself, of the visitor and his com-

munication. I expressed some scepticism on the subject, on which she left me, and Shelley came in, with my hat in his hand. He said, 'Mary tells me, you do not believe that I have had a visit from Williams.' I said, 'I told her there were some improbabilities in the narration.' He said, 'You know Williams of Tremadoc?' I said, 'I do.' He said, 'It was he who was here to-day. He came to tell me of a plot laid by my father and uncle, to entrap me and lock me up. He was in great haste, and could not stop a minute, and I walked with him to Egham.' I said, 'What hat did you wear?' He said, 'This, to be sure.' I said, 'I wish you would put it on.' He put it on, and it went over his face. I said, 'You could not have walked to Egham in that hat.' He said, 'I snatched it up hastily, and perhaps I kept it in my hand. I certainly walked with Williams to Egham, and he told me what I have said. You are very sceptical.' I said, 'If you are certain of what you say, my scepticism cannot affect your certainty.' He said, 'It is very hard on a man, who has devoted his life to the pursuit of truth, who has made great sacrifices and incurred great sufferings for it, to be treated as a visionary. If I do not know that I saw Williams, how do I know that I see you?' I said, 'An idea may have the force of a sensation ; but the oftener a sensation is repeated, the greater is the probability of its origin in reality. You saw me yesterday, and will see me to-morrow.' He said, 'I can see Williams to-morrow if I please. He told me he was stopping at the Turk's Head Coffee-house, in the Strand, and should be there two days. I want to convince you that I am not under a delusion. Will you walk with me to London to-morrow, to see him?' I said, 'I would most willingly do so.' The next morning after an early breakfast, we set off on our walk to London. We had got half way down Egham-hill, when he suddenly turned round, and said to me, 'I do not think we shall find Williams at the Turk's Head.' I said, 'Neither do I.' He said, 'You say that, because you do not think he has been there; but he mentioned a contingency under which he might leave town yesterday, and he has probably done so.' I said, 'At any rate, we should know that he has been there.' He said, 'I will take other means of convincing you. I will write to him. Suppose we take a walk through the forest.' We turned about on our new direction, and were out all day. Some days passed, and I heard no more of the matter. One morning he said to me, 'I have some news of Williams; a letter and an enclosure.' I said, 'I shall be glad to see the letter.' He said, 'I cannot show you the letter; I will show you the enclosure. It is a diamond necklace. I think you know me well enough to be sure I would not throw away my own money on such a thing, and that if I have it, it must have been sent me by somebody else. It has been sent me by Williams.' 'For what purpose?' I asked. He said, 'To prove his identity and his sincerity.' 'Surely,' I said, 'your showing me a diamond necklace will prove nothing but that you have one to show.' 'Then,' he said, 'I will not show it you. If you will not believe me, I must submit to your incredulity.' There the matter ended. I never heard another word of Williams, nor of any other mysterious visitor. I had on one or two previous occasions argued with him against similar semi-delusions, and I believe if they had always been received with similar scepticism, they would not have been often repeated; but they were encouraged by the ready credulity with which they were received by many, who ought to have known better. I call them semi-delusions, because, for the most part, they had their basis in his firm belief that his father and uncle had designs on his liberty. On this basis, his imagination built a fabric of romance, and when he presented it as substantive fact, and it was found to contain more or less of inconsistency, he felt his self-esteem interested in maintain-

ing it by accumulated circumstances, which severally vanished under the touch of investigation, like Williams's location at the Turk's Head Coffee-house.

I must add, that in the expression of these differences, there was not a shadow of anger. They were discussed with freedom and calmness; with the good temper and good feeling which never forsook him in conversations with his friends. There was an evident anxiety for acquiescence, but a quiet and gentle toleration of dissent. A personal discussion, however interesting to himself, was carried on with the same calmness as if it related to the most abstract question in metaphysics.

Indeed, one of the great charms of intercourse with him was the perfect good humour and openness to conviction with which he responded to opinions opposed to his own. I have known eminent men, who were no doubt very instructive as lecturers to people who like being lectured; which I never did; but with whom conversation was impossible. To oppose their dogmas, even to question them, was to throw their temper off its balance. When once this infirmity showed itself in any of my friends, I was always careful not to provoke a second ebullition. I submitted to the preachment, and was glad when it was over.

The result was a second trip to Switzerland. During his absence he wrote me several letters, some of which were subsequently published by Mrs. Shelley; others are still in my possession. Copies of two of these were obtained by Mr. Middleton, who has printed a portion of them. Mrs. Shelley was at that time in the habit of copying Shelley's letters, and these were among some papers accidentally left at Marlow, where they fell into unscrupulous hands. Mr. Middleton must have been aware that he had no right to print them without my consent. I might have stopped his publication by an injunction, but I did not think it worth while, more especially as the book, though abounding with errors adopted from Captain Medwin and others, is written with good feeling towards the memory of Shelley.

During his stay in Switzerland he became acquainted with Lord Byron. They made together an excursion round the Lake of Geneva, of which he sent me the detail in a diary. This diary was published by Mrs. Shelley, but without introducing the name of Lord Byron, who is throughout called 'my companion.' The diary was first published during Lord Byron's life; but why his name was concealed I do not know. Though the changes are not many, yet the association of the two names gives it great additional interest.

At the end of August, 1816, they returned to England, and Shelley passed the first fortnight of September with me at Marlow. July and August, 1816, had been months of perpetual rain. The first fortnight of September was a period of unbroken sunshine. The neighbourhood of Marlow abounds with beautiful walks; the river scenery is also fine. We took every day a long excursion, either on foot or on the water. He took a house there, partly, perhaps principally, for the sake of being near me. While it was being fitted and furnished, he resided at Bath.

In December, 1816, Harriet drowned herself in the Serpentine river, not, as Captain Medwin says, in a pond at the bottom of her father's garden at Bath. Her father had not then left his house in Chapel-street, and to that house his daughter's body was carried.

On the 30th of December, 1816, Shelley married his second wife; and early in the ensuing year they took possession of their house at Marlow. It was a house with many large rooms and extensive gardens. He took it on a lease for twenty-one years, furnished it handsomely, fitted up a library in a room large enough for a ball-room, and settled himself down, as he supposed, for life. This was an agreeable year to all of us. Mr. Hogg was a frequent visitor. We had a good deal of rowing and sailing, and we took long walks in all directions. He

had other visitors from time to time. Amongst them were Mr. Godwin and Mr. and Mrs. Leigh Hunt. He led a much more social life than he had done at Bishopgate; but he held no intercourse with his immediate neighbours. He said to me more than once, 'I am not wretch enough to tolerate an acquaintance.'

In the summer of 1817 he wrote the *Revolt of Islam*, chiefly on a seat on a high prominence in Bisham Wood, where he passed whole mornings with a blank book and a pencil. This work, when completed, was printed under the title of *Laon and Cythna*. In this poem he had carried the expression of his opinions, moral, political, and theological, beyond the bounds of discretion. The terror which, in those days of persecution of the press, the perusal of the book inspired in Mr. Ollier, the publisher, induced him to solicit the alteration of many passages which he had marked. Shelley was for some time inflexible; but Mr. Ollier's refusal to publish the poem as it was, backed by the advice of all his friends, induced him to submit to the required changes. Many leaves were cancelled, and it was finally published as *The Revolt of Islam*. Of *Laon and Cythna* only three copies had gone forth. One of these had found its way to the *Quarterly Review*, and the opportunity was readily seized of pouring out on it one of the most malignant effusions of the *odium theologicum* that ever appeared even in those days, and in that periodical.

During his residence at Marlow we often walked to London, frequently in company with Mr. Hogg. It was our usual way of going there, when not pressed by time. We went by a very pleasant route over fields, lanes, woods, and heaths to Uxbridge, and by the main road from Uxbridge to London. The total distance was thirty-two miles to Tyburn turnpike. We usually stayed two nights, and walked back on the third day. I never saw Shelley tired with these walks. Delicate and fragile as he appeared, he had great muscular strength.

We took many walks in all directions from Marlow, and saw everything worth seeing within a radius of sixteen miles. This comprehended, among other notable places, Windsor Castle and Forest, Virginia Water, and the spots which were consecrated by the memories of Cromwell, Hampden, and Milton, in the Chiltern district of Buckinghamshire. We had also many pleasant excursions, rowing and sailing on the river, between Henley and Maidenhead.

Shelley, it has been seen, had two children by his first wife. These children he claimed after Harriet's death, but her family refused to give them up. They resisted the claim in Chancery, and the decree of Lord Eldon was given against him.

The grounds of Lord Eldon's decision have been misrepresented. The petition had adduced *Queen Mab*, and other instances of Shelley's opinions on religion, as one of the elements of the charges against him; but the judgment ignores this element, and rests entirely on moral conduct. It was distinctly laid down that the principles which Shelley had professed in regard to some of the most important relations of life, had been carried by him into practice; and that the practical development of those principles, not the principles themselves, had determined the judgment of the Court.

Lord Eldon intimated that his judgment was not final; but nothing would have been gained by an appeal to the House of Peers. Liberal law lords were then unknown; neither could Shelley have hoped to enlist public opinion in his favour. A Scotch marriage, contracted so early in life, might not have been esteemed a very binding tie: but the separation which so closely followed on a marriage in the Church of England, contracted two years and a half later, presented itself as the breach of a much more solemn and deliberate obligation.

It is not surprising that so many persons at the time should have supposed that the judgment had been founded, at least partly, on religious grounds. Shelley himself told me, that Lord Eldon had expressly stated that such grounds were excluded, and the judgment itself showed it. But few read the judgment. It did not appear in the newspapers, and all report of the proceedings was interdicted. Mr. Leigh Hunt accompanied Shelley to the Court of Chancery. Lord Eldon was extremely courteous, but he said blandly, and at the same time determinedly, that a report of the proceedings would be punished as a contempt of Court. The only explanation I have ever been able to give to myself of his motive for this prohibition was, that he was willing to leave the large body of fanatics among his political supporters under delusion as to the grounds of his judgment; and that it was more for his political interest to be stigmatized by Liberals as an inquisitor, than to incur in any degree the imputation of theological liberality from his own persecuting party.

Since writing the above passages I have seen, in the *Morning Post* of November 22nd, the report of a meeting of the Juridical Society, under the presidency of the present Lord Chancellor, in which a learned brother read a paper, proposing to revive the system of persecution against 'blasphemous libel;' and in the course of his lecture he said— 'The Court of Chancery, on the doctrine *Parens patriæ*, deprived the parent of the guardianship of his children when his principles were in antagonism to religion, as in the case of the poet Shelley.' The Attorney-General observed on this: 'With respect to the interference of the Court of Chancery in the case of Shelley's children, there was a great deal of misunderstanding. It was not because their father was an unbeliever in Christianity, but because he violated and refused to acknowledge the ordinary usages of morality.' The last words are rather vague and twaddling, and I suppose are not the *ipsissima verba* of the Attorney-General. The essence and quintessence of Lord Eldon's judgment was this: 'Mr. Shelley long ago published and maintained the doctrine that marriage is a contract binding only during mutual pleasure. He has carried out that doctrine in his own practice; he has done nothing to show that he does not still maintain it; and I consider such practice injurious to the best interests of society.' I am not apologizing for Lord Eldon, nor vindicating his judgment. I am merely explaining it, simply under the wish that those who talk about it should know what it really was.

Some of Shelley's friends have spoken and written of Harriet as if to vindicate him it were necessary to disparage her. They might, I think, be content to rest the explanation of his conduct on the ground on which he rested it himself—that he had found in another the intellectual qualities which constituted his ideality of the partner of his life. But Harriet's untimely fate occasioned him deep agony of mind, which he felt the more because for a long time he kept the feeling to himself. I became acquainted with it in a somewhat singular manner.

I was walking with him one evening in Bisham Wood, and we had been talking, in the usual way, of our ordinary subjects, when he suddenly fell into a gloomy reverie. I tried to rouse him out of it, and made some remarks which I thought might make him laugh at his own abstraction. Suddenly he said to me, still with the same gloomy expression: 'There is one thing to which I have decidedly made up my mind. I will take a great glass of ale every night.' I said, laughingly, 'A very good resolution, as the result of a melancholy musing.' 'Yes,' he said; 'but you do not know why I take it. I shall do it to deaden my feelings: for I see that those who drink ale have none.' The next day he said to me: 'You must have thought me very unreasonable yesterday evening?' I said, 'I did, certainly.' 'Then,' he said, 'I will tell you what I would not tell any one else. I was thinking of Harriet.' I told him, 'I had no idea of such a thing: it was so

long since he had named her. I had thought he was under the influence of some baseless morbid feeling; but if ever I should see him again in such a state of mind, I would not attempt to disturb it.'

There was not much comedy in Shelley's life; but his antipathy to 'acquaintance' led to incidents of some drollery. Amongst the persons who called on him at Bishopgate, was one whom he tried hard to get rid of, but who forced himself on him in every possible manner. He saw him at a distance one day, as he was walking down Egham Hill, and instantly jumped through a hedge, ran across a field, and laid himself down in a dry ditch. Some men and women, who were haymaking in the field, ran up to see what was the matter, when he said to them, 'Go away, go away: don't you see it's a bailiff?' On which they left him, and he escaped discovery.

After he had settled himself at Marlow, he was in want of a music-master to attend a lady staying in his house, and I inquired for one at Maidenhead. Having found one, I requested that he would call on Mr. Shelley. One morning Shelley rushed into my house in great trepidation, saying: 'Barricade the doors; give orders that you are not at home. Here is —— in the town.' He passed the whole day with me, and we sat in expectation that the knocker or the bell would announce the unwelcome visitor; but the evening fell on the unfulfilled fear. He then ventured home. It turned out that the name of the music-master very nearly resembled in sound the name of the obnoxious gentleman; and when Shelley's man opened the library door and said, 'Mr. ——, sir,' Shelley, who caught the name as that of his *Monsieur Tonson*, exclaimed, 'I would just as soon see the devil!' sprang up from his chair, jumped out of the window, ran across the lawn, climbed over the garden-fence, and came round to me by a back path: when we entrenched ourselves for a day's siege. We often laughed afterwards at the thought of what must have been his man's astonishment at seeing his master, on the announcement of the musician, disappear so instantaneously through the window, with the exclamation, ' I would just as soon see the devil !' and in what way he could explain to the musician that his master was so suddenly ' not at home.'

Shelley, when he did laugh, laughed heartily, the more so as what he considered the perversions of comedy excited not his laughter but his indignation, although such disgusting outrages on taste and feeling as the burlesques by which the stage is now disgraced had not then been perpetrated. The ludicrous, when it neither offended good feeling, nor perverted moral judgment, necessarily presented itself to him with greater force.

Though his published writings are all serious, yet his letters are not without occasional touches of humour. In one which he wrote to me from Italy, he gave an account of a new acquaintance who had a prodigious nose. ' His nose is something quite Slawkenbergian. It weighs on the imagination to look at it. It is that sort of nose that transforms all the g's its wearer utters into k's. It is a nose once seen never to be forgotten, and which requires the utmost stretch of Christian charity to forgive. I, you know, have a little turn-up nose, H—— has a large hook one ; but add them together, square them, cube them, you would have but a faint notion of the nose to which I refer.'

I may observe incidentally, that his account of his own nose corroborates the opinion I have previously expressed of the inadequate likeness of the published portraits of him, in which the nose has no turn-up. It had, in fact, very little ; just as much as may be seen in the portrait to which I have referred, in the Florentine Gallery.

The principal employment of the female population in Marlow was lace - making, miserably remunerated. He went continually amongst this unfortunate population, and to the extent of his ability relieved the most pressing cases of distress. He had a list of pensioners, to whom he made a weekly allowance.

Early in 1818 the spirit of restlessness again came over him. He left Marlow, and, after a short stay in London, left England in March of that year, never to return.

I saw him for the last time, on Tuesday the 10th of March. The evening was a remarkable one, as being that of the first performance of an opera of Rossini in England, and of the first appearance here of Malibran's father, Garcia. He performed Count Almaviva in the *Barbiere di Siviglia*. Fodor was Rosina ; Naldi, Figaro ; Ambrogetti, Bartolo ; and Angrisani, Basilio. I supped with Shelley and his travelling companions after the opera. They departed early the next morning.

Thus two very dissimilar events form one epoch in my memory. In looking back to that long-past time, I call to mind how many friends, Shelley himself included, I saw around me in the old Italian Theatre, who have now all disappeared from the scene. I hope I am not unduly given to be *laudator temporis acti*, yet I cannot but think that the whole arrangement of the opera in England has changed for the worse. Two acts of opera, a divertissement, and a ballet, seem very ill replaced by four or five acts of opera, with little or no dancing. These, to me, verify the old saying, that ' Too much of one thing is good for nothing ;' and the quiet and decorous audiences, of whom Shelley used to say, ' It is delightful to see human beings so civilized,' are not agreeably succeeded by the vociferous assemblies, calling and recalling performers to the footlights, and showering down bouquets to the accompaniment of their noisy approbation.

At the time of his going abroad, he had two children by his second wife—William and Clara ; and it has been said that the fear of having these taken from him by a decree of the Chancellor had some influence on his determination to leave England ; but there was no ground for such a fear. No one could be interested in taking them from him ; no reason could be alleged for taking them from their mother ; the Chancellor would not have entertained the question, unless a provision had been secured for the children ; and who was to do this ? Restlessness and embarrassment were the causes of his determination ; and according to the Newtonian doctrine, it is needless to look for more causes than are necessary to explain the phenomena.

* ★ ☆

So perished Percy Bysshe Shelley, in the flower of his age, and not perhaps even yet in the full flower of his genius ; a genius unsurpassed in the description and imagination of scenes of beauty and grandeur ; in the expression of impassioned love of ideal beauty ; in the illustration of deep feeling by congenial imagery ; and in the infinite variety of harmonious versification. What was, in my opinion, deficient in his poetry, was, as I have already said, the want of reality in the characters with which he peopled his splendid scenes, and to which he addressed or imparted the utterance of his impassioned feelings. He was advancing, I think, to the attainment of this reality. It would have given to his poetry the only element of truth which it wanted ; though at the same time, the more clear development of what men were would have lowered his estimate of what they might be, and dimmed his enthusiastic prospect of the future destiny of the world. I can conceive him, if he had lived to the present time, passing his days like Volney, looking on the world from his windows without taking part in its turmoils ; and perhaps like the same, or some other great apostle of liberty (for I cannot at this moment verify the quotation), desiring that nothing should be inscribed on his tomb, but his name, the dates of his birth and death, and the single word,

'DÉSILLUSIONNÉ.'

T. L. PEACOCK.

* ★ ☆

PERCY BYSSHE SHELLEY.

SUPPLEMENTARY NOTICE.

IN *Macmillan's Magazine* for June, 1860, there is an article entitled 'Shelley in Pall-Mall; by Richard Garnett,' which contains the following passage :—

Much has been written about Shelley during the last three or four years, and the store of materials for his biography has been augmented by many particulars, some authentic and valuable, others trivial or mythical, or founded on mistakes or misrepresentations. It does not strictly fall within the scope of this paper to notice any of these, but some of the latter class are calculated to modify so injuriously what has hitherto been the prevalent estimate of Shelley's character, and, while entirely unfounded, are yet open to correction from the better knowledge of so few, that it would be inexcusable to omit an opportunity of comment which only chance has presented, and which may not speedily recur. It will be readily perceived that the allusion is to the statements respecting Shelley's separation from his first wife, published by Mr. T. L. Peacock, in *Fraser's Magazine* for January last. According to these, the transaction was not preceded by long-continued unhappiness, neither was it an amicable agreement effected in virtue of a mutual understanding. The time cannot be distant when these assertions must be refuted by the publication of documents hitherto withheld, and Shelley's family have doubted whether it be worth while to anticipate it. Pending their decision, I may be allowed to state most explicitly that the evidence to which they would in such a case appeal, and to the nature of which I feel fully competent to speak, most decidedly contradicts the allegations of Mr. Peacock.

A few facts in the order of time will show, I will not say the extreme improbability, but the absolute impossibility, of Shelley's family being in possession of any such documents as are here alleged to exist.

In August, 1811, Shelley married Harriet Westbrook in Scotland.

On the 24th of March, 1814, he married her a second time in the Church of England, according to the marriage certificate printed in my article of January, 1860. This second marriage could scarcely have formed an incident in a series of 'long-continued unhappiness.'

In the beginning of April, 1814, Shelley and Harriet were together on a visit to Mrs. B., at Bracknell. This lady and her family were of the few who constituted Shelley's most intimate friends. On the 18th of April, she wrote to Mr. Hogg:—'Shelley is again a widower. His beauteous half went to town on Thursday with Miss Westbrook, who is gone to live, I believe, at Southampton.'*

Up to this time, therefore, at least, Shelley and Harriet were together; and Mrs. B.'s letter shows that she had no idea of estrangement between them, still less of permanent separation.

I said in my article of January, 1860 : 'There was no estrangement, no shadow of a thought of separation, till Shelley became acquainted, not long after the second marriage, with the lady who was subsequently his second wife.'

When Shelley first saw this lady,

---

* Hogg's *Life of Shelley*, vol. ii. p. 533.

she had just returned from a visit to some friends in Scotland; and when Mr. Hogg first saw her, she wore 'a frock of tartan, an unusual dress in London at that time.'* She could not have been long returned.

Mr. Hogg saw Mary Godwin for the first time on the first day of Lord Cochrane's trial. This was the 8th of June, 1814. He went with Shelley to Mr. Godwin's. 'We entered a room on the first floor. . . . William Godwin was not at home. . . . The door was partially and softly opened. A thrilling voice called "Shelley!" A thrilling voice answered "Mary!" And he darted out of the room like an arrow from the bow of the far-shooting king.'*

Shelley's acquaintance with Miss Godwin must, therefore, have begun between the 18th of April and the 8th of June; much nearer, I apprehend, to the latter than the former, but I cannot verify the precise date.

On the 7th of July, 1814, Harriet wrote to a mutual friend, still living, a letter in which 'she expressed a confident belief that she must know where Shelley was, and entreating his assistance to induce him to return home.' She was not even then aware that Shelley had finally left her.

On the 28th of the same month, Shelley and Miss Godwin left England for Switzerland.

The interval between the Scotch and English marriages was two years and seven months. The interval between the second marriage and the departure for Switzerland, was four months and four days. In the estimate of probabilities, the space for voluntary separation is reduced by Mrs. B.'s letter of April 18, to three months and thirteen days; and by Harriet's letter of July 7, to twenty-one days. If, therefore, Shelley's family have any document which demonstrates Harriet's consent to the separation, it must prove the consent to have been given on one of these twenty-one days. I know, by my subse-

quent conversation with Harriet, of which the substance was given in my article of January, 1860, that she was not a consenting party; but as I have only my own evidence to that conversation, Mr. Garnett may choose not to believe me. Still, on other evidence than mine, there remain no more than three weeks within which, if at all, the 'amicable agreement' must have been concluded.

But again, if Shelley's family had any conclusive evidence on the subject, they must have had some clear idea of the date of the separation, and of the circumstances preceding it. That they had not, is manifest from Lady Shelley's statement, that 'towards the close of 1813, estrangements, which for some time had been slowly growing between Mr. and Mrs. Shelley, came to a crisis: separation ensued, and she returned to her father's house.† Lady Shelley could not have written thus if she had known the date of the second marriage, or had even adverted to the letter of the 18th of April, 1814, which had been published by Mr. Hogg long before the production of her own volume.

———

I wrote the preceding note immediately after the appearance of Mr. Garnett's article; but I postponed its publication, in the hope of obtaining copies of the letters which were laid before Lord Eldon in 1817. These were nine letters from Shelley to Harriet, and one from Shelley to Miss Westbrook after Harriet's death. These letters were not filed; but they are thus alluded to in Miss Westbrook's affidavit, dated 10th January, 1817, of which I have procured a copy from the Record Office :—

Elizabeth Westbrook, of Chapel-street, Grosvenor-square, in the parish of Saint George, Hanover-square, in the county of Middlesex, spinster, maketh oath and saith, that she knows and is well acquainted with the handwriting of Percy Bysshe Shelley, Esquire, one of the de-

---

* Hogg, vol. ii. p. 537-8.
† *Shelley Memorials*, pp. 64-65.

fendants in this cause, having frequently seen him write ; and this deponent saith that she hath looked upon certain paper writings now produced, and shown to her at the time of swearing this her affidavit, and marked respectively 1, 2, 3, 4, 5, 6, 7, 8, 9 ; and this deponent saith that the female mentioned or referred to in the said letters, marked respectively 2, 4, 6, 9, under the name or designation of ' Mary,' and in the said other letters by the character or description of the person with whom the said defendant had connected or associated himself, is Mary Godwin, in the pleadings of this cause named, whom the said defendant, Percy Bysshe Shelley, in the lifetime of his said wife, and in or about the middle of the year 1814, took to cohabit with him, and hath ever since continued to cohabit, and still doth cohabit with ; and this deponent saith that she hath looked upon a certain other paper writing, produced and shown to this deponent now at the time of swearing this her affidavit, and marked 10 ; and this deponent saith that the same paper writing is of the handwriting of the said defendant, Percy Bysshe Shelley, and was addressed by him to this deponent, since the decease of her said sister, the late wife of the said Percy Bysshe Shelley. And this deponent saith that the person referred to in the said last mentioned letter as ' *the Lady whose union with the said defendant this deponent might excusably regard as the cause of her Sister's Ruin,*' is also the said Mary Godwin.

The rest of the affidavit relates to ' Queen Mab.'

The words marked in italics could not possibly have been written by Shelley, if his connexion with Miss Godwin had not been formed till after a separation from Harriet by mutual consent.

In a second affidavit, dated 13th January, 1817, Miss Westbrook stated in substance the circumstances of the marriage, and that two children were the issue of it : that after the birth of the first child, Eliza Ianthe, and while her sister was pregnant with the second, Charles Bysshe, Percy Bysshe Shelley deserted his said wife, and cohabited with Mary Godwin ; and thereupon Harriet returned to the house of her father, with her eldest child, and soon afterwards the

youngest child was born there ; that the children had always remained under the protection of Harriet's father, and that Harriet herself had resided under the same protection until a short time previous to her death in December, 1816. It must be obvious that this statement could not have been made if the letters previously referred to had not borne it out ; if, in short, they had not demonstrated, first, that the separation was not by mutual consent ; and secondly, that it followed, not preceded, Shelley's first acquaintance with Mary Godwin. The rest of the affidavit related to the provision which Mr. Westbrook had made for the children.

Harriet suffered enough in her life to deserve that her memory should be respected. I have always said to all whom it might concern, that I would defend her, to the best of my ability, against all misrepresentations. Such are not necessary to Shelley's vindication. That is best permitted to rest, as I have already observed, on the grounds on which it was placed by himself.*

———

The *Quarterly Review* for October, 1861, has an article on Shelley's life and character, written in a tone of great fairness and impartiality, with an evident painstaking to weigh evidence and ascertain truth. There are two passages in the article, on which I wish to offer remarks, with reference solely to matters of fact.

Shelley's hallucinations, though not to be confounded with what is usually called insanity, are certainly not compatible with perfect soundness of mind. They were the result of an excessive sensibility, which, only a little more severely strained, would have overturned reason altogether. It has been said that the horror of his wife's death produced some such effect, and that for a time at least he was actually insane. Lady Shelley says nothing about this, and we have no explicit statement of the fact by any authoritative biographer. But it is not in itself improbable.—p. 323.

It was not so, however. He had at that time taken his house at Marlow, where I was then living. He was residing in Bath, and I was looking after the fitting-up of the house and the laying out of the grounds. I had almost daily letters from him or Mary. He was the first to tell me of Harriet's death, asking whether I thought it would become him to interpose any delay before marrying Mary. I gave him my opinion that, as they were living together, the sooner they legalized their connexion the better. He acted on this opinion, and shortly after his marriage he came to me at Marlow. We went together to see the progress of his house and grounds. I recollect a little scene which took place on this occasion. There was on the lawn a very fine old wide-spreading holly. The gardener had cut it up into a bare pole, selling the lop for Christmas decorations. As soon as Shelley saw it, he asked the gardener, 'What had possessed him to ruin that beautiful tree?' The gardener said, he thought he had improved its appearance. Shelley said: 'It is impossible that you can be such a fool.' The culprit stood twiddling his thumbs along the seams of his trousers, receiving a fulminating denunciation, which ended in his peremptory dismissal. A better man was engaged, with several assistants, to make an extensive plantation of shrubs. Shelley stayed with me two or three days. I never saw him more calm and self-possessed. Nothing disturbed his serenity but the unfortunate holly. Subsequently, the feeling for Harriet's death grew into a deep and abiding sorrow: but it was not in the beginning that it was felt most strongly.

It is not merely as a work of art that the *Revolt of Islam* must be considered. It had made its first appearance under the title of *Laon and Cythna*, but *Laon and Cythna* was still more outspoken as to certain matters than the *Revolt of Islam*, and was almost immediately withdrawn from circulation, to appear with alterations under its present name. There is something not quite worthy of Shelley in this transaction. On the one hand, merely prudential reasons, mere dread of public indignation, ought not to have induced him to conceal opinions which for the interest of humanity he thought it his duty to promulgate. But those who knew most of Shelley will be least inclined to attribute to him such a motive as this. On the other hand, if good feeling induced him to abstain from printing what he knew must be painful to the great majority of his countrymen, the second version should have been suppressed as well as the first.'—pp. 314-15.

Shelley was not influenced by either of the motives supposed. Mr. Ollier positively refused to publish the poem as it was, and Shelley had no hope of another publisher. He for a long time refused to alter a line: but his friends finally prevailed on him to submit. Still he could not, or would not, sit down by himself to alter it, and the whole of the alterations were actually made in successive sittings of what I may call a literary committee. He contested the proposed alterations step by step: in the end, sometimes adopting, more frequently modifying, never originating, and always insisting that his poem was spoiled.

T. L. PEACOCK.

NOTES

p. 347, l. 24: '*Ut vidi! ut perii!*': 'as soon as I saw her I was lost'

p. 347, ll. 38–40: 'suffering, like a little kingdom, the nature of an insurrection': adapted from Shakespeare's *Julius Caesar*, 2.1. lines 67–9

p. 349, l. 13: '*simplex munditiis*': Horace, *Odes*, Book I, v, line 5: 'of simple elegance'

p. 354, l. 58: the *ipsissima verba*': 'the exact words'

p. 356, l. 31: '*laudator temporis acti*': Horace, *De Arte Poetica*, line 173: 'praising the acts of those (past) times'

p. 357, l. 16: Volney: Constantin de Chasseboeuf, comte de Volney, was a French intellectual, much admired by both Peacock and Shelley, in particular for his rationalist (and anti-religious) account of the history of civilization, *Les Ruines* (1791), translated into English as *Ruins of Empire* (1795). Long passages are quoted in Shelley's notes to *Queen Mab*, and it is one of the books by which the monster is educated in Mary Shelley's *Frankenstein*

Thornton Hunt, 'Shelley. By One Who Knew Him', in *The Atlantic Monthly*, February, 1863

Thornton Hunt, Leigh Hunt's eldest son, is now best known as the man by whom Agnes Lewes, the wife of George Eliot's partner G. H. Lewes, had four children. His marginal role in the story of the relationship between Lewes and Eliot is, in fact, of some relevance to this memoir. For Lewes and Hunt, who were friends and co-founders of a periodical called *The Leader*, were both admirers of Shelley and sympathised with his ideals of free love. The American readership of Hunt's article would not have known it, but the author was himself living with a woman who was not his wife, and who was hrself married to another man. It is difficult for the reader now not to think that this shaped Hunt's treatment of Shelley's relationships with Mary and Harriet. It is his entirely unevidenced claim that, after Shelley had left his first wife for Mary Godwin, 'Harriet remained in amicable correspondence with Shelley: and not only so, but, while she altogether abstained from opposing his new connection, she was actually on friendly terms with Mary' (Hunt, 'Shelley', *Atlantic Monthly*, Feb. 1863, p. 195). He must do all that he can to persuade others, and perhaps himself, that members of the Westbrook family, hoping to profit from her marriage to Shelley, were to blame for Harriet's misery and that Shelley and Mary both demonstrated all proper 'compassion' for 'the unfortunate girl'.

Of course, Hunt, who earned his living from the pen (from 1855 he had been on the staff of the *Daily Telegraph*), had even simpler reasons for wanting to put together his supposed recollections. He was responding to a mid-century flurry of biographical accounts of Shelley, and cashing in on his early brush with the poet. He begins with his father's imprisonment 'for critical remarks which at the present day would scarcely attract attention' (ibid, p. 184 – see the headnote in this volume to Leigh Hunt's *Lord Byron and Some of His Contemporaries* for an account of this) and his father's description of 'the young stranger who came to him breathing the classic thoughts of college, ardent with aspirations for the emancipation of man from intellectual slavery, and endowed by Nature with an aspect truly "angelic"' (ibid, p. 185). What is made less clear than his knowledge of Shelley through Leigh Hunt is the fact that most of the encounters that he so clearly recalls date from a time when he was six or seven years old (Thornton Hunt was born in 1810). It is difficult, therefore, to have much trust in what we are given, except as telling us something of the version of Shelley that Hunt might indeed have learned from his father. Yet the very fact of the article, published in 'A Magazine of Literature, Art, and Politics' (the periodical's subtitle) aimed at a respectable, self-improving readership, indicates that there were counter-currents to the campaign of Lady Shelley and her allies.

It was at this time that the incident happened which has been mentioned by my father. A poor woman had been attending her son before a criminal court in London. As they were returning home at night, fatigue and anxiety so overcame her that she fell on the ground in convulsions, where she was found by Shelley. He appealed to a very opulent person, who lived on the top of the hill, asking admission for the woman into the house, or the use of the carriage, which had just set the family down at the door. The stranger was repulsed with the cold remark that impostors swarmed everywhere, and that his own conduct was "extraordinary." The good Samaritan, whom the Christian would not help, warned the uncharitable man that such treatment of the poor is sometimes chastised by hard treatment of the rich in days of trouble; and I heard Shelley describe the manner in which the gentleman retreated into his mansion, exclaiming, "God bless me, Sir! dear me, Sir!" In the account of the occurrence given by my father, he has omitted to mention that Shelley and the woman's son, who had already carried her a considerable way up the main hill of Hampstead, brought her on from the inhospitable mansion to our house in their arms; and I believe, that, the son's strength failing, for some

way down the hill into the Vale of Health Shelley carried her on his back. I cannot help contrasting this action of the wanderer with the careful self-regard of another friend who often came to see us, though I do not remember that any of us were ever inside his doors. He was, I believe, for some time actually a pensioner on Shelley's generosity, though he ultimately rose to be comparatively wealthy. One night, when he had been visiting us, he was in trouble because no person had been sent from a tavern at the top of the hill to light him up the pathway across the heath. That same self-caring gentleman afterwards became one of the apologists who most powerfully contributed to mislead public opinion in regard to his benefactor.

Shelley often called me for a long ramble on the heath, or into regions which I then thought far distant; and I went with him rather than with my father, because he walked faster, and talked with me while he walked, instead of being lost in his own thoughts and conversing only at intervals. A love of wandering seemed to possess him in the most literal sense; his rambles appeared to be without design, or any limit but my fatigue; and when I was "done up," he carried me home in his arms, on his shoulder, or pickback. Our communion was not always concord;

as I have intimated, he took a pleasure in frightening me, though I never really lost my confidence in his protection, if he would only drop the fantastic aspects that he delighted to assume. Sometimes, but much more rarely, he teased me with exasperating banter; and, inheriting from some of my progenitors a vindictive temper, I once 'retaliated severely. We were in the sitting-room with my father and some others, while I was tortured. The chancery-suit was just then approaching its most critical point, and, to inflict the cruellest stroke I could think of, I looked him in the face, and expressed a hope that he would be beaten in the trial and have his children taken from him. I was sitting on his knee, and as I spoke, he let himself fall listlessly back in his chair, without attempting to conceal the shock I had given him. But presently he folded his arms round me and kissed me; and I perfectly understood that he saw how sorry I was, and was as anxious as I was to be friends again. It was not very long after that we were playing with paper boats on the pond in the Vale of Health, watching the way in which the wind carried some of them over, or swamped most of them before they had surmounted many billows; and Shelley then playfully said how much he should like it, if we could get into one of the boats and be shipwrecked, — it was a death he should like better than any other.

After the death of Harriet, Shelley's life entirely changed; and I think I shall be able to show in the sequel that the change was far greater than any of his biographers, except perhaps one who was most likely to know, have acknowledged. Conventional form and Shelley are almost incompatible ideas; as his admirable wife has said of him, "He lived to idealize reality, — to ally the love of abstract truth, and adoration of abstract good, with the living sympathies. And long as he did this without injury to others, he had the reverse of any respect for the dictates of ortho-

doxy or convention." As soon, therefore, as the obstacle to a second marriage was removed, he and Mary Wollstonecraft Godwin were regularly joined in matrimony, and retired to Great Marlow, in Buckinghamshire. A brief year Shelley passed in the position of a country-gentleman on a small scale. His abode was a rough house in the village, with a garden at the back and nothing beyond but the country. Close to the house there was a small' pleasure-ground, with a mound at the farther end of the lawn slightly inclosing the view. Behind the mound there was a kitchen-garden, not unintermixed with flowers and ornamental vegetation; and farther still was a piece of ground traversed by a lane deeply excavated in the chalk soil. At that time Shelley had a thousand a year allowed to him by his father; but although he was in no respect the unreckoning, wasteful person that many have represented him to be, such a sum must have been insufficient for the mode in which he lived. His family comprised himself, Mary, William their eldest son, and Claire Claremont,—the daughter of Godwin's second wife, and therefore the half-sister of Mary Shelley, — a girl of great ability, strong feelings, lively temper, and, though not regularly handsome, of brilliant appearance. They kept three servants, if not a fourth assistant: a cook; Élise, a Swiss *gouvernante* for the child; and Harry, a man who did the work of gardener and man-servant in general. He kept something like open house; for while I was there with my father and mother, there also came, for a short time, several other friends, some of whom stopped for more than a passing visit. He played the Lord Bountiful among his humbler neighbors, not only helping them with money or money's-worth, but also advising them in sickness; for he had made some study of medicine, in part, I suspect, to be the more useful.

I have already intimated that he had assisted certain of his companions;

and I am convinced that these circumstances contributed to the resolution which Shelley formed to leave England for Italy in the year 1818, although he then ascribed his doing so to the score of health, — or rather, as he said, of life. He then believed himself to be laboring under a tendency to consumption, not without medical warnings to that effect, although there were strong reasons for doubting the validity of the belief, which was based upon less precise grounds before the introduction of auscultation and the careful examinations of our day. It was, however, characteristic of Shelley to rest his actions upon the dominant motive; so that, if several inducements operated to the same end, he absolutely discarded the minor considerations, and acted solely upon the grand one. I can well remember, that, when other persons urged upon him cumulative reasons for any course of action, whether in politics, or morality, or trifling personal matters of the day, he indignantly cast aside all such makeweights, and insisted upon the one sufficient motive. I mention this the more explicitly because the opposite course is the most common, and some who did not sympathize with his concentration of purpose afterwards imputed the suppression of all but one, out of several apparent motives, to reserve, or even to a want of candor. The accusation was first made by some of Shelley's false friends, — creatures who gathered round him to get what they could, and afterwards made a market of their connection, to his disadvantage. But I was shocked to find a sanction for the notion under the hand of one of Shelley's first and most faithful friends, and I discovered it, too, when death had barred me from the opportunity of controverting the mistake. It was easily accounted for. The writer to whom I allude was himself a person whose scrupulous conscience and strong mistrust of his own judgment, unless supported on every side, induced him to accumulate and to avow as many motives as possible

for each single act. He could scarcely understand or believe the existence of a mind which, although powerful and comprehensive in its grasp, should nevertheless deliberately set aside all motives but one, and actually proceed upon that exclusive ground without regard to the others.

Both Shelley and his friends seem to have underrated his strength, and one little incident will illustrate my meaning. He kept no horse or carriage; but in accordance with his ruling passion he had a boat on the river of sufficient size to carry a numerous party. It was made both for sailing and rowing; and I can remember being one of an expedition which went some distance up the Thames, when Shelley himself towed the boat on the return home, while I walked by his side. His health had very much improved with the change that had taken place in his mode of life, his more settled condition, and the abatement of anxiety, with the absolute removal of some of its causes. I am well aware that he *had* suffered severely, and that he continued to be haunted by certain recollections, partly real and partly imaginative, which pursued him like an Orestes. He frequently talked on such subjects; but it has always appeared to me that those who have reported what he said have been guilty of a singular confusion in their interpretations. As I proceed, you will find that certain facts in his life have never yet been distinctly related, and I have a strong reason for believing that some circumstances of which I became accidentally aware were never disclosed at all, except to Mary; while in her writings I can trace allusions to them, that remind me of passages in ancient authors, — in Ovid, for instance, — which would have been absolutely unintelligible, except for accidental references. In spite, however, of the rude trials to which his constitution had been subjected, and of new symptoms supposed to indicate pulmonary weakness, there was a marked improvement in his aspect since he had visited London. He still had that ultra-youthful figure that partook the traits of the hobbledehoy, arrived at man's stature, but not yet possessing the full manly proportions. His extremities were large, his limbs long, his face small, and his thorax very partially developed, especially in girth. An habitual eagerness of mood, thrusting forward his face, made him stoop, with sunken chest and rounded shoulders; and this was even more apparent in the easy costume of the country than in London dress. But in his countenance there was life instead of weariness; melancholy more often yielded to alternations of bright thoughts; and paleness had given way to a certain freshness of color, with something like roses in the cheeks. Notwithstanding the sense of weakness in the chest, which attacked him on any sudden effort, his power of exertion was considerable. Once, returning from a long excursion, and entering the house by the back way, up a precipitous, though not perpendicular bank, the women of the party had to be helped; and Shelley was the most active in rendering that assistance. While others were content to accomplish the feat for one, he, I think, helped three up the bank, sliding in a half-sitting posture when he returned to fetch a new charge. I well remember his shooting past me in a cloud of chalk-dust, as I was slowly climbing up. He had a fit of panting after it, but he made light of the exertion. I can also recollect, that, although he frequently preferred to steer rather than to put forth his strength, yet, if it were necessary, he would take an oar, and could stick to his seat for any time against any force of current or of wind, not only without complaining, but without being compelled to give in until the set task was accomplished, though it should involve some miles of hard pulling. These facts indicate the amount of "grit" that lay under the outward appearance of weakness and excitable nerves.

Shelley's fulness of vitality did not at that time seem to be shared by the partner of his life. Mary's intellectual powers had already been manifested. He must to some extent have known the force of her affection, and the tenderness of her nature; but it is remarkable that her youth was not the period of her greatest beauty, and certainly at that date she did not do justice to herself either in her aspect or in the tone of her conversation. She was singularly pale. With a figure that needed to be set off, she was careless in her dress; and the decision of purpose which ultimately gained her the playful title of "Wilful Woman" then appeared, at least in society, principally in the negative form, — her temper being easily crossed, and her resentments taking a somewhat querulous and peevish tone. Both of the pair were still young, and their ideas of education were adverse to the received doctrines of the day, rather than substantive; and their own principles in this matter were exemplified somewhat perversely by little William. Even at that early age the child called forth frequent and poignant remonstrances from his *gouvernante*, and occasionally drew perplexed exclamations or desponding looks from his father, who took the child's little perversities seriously to heart, and sometimes vented his embarrassment in generalized remarks on human nature.

☆ ★ ☆

☆ ★ ☆

In the "Memorials" and the "Relics" there is no further allusion to the circumstances which preceded Harriet's suicide; but it appears to me very desirable that the whole story should be brought out much more distinctly, and I can at least show why I say so. The correspondence in question took place in the middle of December, 1816. Shelley was married to Mary about a fortnight later; and in the most emphatic terms he alluded not only to the solace which he derived from the conversation of his host, but to the manner in which my father spoke of Mary. My own recollection goes back to the period, and I have already testified to the state of Shelley's mind. He was just then instituting the process to recover the children, and he caught at an opinion that had been expressed, that, in the event of his again becoming contracted in marriage, there would be no longer any pretence to deprive him of the children.

Let me for a moment pause on this incident, as it establishes two facts of some interest. In the first place, it shows some of the grounds of the very strong and unalterable friendship which subsisted betweeen my father and Mary, — a friendship which stood the test of many vicissitudes, and even of some differences of opinion ; both persons being very sensitive in feeling, quick in temper, thoroughly outspoken, and obstinately tenacious of their own convictions. Secondly, it corroborates what I have said with regard to the community of spirit that Shelley found in his real wife, — the woman who became the companion of his fortunes, of his thoughts, of his sufferings, and of his hopes. It will be seen, that, even before marriage with his second wife, he was counting upon Mary's help in preventing his separation from the two children already born to him. She was a woman uniting intellectual faculties with strong ambitions of affection as well as intellect; and esteem thus substantially shown, at that early age, by two such men as Percy Shelley and Leigh Hunt, must have conveyed the deepest gratification.

Throughout these communications Shelley evinced the strong pity that he felt for the unhappy being whom he had known. Circumstances had come to his knowledge which had thrown considerable light upon his relations with Harriet. There can be no doubt that one member of the family had hoped to derive gain from the connection with himself, as a person of rank and property. There seems also reason to suppose, that, about the same time, Harriet's father, an aged man, became so ill that his death might be regarded as approaching, and he had something to leave. Poor, foolish Harriet had undoubtedly formed an attachment to Shelley, whom she had been allowed to marry ; but she had then suffered herself to become a tool in the hands of others, and the fact accounted for the idle way in which she importuned him to do things repugnant to his feelings and convictions. She thus exasperated his temper, and lost her own ; they quarrelled. in the ordinary conjugal sense. and. from all I have learned. I am induced to guess. that, when she left him, it was not only in the indulgence of self-will, but also in the vain hope that her retreating would induce him to follow her, perhaps in a more obedient spirit. She sought refuge in her father's house, where she might have expected kindness; but, as the old man bent towards the grave, with rapid loss of faculties, he became more severe in his treatment of the poor woman; and she was driven from the paternal roof. This Shelley did not know at the time; nor did he until afterwards learn the process by which she arrived at her fate. Too late she became aware how fatal to her interests had been the intrigues of which she had been the passive instrument; and I suspect that she was debarred from seeking forgiveness and help partly by false shame, and partly by the terrible adaptability of weak natures to the condition of the society in which they find themselves. I have said that there is not a trace of evidence or a whisper of scandal against her before her voluntary departure from Shelley. and I have indicated the most probable motives of that step: but subsequently she forfeited her claim to a return, even in the eye of the law. Shelley had information which made him believe that she fell even to the depth of actual prostitution. If she left him. it would appear that she herself was deserted in turn by a man in a very humble grade of life; and it was in consequence of this desertion that she killed herself.

The change in his personal aspect that showed itself at Marlow appeared also in his writings, — the most typical of his works for this period being naturally the most complete that issued from his pen, the "Revolt of Islam." We find there identically the same doctrine that there is in "Queen Mab," — a systematic abhorrence of the servility which renders man captive to power, denunciation of the love of gain which

blinds his insight and destroys his energy. of the prostitution of religious faith. and, above all. of the slavery of womanhood. But by this time the doctrine has become more distinct in its expression. and far more powerful in its utterance.

> "Man seeks for gold in mines, that he may weave
> A lasting chain for his own slavery;
> In fear and restless care that he may live.
> He toils for others, who must ever be
> The joyless thralls of like captivity:
> He murders, for his chiefs delight in ruin;
> He builds the altar, that its idol's fee
> May be his very blood; he is pursuing.
> O blind and willing wretch! his own obscure undoing.

> "Woman! — she is his slave, she has become
> A thing I weep to speak, — the child of scorn,
> The outcast of a desolated home.
> Falsehood and fear and toil, like waves. have worn
> Channels upon her cheek, which smiles adorn,
> As calm decks the false ocean. Well ye know
> What woman is; for none of woman born
> Can choose but drain the bitter dregs of woe,
> Which ever from the oppressed to the oppressors flow."

The indignation against the revolting subjugation of womanhood comes out still more distinctly in the preceding canto, where Cythna relates the horrors to which she was subjected.

> "One was she among many there, the thralls
> Of the cold tyrant's cruel lust: and they
> Laughed mournfully in those polluted halls:
> But she was calm and sad, musing alway
> On loftiest enterprise, till on a day
> . . . . . .
> She told me what a loathsome agony
> Is that when selfishness mocks love's delight,
> Foul as in dreams' most fearful imagery
> To dally with the mowing dead; — that night
> All torture, fear, or horror made seem light
> Which the soul dreams or knows."

The poet bears testimony to the spiritual power which rules throughout Nature; the monster recovering his dignity while he is under the higher influence.

" Even when he saw her wondrous loveliness,
One moment to great Nature's sacred power
He bent and was no longer passionless;
But when he bade her to his secret bower
Be borne a loveless victim, and she tore
Her locks in agony, and her words of flame
And mightier looks availed not, then he
    bore
Again his load of slavery, and became
A king, a heartless beast, a pageant and a
    name.

        . . . . " When the day
Shone on her awful frenzy, from the sight,
Where like a spirit in fleshly chains she lay
Struggling, aghast and pale the tyrant fled
    away.

" Her madness was a beam of light, a power
Which dawned through the rent soul; and
    words it gave,
Gestures and looks, such as in whirlwinds
    bore
Which might not be withstood."

The doctrine involved in this passage is very clear, and it marks a decided progress since the days of " Queen Mab." It will be observed that Shelley's mind had become familiarized with the idea of a spirit ruling throughout Nature, obedience to which constitutes human power. Most remarkable is the passage in which the tyrant recovers his faculties through his subjection to this spirit; because it indicates Shelley's faithful adhesion to the universal, though oft obscurely formed belief, that the ability to *receive* influence is the most exalted faculty to which human nature can attain, while the exercise of an arbitrary power centring in self is not only debasing, but is an actual destroyer of human faculty.

E. J. Trelawny, *Records of Shelley, Byron, and the Author*, 2 vols (London, 1878)

In 1878, when Trelawny was eighty-six, three years before his death, he was persuaded by William Michael Rossetti, brother of Dante Gabriel Rossetti and enthusiastic Shelleyan, to issue an expanded version of his 1858 *Recollections* as *Records of Shelley, Byron, and the Author*. The inclusion of 'the Author' in the title conceded what had always been the case: Trelawny's memoirs were unashamedly stories of himself as well as of his famous friends (Shelley and Byron were both dead well before the reader got to the end of the *Recollections*). His records are subjective in ways that have led later literary historians to ignore them. For there is little evidence that the aged Trelawny returned to any documentary sources, let alone found new ones. Instead he seems to have turned to his own memories and to senses of allegiance that had altered since his memoir of the 1850s.

William St Clair, his most informative modern biographer, sums up Trelawny's rewriting of his own earlier account thus: 'He took every opportunity to run down Byron at the expense of Shelley and he was bitterly untruthful and unfair to Mary' (St Clair, *Trelawny*, p. 180). In broad outline, this is right. Time had hardened his sense of Shelley's superiority to Byron, which, by the late nineteenth century, was, as a literary judgement, no longer an unconventional preference. His new antipathy to Mary Shelley is more surprising. His *Recollections* had been complimentary to her, and she had, of course, been dead long before that work appeared. In his last years, spent living near Worthing with his so-called 'niece', Emma Taylor, the last in a sequence of young women who were his companions, he clearly changed his mind about Mary Shelley's role in the story he had to tell. That the thoughts were recent ones is indicated by the fact that his 'character' of her is given in an appendix – as if the truth had just rushed upon him. 'As this re-edition is passing through the press, it occurs to me to add a few particulars, all relating more or less to Shelley', he says (Trelawny, *Records*, II, p. 229), but the 'particulars' are mostly dismissive judgements of the poet's wife. 'Mrs. Shelley was of a soft, lymphatic temperament, the exact opposite to Shelley in everything; she was moping and miserable when alone, and yearning for society. Her capacity can be judged by the novels she wrote after Shelley's death, more than ordinarily commonplace and conventional' (ibid, II, p. 229). Apparently she was distinguished only by her 'littleness' – a woman tormented, after Shelley's death, by 'the memory of how often she had irritated and vexed him' (ibid, II, pp. 229–30). Worst of all, she was also religiously conventional, attending church whenever possible and grieving at her husband's stubborn atheism. 'Mrs. Shelley did not worry herself with things established that could not be altered, but went with the stream' (ibid, II, p. 231). Perhaps resentful at the posthumous entwining of her name with her husband's, Trelawny had decided to disengage the two.

Elsewhere, his changes are less easily visible and more in keeping with the spirit of his earlier memoir. There too he seemed most concerned with the dramatic truth of characters and episodes. In the *Records*, the latter are often simply padded out – 'developed', we might say – with further detail and dialogue. The additions must be, broadly speaking, inventions, yet were no doubt true to Trelawny's sense of the characters and events that he angrily believed had been traduced by all later biographers save Hogg (another fiction maker, of course). Perhaps the 'conversations' that suddenly appear in the *Records* are based on exchanges that once actually took place, almost sixty years earlier. Yet the new material often seems conveniently to follow and confirm the convictions that Trelawny had clearly been nourishing. New exchanges with Shelley introduce puzzlement at Byron's supposedly truculent behaviour. An account of Shelley's meeting with Mary Godwin shows the poet's head being disastrously turned by her 'resemblance to her mother' (ibid, II, p. 13) and is full of circumstantial detail and and direct speech that Trelawny tells us he gathered 'from words dropped from Mary at various times' (ibid, II, p. 12). The fact that he can expect his reader to trust to this material is sufficient indication that his fierce belief in the truth of his memories had long since transcended any need for evidence.

PREFACE.

" No living poet ever arrived at the fulness of his fame; the jury which sits in judgment upon a poet, belonging as he does to all time, must be composed of his peers: it must be impannelled by Time from the selectest of the wise of many generations."—SHELLEY's *Defence of Poetry.*

" There they saw a man clothed in white, and two men, Prejudice and Ill-will, continually casting dirt upon him. Now behold the dirt, whatsoever they cast at him, would in a little time fall off again, and his garments would look as clear as if no dirt had been cast thereat."—*Pilgrim's Progress.*

THESE two men who have left a stamp on the annals of our literature, Shelley and Byron, will interest a sect who, without priests or temples, believe in the divinity of the Muses and worship them. They alone will appreciate these records, and for them I am induced to state particulars which otherwise would die with me.

If our literature were confined to statistics and dry facts, it would be eternal winter. All our pains and aches and misadventures are dry facts, and all our pleasures spring from our imagination, which, like the sun, adorns everything. The poets create; they fill us with illusions which only Death proves delusions.

Our libraries are crammed with lives of distinguished men, and yet how rare it is to get a glimpse of the real man as he was in life. It is like unrolling an Egyptian mummy, wrapped in countless cerecloths and containing nothing but dry bones. In my brief records, first issued in 1858 and now re-issued with very large augmentations, I have endeavoured to portray men as men, as they were in their every-day lives. In public life men say and do the same things, and are as difficult to distinguish one from the other as sheep. Their writings are open to all the world; individual censure or praise should go for nothing.

Few, if any, can look backward on their lives with satisfaction. Hitherto the highest mental attainments have proved incompatible with that which everyone is seeking—Happiness. Gray says:—

> " When ignorance is bliss,
> 'Tis folly to be wise."

The happiest human animals I have known bore the strongest affinity to house-dogs—satisfied with food and shelter, and only disturbed at the approach of beggary and rags, with stagnant brains and active instincts.

I knew Shelley the last year of his life, and Byron the last three years of his life. I was on the most intimate terms with both, and saw them almost every day. On my return to England after Shelley's death, I became more or less intimate with all the friends whom Shelley had in England, and I continued to know Mrs. Shelley till her death.

That young men fresh from College and inflated with records of Greek and Roman history should rail at our humdrum life, and dissent from the institutions which had reduced us to this state, is no uncommon occurrence; but when they come in contact with the world these elevated notions are quickly rubbed off. It was not so with Shelley. Beginning at Oxford to question all things that were established in State and Church from time immemorial was considered by the orthodox as unprecedented audacity, and his being expelled from College and cast off from all his family, a just punishment. But the young reformer, with un-tamed energy of mind and body, fearlessly pursued his erratic course. As the pillory and imprison-ment had been foolishly laid aside, there was no ready remedy to check the blasphemy spreading like a pestilence throughout the land.

If authors write their own lives, or if publishers get lives written of them, they are so anxious the author should cut a good figure that they sacrifice everything for that one object. They may tell the truth, but not the whole truth. It was so in Byron's memoirs written by himself. If Shelley had undertaken the same task, he would not have mentioned himself; he never did allude to himself, he ignored self. What the orthodox wrote against him was brief, and bitter; that soothes our self-complacency, and so we read it. If praise were as brief we could endure it; but to make an idol of a man, endowing him with every virtue, and de-claring him infallible and guiltless of all human frailties, as a small sect of enthusiasts now do in chapter after chapter of eulogium, is nauseous and repulsive to every well-constituted mind. When

Shelley was alive, fanatics have asked me if he was not the worst of men; now he is dead, another set of fanatics ask me if he was not perfect.

Shelley never was a boy in mind: whilst they of his age were playing marbles, he was reading. His mental hunger for knowledge was insatiable—no one ever saw him without a book in his hand or pocket.

At Eton, after an illness, the doctor who attended him took a liking to him, and Shelley borrowed his medical books and was deeply interested in chemistry from that time, and, unlike doctors, he experimented with some of the drugs on himself. The power of laudanum to soothe pain and give rest especially delighted him; he was cautioned, and knew it was wrong; the seductive power of that drug retained a hold on him during the rest of his life, used with extreme caution at first and at long intervals. People who take to opiates are enslaved and never abandon them; these may be traced in some of Shelley's flights of imagination, and fancies of supernatural appearances. On one occasion in London, and again in Italy, he so over-dosed himself that his life was only saved by those measures that are used to counteract the drug; but it must not be thought that, like De Quincey and many others, he habitually used it: he only took it on rare occasions, when in deep dejection. He was impatient of remonstrance, and so made a mystery of it. The effect of opiates is to deaden pain, but they benumb the vital powers and derange our vital organs; with Shelley they caused spasms. The professor of anatomy at the University of Pisa, Vaccà, was renowned for his skill in surgery and medicine, and he came to the conclusion that Shelley was drugging himself, and earnestly interdicted medicine in all its forms; he said that Shelley was perfectly well constituted and of a healthy and vigorous frame—he recommended his varying his diet. I often saw him in a state of nudity, and he always reminded me of a young Indian, strong-limbed and vigorous, and there were few men who would walk on broken ground at the pace he kept up; he beat us all in walking, and barring drugs and accidents, he might have lived as long as his father—to ninety.

Those desirous of knowing what Shelley really was in his natural state and habits, will find it in Jefferson Hogg's book, and in no other that I have seen. Hogg has painted him exactly as I knew him : his is the only written likeness that I have ever read of him ; at the same time it is necessary to know that Hogg despised poetry, he thought it all nonsense, and barely tolerated Shakespeare. When I asked him why he did not continue the Life, he said, " Those who asked me to write it did not want a likeness of the poet as he was, but as they thought he should be ; there are literary men who undertake such jobs ; Tom Moore and others, who compile Lives and will say anything that is desired ; they would introduce their man as a heathen deity, with a flourish of trumpets, a big drum, and mad poets dancing, the muses singing, and the poet in a triumphal car, covered with spangles, and crowned with tinsel.   I don't puff : I described him as he was, and they were shocked.   It was his rare talents as a scholar that drew me to him.   The greatest men are those who composed our laws and the judges who administer them, and if Shelley had put all his mind into the study of the law, instead of writing nonsensical rhapsodies, he would have been a great benefactor to the world, for he had the most acute intellect of any man I ever knew." This being Hogg's idiosyncrasy—contempt of poets

—it is unnecessary to say his criticism of Shelley's poetry was of no value; but what he says of the poet as a man is perfectly true, and so, valuable.

Leigh Hunt often said that he was the dearest friend Shelley had; I believe he was the most costly. His theory was that between friends everything should be in common; he said you could not do your friend a greater favour than constitute him your banker, and that he could receive no greater pleasure than answering your drafts : as Leigh Hunt had an ailing wife and seven children, those drafts were frequent. Mrs. Shelley's father, Godwin, was another dear friend; his theory was that a man, labouring as he did for the advancement of knowledge, should be supported by those who agreed with the justness of his views. These two dear friends being heavily in debt, the poet had not the means of paying those debts, but the worldly philosopher, Godwin, having ascertained the poet's exact pecuniary position, as the heir of an entailed estate, suggested to him the antedating his inheritance, by raising money on post-obit bonds, and satisfied Shelley as to the expediency of so doing. The poet, always prepared for martyrdom, assented, and Godwin found the ready means of executing the project. Money was raised at cent. per cent.; both his dear friends' debts were paid. But experience proves that this practice is not effective: those who are in the habit of allowing their expenses to exceed their earnings will not alter those habits whilst they have credit, and the debts of these claimants being paid their credit was strengthened. Shelley repeated the process in vain. Besides these dear friends, Shelley had less costly friends, who dipped their hands into his purse.

Borrowers remain borrowers as long as they can find lenders, and if this small sample of communism became general, it would rapidly lead us back to a primitive state. We all dislike work, and we are only supported in our labour by the hope of rest; but with a general system of communism there would be no urgent stimulant to compel us to work; probably we should return to cannibalism until a new beginning was made of civilization.

When Shelley had a son and heir he doubted his right to pauperize him; of himself he thought nothing, but he doubted his right to give away his son's inheritance, and so he stopped that ruinous system of post-obits, but he continued to the last to keep for himself only what was absolutely necessary, and to bestow the rest on his dear friends. Giving money without well considered, specific, and well defined objects is always foolish. It was fortunate Shelley had so few friends, for with the exception of Jefferson Hogg and Horace Smith they all used him as their purse. Schoolboys have an apt saying, if they get hold of a generous, open-handed boy, "What's yours is mine, what's mine is my own;" and sailors say, "Everyone for himself and the devil for us all." This boys' saying was verified by Shelley's friends.

I one day pointed out to Shelley a picture which had great natural beauty, a sylvan scene; there was a clear pool of water, with wild fowl, a doe and two fawns in the foreground, a timid hare with two leverets, and an impudent magpie, a ledge of rocks and a dense wood in the background; it was richly coloured, the sun just disappearing. I said, "That's a picture that would be a pleasure for ever —all solemnity and solidity; it's a bit of heaven; any carnivorous animal, a fox, or a dog, or a man with a gun, would transform it into a semblance of hell. Why I like your poetry is, that you have none of these vermin. If you must have men or women, you create them to suit your ideal subjects. The poem you plume yourself on most is the 'Prometheus Unbound.'" Shelley said: "If that is not durable poetry, tried by the severest test, I do not know what is. It is a lofty subject, not inadequately treated, and should not perish with me." I answered: "A man's mind must be richly stored before he can appreciate that poem. Williams and I talking of your poetry, he said he preferred the 'Cenci;' I prefer the 'Epipsychidion.'" He opened his eyes wider. I observed: "Our opinions are worth nothing. We both went to sea when we were eleven, and could have had no education; until near thirty we were wandering about the world, and had no leisure." Shelley replied: "You have the advantage; you saw the things that we read about; you gained knowledge from the living, and we from the dead." This conversation took place in a room while we were waiting for a friend at Leghorn.

Shelley rarely read any book through; he was

eager to get at the matter stripped of the verbiage. Novels were totally uninteresting to him, there was no reality or imagination in them; but he retained some of his early fondness for romances. After glancing at an old Italian romance, in which a Knight of Malta throws down the gauntlet defying all infidels, he remarked: "I should have picked it up. All our knowledge is derived from infidels."

There was a marked individuality in Shelley. In habits, manners, and all the ordinary occurrences of life, he never changed. He took no notice of what other people did; brave, frank, and out-spoken, like a well-conditioned boy, well-bred and considerate for others, because he was totally de-void of selfishness and vanity. He did not laugh or even smile, he was always earnest. He had ob-served that people laughed at the misadventures of others, and therefore thought it cruel; but his eyes and face were so expressive that you could see all the workings within his mind in joy or sorrow. Beauty is said to be a fatal gift to women, and it may be added that genius is a fatal gift to men; they are born before their time and out of harmony with the things about them.

Byron, for eleven or twelve years, was the choice spirit of his age, and cheered on his way by the applause of multitudes; Shelley, on the contrary, for about the same space of time, as he himself said, was denounced as a Pariah; wherever recognized he was shunned. No two men could be more dissimilar in all ways, yet I have seldom known two men more unhappy.

I have been thus particular in describing the younger poet, as he was of a rare variety of the human species. I have met men similar to Byron, but never to Shelley; he was the ideal of what a poet should be.

E. J. T.

March 1878.

* ★ *

The day I found Shelley in the pine-forest he was writing verses on a guitar. I picked up a fragment, but could only make out the first two lines : —-

> " Ariel to Miranda : Take
> This slave of music."

It was a frightful scrawl; words smeared out with his finger, and one upon the other, over and over in tiers, and all run together " in most admired disorder ;" it might have been taken for a sketch of a marsh overgrown with bulrushes, and the blots for wild ducks ; such a dashed-off daub as self-conceited artists mistake for a manifestation of genius. On my observing this to him, he answered,

" When my brain gets heated with thought, it

soon boils, and throws off images and words faster than I can skim them off. In the morning, when cooled down, out of the rude sketch, as you justly call it, I shall attempt a drawing. If you ask me why I publish what few or none will care to read, it is that the spirits I have raised haunt me until they are sent to the devil of a printer. All authors are anxious to breech their bantlings."

When I first knew Shelley, I met an old friend and his wife walking by the Arno. I said to Shelley,

" That man was a gay, frank, and cheerful companion ; a widow immeshed him as a spider ensnares a fly and sucks his blood. She is jealous and torments him ; when I remonstrated with her, she said it was excess of love made her so."

Shelley answered,

" Love is not akin to jealousy ; love does not seek its own pleasure, but the happiness of another. Jealousy is gross selfishness ; it looks upon everyone who approaches as an enemy: it's the idolatry of self, and, like canine madness, incurable."

His eyes flashed as he spoke. I did not then know that the green-eyed monster haunted his own house.

CHAPTER IX.

So as we rode, we talked; and the swift thought
Winging itself with laughter, lingered not,
But flew from brain to brain.

SHELLEY.

There are several kinds of divine madness. That which proceeds from the Muses' taking possession of a tender and unoccupied soul, awakening and bacchically inspiring it towards songs and other poetry, adorning myriads of ancient deeds, instructs succeeding generations; but he who, without this madness from the Muses, approaches the poetical gates, having persuaded himself that by art alone he may become sufficiently a Poet, will find in the end his own imperfection, and see the poetry of his cold prudence vanish into nothingness before the light of that which has sprung from divine insanity.—SOCRATES.

AT 10 a.m. by appointment I drove to Shelley's house and hailed him; he was always prompt as a seaman in a squall, and rushing downstairs, was brought to by his wife on the first landing:—

" Percy, do change your cap and jacket; you promised Tre to call on his Yankee girl and Highland beauty at Leghorn. Caterina! bring down the padrone's coat and hat."

The Poet, reluctantly submitting, muttered,

"Our bones should be outside, or our skins as tough as alligators'; the thing you have put on my head feels like a crown of thorns, and the ligature round my throat a halter. I bear what I can, and suffer what I must."

No personal vexations could extort harsher words than these from him, and he often used them. To avoid any further manipulation he sprang down the stairs, and striding adroitly over a fair fat child squatting on the doorstep beside its nurse, stepped into my chaise at the door. The child cried.

SHELLEY :

> "When we are born, we cry that we are come
> To this great stage of fools."

TRE. : Whose child is it ?

POET (looking at it): Don't know.

MRS. SHELLEY (from open casement) : That's too bad, not to know your own child. Why, you goose, it is Percy !

TRE. : You are not the wise man who knows his own child.

SHELLEY : The wise men have none.

TRE.: Those wise men must be in the moon; there are few such on the earth.

As we turned off the Lung' Arno, a friendly puff of wind relieved the Poet of his obnoxious head-gear, and the hat trundled along. I stopped the horse.

SHELLEY : Oh, don't stop ! It will get into the river and I shall find it at Leghorn.

TRE. : That will depend on wind and current.

Two Florentine gentlemen ran and picked it up, wiped the dust off, and brought it to us.

SHELLEY : They say that beavers are nearly exterminated ; if hats go too, I cannot mourn for them.

Outside of the Port, on the Leghorn road, half-a-dozen small children were clustered round a ruined building, tormenting a family of beautiful bright green-and-gold coloured lizards.

SHELLEY : The young demons !

TRE.: You are blaspheming, for is it not said, "Of such is the kingdom of heaven"? Children, until restrained, kill everything that runs from them ; but if a beetle or a mouse moves towards them they fly in terror : cruel and cowardly; and that is the nature of man.

SHELLEY: He is in process of training.

TRE. : It is very slow.

SHELLEY: The animals that subsist on herbs are docile, the flesh-eaters are untamable.

TRE.: In the tropics we can live on fruits, not in the north. The Brahmins live on grains and fruit and are docile, the flesh-eaters make serfs of them. Mrs. Shelley says I am as eccentric as you; I wish I were as reasonable.

SHELLEY: Mary is under the dominion of the mythical monster "Everybody." I tell her I am of the Nobodies. You have been everywhere; have you seen the ubiquitous demon Everybody?

TRE.: Yes, in Egypt; a harmless and most useful beast. The loaded camels of a caravan are piloted by a donkey. His head-stall is decorated with bells; he leads the way and the docile animals follow, guided by the jingling. Without him they stray always. So you see the much-abused donkey is not the most stupid of animals; "Everybody" follows him.

SHELLEY: You have solved the mystery. You must tell Mary. Wise men in all ages have declared everything that is, is wrong; those who stray away find something that is right. A donkey decorated is a guide for those that are as stupid as camels; we stray, we are eccentric.

Soon after we passed some masons building a chapel, and women acting as bricklayers' labourers, carrying heavy stones and mortar.

SHELLEY: See the barbarism that the priests have reduced Italy to.

TRE.: It is the primitive state of things. In the earliest records of the human race the duty of men was as hunters and warriors, and women did all the drudgery—fetched the wood and water. The professor of anatomy at the university of Pisa—and he is a high authority—says that women, though not the strongest, are the toughest. He says the female of all races of animals are less highly organized than the male; they are not so subject to diseases, and wounds more readily heal with them than with the male. It is the poets, artists, and others of imagination who have reversed the natural order of things, and who have placed women where we should be.

SHELLEY: We are indebted to the poets for having transformed women from what they were to what they are—a solace and delight.

TRE.: No; they have overshot their mark. They tell us that our principal object, aim, and end is to seek in the world for a fair skin, silky hair, and bright eyes ; the emptier the mind the better ; and that this is all life has to bestow. It is the old story—the sirens luring one to the sea-beach paved with human bones. Nature has lavished all its beauties on the male in the animal races as well as the human. Look at the hen pheasant and the pea-hen, and the singing birds, it is only the male that sings. Now we search the four corners of the earth to transform a dowdy into a fine lady. Half the world pass their lives in searching for gems and silks and satins to ornament them, and what torments does one suffer when captured by one of these dragon-flies ! Men have nothing to cover themselves with but the cast-off winter clothing of sheep.

The poet, when he was in a placid humour, delighted in amplifying notions the most adverse to his real opinions.

I said,

" The primitive people in the Indian Archipelago and other countries alone preserve the natural order of things. I once put into a bay on the eastern coast of Madagascar for fresh provisions and water. A great chief came down to barter with a retinue of nude followers, he himself being distinguished by having a gold-laced cocked hat with feathers, such as worn by generals of division, and hunting boots, otherwise as naked as Adam; his face and body elaborately ornamented by tattooing with colours which I had never seen before."

SHELLEY: In youth I thought the reasoning faculties, if fairly developed, would triumph, but passions overpower all our faculties. The animals are guided by their instincts, we by our cultivated cunning and blind passions.

TRE.: And reason.

SHELLEY: No, that faculty is paralysed by the priests. . . . .

Of such stuff was our ordinary talk, to keep him awake from his dreamy reveries, and so we reached Loghorn.

During our return I said to him,

"You had better dine with me."

He replied,

"What for?" (I saw he was disturbed.) "When?"

I said,

"Now," and produced a basket of all the fresh fruits of the season, saying,

" The Muses might dine on this food."

He answered,

" No; they live in the blue regions of the air."

Notwithstanding his protest, he went on picking the grapes and eating the fruit, unconscious of what he was doing. He invariably read when he was eating. He now had in his hand a monthly review, sent to him from England. He never in such cases laughed, but I saw by his eyes that he was amused.   I said,

" What is it that amuses you ?"

SHELLEY : The " Epipsychidion," that you like so much, the reviewer denounces as the rhapsody of a madman. That it may be a rhapsody I won't deny, and a man cannot decide on his own sanity.   Your dry, matter-of-fact men denounce all flights of imagination as proofs of insanity, and so did the Greek sect of the Stoics. All the mass of mankind consider everyone eccentric or insane who utters sentiments they do not comprehend.

There was other abuse of him in the magazine. I said,

"The Persian poet Hafiz would have consoled you by saying, 'You are like the shell of ocean that fills with pearls the hand that wounds you.' "

He was delighted with the Eastern metaphors, and I repeated many others to him, talking of Eastern civilization, from which all poetry had originated.

In answer to my questions Shelley once said,

" In writing the ' Cenci ' my object was to see how I could succeed in describing passions I have never felt, and to tell the most dreadful story in pure and refined language. The image of Beatrice haunted me after seeing her portrait. The story is well authenticated, and the details far more horrible than I have painted them. The ' Cenci ' is a work of art; it is not coloured by my feelings, nor obscured by my metaphysics. I don't think much of it. It gave me less trouble than anything I have written of the same length.

" I am now writing a play for the stage. It is affectation to say we write a play for any other purpose. The subject is from English history;[1] in style and manner I shall approach as near our great dramatist as my feeble powers will permit. ' King Lear ' is my model, for that is nearly perfect. I am amazed at my presumption. Poets should be modest. My audacity savours of madness.

[1] Charles the First.

☆ ★ ☆

His flashing eyes and vehement eager manner determined on the instant execution of any project that took his fancy, however perilous.   He over-bore all opposition in those less self-willed than he was, and women are of a trusting nature and have faith in an earnest man.   So Jane impulsively and promptly squatted in the bottom of the frail bark with her babies.   The Poet proud of his freight triumphantly shoved off from the shore, and to ex-hibit his skill as a mariner rowed round a jutting promontory into deep blue water.   The sea is very shallow for a considerable distance from the land in the bay, and Jane understood that Percy intended to float on the water near the shore, for the gun-wale of the boat was only a hand's breadth out of the water ; a puff of wind, a ripple on the water, or an incautious movement of the Poet, or herself or children, and the tub of a thing that could barely sustain the weight within it would cant over and fill and glide from under them.   There was no eye watch-ing them, no boat within a mile, the shore fast receding, the water deepening, and the Poet dreaming. As these dismal facts flashed on Jane's mind, her insane folly in trusting herself to a man of genius, but devoid of judgment, prudence, or skill, dismayed her.

After pulling out a long way, the Poet rested on his oars, unconscious of her fears and apparently of where he was, absorbed in a deep reverie, probably reviewing all he had gone through of suffering and wrong, with no present or future.

He was a brooding and silent man, feeling acutely, but never complaining—the wounds that bleed inwards are the most fatal. He took no heed of the occurrences of daily life, or men's selfish hopes or fears ; his mind was so organized that it required a nice perception to know when and how to strike the chord that would excite his attention. Spellbound by terror, she kept her eyes on the awful boatman : sad and dejected, with his head leaning on his chest, his spirit seemed crushed ; his hand had been for every man, and every man's hand against him. He was "the shorn lamb, but the wind was not tempered." At any other time or place Jane would have sympathized deeply with the lorn

and despairing bard. She had made several remarks, but they met with no response. She saw
death in his eyes. Suddenly he raised his head,
his brow cleared and his face brightened as with a
bright thought, and he exclaimed joyfully,

"Now let us together solve the great mystery."

An ordinary lady-kind would have screamed or
got up to implore, or pray, or reason, and thus herself have accomplished what she most dreaded—the
Poet's suggestion; but Jane, with a true woman's
keen instinct—a safer guide in sudden perilous
emergencies than could be found in a senate of
sages—knowing Shelley was unlike all other men,
felt that to be silent or strike a discordant note to
his feelings might make him stamp his foot, and
the leaden waters would roll over and wrap round
them as a winding-sheet; that her only chance was
to distract his thoughts from his dismal past life to
the less dreary present—to kindle hope. In answer
to his kind and affectionate proposal of "solving the
great mystery," suppressing her terror and assuming
her usual cheerful voice, she answered promptly,

"No, thank you, not now; I should like my dinner
first, and so would the children."

This gross material answer to his sublime proposition shocked the Poet, as showing his companion could not enter into the spirit of his idea.

" And look," she continued, " the sea breeze is coming in, the mist is clearing away, and Edward is coming on shore with Trelawny ; they have been out since light and must be famished, they took nothing with them, and to-morrow you are to have the boat-race to see if you can beat the 'Bolivar.'   I wish we were on shore ; they'll be so surprised at our being out at this time, and Edward says this boat is not safe."

" Safe ! " said the Poet ; " I'd go to Leghorn or anywhere in her."

Death's demon, always attending the Poet on the water, now spread his wings and vanished.   Jane felt his thoughts were veering round and continued,

" You haven't written the words for the Indian air."

" Yes, I have," he answered, " long ago. I must write them out again, for I can't read what I compose and write out of doors.   You must play the air again and I'll try and make the thing better."

The weird boatman now paddled to where our

boat had landed. Williams, not finding his wife in the house, came down to the beach in dismay, when I pointed her out to him in the skiff: the fisherman's boat that landed us had shoved off.

The Poet, deluded by the wiles of a woman into postponing his voyage to solve the great mystery, paddled his cockle shell of a boat into shallow water.

As soon as Jane saw the sandy bottom, she snatched up her babies and clambered out so hurriedly that the punt was capsized. Edward and I picked them up; the bard was underneath the boat and rose with it partly on his back, and was not unlike a turtle, or a hermit crab that houses itself in any empty shell it can find. Edward, surprised at his wife's lubberly way of getting out of the boat, said,

" We would have hauled the boat up, if you had waited a moment."

" No, thank you. Oh, I have escaped the most dreadful fate; never will I put my foot in that horrid coffin. Solve the great mystery? Why, he is the greatest of all mysteries. Who can predict what he will do?—and he casts a spell over everything.

You can form some notion of what other people will do as they partake of our common nature—not what he will do. He is seeking after what we all avoid, death. I wish we were away, I shall always be in terror."

Leaving them to their cogitation, I went to make my toilet, the sea my washing-basin—there was no other. As usual we had a fish dinner. Jane ate nothing; the sight of the natives of the deep was enough. Condemned men can eat, but not the suddenly reprieved.

"You won't catch me in a boat with Shelley alone," said Jane.

The Poet hearing his name—for all his faculties were marvellously acute—glided into the room, with his boyish face and radiant expression. He seized some bread and grapes—his usual food. He fed his brain as well as body; he was then reading the Spanish dramas. His body was with us but his brain in Spain. His young face looked as innocent of all guile as a cherub, and so he was. Simple, frank, and confiding, any one would trust him at sight. His mild, earnest manners won all hearts, gentle and simple. There was no limit to his generosity and self-negation to serve a friend, and he considered all the poor and oppressed as his friends. But then he avowed that he did not believe the State religion, and repeated what many have said before him and more have thought, that priests of all denominations only consider religion as the means of obtaining that which all are desirous of—power. When Lord Eldon was Chancellor, the Church of England excommunicated unbelievers more effectually than the Church of Rome.

The ground floor of the Poet's villa was appropriated, as is often done in Italy, for stowing the implements and produce of the land, as rent is paid in kind there. In the autumn you find casks of wine, jars of oil, tools, wood, occasionally carts, and, near the sea, boats and fishing-nets. Over this floor there were a large saloon and four bedrooms, and nothing more; there was an out-building for cooking, and a place for the servants to eat and sleep in. The Williamses had one room and Shelley and his wife occupied two more, facing each other.

☆ ★ ☆

Well-constituted minds, not influenced by personal considerations, are shocked at every act of injustice committed in the world; and as I see indications that the reputation of Harriet Shelley, the first wife of the Poet, will be slandered by an evil tongue, to remove the only great error in that Poet's life, I desire, as I am the last person who can do so, to leave on record what evidence I could collect regarding the separation that ensued between Shelley and his first wife.

And first as to their marriage. Shelley had one or two of his sisters at a boarding-school in London. He often visited them, and found a girl named Harriet Westbrook with them. In one of these visits the girls were discussing the difficulty that her father had with her; the arbitrary tyranny of his own father caused Shelley to sympathize with her. The perplexed girls not seeing their way out of the difficulty, Shelley said abruptly, " I will marry her." They were both startled, for Shelley had shown no symptoms of individual liking for the girl,

nor any special interest regarding her. The thought
had flashed from his mind to meet a sudden emergency. As both were under age, Shelley with his
usual impetuosity posted to Scotland, and there this
boarding-school Miss and the expelled Oxford boy
were married, and, as the novelists would end their
story by saying, they were ever after happy. Harriet
and Shelley were both thoroughly ignorant of life
as it is, and essentially different in their minds and
bringing up. Harriet was made of plastic clay and
could be readily stamped into any form; but her
elder sister Eliza was of the fire-brick clay, and
once pressed into a form was unalterable.

I was assured by the evidence of the few friends
who knew both Shelley and his wife—Hookham,
who kept the great library in Bond Street; Jefferson
Hogg, Peacock, and one of the Godwins—that
Harriet was perfectly innocent of all offence. Shelley had early been a convert to Godwin's and Mary
Woolstonecraft's theories regarding marriage: that
the sexes should not be held together when their
minds become thoroughly estranged. In five or ten
thousand years this theory may be practicable; it is
not so now. Shelley indoctrinated his wife with

these impracticable theories. Harriet felt Shelley's
great superiority to herself, and placed implicit
confidence in his judgment. She was innocent of
all knowledge, beyond the ordinary routine of a
boarding-school education. The poet, at the date
of his marriage, was nineteen years of age, and his
bride sixteen.

Harriet, as already intimated, was of an easy,
trusting, and pliant nature, that any person could
have lived with. Her sister Eliza—so admirably
described by Jefferson Hogg in his " Life of Shelley "—was a woman composed of all those ingredients which constitute a she-devil, that no man can
live with. She was a perpetual torment to the Poet.
Shelley knew that animals can't alter their nature.
He could not reason with his tormentor, because she
was devoid of reasoning faculty. Eliza was much
older than Harriet; and, when the latter was not at
school, Eliza domineered over her. Eliza considered
Shelley and her sister as young people utterly ignorant of the ways of the world, and deemed it her
duty to set them right. Their irregular habits, and
neglect of all forms and ceremonies, as practised by
well-conducted families, perplexed and irritated

Eliza, and she was perpetually lecturing the Poet on proper behaviour. Harriet, from being used to her admonitions, was callous to them; Shelley's sensitive nature could not endure the process, and it generally ended in driving him out of the room.

If our universities cannot teach our boys how to act their parts as men, our female schools do not teach our girls how to act *their* parts as women; otherwise Harriet would have seen that the only prudent course was to get rid of her sister. Shelley's excessive toleration was dangerous, and misled unobservant people; but an observer could see by his face how much he suffered in consequence of what he considered ungenerous or unjust assertions. His indignation was suppressed; he never contradicted or used harsh words to his opponent, and sometimes foolish opponents were absurd enough to think they were converting him to their opinions. He retreated into his burrow to avoid them.

Thus Eliza became a perpetual torment to him with her platitudes and commonplaces. She was bristling all over with knowledge of the ways of the world; and what the world did she thought must be as orthodox as the Gospel. She looked upon

Shelley and Harriet as infants who knew little or nothing. She tried her hand upon Shelley, but considered that he was incorrigibly perverse, and was making her sister as bad as himself. She complained to her friends bitterly of the mean way in which they had been married in Scotland, saying that the great event of a girl's life was the marriage ceremony, and of this Harriet had been defrauded; that she had been taken away like a piece of smuggled goods into a strange country where they had no relatives or friends, no one to give her away, no wedding dress of silk or satin, no wreath of orange flowers, no presents of trinkets, no public breakfast, or wedding cake, or chaise-and-four with postillions, white gloves, and favours, and nowhere to go to but a paltry lodging. It was a pauper wedding: this grievance rankled in Eliza's mind, and often found vent. Girls look to a triumphant marriage as the great event of their lives; but Harriet was so simple-minded that she laughed at the affair, and thought it good fun.

Eliza was arbitrary and energetic. Harriet had the difficult task of pacifying her sister, and following in the footsteps of her husband. They wandered into the Northern Lake district, then into Ireland and Wales, and back to London—as Eliza said, like tramps or gipsies—for nearly three years; then the Poet, lured by a new light, broke his chain, and fled. Harriet sought a refuge with her father. The father at last was confined to his room by sickness, and the sister refused her entrance there. Friendless, and utterly ignorant of the world and its ways, deserted by her husband and family, Harriet was the most forlorn and miserable of her sex—poor and outcast. It is too painful to trace her faltering steps. She made one effort to hold on to life. A man professed to be interested and to sympathize in her fate. He was a captain in the army, and was suddenly ordered to join his regiment abroad. He promised to correspond with her. Her poverty compelled her to seek a refuge in a cheaper lodging; her former landlady refused to forward her letters to her new address. In this deplorable state, fancying that no human being could take the least interest in her, and believing in Shelley's doctrine—that when our last hopes are extinguished, and life is a torment, our only refuge is death—blighted, benighted, and crushed, with hurried steps she hastened into the Park, and threw herself off the bridge into the Serpentine.

Shelley had lately been on the Continent, and knew nothing of this train of events, supposing Harriet was with her family. The calamity very much changed his character, and was a torment to him during the rest of his life.

☆ ★ ☆

5.—*Remarks on Mr. Barnett Smith's volume, " Shelley, a Critical Biography."*

Minute particulars regarding the death of Shelley are sought for and narrated by different writers in different ways. I see the latest by Mr. Barnett Smith has many errors. Details can only be interesting from their authenticity, and everything that was done from first to last was done by me alone.

Mr. Barnett Smith gives a different version of the details from that which I have published ; and

he can have no authority for so doing. Amongst
other things he says that, when Shelley's body was
washed on shore he had firmly grasped in his
hand a volume of Æschylus. I have stated in my
former account of the poet's death that Shelley's
body had been eight days in the water, and his
comrade Williams the same, and that all parts of the
body not protected by clothes were torn off by dog-
fish and other sea-vermin, even to their scalps; the
hands were torn off at the wrists. That disposes of
the Æschylus story. When I parted from Shelley
on his embarking on his last voyage, he had a black
single-breasted jacket on, with an outside pocket
as usual on each side of his jacket. When his body
was washed on shore, Æschylus was in his left
pocket, and Keats's last poem was in his right,
doubled back, as thrust away in the exigency of the
moment. Shelley knew that Keats was ripening
into a true poet, and was very anxious to read this
his last poem; Leigh Hunt had lent it to him.
When reading a Greek poet, he would carry the
book about with him for months, as he said there
were often passages in it that perplexed him. That
Greek volume, after I had had it in my possession
for twenty or thirty years, I gave to his son Sir
Percy. Excepting their wives, no one could have

412 LIVES OF THE GREAT ROMANTICS: SHELLEY

identified the bodies of Shelley and Williams except
myself, and no one but I saw them. If I had not
been there, probably they never would have been
identified, and I could do this only by familiarity
with their dress.

Then Mr. Barnett Smith says, the Shelley family
were never satisfied with the account of the wreck,
as being the right one. Except Shelley's wife, and
his son, who was under three years old, there were
no Shelleys that were in any degree interested, or
knew anything about it, except from the papers.
Neither Mrs. Shelley, Byron, nor Leigh Hunt,
knew anything but what I told them.

When I burnt the bodies, Shelley's heart was
not consumed when other portions of the body
were. In drowning, the blood rushes to the heart;
and the heart of Shelley was gorged with blood, so
it was no miracle that it would not burn. Ultimately I gave the heart to his wife, and she inconsiderately gave it to Leigh Hunt, and some years
ago it was given to Sir Percy Shelley by the Hunts.
Mr. Barnett Smith says the heart was buried in
Rome. It never was in Rome, and it is now at
Boscombe, and, for anything I know to the contrary,
in an ornamental urn on the mantel-shelf. I purchased ground in the burying-ground of the Pro-

testants at Rome, and there I myself buried not
Shelley's heart but his ashes; not near Keats's
grave, but isolated; from which place (so I am told,
but I cannot affirm it of my own knowledge) the
ashes have been surreptitiously taken, and are now
in the possession of Lady Shelley.

Mr. Barnett Smith also says—The fishermen who
ran down Shelley's boat intended keeping Byron
till they got a large ransom for him.   This is nonsense; there was no brigandage in Tuscany.   Their
real game was that which they executed.   They
knew there would be a squall; in that squall they
would run down the "Don Juan," drown the three
people on board, and get the bag of dollars which
they had seen taken on board.   That was what
tempted them.   They succeeded in all but the last
part; the boat's sinking so suddenly defeated their
getting the money.   If they had saved any of the
lives they would have been subjected to fourteen
days' quarantine, besides the investigation which
would have followed.

There are many other inaccuracies in Mr. Smith's
book.

The principal fault I have to find is that the
Shelleyan writers, being Christians themselves,
seem to think that a man of genius cannot be an

Atheist, and so they strain their own faculties to disprove what Shelley asserted from the earliest stage of his career to the last day of his life. He ignored all religions as superstitions. Some years ago, one of the most learned of the English Bishops questioned me regarding Shelley; he expressed both admiration and astonishment at his learning and writings. I said to the Bishop, " You know he was an Atheist." He said, " Yes." I answered : " It is the key and the distinguishing quality of all he wrote. Now that people are beginning to distinguish men by their works, and not creeds, the critics, to bring him into vogue, are trying to make out that Shelley was not an Atheist, that he was rather a religious man. Would it be right in me, or anyone who knew him, to aid or sanction such a fraud ? " The Bishop said : " Certainly not, there is nothing righteous but truth." And there our conversation ended.

Certainly there were men of genius before the Christian era : there were men and nations not equalled even at the present day.

A clergyman wrote in the visitors' book at the Mer de Glace, Chamouni, something to the following effect : " No one can view this sublime scene, and deny the existence of God." Under which Shelley, using a Greek phrase, wrote, " P. B. Shelley, Atheist," thereby proclaiming his opinion to all the world.   And he never regretted having done this.

The Diary of Dr. John William Polidori 1816, (London, 1911)

Polidori's diary might appear anomalous alongside the other texts included in this anthology, all of which carefully shape their recollections of Shelley for public consumption. Yet the diary is not quite what it seems. When John Polidori, at the age of only twenty, became travelling physician to Lord Byron in the Spring of 1816, John Murray, Byron's publisher, offered him £500 for an account of the tour of Europe on which he was about to embark with his employer. An intimate account of the lordly poet would be a highly saleable commodity. Polidori therefore began to keep a journal – a text designed from the first as the basis of a future publication. Just as Medwin sought conversations with Byron in order to obtain material for a book, so Polidori, in his unsystematic way, scribbled a record of his time in Switzerland with Byron and his friends in order to make an account that could be published. As it was, Byron and Polidori parted company sooner than Murray can have expected: the 'diary' was begun on April 24th, 1816, when they left London on the first leg of their journey, and recorded September 16th, less than four months later, as the date of their separation. 'L[ord] B[yron] determined upon our parting, – not upon any quarrel, but on account of our not suiting' (*The Diary of Dr. John William Polidori*, ed. Rossetti, p. 152).

Polidori was evidently a trying, sometimes impossible, companion – hot-tempered enough, during one altercation, to challenge Shelley to a duel (see Holmes, p. 330 – the story derives from Moore's *Life of Byron*). Byron was to tell Murray, 'I know no great harm of him; but he had an alacrity of getting into scrapes' (cited in Marchand, II, p. 651). It was clear to those close to Byron that Polidori had had to be dismissed, and, on his return to England from his 1816 journey to the Continent, Shelley was to write to express his relief at hearing this (see Jones, *Letters*, I, p. 505). Yet Polidori's short time with Byron had included Byron's first meeting with Shelley and Mary Godwin, and the evenings together at the Villa Diodati that stimulated Mary to write *Frankenstein*. So, although he never did publish his account, the so-called 'diary' that has come down to us has provided some of the best material for one of the most famous chapters in Shelley's life. Polidori himself was dead before either of the two poets of whom he wrote. After parting from Byron, he travelled on to Italy, but was back in London by the beginning of 1817, and then tried to resume a medical career in Norwich. He relinquished this for a legal training, but, in August 1821, apparently encumbered with gambling debts, he committed suicide by poisoning himself.

After his death, Polidori's journal came into the possession of his sister, Charlotte, and was consulted by William Michael Rossetti when he was preparing a biographical sketch of Shelley for his 1870 edition of his poems. Rossetti, brother of Dante Gabriel, was one of those enthusiastic Shelleyans allowed access to the Boscombe relics by Lady Jane Shelley (see the head-note in this volume to Lady Jane Shelley, *Shelley Memorials*) and knew Trelawny (see the headnote to Trelawny's *Records*). He was also Polidori's nephew (Polidori's sister was his mother). In 1911 he edited the *Diary*, and gave a history of the text that he was using. Charlotte Polidori, a woman possessing 'the severe virtue so characteristic of an English maiden aunt', had found in it 'some few passages which she held to be "improper"' (*Diary*, ed. Rossetti, p. 11). These included 'one about Byron and a chambermaid at Ostend'. 'My aunt therefore took the trouble of copying out the whole Diary, minus the peccant passages, and she then ruthlessly destroyed the original MS'. After her death in 1890, Rossetti was left with only his aunt's expurgated transcript, and it was this that he published. The extracts below (here reset) are taken from his edition. Rossetti was to observe that, had his aunt been 'an adept in Shelleian detail' (ibid, p. 103), the very first comment about Shelley and Godwin's daughters 'who practise his theories' (i.e. free love) would not have survived.

Found letter from De Roche inviting me to breakfast to-morrow; curious with regard to L[ord] B[yron]. Dined; P[ercy] S[helley], the author of *Queen Mab*, came; bashful, shy, consumptive; twenty-six; separated from his wife; keeps the two daughters of Godwin, who practise his theories; one L[ord] B[yron]'s.

☆ ★ ☆

Was introduced by Shelley to Mary Wollstonecraft Godwin, called here Mrs. Shelley. Saw picture by Madame Einard of a cave in the Jura where in winter there is no ice, in summer plenty. No names announced, no ceremony – each speaks to whom he pleases. Saw the bust of Jean Jacques erected upon the spot where the Geneva magistrates were shot. L[ord] B[yron] said it was probably built of some of the stones with which they pelted him.[1] The walk is deserted. They are now mending their roads. Formerly they could not, because the municipal money always went to the public box.

May 29. – Went with Mr. Hentsch to see some houses along the valley in which runs the Rhone: nothing. Dined with Mr. and Mrs. Percy Shelley and Wollstonecraft Godwin. Hentsch told us that the English last year exported corn to Italy to a great amount.

May 30. – Got up late. Went to Mr. and Mrs. Shelley; break-fasted with them; rowed out to see a house together. S[helley] went from Lucerne with the two, with merely £26, to England along the Rhine in bateaux. Gone through much misery, thinking he was dying; married a girl for the mere sake of letting her have the jointure that would accrue to her; recovered; found he could not agree; separated; paid Godwin's debts, and seduced his daughter; then wondered that he would not see him. The sister left the father to go with the other. Got a child. All clever, and no meretricious appearance. He is very clever; the more I read his *Queen Mab*, the more beauties I find. Published at fourteen a novel; got £30 for it; by his second work £100. *Mab* not published. – Went in calèche with L[ord] B[yron] to see a

---

[1] I don't think there was any such stone-pelting in Geneva: it took place elsewhere in Switzerland.

house; again after dinner to leave cards; ·then on lake with L[ord] B[yron]. I, Mrs S[helley], and Miss G[odwin], on to the lake till nine. Drank tea, and came away at 11 after confabbing. The batelier went to Shelley, and asked him as a favour not to tell L[ord] B[yron] what he gave for his boat, as he thought it quite fit that Milord's payment be double; we sent Berger to say we did not wish for the boat.

☆ ★ ☆

Shelley is another instance of wealth inducing relations to confine for madness, and was only saved by his physician being honest. He was betrothed from a boy to his cousin, for age; another came who had as much as he *would* have, and she left him "because he was an atheist." When starving, a friend to whom he had given £2000, though he knew it, would not come near him. Heard Mrs. Shelley repeat Coleridge on Pitt, which persuades me he is a poet.

☆ ★ ☆

June 18. – My leg much worse. Shelley and party here. Mrs. S[helley] called me her brother (younger). Began my ghost-story after tea. Twelve o'clock, really began to talk ghostly. L[ord] B[yron] repeated some verses of Coleridge's *Christabel*, of the witch's breast; when silence ensued, and Shelley, suddenly shrieking and putting his hands to his head, ran out of the room with a candle. Threw water in his face, and after gave him ether. He was looking at Mrs. S[helley], and suddenly thought of a woman he had heard of who had eyes instead of nipples, which, taking hold of his mind, horrified him. – He married; and, a friend of his liking his wife, he tried all he could to induce her to love him in turn. He is surrounded by friends who feed upon him, and draw upon him as their banker. Once, having hired a house, a man wanted to make him pay more, and came trying to bully him, and at last challenged him. Shelley refused, and was knocked down; coolly said that would not gain him his object, and was knocked down again. – Slaney called.

The Prisoners
of the
Thirteenth Floor

BY MICHAEL DAHL

ILLUSTRATED BY LISA K. WEBER

STONE ARCH BOOKS™
a capstone imprint

3 THE ABRACADABRA HOTEL

Table of

Contents

Shifting Shadows

Charlie Hitchcock had never slept in a magician's house before.

It was disappointing. No unearthly moans. No rattling chains. No phantoms flitting through walls. Charlie would have welcomed them, and would have spent the rest of the night trying to solve the mystery of what they really were. He loved solving puzzles.

Charlie yawned and pulled the blanket to his chin. Counting ghosts would have been a lot more fun than lying there counting sheep. Instead, he listened to the rumbling of the thunderstorm outside and to the ticking of a grandfather clock. The clock faced the sofa on which he was trying to fall asleep. A flash of lightning lit up the dial.

Almost three o'clock? he thought. *Only four more hours!* He groaned and rolled over, gazing around Brack's sitting room.

Brack — also known as Abracadabra, the legendary magician — was the founder and owner of the world-famous Abracadabra Hotel, the only hotel made by and for retired magicians, and Brack's home was a special penthouse on the windy roof of the building. But Brack was not there. The old magician was missing.

Groans came from the closet.

For a nanosecond, Charlie hoped it was a ghost, but he knew the sound was just old floorboards settling in the storm.

The boy glanced over at the magician's big, wooden desk. The pile of books and papers covering the desk was the reason he was staying overnight. They had also led Charlie into his latest adventure, along with Tyler Yu.

The hotheaded Tyler was known at Blackstone Middle School for having enemies. But he and Charlie made a good team. They had solved a number of weird puzzles in the old hotel. This newest mystery was the weirdest. Brack was missing, and Tyler had also vanished.

On the magician's desk lay a clue that Charlie hoped would lead him to his friends. It was a sheet of paper that held an unusual list of words:

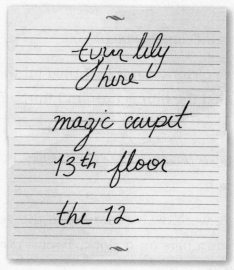

Charlie was convinced that "lily," written in Brack's spidery handwriting, referred to a flower in the hallway of the hotel's fourteenth floor. A flower that stood out strangely from the rest of the old-fashioned wallpaper.

But it was the last entry in the list that bothered him the most. *THE 12.* Did that mean the twelfth floor?

Then why hadn't Brack written it the way he wrote *13th floor* just above it?

Dnnng! Dnnng! Dnnng!

Three o'clock. Charlie shifted on the sofa and pulled the blanket around himself more tightly.

What — or who — are the Twelve? he wondered.

There were twelve months in the year. Twelve numbers on a clock. Twelve days of Christmas.

Twelve signs of the *Zzzzz* . . .

Brack's sitting room soon echoed with the thunder-like rumbling of Charlie's snores.

And while the boy slept, a dark figure — waiting patiently in the shadows — slipped from the closet, made its way to the front door, and darted away from the magician's house.

* * *

Four hours later, Charlie yawned and stepped off the elevator, shuffling through the vast lobby of the Abracadabra, which was also known as the Hocus Pocus Hotel to the staff and its guests.

"Charlie! Over here!" came a voice.

Charlie rubbed his eyes and saw Annie Solo waving furiously near the front desk. Another girl stood next to her.

"Charlie," said Annie, smiling widely. "This is Cozette. She's new here. Just started a couple weeks ago."

The other girl held up a hand and said, "Hey." She had thick dark hair and bright eyes, and wore pink shoes that matched her fingernail polish.

"Cozette's going to help us," said Annie. "I figured two heads are better than one, and, well, three heads are better than two."

Before Charlie could ask a question, Annie grabbed his hand and pulled him, along with Cozette, toward the hotel restaurant. "Come on, I'm starving," she said.

Tyler's dad, Walter Yu, was the head chef of the Top Hat restaurant. He showed them to a table. "Breakfast is on the house," he said. "Thanks to you, Annie, and your friend here, we can all keep our jobs. And the hotel is safe!"

Cozette looked puzzled, so Annie said, "I'll explain it all later."

And she did, with help from Charlie, while the three of them dug into eggs, toast, bacon, and fruit.

Annie explained how the two of them, but mostly Charlie, had saved the hotel from falling into the hands of a magician known as Theopolis.

"That snake threatened to take away the Hocus Pocus if Mr. Brack didn't pay the rent," said Annie.

"But Mr. Brack is missing," said Cozette.

Annie and Charlie nodded. Charlie had kept Theopolis from stealing the hotel, by threatening to reveal one of his most amazing magic tricks. But who knew how long that would keep the evil magician quiet? Charlie was afraid the man would come up with another awful plan. And soon.

"That's why we have to find Brack," said Charlie.

"And Tyler, too," added Annie. "They're both in trouble."

"We told Ty's parents that he's been helping us look for Brack," said Charlie. "But if we don't find him soon, Mrs. Yu's going to get suspicious.

"You should call the police," said Cozette.

"We will," said Annie. "Tomorrow. If we still can't find them by the end of the day. But we know they're somewhere in the hotel."

"On the thirteenth floor," said Charlie.

"Thirteen?" said Cozette. Her eyes grew wide. "That seems unlucky."

"But we'll go to the fourteenth floor first," said Charlie.

"Right," said Annie. "The lily."

Cozette put down a forkful of eggs. "Lily who?"

"No, it's lily what," said Annie. "A flower."

"But not really a flower," said Charlie.

Cozette sighed. "I don't know why you talked me into this, Annie."

"Because we have to help Tyler," said her friend.

Cozette and Charlie shared a glance. They knew Annie liked Tyler. Really liked him.

Cozette patted her lips with her napkin and then dropped it on the table. "Okay then," she said. "Let's go rescue Tyler."

When they got off the elevator at the fourteenth floor, Charlie led them to the hallway he and Annie had investigated the day before. Annie waved toward two doors, side by side. "That's where the magicians are staying this week. Theopolis there, and Mr. Dragonstone there."

"David Dragonstone?" said Cozette. "He is so cute! Do you think he'll come out if we knock on the door? Will he be wearing his cute white suit?"

"We're here to look for Tyler, remember?" said Annie.

"Besides, David Dragonstone might be involved in this," added Charlie.

"Charlie figured out how Mr. Dragonstone did his magic tricks," said Annie. "Figured it all out by himself. Except for one thing."

"What's that?" asked Cozette.

"The trick where he walks through a glass door down on the twelfth floor," Annie said. "Charlie knows how he got through the glass. But he doesn't know how he got to the twelfth floor in the first place."

Charlie walked down the hall. "Tyler stood at one end of that hallway. The solid glass door was at the other end. But somehow Dragonstone appeared in the middle," he said.

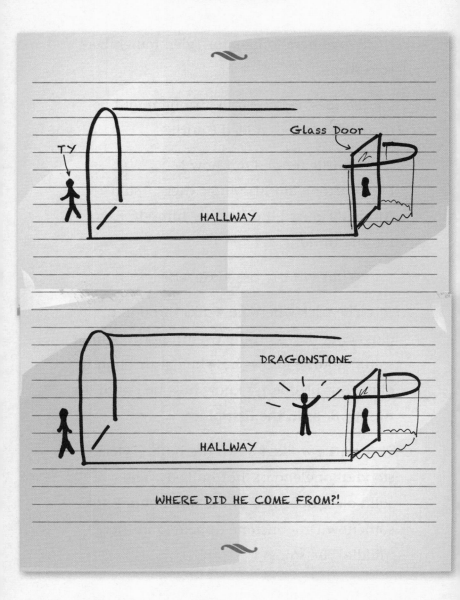

"How?" asked Cozette.

Charlie was staring carefully at the wall. "I think it has something to do with this."

The two girls rushed over to him.

"That's the lily!" said Annie. The dark wallpaper was covered with patterns of lilies. The flower Charlie was staring at, however, was not printed on the wallpaper. It was made of plaster and sat on top of the paper, in three dimensions, but blended in with the flowers around it. If a person hadn't been looking for it, they would have overlooked it in the flowing pattern.

"Brack's writing," said Charlie, referring to the paper he had found the day before, "had the words 'turn lily there.'"

"I figured out that part," said Annie.

"So, how do we turn it?" asked Cozette.

"I'm not exactly sure," said Charlie. He took a few steps back for a better view. On the floor beneath his shoes was a rectangle. It was the only shape in the otherwise plain, red carpet. A rectangle made of twisting lines of gold and emerald and cream. Charlie was sure that the two items that didn't fit in, the rectangle and the flower, were parts of the same puzzle.

Cozette shrugged. "Why don't you just try turning it?"

She reached out and grabbed the plaster lily. With a small crunch, it turned in her grip like a doorknob.

Something thudded in the hallway and shook the floor. Annie gasped. The rectangle in the carpet tilted downward, like a waterslide, into a dark rectangular space. The last things Charlie saw were Cozette's pink shoes.

He fell through the floor, then rolled into something hard. With another thump, the carpet above him tilted back up and the light disappeared.

Charlie heard a wrenching sound, a scream, and then nothing. He was in darkness.

The Thirteenth Floor

True, deep darkness.

Charlie felt his heart pumping faster. He started breathing harder.

Then he heard something.

. . . beep . . . beep . . .

"Ty, is that you?" he called.

"Yeah, it's my stupid beeper," came Tyler's familiar voice. "It's gone off about a million times. If my parents had given me a phone, then maybe I could have called them and gotten out of this hole, but no, I'm not responsible enough. Even though I do all the work around here."

The darkness in front of Charlie's eyes appeared to swirl. A shadow separated from the others. A silhouette.

"You've been on the thirteenth floor the whole time?" asked Charlie.

"Yeah, and I'm not the only one, brainiac. Brack's here too. But I think he's hurt."

"You think? Don't you know?"

"I can't see him," said Ty.

Charlie's heart began beating harder again. "There's no lights in here?!" he said.

"Well, there aren't any windows on this floor, but there's a few lights. But that's not the problem. He's locked behind a door and neither of us can open it. So I've been looking for a way out for hours!"

Light burst above them. Charlie could see that he and Ty were sitting in a hall that resembled the others in the hotel.

The secret rectangular door had re-opened overhead and slanted toward them. Annie and Cozette ran down the carpeted ramp.

"Tyler!" exclaimed Annie. "I'm so glad you're all right."

"Yeah!" said Ty. "Now we can get out of here."

But as soon as the two girls stepped off the ramp, it sprang quickly back into place, and out of reach.

"Don't worry," said Charlie. "I think I know how we can get out of here."

"You do?" said Ty. "Then why did you take so long? I've been starving!"

"I waited so long because I just figured it out," answered Charlie.

"We just figured it out," said Cozette. "I was the one who turned that weirdo lily thing."

"We need to get Brack," said Ty

"I've got a phone," said Cozette. She turned it on and its pale blue light helped guide them through the hallway.

Tyler Yu looked the way he always did. Spiky black hair, jeans, boots, and a scowl on his face. He stopped before a door. "We have a slight problem," he said.

"Now what?" asked Annie.

"It's locked," Ty said. "Brack's inside."

"I have a passkey!" Charlie said. He pulled the keycard out of his pocket.

Charlie heard a low moan from the other side of the door. "Brack!" he called. "It's us!" Cozette's phone light made it bright enough to see the door.

Charlie looked at the door and then stopped. "Uh, where's the slot for the passkey?" The old wooden door had a traditional lock and keyhole.

"These old doors don't have the new electronic system," said Annie. "We need an old-school metal key."

"And that's probably been missing for fifty years," said Charlie, groaning.

"Now that you mention it," said Annie, "there are some old keys hanging behind the desk."

"You mean these?" asked Cozette. She held out a small ring of dark metal keys.

"How did you —?" Annie started.

"I figured if we were going into the old part of the Hocus Pocus, we might need them," said Cozette.

"You're smarter than you look," said Ty.

"Stand aside," said Cozette. She tried a few of the keys in the lock. Finally, there was a click.

The door opened, and in the phone's blue light, they saw a closet door just inside.

"Brack!" called Ty.

A groan came from within the closet. Ty twisted a deadbolt knob on the door and opened it. The four companions saw an old man on the floor inside, his thin back against the wall, his wrinkled face stretched in a grimace of pain.

The Twelve

"Master Hitchcock!" said the man in a tired, raspy voice. "And Master Yu. And Miss Solo."

"How are you, Brack?" asked Charlie.

"Body and soul still together, young man," said Brack, pushing himself into a better position. "And this charming young woman must be Miss Bailey."

Cozette stared. "You know who I am?" she said. "I've only worked here a few weeks."

"We need to get you out of here," said Ty.

"Carefully," said Brack. "I think I may have sprained an ankle."

"Who did this to you?" said Charlie.

"I have an idea," said Brack. "But I don't have any evidence, of course. It was dark when I woke up here. The last thing I remember was sitting in my house."

"With Theopolis!" said Charlie.

Brack blinked, surprised. "Why, yes. At least, that's who he turned out to be. He was wearing a disguise."

"A red beard," said Annie.

"Somebody better explain what's been going on," said Ty. "And I mean now."

"First things first," said Brack. He lifted a shaking hand and pointed. "I believe there's a men's room in that direction. I could hear the pipes through the wall."

Ty gently hoisted Brack to his feet and hunkered under one of the older man's shoulders. Charlie and Annie supported him on the other side. Cozette raised her phone and a door loomed out of the darkness. While Ty helped Brack walk inside, the other three turned and gasped.

A hand reached out toward them. Icy white fingers. Annie screamed. Charlie couldn't speak. Ty stepped out of the bathroom, closing the door behind him. "What's going on?" he asked.

Cozette pointed. The clutching white fingers hadn't moved. They could see the hand was attached to a bare white arm that led to a naked shoulder.

"Look out!" said Ty. As Cozette's light traveled up the mysterious white shape, Ty saw another figure close behind.

Neither of the white shadows moved. "Who are you?" Ty demanded.

The four companions jumped as something moved behind them. It was Brack, who had opened the bathroom door and was grasping the side of the doorway for balance. "I'm afraid he can't answer you," he said. "None of them can."

Cozette lifted her light. They saw more and more figures crowded in front of them.

All pale, all frozen in place, all silent.

"Statues," said Charlie.

Brack nodded. "They are the great secret of the thirteenth floor," he said. "A secret I thought was a rumor until I saw them just now with my own eyes."

"Who are they?" asked Ty.

"The Twelve," said Brack.

Charlie looked closer at the blurry, bluish shapes in the cellphone's gleam. One of them brandished a sword. Another held a spear with three sharp prongs. A female figure wore an old-fashioned helmet and carried a shield.

I've seen them before, thought Charlie. He had a memory that held onto images like a computer hard drive. "Acute visual memory," his teachers called it. Other people might call it a photographic memory.

Once Charlie saw a picture or a movie or a show, he never forgot it. For example, the photo he had seen in an old book at the library of some statues. The same statues he'd seen on a show on the History Channel.

"The Twelve Olympians," said Charlie.

"You mean, like athletes?" asked Annie,

Ty rolled his eyes. "Like the Greek gods," he said. "*Clash of the Titans*, The Immortals, Percy Jackson."

"You read?" said Cozette in a quiet voice.

Ty ignored her. "That must be Ares," he said, pointing at the statue with the sword.

"And Poseidon and Athena," said Charlie. He saw a statue of a beautiful woman with long hair, holding a stone apple in her cold marble hand. "That one is Aphrodite, the goddess of beauty."

"Yeah," said Ty. "Some dude gave her that apple because she was the prettiest."

"The Twelve," said Brack. "These statues were a gift to the hotel many, many years ago. They were the handiwork of a famous Spanish sculptor, Ernesto Endriago."

"One guy made them?" asked Cozette.

"One very talented guy, yes," said Brack. "He sent them to the hotel as a gift. He came from a long line of magicians — he was the only sculptor, and a disappointment to his father. But these magnificent statues were delivered here and then forgotten. I knew they had been sent, but never saw them. It was a very busy time. Deliverymen must have put them on this floor by mistake."

"Wow," said Annie. "So, we're like the first people to see them since Ernesto!"

"Where were they supposed to go?" asked Charlie.

"Endriago designed them to be installed on the roof," said Brack. "The twelve gods of Greek mythology gazing down on humans from on high. Just as they once did from Mount Olympus."

"Awesome," said Tyler.

"Awesome indeed, but it wasn't a good idea," said Brack. "They're far too valuable to be exposed to the elements."

"Um, how valuable?" said Charlie.

"Endriago was killed in the Second World War," Brack said. "These are the last — and the greatest — works from his hand. They must be priceless."

Charlie wondered how much a single statue would cost. A million? A hundred million? That would pay for the hotel a thousand times over. Brack would be able to pay for the whole thing, and Theopolis would be out of his life forever.

Charlie was too busy thinking about dollar signs to notice the shadowy figure moving beyond the circle of light cast from Cozette's phone. It moved from the statue of Apollo to Hermes, and then hid behind Hades, the lord of the dead. Then it smiled.

The Old Magic Returns

Tyler sighed. "I'm starving here, people. And we need a doctor to look at Brack's ankle."

Cozette turned to Charlie. "You said you knew a way out of here."

"Right," said Charlie. "Let's go back to the hall we first landed in."

It took longer to retrace their steps with the injured Brack, but soon they were back in the hallway.

"See?" said Charlie, pointing to the floor. "I knew it was there." In the glow of the phone they saw a familiar shape on the carpet.

"Aladdin's magic carpet," said Annie. "Or at least it looks like it."

"Just like the rectangle above us, on the fourteenth floor," said Charlie.

"You mean it was right there all the time?" said Ty.

Charlie began running his hands along the wall, searching for another hidden switch. "I figured they'd be right on top of each other," he said. "Ah, here it is." His left hand touched a bumpy shape protruding from the wallpaper.

Another flower. This one was a sunflower. "Stand back," he yelled. Then he twisted the plaster flower just as Cozette had twisted the lily.

Something banged against the floor. Gears rattled and walls shook as the floor began to sag. Light shot up from below as the rectangle in the carpet slanted downward to reveal a lit hallway on the twelfth floor.

Carefully, they helped Brack down the ramp. As soon as they all stepped into the lower hallway, the ramp snapped up like the end of a teeter-totter.

"This is the hallway with the glass door," said Ty. "This is where I went up. After you took off for the elevators, the ramp came down again."

"So why didn't you just come back the same way?" asked Annie.

"I didn't know how it worked," said Ty.

"Well, that's how David Dragonstone got into the hallway without you seeing him enter it," said Charlie. "Remember how you said you saw the black curtains dropping down over the glass door? That's what clued me in to this secret ramp. The black curtains used in the magic trick moved from side to side, on a frame, like regular curtains. When you said you saw them drop down, from the far end of the hall where you were standing, I knew you must have seen something else dropping down."

"After you left the hall, I took one last look around," said Ty. "And then, for no reason, the ceiling began to open up and the ramp came down. That's when I went up to the thirteenth floor and got stuck. Hey, how many of those ramps are there?" he asked Brack.

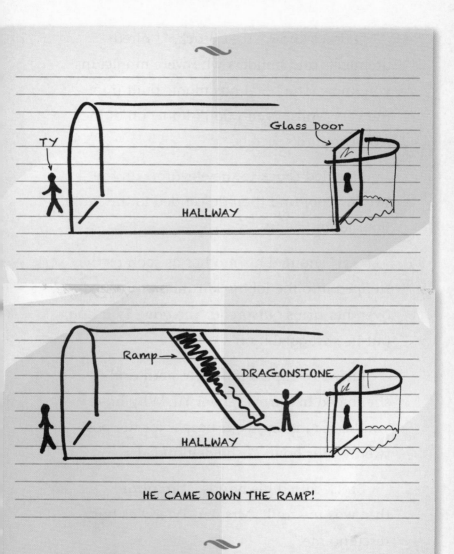

HE CAME DOWN THE RAMP!

"I don't know," said Brack. "I hired architects and builders who were magicians, you know. The hotel has magic built into the very walls. Even I don't know all of the Abracadabra's secrets."

They led Brack to the elevators on the twelfth floor and then descended to the main floor lobby.

"Ty!" shouted his mother as soon as they stepped into the lobby. Miranda Yu rushed over, her arms outspread. She gave Ty a hug, but he shrugged it off.

Mrs. Yu's expression grew stern and she folded her arms. "Tyler Yu. Why have you been ignoring your beeper for the past twenty-four hours?" she demanded.

Brack raised his hands. "I'm afraid that was my fault, Mrs. Yu. Tyler was busy rescuing me."

Once the magician explained how Tyler had been trying to help him, and how he had hurt his ankle during his abduction, Miranda Yu's anger drained away. She ordered Brack to wait in the lobby while she phoned a doctor.

Brack settled into a plump, overstuffed chair. Meanwhile, Cozette peppered Annie with dozens of questions about David Dragonstone and whether they could go back upstairs for his autograph. A flash of lightning blazed through the vast lobby. It flickered on a forest of columns and a jungle of potted plants.

"I thought that storm was over," said Charlie.

"We all make mistakes," came a booming voice from the center of the room. A tall man in a swirling cape, with a black mustache and cruel eyes, appeared.

"Theopolis!" said Ty.

"I heard the wonderful news of your return, old friend," said the man, bowing toward the seated Brack.

"We just got here," said Charlie. "How could you have heard anything?"

Theopolis slowly shook his head. "Still doubting my mystical abilities, I see," he said. "Well, Brack, I'm so glad you haven't left us. For good, I mean. Oh, I was so worried."

"Did you really think I would leave this place?" asked Brack with a grim smile.

"Never," said Theopolis. "I know how much this stuffy old fleabag means to you. In fact, I know exactly how much."

Yeah. Down to the penny, I bet, thought Charlie.

"And now that you're back," said Theopolis, "you must attend one of David Dragonstone's performances. It would mean so much to the young man to have one of magic's oldest practitioners in the audience."

"I have heard all about Dragonstone's tricks from my young friends," said Brack.

"Well," said Theopolis, giving Charlie a sour smile. "Don't believe everything you hear. Ah well, you're here, these brats are here, and everything is back to normal. Charming. I must talk to my partner about his next show. We're planning something really big."

"I can't wait," said Brack.

Theopolis swirled his cape and strode toward the elevators. "How can Brack just sit there and not say anything to that weasel?" said Ty. "He didn't even ask that creep for an apology for locking him in that room."

Charlie straightened his shirt. "Like Brack said, he doesn't have any evidence against Theopolis," he said. "I mean, Brack didn't exactly see who trapped him on the thirteenth floor."

"Then we're gonna find evidence," said Ty. "Yeah, that's it. I know how to catch him red-handed." Ty looked down at Charlie. "Come on, Hitchcock. We're going back to the thirteenth floor."

"What?" squawked Charlie.

"The Twelve," said Ty. "Those statues. You heard Brack say they were priceless. I'll bet that's what Theopolis is up to. He's gonna steal them and make millions. But we're gonna sit in that room and grab him as soon as he makes his move."

Standing Guard

This time they brought flashlights. Annie had to help Mrs. Yu in the office with some paperwork, so Charlie, Ty, and Cozette returned to the fourteenth floor, to the hallway outside Dragonstone and Theopolis's bedrooms.

After fiddling with the plaster lily a few dozen times, they were able to keep the ramp stuck in a diagonal position.

Once they stepped down to the thirteenth floor, they did the same with the sunflower and the second ramp. Now both ramps were stuck in the "down" position, and light flooded into the old, hidden hallway from above and below.

"The door's over there, around the corner," said Ty. "Room 1308."

Their flashlights were able to pick out more details of the fantastic statues.

"Who's the lady in the helmet?" asked Cozette.

Charlie joined her. "That's Athena. Also called Minerva. The goddess of wisdom."

"Why would a smart woman need a helmet and a shield?" asked Cozette.

"Because she was smart," said Ty. "There were a lot of crazy, scary dudes back in the Greek days."

"And who's this with the wings on his feet?" she asked.

"He's one of my favorites," said Charlie. "He's Hermes, the messenger of the gods. The wings helped him travel back and forth between Mount Olympus and Earth."

"Hitchcock has a favorite Greek god?" Tyler said, smirking. "Nerd alert."

"He looks cute," said Cozette.

"Hitchcock?!" said Ty.

Cozette's face flushed deep red. "No! The messenger guy."

Charlie's face felt hot. He quickly tried changing the subject by pointing at the statue of a tall male holding a bow. A quiver of arrows hung at his back, and a small sun beamed from his brow. "That's Apollo. He's supposed to be the god of the sun and beauty and —"

"And who's this creepy guy with the frown?" asked Ty.

Charlie and Cozette walked over to the statue Ty was facing. In the small space with all the statues' bodies jammed together, it was hard to see them all at once.

"I'm not sure," said Charlie. "But I think he's Hades. The god of the underworld."

Cozette shivered. "You mean, like dead people and stuff? I'm getting out of here."

Ty turned to her. "I thought you wanted to help us guard this place."

"You guys guard it. I have work to do," said Cozette. "Besides, these statues aren't going anywhere. They weigh a ton."

To prove her wrong, Ty bent his knees, grasped Hades, and tried straightening up. He strained and grunted, and did manage to shift the statue from its base slightly.

"See? No sweat," said Tyler, wiping his forehead.

"Like I said, they weigh a ton," replied Cozette.

"Wait a minute, Cozette," said Charlie. "So, Ty, what exactly is your plan? What do you want us to do?"

Tyler stared at Charlie as if he had just arrived on the planet. "Stand. Guard. Over. The. Statues," he said. "And catch that creep Theopolis when he comes in to steal them."

"Stay up here?" said Cozette.

"We'll take turns," said Ty. "You wimps go do your work, or read more books, or talk about your favorite gods. And I'll stay up here, with the door locked. Then you come back in an hour, and Charlie takes over. Bring plenty to eat. See if you can get my dad to make a pizza."

Tyler hurried him out of the room. A moment later, Cozette was also rushed into the hall, the door closing behind her. She turned, as if to re-enter, but the doorknob jiggled uselessly in her hand.

Cozette sighed. "Let's go back to the elevators and . . ." She hesitated. Charlie guessed she was thinking about the fourteenth floor, and how close they were to David Dragonstone's room.

"Did you hear something?" asked Cozette. "Like a thump or something?"

Charlie tried the knob, but the door was locked. The two of them pounded on the door. "Let us in!" shouted Charlie.

Not a sound came from the room of statues.

The Locked Door

Cozette handed Charlie her set of keys while she used her phone to call for help.

"The key's not working, Cozette," said Charlie.

"Tyler must have turned the deadbolt," said Cozette. "I don't see a keyhole for that."

"I hope someone comes soon," Charlie said.

Annie and Rocky were the first to arrive. Rocky Brown was a teenage boy with long blond hair who also worked at the front desk. Charlie quickly explained what happened.

"Stand back," said Rocky. He rammed the door with his shoulder. It wouldn't give.

"That only works on TV," said Cozette.

"I just need a little more momentum," said Rocky. "Now, look out. I don't want you guys to get hurt." He took several steps back, drew in a deep breath, and then ran toward the door. His shoulder slammed into the wood like a linebacker tackling a tight end. The frame shattered, and splinters flew into the hall. "I broke my shoulder!" Rocky screamed.

Charlie and Cozette beamed their flashlights into the darkness.

"Tyler!" cried Annie.

Just inside the room, on the floor, lay the motionless body of Tyler Yu.

"Could someone call a doctor?" asked Rocky. He sat out in the hall, holding his left shoulder.

Then, things became even more confusing. Over Rocky's groans and Annie's cries, Charlie heard more people arriving. Walter and Miranda Yu shoved their way to the door. Brack hobbled in on a cane. Theopolis and David Dragonstone, obviously alerted by the noises drifting up to their rooms through the open ramp, joined the crowd. Charlie heard some of the hotel's residents as well, ex-magicians and performers like Mr. Madagascar, Dottie Drake, and the reclusive juggler Mr. Thursday, who had just moved into the hotel the week before.

Charlie found himself in the room, kneeling over Tyler, although he didn't remember how he got there. And as he glanced up, he saw more and more onlookers stepping through the broken doorframe and entering the dark room that had been unused for fifty years.

"Oh my dear, is that Tyler?"

"Is he alive?"

"What are all these statues doing here?"

"What is this place?"

"He's breathing. He's breathing!"

"I think I'm going to faint. Do you think the floor is clean enough?" That was Dottie Drake, at one time a famous magician's assistant. Her silver hair was swept up in a tall pile and she clutched her throat in terror. "Oh, that poor boy," she said. "The poor boy. I really do feel faint."

"Everyone move back!" yelled Miranda Yu. Even in an emergency she looked cool and professional. "And no fainting!" she said. "We don't have time for that. Someone call a doctor. The rest of you, wait outside."

Out in the hall, the scene reminded Charlie of a dentist's waiting room. Except for the crying. Annie was weeping softly as Dottie Drake hugged her. Rocky was weeping rather loudly.

Charlie stared at Theopolis, but the magician would not meet his gaze.

I know he has something to do with this, thought Charlie. *But I need evidence. How did he do it? How did he get into a locked room with Ty, when Cozette and I were standing right outside the door? And — more importantly — how did he get back out?*

Wait!

Charlie stood up. He grabbed his flashlight and headed back inside the room. Mrs. Yu was sitting on the floor, gently rubbing Tyler's back. Her head snapped up. "Outside, Charlie," she ordered.

"But I have to look at something —"

"Out," she repeated.

Charlie had learned early on not to mess with the Yus. They all meant business, each in their own way. He stood for a moment, gripping his flashlight, not saying a word. He simply looked at Tyler's motionless body.

He had never seen the boy so quiet, so vulnerable. It was like looking at a fallen soldier. Above Ty's body stood the statue of Ares with his outstretched sword.

Then Charlie turned and walked out, just as the ambulance team was hurrying in with their bags and a stretcher.

No Way Out

Once Tyler and Rocky had been taken away on stretchers by the EMTs, the hallway emptied quickly.

A half hour later, the last ones remaining were Charlie, Brack, and Mr. Yu, who frowned, examining the splintered door frame. "I can't leave it like this," he muttered. "What a terrible accident."

"I don't believe it was an accident at all," said Brack. "Do you still have your flashlight, Charlie?"

Charlie nodded. He didn't need to hear another word from the old magician. He turned on his light and stepped into the room. Back and forth, he swung the flashlight's beam.

It was a single open room, a large hotel room with only ancient gods and spiderwebs for guests. He saw the statues. He saw the door to the bathroom that Brack and Tyler had both used. He saw a few pieces of old furniture. He saw an open space that was probably supposed to have been a closet but never had a door attached to it. The one thing that Charlie did not see in the glare of his flashlight: another door or window.

"Do you see what's missing?" whispered Brack.

"Yeah," said Charlie. "No way out."

"That's not what I meant," said Brack. "Something else."

Charlie swung the light some more. What else was not there that should have been? Did Brack mean — no, it was impossible.

Charlie used the flashlight as a spotlight on each of the Twelve. Zeus, Hera, Poseidon, Ares, Hermes, Apollo, Athena, Hades, Artemis, Demeter, Hephestus, and . . .

Where was the beautiful woman holding the apple? He counted them a second time.

"Aphrodite is missing," Charlie said. "But, Brack, how could that be? I saw Aphrodite when we first came in to get you."

"I saw her too, Charlie," he replied. "But someone got to her."

Charlie shut his eyes. He tried to think back. When he first entered the room, he had seen all of the Twelve, even if he saw a few only out of the corner of his eye. He could count them all.

And then he pictured the second time he came back, with Ty and Cozette. He remembered how crowded it had felt, walking through the forest of frozen figures in the stuffy room. But, yes, he had counted then, too.

There had been twelve gods and goddesses of stone. He was sure of it. They sometimes seemed to twitch and blink in the moving beams of light from the flashlights and Cozette's phone. The muscles in their fingers flexed, the veins in their necks pulsed. But there had been the Twelve.

Where was the goddess of beauty? She couldn't walk out on her carved stone feet.

Or could she? Maybe that sculptor, Ernesto Endriago, was a magician after all. Maybe he possessed some genius skill for building stone figures that moved on their own.

But that still didn't solve the bigger mystery. How did Ty's attacker — and the goddess Aphrodite — leave the room while it was locked from the inside? And while Charlie and Cozette stood guard outside?

"My stupid ankle!" cried Brack. "If only I hadn't hurt it, this wouldn't have happened! The statue would still be here."

"You don't think it was alive too, do you?" whispered Charlie. But Brack didn't answer. He just stared at the statues.

Mr. Yu was standing outside by the broken door frame. Charlie could hear him on his phone trying to get a carpenter and a locksmith to the hotel as quickly as possible.

Then he heard him talking to his wife, telling her that he would soon join her at the hospital.

"You don't, do you?" repeated Charlie. "Think it was alive?"

A stone cold shiver ran down Charlie's spine. The air in the dark room grew darker. He thought the statues were shuffling closer.

Brack smiled. "Magic can always be explained," he said. "You've proven that before, Master Hitchcock, time and again. And this can be explained too. I know that you'll solve this mystery, just as you have the others."

I'm not so sure about that, thought Charlie. He looked into Brack's eyes, and the feeling that the statues crowded in on him faded away. But his doubts remained. There was only one thing he was sure about. He couldn't let his friends down.

The Third Flower

How does a human get into a locked room?
Charlie asked himself. *With a key.* A light
went on in Charlie's brain.

Key!

He needed to ask Cozette about her ring
of keys, and why they didn't work when he
tried unlocking the door to help Tyler.

Charlie imagined Tyler, lying in a hospital room. The last time he'd seen Tyler, the other boy was trying to lift the Hades statue. And he did, sort of. It was heavy, but not impossible to lift. If you had help.

"Brack," said Charlie. "How did those statues get here in the first place? I mean, they're heavy."

Brack paused, both hands gripping the top of his cane. "Well, I'm sure Endriago had them shipped here from Spain."

Charlie shook his head. "I mean, here. This floor. Those statues are heavy."

"Most of the heavy objects, like furniture for the guests rooms, were hauled up on the freight elevator at the rear of the hotel," Brack explained.

Charlie knew that the hotel's elevators didn't stop at the thirteenth floor.

But he wasn't so sure about the freight elevators. He hadn't seen them or used them before. That reminded him of the blueprints he'd found while looking for clues. They showed every part of the hotel. Charlie slipped his backpack off his shoulder and dug inside.

"Recognize these?" he said proudly to Brack, pulling out the big roll of paper.

"My blueprints!" the old man exclaimed.

"I found them in the magicians' dressing room backstage," said Charlie. He had discovered them the day before while searching for clues to Brack's disappearance.

Charlie pulled out the huge sheet that showed the 3-D version of the entire Abracadabra Hotel. Each floor of the hotel was outlined in faint white lines against a blue background. Every hall, every room could be seen.

"Here's where we are now," Charlie said, pointing to the page.

"And here are the freight elevators in back," said Brack, indicating a tall vertical tube at the back of the hotel.

Charlie cried out, "Yes! The freight elevators do stop at this floor!" Without waiting for his friend, he ran down the dark halls, shooting his flashlight's beam ahead of him.

After several minutes of searching, however, he ran his fingers through his rust-colored hair in frustration. "Where are they?"

Brack slowly padded around the corner on his cane. Charlie turned to him. "They're not here," Charlie said. "According to the blueprint, they should be . . ." He trained his flashlight on a wide panel of sunflower wallpaper. ". . . Right there!"

Brack tilted his head. "I hear something rumbling," he said.

Charlie put his ear to the wall. "The elevator?"

The boy scanned the flowers on the wallpaper. Maybe there was a plaster knob like the two that controlled the ramps to the thirteenth floor.

"Yes, yes!" said Charlie. He found a sunflower whose dark brown head, inside its yellow petals, was sunk at least a quarter of an inch deeper into the wall. A button.

Charlie pressed the button and the flower immediately lit up. "Cool!" he cried. Within a minute a panel, covered in wallpaper, slid soundlessly up and into the ceiling, revealing the freight elevator.

"And look there!" said Charlie. He aimed his flashlight at a far corner of the elevator. The light picked out an orange metal trolley. Thick canvas straps lay at its wheels.

"That would be really useful for moving a statue," said Charlie.

They entered the elevator and Charlie pushed the button for the first floor. With a rumble, the door slid shut. There was no light inside the elevator, so Charlie kept the flashlight on. He did not want to be trapped in the dark again. When the elevator finally jerked to a stop, the back wall opened up, revealing the alley behind the hotel.

The loading docks, thought Charlie.

The storm was gone. Overhead, they could see gray clouds moving in the narrow stretch of sky between old, brick buildings. A cool breeze blew into Charlie's face.

A truck delivering bread was backed up to another door alongside them. "This has to be where the crook took the Aphrodite statue," said Charlie. "This is how he got it downstairs. Now we just have to figure out how he got it out of that room, while Tyler was locked inside!"

Shadow Man

Charlie saw a frown of pain flash across Brack's face.

"I think some rest and recuperation is needed," Brack whispered to Charlie.

The boy helped the limping magician back to his house on the roof. Charlie made him lie down on his sofa in the sitting room. Then he waited with his friend while two hours passed across the face of the grandfather clock.

"Hand me that phone," said Brack. "I'm going to see what's holding up that doctor. And you have been wasting far too much time with me." He waved the boy out of the house. "Go! Go investigate!"

Charlie grinned and went looking for Annie at the front desk. Annie smiled when she saw him. "Two words," said Charlie. "Surveillance. Camera."

"You sound just like Tyler," said Annie, leading him into the security room behind. "He's better, by the way. Mrs. Yu called and said he has a slight concussion. And why do you need to see the surveillance camera?"

"I need to see the tapes from today," Charlie said. "By the way, where's Cozette?"

"She said she had a family emergency."

"Oh," said Charlie. "I was going to ask her about those old keys."

"She still has them," said Annie. "At least, I don't see them here at the desk."

She still has them? thought Charlie. *Weird.*

"Which tapes do you need to see?" asked Annie.

"The ones from the loading docks."

"Something happened back there, too?" said Annie.

Charlie explained how he and Brack had discovered that the freight elevator stopped at the thirteenth floor.

It took Annie a while to find the right tapes. Charlie thought he'd go crazy while she typed commands into the computer.

Finally, Annie found the right files and played them back on one of the screens. She asked, "What are you looking for?"

"That!" said Charlie.

The computer screen showed a perfect view of the loading dock next to the freight elevator. A man, dressed all in black, with a black ski mask, was struggling with a heavy object strapped to a trolley, draped in black.

"Who is it?" asked Annie. They both stared closer at the screen.

Charlie frowned. "I can't tell."

They watched the shadowy figure lug the shrouded statue into the back of an SUV. Then the man — they assumed it was a man — closed the loading dock doors, locked the SUV, and walked back into the hotel.

"Now where's he going?" said Annie.

"To get another statue?" said Charlie.

"But that's when we were all upstairs," said Annie. "Look at the time." She pointed to a digital display on the videotape. 12:00. "We got the call from Cozette at 12:30."

"12:30? Are you sure?" said Charlie.

Annie nodded. "I looked at the clock over the front counter when the call came. Then I told a guest who was checking in that I had an emergency and would be right back."

Charlie was confused. "If Ty was attacked right before she called, say 12:29, that means the statue was stolen fifteen minutes before that! But that's impossible! All twelve statues were in the room before Ty pushed us out and locked the door. I saw it!"

At least, I thought I did. I counted twelve statues. Twelve white figures in the darkness.

"I wish we could see who that guy was under all those black clothes," said Annie, staring at the screen again while she replayed the theft. "He was smart to cover up the statue, too," she added. "That way no one could tell what he was moving."

They stared at the frozen image on the screen. The white statue hidden under the black cloth. *That's not a cloth,* Charlie realized. *It's a cape!*

"What's up, you two?" Cozette walked in the room.

"Cozy, I thought you were with your family," said Annie.

Cozette dismissed it with a wave. "Oh, it was a big deal about nothing. It's fine."

"Do you remember what time you called us about Ty?" said Annie.

Cozette pulled out her phone and checked. "It was 12:30. Why?"

"That's what I told Charlie."

Cozette's expression changed. "Um, now that things are a little quieter," she said, "do you think we could go get David Dragonstone's autograph?"

"Oh, Cozette . . ."

"You could take a picture of me next to him," said Cozette. She giggled.

"Oh, that reminds me," said Annie. "I have to send out his white suit to get cleaned before tonight's magic show."

White? thought Charlie. *White and black. Black and white. A black covering over the white statue . . . is that how it was done?*

Twelve statues . . . but not really.

And there was Theopolis standing in the hall, next to Dragonstone, after Ty was attacked. And he would not meet Charlie's gaze. Charlie knew that man would stop at nothing to get the hotel.

Aha! thought Charlie. *Now I know how he did it.*

It was just another magician's trick. And some magicians had assistants.

Ty and the Trap

The twelve priceless statues of Enrico
Endriago had been locked in Room 1308 for
fifty years. They had been prisoners of the
thirteenth floor. And if Charlie was right
about who attacked Tyler and why, it all
made sense. It explained why, after fifty
years, the statues would now be the target of
a shadowy figure.

But how could Charlie get the evidence he needed? And how could he tell Annie who he suspected? She'd never believe him.

Annie shook her head at her friend. "Oh, Cozette," she said. "I just don't think it's a good — Tyler!" Annie screamed.

Charlie looked up just as Tyler Yu walked through the door. He wore the same clothes he did when he was carried out on the stretcher four hours earlier. The only thing new about him was a bandage over one eye. Some of his hair was missing at the back of his head. "What are you wimps doing here?" he asked.

"Charlie found the guy who attacked you," said Annie.

The taller boy smacked his hands together. "Yeah? Well, just give me the dude's name. I'll show him. That freak gave me six stitches."

Charlie showed Ty the tape. But Ty was not happy. His spiky hair seemed to grow angrier and spikier. "You can't see who it is!"

"But, uh, I think I might, uh —" said Charlie.

"Hitchcock!" said Ty. "You solved it again?"

"I think so," Charlie said. "But I don't have proof yet."

"Do you have evidence?" asked Cozette. She looked worried.

"Forget proof," said Ty. "Let's go catch this guy!"

"You need evidence," said Cozette. "Otherwise it's just your word against his."

"Or hers," added Annie.

"It's probably a guy," said Cozette. "It usually is."

"Maybe you're right, Ty," said Charlie. "Maybe we do catch him. Or her. But first, we need a trap!"

When Charlie explained his idea, Ty thought it was genius. The two girls were more skeptical, but it was the only way to get the evidence that Brack needed.

Then they started to put the plan into action. First they printed out a special message on the computer. The message read:

We are happy to announce that Tyler Yu is back and feels much better. He now remembers a valuable clue he left behind in room 1308. He will be sharing that clue with the police tomorrow, and we hope that Ty's attacker will be found and arrested. Then the residents of The Abracadabra can all feel safe once more.

The second step in the trap was to give copies of the message to several people in the hotel. They waited until dinnertime, when they knew people would be busy. Charlie didn't want to meet anyone face to face. Also, preparations for that Saturday night's performance would be in full swing. So they slid the copies under the doors of Dottie Drake, Mr. Madagascar, and Mr. Thursday. A copy was dropped off in the dressing room backstage. They even left one at the front desk so that Rocky would see it. Then Charlie made a few phone calls from the hotel office, spent a few minutes Googling on the computer, and made sure his flashlight batteries were working.

"I think that's everything," said Charlie, when they all met back in the lobby.

"Now's the fun part," said Ty, smacking his fist into his palm.

"Do we have to do this?" asked Cozette, a nervous look on her face.

Annie patted her friend's shoulder. "We'll all be together," she said. "Besides, it will be fun!"

Cozette lifted an eyebrow. "Really? Fun?"

"Thrilling?" suggested Annie.

"How about 'terrifying'?" said Cozette.

Charlie agreed. He wasn't looking forward to this part of the plan. And less than twenty minutes later, as he stood in Room 1308 in pitch darkness, he had to force down panic. It bubbled up inside his chest and into his throat. *I am not going to scream*, he told himself.

Charlie was standing behind the statue of Hades, lord of the dead. The other three kids were hidden behind various statues.

Charlie felt dizzy. He leaned against the statue.

"I hear something," whispered Annie.

They all froze. "I think that's my heart pounding," said Cozette. "I have something I need to confess."

Charlie's mind rapidly pieced new clues together. Had he been wrong all this time? Was the criminal Cozette? She carried keys to the old rooms of the thirteenth floor. She had recently started working at the hotel, right before Brack disappeared. When she came out of Room 1308 when Tyler was hurt, she could easily had locked the room behind her. After she had knocked him out!

And when Charlie tried to unlock it, and the key wouldn't work, there was only one explanation. She had given him the wrong key on purpose.

Cozette could have moved that statue by herself, too. She could have used the trolley. And when the thief was caught on videotape, where was she?

But why would she do it?

Charlie heard Cozette gasp. A flashlight beam, from outside the room, was traveling along the bottom edge of the door. Someone was standing just outside.

Someone gripped the doorknob. Charlie heard a scrape, then a rustle. The lock was being fiddled with. Then — *click*!

Charlie took a deep breath. He felt the hairs on the back of his neck prickling up like ant feelers. "Lights!" Charlie shouted. The four of them switched on their flashlights as one, aiming at the intruder.

The figure lifted its arms. It tried to hide, but they could see exactly who it was.

Ancestors

"David Dragonstone!"

The young magician lowered his arms and squinted into their flashlights. "What — what's going on?"

Tyler stepped out from behind a statue that held twin thunderbolts. Charlie thought his friend looked angry enough to start throwing thunderbolts of his own. "You're the jerk who hit me!" Ty said.

"It was an accident," cried Dragonstone.

"It was no accident when you stole that statue of Aphrodite," said Annie.

"You kids are nuts," said Dragonstone. He quickly turned to exit the room, but the door was locked. He rattled the knob, but it still wouldn't open.

"How do you like our magic trick?" said Ty.

Dragonstone turned to face them. His eyes gleamed angrily. "What are you doing in here, anyway?" he demanded.

"What are you doing here?" asked Annie.

"He's looking for that clue I supposedly remembered that would point to his guilt," said Ty. "But there is no clue, Dragonstone. We just made that up."

"It's a trap," said Charlie.

A feeling of relief hit him like sunshine through an open door. He was glad his first hunch was right. Cozette was innocent. But then, what had she been close to confessing before Dragonstone arrived?

Dragonstone laughed. "A trap? Don't be stupid. I just came in here to take a look at these incredible sculptures."

"But you've seen them before," said Charlie. "Plenty of times. Probably in old photographs that belonged to your grandfather. Or was it your uncle?"

Dragonstone was silent.

"I looked him up on the computer," said Charlie. "Ernesto Endriago. Endriago means 'dragon' in Spanish. And that's where you're from. Spain."

"Anyone could have known about these statues," said the magician.

"Only Brack and Ernesto knew about them," said Charlie. "They got delivered to the wrong floor and ended up locked in this room for years. Only those two men knew about them. Or whoever they told. And I thought it was weird that in all this time, after fifty years, that now is the time when someone actually tried to steal them. The first time you ever performed here."

"Pure coincidence," said Dragonstone, folding his arms. "I have nothing to do with this."

"You just said it was an accident that you hit Tyler!" Annie pointed out.

"Did I?" said Dragonstone. "I must have been shocked by the flashlights. I didn't know what I was saying. Besides," he added, "it's my word against yours. You have no proof."

"We got plenty of proof, you creep," said Ty.

Charlie noticed a bead of sweat forming on Dragonstone's pale forehead.

"We have a videotape," Charlie said. "It shows a man carrying a statue into an SUV."

"Does it really?" said Dragonstone. "Does it show me? Can you see my face?"

"You know we can't," said Charlie. "Because you were wearing a mask. But we did see something. We saw the SUV. And we saw the license plate. We can give that number to the police and find out who owns it."

Suddenly, the door swung open. "We already have," said Brack. Behind him stood three police officers.

The men crowded into the room. "We also found a pair of keys belonging to the SUV in your room, Mr. Dragonstone," said one of the officers. "Right now we're examining the SUV. We found it parked a few blocks away from the hotel."

"This is ridiculous," said Dragonstone. "First of all, how could I possibly have been in this room, when your friend here got injured, when I was outside all the time?"

Charlie smiled. "Because you weren't outside. You were inside all the time!" Then he explained how the magician had managed his trick.

Dragonstone had stolen the statue of Aphrodite, loading it off the dock and into his SUV. That was around 12:15.

Then he returned to the hotel. He planned to steal a second statue. Dragonstone was inside Room 1308 when Charlie, Ty, and Cozette entered. It was too late to find a hiding place, so Dragonstone stood off in a corner, frozen still. In the dim light of a flashlight, and wearing his trademark white suit, he would blend in with the statues.

Charlie had seen him out of the corner of his eyes, but mistook the magician for a statue. That's why Charlie had thought all twelve of the statues were in the room at that time. Then, after Ty pushed Cozette and Charlie into the hall and locked the door, Dragonstone tried to find a better hiding place. But he was afraid Ty might see him. So he knocked him out.

"I would never be so brutal," cried Dragonstone.

"That's where you're wrong," came a voice from the doorway.

"Theopolis!" cried Charlie.

The evil magician, wearing his dark cape, looked angry and sad at the same time. He starred at his young partner. "You and I had coffee with Brack in his home the other night," he said. "I was in disguise, because I know how Brack feels about me."

Brack was silent.

"And then when he unmasked me," continued Theopolis, "I left and returned to my room. But you stayed behind."

He pointed to Dragonstone. "I found out that Brack had vanished the next day. I decided to use it to my advantage and finally take over this hotel. But I did not realize *who* had kidnapped Brack, until I saw this room today. Then I knew. You are the grandson of the famous Ernesto Endriago, and I knew he had sent the statues here. Brack had told me about them, many years ago. But I had forgotten all about them. Until today."

Theopolis turned to Brack.

"I am sorry about all this," Theopolis said in a low voice. "I had no idea to what depths Ernesto's grandson would sink!"

"That still doesn't explain how we saw Mr. Dragonstone come in from the hall after Tyler was attacked," said Cozette. "How could he get out of the room?"

"He never did!" said Charlie. "After hitting Ty, he hid beside the door, in the dark. He used the black cape that he covered up the statues with, to hide himself. To melt into the shadows. Then when Rocky broke down the door, everyone started crowding into the room. Dragonstone just joined the crowd. No one noticed how he got there. We were all too busy looking at Ty."

"Look!" shouted Annie. She aimed her flashlight at a dark corner of the room near the door. "There's the cape! It's proof!"

Then the room burst into chaos.

Dragonstone waved his hand and an explosion lit up the room like a firework.

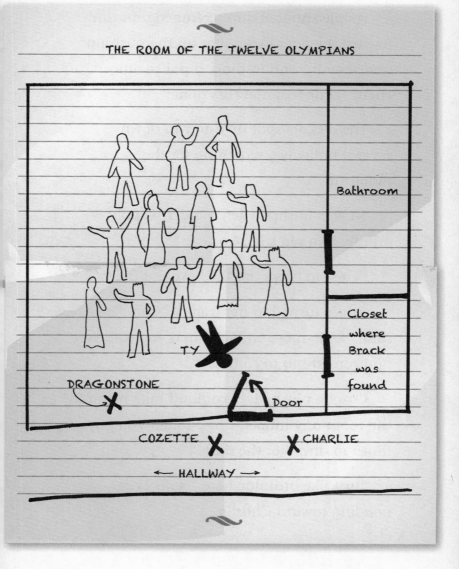

People shouted and screamed and ran toward the door. And after all the pushing and shoving and jostling, a police officer cried, "Dragonstone! He's gone!"

The officers split up and ran down several hallways, searching for the magician.

"It was flashpowder," said Theopolis grimly. "An old trick."

"The old tricks are the best," said Brack.

Annie turned to her friend. "Cozy," she said. "Remember earlier, when you said you had something to confess?"

Cozette blushed. "I couldn't take being in the room any longer. I had to tell you guys that I'm afraid of the dark!"

"Just like brainiac here," said Tyler, nodding toward Charlie.

Theopolis cleared his throat loudly and then said, "I shall go and tell our audience there's been a change of plans."

"Wait!" said Brack, holding up a hand. "A change, yes. But not a cancellation."

Theopolis stared at his former partner and frowned. "You mean —?"

"We'll go on instead," said Brack. "You and I. I'm sure we can improvise a show. A good show, too."

"But what about Dragonstone?" asked Charlie.

"Oh, I doubt if the police will find him this time," said Brack. "He's far too clever. But at least you and your friends foiled his plans. And saved the hotel from losing millions of dollars worth of art!"

"What do we do now?" asked Tyler.

Brack bowed to him over his cane. "You run downstairs and grab the best seat in the house, young man. For the show must go on!"

ABOUT THE AUTHOR

MICHAEL DAHL grew up reading everything he could find about his hero Harry Houdini, and worked as a magician's assistant when he was a teenager. Even though he cannot disappear, he is very good at escaping things. Dahl has written the popular Library of Doom series, the Dragonblood books, and the Finnegan Zwake series. He currently lives in the Midwest in a haunted house.

ABOUT THE ILLUSTRATOR

LISA K. WEBER is an illustrator currently living in Oakland, California. She graduated from Parsons School of Design in 2000 and then began freelancing. Since then, she has completed many print, animation, and design projects, including graphic novelizations of classic literature, character and background designs for children's cartoons, and textiles for dog clothing.

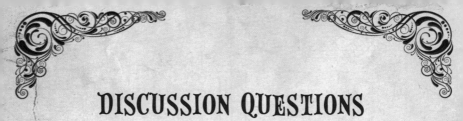

DISCUSSION QUESTIONS

1. Explain how the Hocus Pocus Hotel could be in danger if Brack is not found quickly.

2. Have you been in a performance? Talk about what kind of show you were in.

3. Would you try to rescue your friends (like Annie and Cozette) if you were at risk of getting stuck too? Why or why not?

WRITING PROMPTS

1. Try writing a chapter from Theopolis's point of view. How does the story change? What does Theopolis see, hear, think, and feel?

2. Charlie likes solving mysteries, even though it can be a little bit scary. Write about something you enjoy doing that can be scary sometimes.

3. Charlie and his friends use maps and blueprints to try to find their way out of the trap. Write about a time when you were lost. How did you find your way back?

GLOSSARY

acute (uh-KYOOT)—sharp

coincidence (koh-IN-si-duhns)—a surprising or remarkable event that seems to happen by chance

concussion (kun-KUSH-uhn)—an injury to the brain caused by a heavy blow to the head

evidence (EV-i-duhns)—information that helps prove something is true or not true

grimace (GRIM-is)—a facial expression that usually expresses a negative reaction

hotheaded (hot-HED-id)—easily angered

mythology (mi-THAH-luh-jee)—a group of myths, especially ones that belong to a particular culture or religion

protrude (proh-TROOD)—to extend beyond

silhouette (sil-oo-ET)—a dark outline of someone or something, visible against a light background

skeptical (SKEP-ti-kuhl)—doubting that something is really true

unearthly (uhn-URTH-lee)—unnaturally strange and frightening

MULTIPLYING MONEY

Everybody likes having plenty of money. Magic with money really grabs people's attention. This trick will make the audience wish their money could multiply this fast!

<table>
<tr><td>YOU NEED:</td><td>• six coins
• two popsicle sticks
• tape</td><td>• a table and chair
• a magic wand.</td></tr>
</table>

PREPARATION:

1. First, create a secret pocket by taping the popsicle sticks to the bottom of the table as shown. The space between them should be a little smaller than the coins are wide. Be sure the pocket is near the side of the table you'll be sitting at.

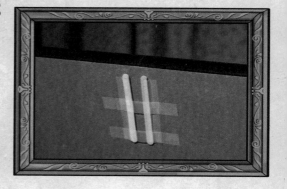

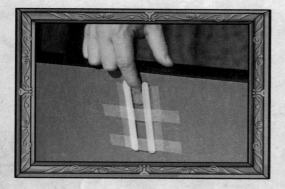

2. Next, slide one or two coins into the secret pocket made by the popsicle sticks. The gap between the sticks should allow you to easily get at the coins.

PERFORMANCE:

3. Start by laying out the rest of the coins on the table. Tell your audience, "Making money is easy. I can make these coins multiply." Ask a volunteer to count the coins on the table.

4. Now slide the coins off the edge of the table with one hand so they drop into your other hand.

5. At the same time, use your second hand to slide a coin out of the secret pocket as shown.

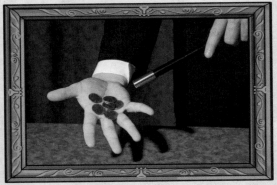

6. Close your hand around the coins, then wave your magic wand over your hand in a mystical way and say a few magic words. Finally, open your hand and have the volunteer recount the coins. The audience will be stunned when they see that the coins have multiplied!

Like this trick? Learn more in the book *Amazing Magic Tricks: Expert Level* by Norm Barnhart!
All images and text © 2008 Capstone Press. Used by permission.